J. Sai Deepak has begun something here that needs serious attention. It also suggests that significant support is required to develop its proposals further in directions not yet explored. I hope the book will be read and debated widely, especially in and for the sake of the 'India that is Bharat'.

—Dr. Prakash A. Shah
Reader in Culture and Law, Queen Mary University of London

World over, academic discourse is rife with decolonial arguments that have been explicit in their challenge to the insular homogeneity of historical narratives, nomenclatures and historiographical frameworks emanating from Europe. These movements of reclamation and 'reparatory justice' rely on what is popularly called 'epistemic disobedience' that seeks to reimagine and reconstruct our world, our notions of 'modernity' and 'rationality' from the viewpoint and lived experiences of hitherto enslaved colonies. Much of this scholarship has so far emanated from Latin American and African countries. Asia, in particular India, which has been the longest sufferer of colonialism, is conspicuous by the lack of her adequate representation in this discourse. The tide, however, seems to be changing for the better now. Through this magisterial trilogy, advocate and scholar J. Sai Deepak successfully fills a huge vacuum in the corpus of decolonial scholarship from a uniquely empathetic Indian perspective. In a masterful manner, Sai Deepak traces the global history of colonialism, India's unfortunate tryst with it and, importantly, enquires its impact on the emergence of a colonial consciousness. Combining the skills of an adept lawyer and a tenacious researcher, Sai Deepak references a wide and impressive array of archival literature to make a compelling argument that in the case of India, decoloniality is not merely an option but a civilisational imperative, which we simply cannot afford to delay any further. Gleaning from the works of several Indic as well as Western decolonial scholars and policymakers, and legislative debates, he makes a richly layered case in this eminently readable treatise on how, despite being technically free from colonialism with the achievement of freedom, our minds are far from being decolonised. It is this 'coloniality' that regularly manifests, itself in judicial pronouncements on Indic faith-based matters, the State's continued stranglehold and perverse intervention in the majority's places of worship, or the casual, axiomatic pronouncements of the elite, who debunk the very idea of our existence as a nation ever, pathetically attributing this as well as other economic milestones (railways, schools, etc.) to the Raj. Not the one to fear calling a spade by its name in the interests of political correctness, Sai Deepak convincingly busts each of these myths and symptoms through the heft of his intellect and the might of his fact-based arguments. It would become amply clear to any discerning reader too, just as Sai Deepak rightly concludes by taking recourse to pop culture, that European coloniality is like the matrix—one just needs to become aware of it, after which it is impossible to unsee it, especially in matters of religion, polity, education, economics and the law. A must-read tribute to the Indic civilisation for anyone serious about understanding the pernicious trajectory of invasive colonialism and the lingering colonial consciousness in the 'independent' Indian (or should we term this as he does, Bharatiya) mind, and how to consciously work towards reversing it.

—Dr. Vikram Sampath
Historian, Author and Adjunct Senior Research Fellow at Monash University

Advocate J. Sai Deepak has provided India with a milestone—a step from superficial to integral decolonisation. The coloniser had transferred the exercise of power in 1947–1950, but left in place a legal framework that continues to guide the lives of Indians in considerable detail—a 'steel frame' of perpetual and profound European domination. Few combine the vision of a civilisational liberation, easy to invoke in malleable cultural respects, with the exacting juridical knowledge needed for a precise and workable paradigm shift to deconstruct this lingering submission. In particular, Sai Deepak problematises the version of secularism that actually managed to worsen the imposition of an extraneous model on India's management of plurality. After digesting this conceptual decolonisation, a self-respecting India will have a formidable task in implementing Sai Deepak's analysis of her subtle colonised condition.

—Dr. Koenraad Elst
Scholar and Author of Decolonizing the Hindu Mind

Just a century ago, our scholars and philosophers who were rooted in the Sanatana ethos applied just one word to describe the underlying nature as well as the history of European colonialism—Asuric. This is the exact vocabulary that we must reclaim today if we are to fully reclaim the precolonial narrative of India, which continues to be set by the same European colonisers. This is one of the fundamental contours of the urgent imperative to fully decolonise India. In fact, this decolonisation effort had begun during the era of the modern Indian Renaissance—roughly between the second half of the nineteenth and the second half of the twentieth century. What is notable is that the luminaries of this Renaissance were running a parallel track of stopping the cultural and psychological colonisation of India, even as it was spreading all around them. Another characteristic theme of this Renaissance was to produce a comparative history and analyses of the world from the Sanatana perspective. Tragically, the effort was halted in 1947.

What Christopher Columbus failed but Vasco da Gama succeeded in—discovering India—is underscored by the same motive. In retrospect, Vasco da Gama was the feeble forerunner of a more far-reaching and eminently successful project of colonising the indigenous psyche. Indeed, a measure of the sorry depth of our mental colonisation is visible even in recent history.

In 1998, the Kerala government decided to celebrate the 500th 'anniversary' of Vasco da Gama's 'arrival' in India as though he was a benefactor of sorts. However, this only shows the comprehensive extent of the success of the European colonial project.

Sri Sai Deepak's book is a detailed and multipronged exploration of precisely this phenomenon from the Sanatana standpoint. His book employs the approach derived largely from recent scholarship in the emerging discipline of decoloniality that originated in Latin America. Quite ambitious in its scope and candid in its tenor, the book is essentially a continuation of the ideas that were seeded by the luminaries of the modern Indian Renaissance but uses contemporary academic epistemologies.

What is also notable is Sri Sai Deepak's frank declaration that he has adopted a 'learner's approach', a rare honesty of taking a firm position that is difficult to find in what is today known as mainstream academic scholarship. The wealth of evidence the author marshals in support of his arguments is truly impressive and reflects the rigour of his study. I have no doubt that *India that is Bharat* will be a welcome addition to the nascent corpus of literature in this specialist field. That it has emerged from India is a bonus. I wish the book and its author all the success in getting the recognition it deserves.

—Sandeep Balakrishna
Scholar and Author of Invaders and Infidels

The book is a must-read for everyone who is interested in understanding the relationship between the consciousness of the world's oldest surviving indigenous civilisation and the Constitution of the world's largest democracy.

—Professor Lavanya Vemsani
Professor of History, Shawnee State University,
and Editor-in-Chief, American Journal of Indic Studies

A discourse is understood to have attained a definite level of maturity, momentum and legitimacy when its stated position, defining convictions and operating principles are systematically codified. These constituent elements of a discourse may be reiterated on various occasions and platforms over a period of time, and yet without a proper, systematic and formal codification (such as a book/thesis/manifesto), these same elements may elude those who participate in the discourse, either actively or passively. It is from this point of codification onwards that a discourse starts taking a definite shape; in other words, it becomes theoretically coherent. A discourse that has taken the shape of a theoretically coherent argument usually has more impact on its own age and the ages to come, compared to the stage when the discourse was fragmented by virtue of the ununified utterances of its participants.

Whenever Bharatiya discourses, informed by specific thought-movements and intellectual or spiritual activities within the larger framework of Indic Knowledge Systems, have come of age, they have been codified in one form or other depending on the nature of their content and participants. Therefore, it is only fitting and significantly timely that Advocate J. Sai Deepak has now made a necessary leap from delivering energetic as well as intellectually perspicuous public lectures and frequently writing perceptive articles in newspaper columns to finally putting down his thoughts on the very relevant subjects of colonialism, Indic civilisation and the Indian Constitution in the form of a book.

The publication of this book, together with the promise of upcoming sequels, heralds a marked ripening of the Indic civilisational discourse from a previous stage that was largely characterised by the broadcasting of emotional outbursts and poorly informed opinions on social media. When the future generations of historians chronicle the development of the reawakening of our civilisation through time, they will find it difficult not to recognise the significant role that this book plays in that reawakening.

At the outset, it should be mentioned that the author has built his argument, or rather the premise of his argument that is likely to be unfolded more fully in the sequels to this book, on the scholarship of thinkers associated with the intellectual movement called decoloniality, which is now recognised as a distinct area of scholarship in the humanities and social sciences. The range and depth of the decolonial literature that Sai Deepak has surveyed—first to understand decoloniality and then to create the foundations for its application in explaining the Bharatiya experience of colonialism—is quite impressive.

—Sreejit Datta and Raghava Krishna in *Open* magazine

India

that is

Bharat

India
that is
Bharat

Coloniality, Civilisation, Constitution

J. SAI DEEPAK

BLOOMSBURY
NEW DELHI • LONDON • OXFORD • NEW YORK • SYDNEY

BLOOMSBURY INDIA
Bloomsbury Publishing India Pvt. Ltd
Second Floor, LSC Building No. 4, DDA Complex, Pocket C – 6 & 7,
Vasant Kunj, New Delhi, 110070

BLOOMSBURY, BLOOMSBURY INDIA and the Diana logo
are trademarks of Bloomsbury Publishing Plc

First published in India 2021
This edition published in 2021

ISBN: HB: 978-93-54352-49-2; eBook: 978-93-54350-04-7
8 10 9

Typeset in Fournier MT Std by Manipal Technologies Limited
Printed and bound in India by Thomson Press India Ltd.

To find out more about our authors and books, visit www.bloomsbury.com and sign
up for our newsletters

For Amma, Appa, Akshara and Prasad

सत्येनोत्तभिता भूमि: सूर्येनोत्तभिता द्यौ:।
ऋतेनादित्यास्तिष्ठन्ति दिवि सोमो अधिश्रित:।।
Rig Veda 10.85

Truth is the base that bears the earth;
by Sūrya are the heavens sustained.
By law the Ādityas stand secure;
and Soma holds his place in heaven.

CONTENTS

FOREWORD

The almost accidental journey of J. Sai Deepak, once a student of engineering, towards the legal profession, and then a momentous apparent decision to grapple with the future of his very civilisation, is a fascinating story worth reading for the narrative alone. His awakening is also an account of the growing reawakening of the Indic civilisation itself, the subject of V.S. Naipaul's celebrated book *India: A Million Mutinies Now*. The protagonist of this tale, J. Sai Deepak, did not apparently begin with any remarkable antecedents for this quest, except perhaps, an urgent desire to understand the troubling predicament of his own civilisation. His thirst for deeper knowledge to analyse the vexatious situation of Bharat amounted to a manifestation of *gnana* and an approach that echoes *darshana*. It prompted him to begin a trilogy on the experience of Bharat as a civilisation, with the present volume ending in 1920 and two projected volumes covering the period from the early 1920s and beyond. The civilisational issues evaluate a number of core issues that define its encounter with the modern world. Sai Deepak describes them as the impression on Bharatiya civilisation of the tension between coloniality and Constitution, exhibited specifically by the impact on religion, nature, language, caste and tribe.

Sai Deepak became an autodidact, reading widely and consulting eminent intellectuals of the human sciences. It could not have been an easy task to immerse oneself in a vast literature with which he did not have familiarity, given his educational background in engineering and the law. But he has grasped the

essentials of the vast and complex arguments and put them down
in a readable form in his single-handed endeavour to impact
the course of Bharatiya history. There are and were others
traversing this stony path but he is unique in the import of his
practical focus on the law to bring about concrete change, which
ideological campaigns alone cannot achieve. Reading his book
highlights the clarity and nuance for which he has become justly
admired and respected as a lawyer. His book also encapsulates
the need for even more thoughtful research to fully explicate the
issues raised by Sai Deepak.

Sai Deepak's involvement in historic cases—such as the
Sabarimala Ayyappa Temple case—as a Supreme Court advocate
serves as the trigger for his book because they underline the
critical issue of the historical consciousness of Bharatiyas
evident in how they were presented, argued and received by
the Supreme Court. The apparent dichotomy counterposed
between tradition and the rationality of modernity by those
involved on opposing sides exposed the parameters of the
key intellectual conundrum analysed by Sai Deepak, namely
coloniality and the distorted consciousness, by and large,
of the Bharatiya society. Such perceptual distortions arose
from the unconscious and largely unquestioning acceptance
of ideas of modernity that came to dominate intellectual
life in the nineteenth century and were accepted as valid by
both colonisers and the colonised. The argument advanced
in the book is the exact obverse of the accusation of 'false
religion' levelled by Christian evangelists against Hindus.
What Sai Deepak seeks to unravel is the mystique and veil of
coloniality itself that has profoundly shaped the thinking of the
conquered by White European Christian subjugation since
the advent of Christopher Columbus in 1492 CE.

A key intellectual and political conviction of the argument in the
Latin American decoloniality literature, revisited in Sai Deepak's
tract, is the overpowering nature of colonial consciousness and
the distinctive self-serving mindset of the coloniser as well. It

first locates the origins of the colonial experience at the dawn of the religiously and racially inspired Age of Discovery rather than the subsequent era of the Enlightenment that preoccupies postcolonial analysts, firmly establishing its underlying Christian ideological rationalisation. The decoloniality episteme rejects the unspoken foundational intellectual assumptions of modernity that are, in effect, also subliminally universalised within the very postmodernist and postcolonial critiques of the colonial and imperialist postures of European modernity. In effect, the decolonial framework seeks to reinscribe the primacy of indigeneity, indigenous consciousness and its subjectivity in formerly colonised societies and civilisations.

One of the fundamental questions examined in the book is the rootedness of the entire colonial venture in Christian conceptions derived from Biblical verities. However, what is very rarely understood is the chameleon adaptability of the Christian ideological yearning towards spiritual and psychological enslavement of the 'Other', manifested in the post-Enlightenment world as 'secularism'. Christian theology also proved to be an irresistible handmaiden to the prolonged plunder of colonised lands; it inflicted a particularly devastating tragedy by severing indigenous traditions from the seamless continuity of life with nature, which many non-European societies practised. Of course, brutal violence, cynical contrivance and the manipulation of local divisions and fissures were the important immediate and daily adjuncts to the colonial rule.

Sai Deepak focuses detailed attention on an issue of particular importance to Bharatiyas, which is the likely nature of the colonial impact on their civilisation and the relevance of coloniality to explain their current predicament. In a thoroughly fleshed out exegesis, Sai Deepak reiterates the findings of leading scholars of Bharat on how deeply coloniality has imbued Indic consciousness, which exhibits itself in self-abnegation, even self-loathing. Every aspect of Bharatiya society, including its governance and legal structures, originates in colonial constructs that disavow Bharat's indigeneity. Its continuing adroitness in nurturing extra-national loyalties and tethering Bharat's intellectual life to the interests of extra-civilisational detractors can only be described as dismaying.

Poignantly, the European worldview continues to prevail in former colonies, such as Bharat, without the need to actually espouse Christianity, since it spawned the secular worldview and framework from within its established traditions and scriptural injunctions. This misconceived explanatory framework, which continues to hold sway in Bharat, fails to grasp the nature of the continuing adversarial demonisation of Bharat's indigeneity by mis-specifying the very parameters of the discourse and misdirecting it towards overarching intellectual sources of stupefaction, such as secularism. Sai Deepak also highlights the role of coloniality in Bharat's failure to truly excavate the nature of the Islamic impact on Indic culture, which is itself a product of secular political expediency that enjoins deceit and self-delusion in the alleged interest of buying that elusive social peace. In the same vein, Marxism is also rightly deemed as just another universalising European project, though in Bharat it has been repackaged to accommodate crass contemporary exigencies and has long allied itself opportunistically with both European and Middle Eastern imperialisms. Hence, the imperative of decoloniality is to prevent the decimation of what remains of Bharat's indigeneity.

In a foray into the history of the seventeenth-century British incursion into Bharat, Sai Deepak highlights the cultural and religious nature of the East India Company's motivations, wrongly depicted in most historical accounts as essentially commercial. Propagating the gospel was affirmed as a purpose at the very outset in 1614 and subsequently repeated unequivocally, and the East India Company was specifically authorised to make war on 'heathen nations' by a Charter in 1683. One critical dimension of colonial experiences was the policy of tolerating the scriptural and doctrinal essence of Hinduism and delegitimising popular practices, adjudged by colonial bureaucrats to be superstitious. The intervention imposed a thoroughly distortive Christian paradigm of separation between the religious and the secular, meaningless in terms of Indic/Dharmic philosophical perceptions and practices. The most enduring aspect of colonial interference, prompted by cognisance of temple wealth, was in successive legislative acts introducing State regulation of temples. It is this legacy that haunts the integrity and very durability of Sanatana Dharma in independent Bharat and the insistence of governments of all political stripes to allow the progressive degradation of temples.

In two revelatory concluding chapters, Sai Deepak graphically revisits the debates and legislative acts that preceded Bharat's First War of Independence in 1857 and those that followed the assumption of direct rule over Bharat by the Westminster government and its designated representatives in Bharat. It is amply clear that effective political rule to pre-empt future revolts remained Christian in spirit, despite the Queen's proclamation of religious neutrality in 1858, with all the antecedent precepts of toleration continuing to be deeply imbued with Christian prejudices imposed on Hindu society and practice, viz official hostility towards alleged superstitions, etc. At the same time, the British debate on governing Bharat continued to reiterate the desirability of mass conversions of idolators, publicly and resoundingly articulated by the Archbishop of Canterbury and supported by the then British prime minister. In addition, successive Government of India Acts of the British Parliament modifying the Act of 1858 extended some legislative representation to Bharatiyas, but the underlying ethos of the primacy of European Christian theological inspiration motivating the coloniser remained intact.

In the final analysis, the discerning lawyer, Sai Deepak, underscores the fact that the Government of India Act of 1919 provided the framework for independent Bharat's Constitution of 1950, while the Government of India Act of 1935 provided its architecture, which he promises to explore further in the sequels to this book. Further, interrogation by Sai Deepak of founding documents and pronouncements of leading Western statesmen affirms how the notion of 'civilised nations' to characterise the expanding international order asserted a secular Christian motif to define it at the Paris Peace Conference of 1919 and the Treaty of Versailles. Sai Deepak concludes the book with the hope that Bharat's public institutions, including its judiciary and executive, will reflect thoughtfully on Bharat's indigenous traditions, and that decolonial perspectives will inform their decisions on issues arising in relation to them so that Bharat's enduring coloniality may be overcome. The book is a handsome effort to bring ideas and modes of analysis to the attention of Indian readers that will enable the achievement of true freedom and fresh thinking to embrace their historic cultural antecedents with dignity.

London
9 July 2021

—Dr. Gautam Sen
BSc (Economics), PhD (London),
Co-creator of the graduate programme in International Political
Economy at the London School of Economics and Political Science

ACKNOWLEDGEMENTS

This book, like everything else in life, is not the product of a solo act. The process of writing this book has taught me several life lessons which I hope to never forget. For starters, there is absolutely no substitute for the unconditional love and support of my family, particularly my parents who are my first teachers and from whom I have learnt the value of integrity and determination, among other things. Their fortitude and optimism under all circumstances never ceases to amaze me. For close to nine months from October last year, when I started writing the book, until the release of the pre-order link this July, without so much as a murmur, my parents have put up with my unavailability caused by my professional commitments and writing schedule in equal measure. I thank them for who they are, for this book would not have been possible without their calm presence. Thanks are equally due to my wife Akshara, for her support to my endeavours and unstinting patience with my demanding schedule, and my brilliant younger brother J. Sai Krishna Prasad (better known as JSK), for being a wonderful sounding board. I could not have been blessed with a better set of parents and family by the Gods.

The Gods, at whose feet I prostrate, have put me through an unusual journey, the reasons for which are still beyond my ken and grasp. Be that as it may, I am nothing but grateful to Them for the family and culture I have been born into, the gurus I have been mentored by and learnt from (especially Shri S. Paranjothi, the former Head of Department of the mechanical engineering department from my engineering days), the friends and well-wishers I am surrounded by, the people I have interacted with, the opportunities that have come my way, and the learning curve I have been put through in all spheres and at every step of my life. I thank the Gods for this book, my first, which is the product of an epiphany that triggered my switch to law from engineering, back in 2006, because every decision, according to me, has the hand of the Supreme Consciousness written all over it, which is only revealed in hindsight to the human mind.

Special thanks are owed to Dr. Indumathi Viswanathan, a Hindu-American scholar and educator, who introduced me to the framework of decoloniality and its literature in April 2020 after hosting me on a webinar on the Constitution for the benefit of Indian Americans. Terming my legal arguments before the Supreme Court in defence of the Sabarimala Ayyappa Temple's religious practices as 'decoloniality in action', she urged me to build on decolonial scholarship when I had shared my intent to pen a book on Bharat's civilisation and its relationship with the Constitution. She was also kind enough to be available for extensive and intense discussions when the first section of the book, which deals with coloniality, was being written. Thanks are due to Ms Sumita Ambasta, another scholar to whom I was introduced by Dr. Viswanathan. Ms Ambasta directed me to the literature relating to education, language and development policies of former colonies.

While in search of the right publisher for the book, given the nature of issues it addresses and the diverse audience it caters to, it was Shri Sanjay Dixit, former bureaucrat, lawyer and commentator, who put me in touch with Bloomsbury India. I must convey my thanks to him for the introduction.

If the process of writing a book could be compared with a motor rally, the researcher is the navigator without whom the driver could lose focus and direction. The researcher is the human compass of the writing process, who, apart from providing ammunition for the book, also keeps the author grounded by preventing flights of fancy. Ms Shaktiki Sharma, lawyer and researcher, has performed this role to perfection by grasping the message the book is meant to convey and providing the material needed to convey it. Her commitment to the cause of the Indic Renaissance was balanced by her objectivity as a researcher, which ensured that the book's propositions and conclusions found sufficient basis in scholarly literature and legislative material. My profound thanks to her for being part of this journey.

Given the sheer goldmine of material collected for the book—which necessitated its break-up into a trilogy—the manuscript required a fresh pair of eyes with attention to detail and a flair for editing to ensure clarity, coherence, flow and lucidity in the interest of readability, especially in view of the subject tackled by the book. The invaluable editorial assistance rendered by Ms C. Sai Priya, a doctor by training and an Indic researcher out of passion, has made the book much more readable, for which I thank her.

I would be remiss if I did not acknowledge the creative inputs received towards the conception of the cover design from the brilliant team at Upword helmed by Ashish Dhar, himself an Indic entrepreneur and commentator. In particular, Utkarsh Khanna and Harshit Jadwani of Upword worked with Syed Dilshad Ali of Bloomsbury India to create a cover design whose brilliance stands validated by the universally positive reception it has received upon its release. I also thank Akshara and JSK for their aesthetic inputs on the cover, which significantly contributed to the final outcome.

I would not have been able to embark on this journey of writing the book but for the dependability of my junior colleagues—Advocates Avinash Kumar Sharma and Abhishek Avadhani—who helped me with my professional commitments as I worked on the book. Thanks are also owed to Nupur J. Sharma, Rami Niranjan Desai and Advocate Eashan Ghosh for being constant sources of encouragement, particularly Eashan, for being available for discussions on the mechanics of writing a book, being an author himself. I am also deeply grateful to Senior Advocate Shri P.S. Narasimha for his confidence in my abilities and his supportive disposition to my initiatives.

I thank the team at Bloomsbury India, specifically Shri Praveen Tiwari, Shri Nitin Valecha, Shri Vimal Kumar, Ms Shreya Chakraborti and Ms Megha Dey, for all their efforts towards putting this book together and bringing it out. Praveen's patience with my calls, queries and follow-ups deserves a special mention.

Finally, I offer my deep veneration and gratitude to Indic/ Dharmic icons and scholars of the past and present whose lives, ideas and work I have drawn from, and upon whose majestic shoulders this book rests. I sincerely hope and pray that this book and its sequels contribute, even if a mere pebble, to the cause of reawakening Bharat's civilisational consciousness.

Introduction

If you grew up in the 1990s in a middle-class Hindu family in southern Bharat, not to perpetuate stereotypes, but chances are that a career in engineering or medicine featured right at the top of your life goals. My goals were no different, not just because of my limited means and exposure but also because I was keen on pursuing a career in aerospace engineering. However, eventually, I had to settle for mechanical engineering and committed myself to performing well so that I could pursue a master's in aerospace engineering. By the time I reached the end of the sixth semester in mid-2005, I was well placed to start a career in the core manufacturing sector, in the event I failed to secure admission to a good aerospace programme.

Just when it seemed like I had it all figured out, I started having second thoughts about what I truly wanted to do in the long run. This introspection was partly triggered by my visits to Ramakrishna Math, the writings of Swami Vivekananda, Dr. Arun Shourie's incisive and piercing books[1], and the spike post the elections of May 2004 in the normalised and open hostility directed at specific Indic sub-identities, especially on academic campuses. Had it not been for the writings of Swami Vivekananda and Dr. Shourie, I would have missed the forest for the trees since it was evident that the hostility, while on the face of it, was directed at specific Indic sub-identities in the name of societal reparation, it was, in reality, meant to weaken the larger Indic civilisational edifice. Systematic isolation, ostracisation and acculturation of one Indic strand at a time seemed to be at play. It became clearer with each passing day that this hostility had the previously tacit but increasingly overt support of extra-civilisational, specifically colonial and non-Indic, systems, that stood to benefit from this motivated internecine tussle.

Thanks to my interactions with better-informed people who were civilisationally rooted and had worked on the ground, I gradually came to understand that while the instinctive human reaction would be to protect the sub-identities one was closest to, the priority should be to preserve the civilisational tapestry and its foundations, which enabled the birth, growth and expression of diverse sub-identities. This also meant that protection of Indic civilisational integrity did not require the submergence of its sub-identities at the altar of a well-intentioned, albeit misplaced, grand unity project. On the contrary, history seemed to teach us that the survival of the Indic civilisation *as a civilisation* depended on the flourishing of its sub-identities, with each of the sub-identities realising that they were part of a federal symbiotic whole and that it was in their own existential interest to remain part of the whole. I also learnt that the tumultuous and fissiparous state of affairs that met the eye was the product of sustained long-term investment at a very fundamental level much before 1947. Therefore, it required, at the very least, an equally sustained long-term investment by the society at the most fundamental levels, namely the group and the individual, in order to undo the damage sustained by this living civilisation.

This realisation had a profound effect on me; however, I was not remotely sure of the path I had to take. Any drastic change in career paths required me to take the immediate family into confidence and convince them of my decision, and rightly so, because I had not given them the slightest inkling that I was going through a churn. But before breaking it to them, I wanted to be sure of the path myself, and so, I spent the seventh semester evaluating a career in civil services and alternatively, the law.

In early 2006, in my final semester, I had the opportunity to present a technical paper at the Indian Institute of Technology (IIT) Kharagpur. That is when I learnt that the institution was all set to inaugurate later that year a unique three-year

LLB programme with an in-built specialisation in intellectual property rights under the auspices of its newly established law school, the Rajiv Gandhi School of Intellectual Property Law (RGSOIPL). What made the three-year law programme unique, apart from its marked tilt towards intellectual property law, was the fact that it was open exclusively to the scientific and technological pool of the country. I realised that my future lay in the field of law, which, I believed, would equip me with the skills I needed to act on my convictions. In July 2006, a month after my undergraduation, I joined the programme after clearing the admission process for the IIT law school.

Although I had no known relatives who were part of the legal fraternity and I did not know much about the profession and its inner workings, the only thing I was sure of was my interest in litigation. Despite the specialised nature of the programme and my aptitude for intellectual property law,[2] upon my graduation in July 2009, I was recommended by the Advisor to the law school to pursue a career in constitutional law. In fact, he was kind enough to write a letter recommending me to a Senior Advocate in the Supreme Court who had then just been appointed as one of the top law officers of the country. Though I loved constitutional law, my personal commitments required me to take up commercial litigation. So I started off as a civil commercial litigator in a National Capital Region-based law firm that specialised in intellectual property litigation and allied areas, and practised primarily before the High Court of Delhi.

For the first seven years of my career as a litigator, until mid-2016, while intellectual property law and competition law were my core practice areas, I was given the opportunity to work on a few landmark matters that involved significant questions of constitutional import. In 2010, I was second chair for Greenpeace India in *Tata Sons Limited* v. *Greenpeace International & Anr.*[3] Tata Sons had sued Greenpeace International and Greenpeace India in the High Court of Delhi for alleged trademark infringement and defamation citing Greenpeace India's use of the Tata logo in its Pacman-style game, *Turtle* v. *Tata*. The High Court's judgment in this case, while dismissing Tata's prayer for an interim injunction on the game, laid down the law on the interplay between trademark law, the law of defamation and the right to parody and fair comment as part of the fundamental freedoms of speech and expression under the Constitution. This judgment remains one of the finest in its genre to date and is appreciated for its nuance and clarity.

A few years later, in 2014–2015, I had the opportunity to second chair for the Internet and Mobile Association of India (IAMAI) in its writ petition before the Supreme Court challenging certain provisions of the Information Technology Act, 2000. These provisions required online intermediaries, such as Facebook and Google, to take upon themselves the task of deciding the legality of content posted by its users upon receipt of legal notices from third parties seeking removal of such content. The IAMAI's writ petition was decided in its favour as part of a batch of writ petitions in the landmark judgment of *Shreya Singhal* v. *Union of India*, which is otherwise popular for striking down the draconian erstwhile Section 66A of the IT Act.[4] In the judgment, the Supreme Court recognised the chilling effect of overbroad restrictions on free speech. This judgment too remains a landmark one for its contribution to free speech jurisprudence, especially in the context of online platforms.[5]

While these cases certainly presented me with fantastic opportunities to apply my understanding of constitutional law to IPR and technology-related contexts and vice versa, my brush with constitutional law from a civilisational perspective first and truly began after I set up an independent practice, exclusively as an arguing counsel in June 2016. Fortunately, since I had earned my stripes as a litigator by then, my peers in the legal fraternity supported my decision, which kept me in good stead as an arguing counsel in civil commercial matters as well as in writ petitions before the Delhi High Court and the Supreme Court.

It was around then that Senior Advocate Shri C.S. Vaidyanathan,[6] one of the leading lights of the Supreme Court, recommended me to the team that, to date, steers the writ petition[7] (the HRCE Petition) moved before the Apex Court by the Late Swami Dayananda Saraswati.[8] The HRCE Petition, which is yet to be decided by the Supreme Court, challenges the constitutionality of the key provisions of the Tamil Nadu Hindu Religious and Charitable Endowments (TNHRCE) Act, 1959, the Andhra Pradesh Charitable and Hindu Religious Institutions and Endowments Act, 1987 and the Pondicherry Hindu Religious Institutions Act, 1972 (the HRCE Acts) for violating Articles 14, 15(1), 19(1)(g), 21, 25, 26 and 29 of the Constitution.

The more I read the HRCE Petition and the material assiduously put together by the team in support of the petition, the more it convinced me that there was a clear causal link between State control of Hindu temples and the visible degradation of the temple ecosystem. Also, I came to the jarring realisation that a legal framework as invasive as the HRCE Acts was reserved for Hindu religious institutions alone. I learnt of similar Hindu-specific legislations that were in force in Karnataka, Kerala, Odisha and several other States. Given the significant questions of constitutional law involved in the HRCE Petition, such as the nature and role of the Indian State, its relationship with religion and its treatment of religious institutions of different faiths, I was keen on contributing to the matter. I joined the team as an arguing counsel on a pro bono basis, which gave me the opportunity to work alongside eminent Senior Counsels, such as Shri C.S. Vaidyanathan and Shri R. Venkataramani, who had been spearheading the matter from the beginning. Since I felt strongly about the issue, and there were several myths in the public domain as to who controlled temples and how, I delivered a few lectures on the subject within the broader canvas of civilisation and the Constitution.

Coincidentally, it was around this period that I was approached by the trustees of People for Dharma, an NGO led by women, to represent them as intervenors before the Supreme Court in a writ petition moved by the Indian Young Lawyers' Association in relation to the Sabarimala Sree Ayyappa Temple. The writ petition sought the entry of women of a reproductive age group into the temple as well as the removal of restrictions on entry of women into places of worship/prayer of other faiths as well.[9] People for Dharma had previously launched a phenomenally successful international campaign called 'Ready to Wait' on behalf of the women who supported the rights of the temple to protect its religious practices. I took up the case on behalf of People for Dharma on a pro bono basis, since it presented me with an opportunity to showcase before the highest court of the land the sheer diversity of religious practices, the unique character of religious institutions within the Dharmic fold and the position enjoyed by the deities enshrined within. I also wished to highlight the rights of deities and the devout under the Constitution, and the serious complications arising as a result of the application of non-Indic ontology, epistemology, theology and jurisprudence to Indic ways of life, faiths, practices and institutions. I presented these positions on behalf of People for Dharma before a three-Judge Bench of the Supreme Court, which heard several others in the case. In October 2017, the Bench referred the matter to a Constitution Bench (a bench typically consisting of five judges).

By early 2017, in light of my involvement in the HRCE Petition and the Sabarimala Temple case, the manifest incongruity of having to establish the legitimacy, authenticity and civilisational centrality of Indic/Dharmic religious institutions before an ostensibly Indian court gave me the push I needed to understand the journey of the Indic civilisation better. Despite a demanding professional schedule, I started reading the works of Pandurang Vaman Kane, Jadunath Sarkar, Radha Kumud Mookerji, R.C. Majumdar, K.A. Nilakanta Sastri, K.S. Ramaswami Sastri, S.L. Bhyrappa, R. Nagaswamy, Ram Swarup, Sitaram Goel, Dharampal, Kapil Kapoor, Koenraad Elst, Michel Danino, Shrikant G. Talageri, Meenakshi Jain and Sandeep Balakrishna, apart from the publications of the Ramakrishna Mission Institute of Culture and Bharatiya Vidya Bhavan. This was, of course, in addition to the writings of Swami Vivekananda, Sri Aurobindo and other civilisational icons. My reading was based on the recommendations of better-informed individuals who worked full-time on civilisational issues as trained scholars, historians, civil society advocates, educators and public intellectuals. Also, the diversity of my reading was handicapped by the unfortunate reality that I was more comfortable consuming content in English than in Indian languages, which represented the very problem I hoped to understand better.

On the constitutional front, I revisited the history starting from the Home Rule Scheme in 1889 until the adoption of the Constitution in an effort to better understand whether this document captured the essence of and reflected Bharat's civilisational spirit. B. Shiva Rao's six-volume publication *The Framing of India's Constitution: A Study*, V.P. Menon's *The Story of The Integration of the Indian States* and Justice Rama Jois's *Legal and Constitutional History of India: Ancient, Judicial and Constitutional System* served as some of my principal references in this regard. I also read through commentaries on Bharat's journey towards constitutionalism written between 1933 and the late 1940s, which shed light on the history and the prevalent thought processes on the subject. This exposure enabled me to apply the lessons drawn from the literature to live constitutional matters that had a bearing on the Indic civilisational worldview.

Among them, perhaps the most significant, was the Sabarimala Sree Ayyappa Temple case which was taken up for hearings in July 2018 by a Constitution Bench of the Supreme Court headed by the then Chief Justice of India, Shri Dipak Misra. Fortunately, alongside several stalwarts of the profession, such as Senior Advocate Shri K. Parasaran, I was granted the opportunity by the Bench to present detailed arguments on behalf of People for Dharma and a Delhi-based women's organisation, Chetana, both of which supported the religious practices of the temple and its rights. This included its right to restrict the entry of women of the reproductive age group. Unfortunately, the Constitution Bench ruled in favour of the writ petitioners by a majority of 4–1 on 28 September 2018, against which several review petitions were moved. The review petitions were heard in early 2019, and later that year, acknowledging that the review petitions had merit, seven questions of law were framed by a Constitution Bench headed by the then Chief Justice, Shri Ranjan Gogoi, and referred to a larger nine-Judge Bench. Pending the outcome in the proceedings before the nine-Judge Bench (known as a 'Reference', when a larger Bench is called upon to decide on questions of constitutional import), the next Chief Justice, Shri Sharad Arvind Bobde, declined to grant security to any woman of the reproductive age group who sought entry against the temple's religious practices and beliefs, thereby restoring the status as it existed prior to the first verdict.[10]

Alongside this, in the first half of 2019, in relation to the Sree Padmanabhaswamy Temple in Kerala, I had the privilege of representing the Chief Tantri of the Temple, the Chief Priest of the Chilkur Balaji Temple in Hyderabad and People for Dharma before the Supreme Court in an appeal from the 2011 judgment of the Kerala High Court. In its judgment, the High Court had held that the Travancore Royal Family had no authority over the administration of the Padmanabhaswamy Temple after the abolition of royal titles and privileges by the Constitution (Twenty-Sixth Amendment) Act of 1971. The High Court had also transferred control over the Temple to a trust, which was to be managed by the appointees of the State Government of Kerala. Fortunately, the Supreme Court reversed the verdict of the High Court on 13 July 2020 and upheld the rights of the Travancore Royal Family as well as the authority of the Chief Tantri on religious matters in relation to the temple.[11] My involvement in this case required me to understand, among other things:

1. the nature of Hindu princely States prior to their integration with the Indian Union;

2. the relationship between the heads of Hindu princely States and their titular deities;

3. the circumstances, terms and conditions of integration of Hindu princely States with the Union;

4. the history surrounding the Twenty-Sixth Amendment to the Constitution; and of course,

5. the recurring issue of State control of temples.

Little did I know then that the experience of working on such matters of constitutional and civilisational significance would prepare me better to make sense of what was to transpire between August and December 2019. During this momentous period, Bharat witnessed the following:

1. Amendments were undertaken to Articles 367 and 370 of the Constitution on 5 and 6 August 2019, and the erstwhile State of Jammu and Kashmir was reorganised into two Union Territories with effect from 31 October 2019.

2. A Constitution Bench of the Supreme Court led by the then Chief Justice of India, Shri Ranjan Gogoi, pronounced a unanimous verdict on 9 November 2019 affirming the ownership of the Deity Shri Ram Lalla over His birthplace in Ayodhya, thereby validating a 500-year-old Indic civilisational and religious movement to reclaim Shri Ram Janmabhoomi.

3. The Citizenship Amendment Act, 2019 (the CAA) was promulgated on 12 December 2019, which provided an accelerated access to citizenship for persecuted Hindus, Sikhs, Buddhists, Jains, Parsis and Christians from Muslim-majority countries, such as Pakistan, Bangladesh and Afghanistan.

Each of these developments generated significant debate, which was natural given that these were tectonic shifts in Indian history that touched upon quite a few fault lines and unresolved legacy and civilisational issues. That said, the most troubling aspect of these debates, which kept rearing its head over and over again, was that the very legitimacy and the underlying identity of the Indian State and the Indic society were called into question.

We were being told that Bharat was a synthetic product of colonisation, which had no identity or consciousness of its own before the European coloniser set foot on its soil and stitched it together as one 'nation'. Arguments that were allegedly rooted in the Constitution were being marshalled to support these positions, which effectively turned the Constitution into a battleground of sorts. The extent of the divide was such that I was told on social media that the use of 'Bharat' for India was bigoted and against the Constitution's promise of secularism. The fact that Article 1 of the Constitution expressly spoke of '*India, that is Bharat...*' to declare its roots and heritage to the world was barely known, and even if it was known, the significance of the use of 'Bharat' in the very first Article of the document appeared to have been lost over time. That is when I decided to examine the fundamental question of the relationship between India and Bharat through the prisms of civilisation and the Constitution, and what it meant, if anything, to the State and to society at large.

To this end, I began to write a few pieces for *Firstpost*[12] and *Open*[13] capturing my views. In particular, I argued against approaching the Constitution with a sense of affected and exaggerated religiosity without understanding it in the broader context of the civilisation, which, I contended, was the primary canvas as well as the object of protection. To romanticise and venerate the Constitution, I argued, was to conflate the means with the end to the detriment of the civilisation. In a nutshell, I took the position that the Constitution must be alive to history to serve its intended purpose.

These were my tentative beginnings on this intersection, and my thoughts took better shape when I spoke at a conference in Chennai on the Hindu character of princely States based on the research that was put together for the Sree Padmanabhaswamy

Temple case. Around this time, ideas for a book had started taking shape in my mind and quite a few well-wishers had begun to ask me to pen my thoughts in the form of a book. However, I first wanted to run my ideas through a series of pieces before capturing them coherently in the form of a book. This, I felt, would also help me to assess if I could balance my professional commitments as an arguing counsel with my writing initiatives. While I was still mulling over the prospect of writing a book, the world was hit by the COVID-19 pandemic. I decided to use the respite provided by the lockdown to read up more on civilisational and constitutional aspects before starting a column.

I set out to try and make sense of existing ideological divides across the political spectrum in Bharat. It seemed to me that regardless of labels, there was a common acceptance of the colonialised version of Bharat's history, especially in matters of human rights, religion, education, environment, development, caste and gender. In fact, there seemed to be a shared view across ideologies that there was indeed a 'universal' and uniform moral standard that all 'civilised societies' *must* adhere to. Barring a handful of scholars, such as Ram Swarup, Sitaram Goel, Dharampal, Koenraad Elst, Dr. S.N. Balagangadhara and Dr. Jakob De Roover, very few seemed interested in challenging the Western-normative framework which informed these so-called universal standards. Even those who publicly extolled the Indic civilisation for its spiritual, philosophical, legal and epistemological traditions, seemed more interested in calling out the selective application of such supposedly universal standards. For some reason, they would not question the application of the Western-normative framework that refused to accommodate Indic thought. Critically, the ontological and theological origins of this framework and their effect on non-Western civilisations, such as Bharat, did not seem to get the scrutiny and examination they warranted.

What piqued my attention was that the reservoir of colonial stereotypes about the Indic civilisation, which seemingly opposing sides (or 'wings') dipped into and drew from liberally, pun intended, was the same. While one reinforced the stereotypes to make the case that there existed no connection whatsoever between Bharat and India, the other highlighted the very same stereotypes to make its case for a 'liberal' Bharat, a new idea of India, if you will, citing Bharat's innate openness to new ideas and 'reform'. The former, at least, wore its antipathy to the Indic consciousness openly on its sleeve; the message that was being evangelised by the latter was a repackaged version of the Reformation, in this case, an Indic Reformation. Of course, the latter school of thought pursued its Reformist agenda while paying lip service to Bharat and its civilisational character to placate the larger Indic society with tokenism. This was a critical layer in the national discourse which needed to be unpacked, in my opinion, since the larger goals of reclaiming Indic civilisational consciousness and agency over it were being relegated to the margins by both sides, albeit for different reasons. The net result was the same—Bharat would continue to operate within the coloniser's framework, while its civilisational character would be put to symbolic and ornamental use without any real and lasting impact on policymaking.

To me, this did not bode well even for Bharat's economic aspirations since the premise of an Indic Renaissance, that is, a re-inscription of indigenous consciousness onto contemporary Bharat, was that it was not necessary for Bharat to play by the West's rules in order to achieve economic prosperity. On the contrary, I believed that a civilisational reclamation had the potential to spur confidence and originality of thought, thereby paving the way for economic progress in a way that was consistent with Indic ethos, which valued a balanced approach to nature and development. Critically, the pursuit of economic prosperity through the mere imitation of a Western framework, according to me, would cement the notion that the only viable way was the Western way, which would have irreversible and catastrophic consequences for the survival of Bharat's indigeneity. I believed that it would be unwise to put economics and civilisational priorities in walled gardens because the relationship between the two was too close to risk a silo-based approach. After all, the average person was bound to assume and attribute the West's economic prosperity to the values and ideals it subscribed to, and ultimately to its onto-epistemology and theology (OET).

Also, I asked myself, was it not the ultimate goal to ensure that Indic thought had a respectable seat, its rightful position, at the table of Big Powers? Unless, of course, the true objective was to preserve the hallowed status quo between the seemingly opposing camps, the sacred middle ground where all civilisational enquiry ended regardless of which side of the so-called ideological divide one was on. This was when I started considering the possibility that maybe I was unaware of the existence of an unwritten code that allowed the envelope on the civilisational front to be pushed only so far and no further, thereby maintaining the hegemony of the Western-normative framework in Indian discourse. What else could explain the unquestioned deference with which the framework was being treated by even those who claimed to stand for a living civilisation that placed a premium on self-confidence, critical enquiry and truth?

These questions led me to the view that it was important for people to understand that Bharat as a civilisation was a reality, and reducing that reality and near-unbroken lived experience to a mere talking point to score brownie points over one another was more a proof of expediency than real conviction in the values the Indic civilisation stood for. After all, if one did not believe in the capacity of this civilisation to offer a credible and viable alternative to the Western-normative framework, at least for Bharat, it would be unrealistic to expect the rest of the world to look up to Bharat as the 'Vishwaguru' (literally, teacher or guide to the world). I believed that a people that lacked the courage of their conviction to live by their own civilisational values could hardly expect the world to look up to them for guidance. Also, based on the writings of leonine civilisational icons, such as Swami Vivekananda and Sri Aurobindo, I believed every culture had something of value to contribute to the global pool of thought. It was, therefore, clear to me that recasting Bharat in the mould of the West would kill its originality and character, making it a mere vassal of the West, that too *after* the European coloniser had left its shores. That would be a tragedy of incalculable proportions for which we would have none to blame but ourselves.

To bring out the unconscious and unshakeable belief in the Western-normative framework across the political and ideological spectrum, I began my search for similarly placed movements in other societies which could be compared with the Indic quest for cultural decolonisation. While I was aware of the scholarly work of Dr. Balagangadhara and Dr. De Roover on colonial consciousness in relation to Bharat, I had two reasons for undertaking the search: first, to demonstrate the global presence of such consciousness owing to the scale of European colonialism and its successor Western imperialism; and second, because contemporary Bharat, unfortunately, sought global validation of its position even on cultural decolonisation. Therefore, to make a case for Bharat, I wanted to place its experience within or alongside a global framework in the hope that it would drive home the point better.

Also, as a practising lawyer, I sought a framework that would make it possible for me to strike a balance between civilisational imperatives and constitutionalism, especially in view of the ongoing debates surrounding the Constitution. One of the ways could have been to approach the subject through the prism of the historical school of jurisprudence based on the works of Friedrich Karl von Savigny, Georg Friedrich Puchta and Henry Maine; however, I was interested in a non-Eurocentric framework that was applicable to societies that shared Bharat's colonial experience and transgenerational trauma. My most critical expectation was that the framework must be malleable and conducive to the Indic worldview given that Bharat's colonial experience had aspects that were both similar and dissimilar to the experience of other hitherto colonised societies. Therefore, my objectives were:

1. to continuously apply such a framework to my own personal journey in understanding the Indic civilisation on its own terms and using its own lexicon, warts and all; and

2. to extend the application of this framework in a concrete manner to my area of competence, namely the law, and more specifically to the Constitution, given its manifest importance to the polity of Bharat.

However, my search for a framework was not helped by the fact that I lacked formal training in this area of humanities. It was at this juncture that in April 2020, I was approached to speak on the Indian Constitution at a webinar meant for Indian Americans. After the webinar, Dr. Indu Viswanathan, a Hindu-American scholar and educator whose brainchild the session was, happened to remark that my work on reconciling the Constitution with Indic civilisational perspectives fell within the purview of 'decoloniality'. To put it in her words, she called it 'decoloniality in action', which several other similarly placed societies had witnessed. She urged me to look into decoloniality in order to understand its applicability to the Indic position and was kind enough to share some of the literature on the subject. As a result, I started reading the works of scholars, such as Aníbal Quijano, Walter D. Mignolo, Sylvia Wynter, Ramón Grosfoguel, Catherine E. Walsh and Nelson Maldonado-Torres, among others. Dr. Viswanathan also put me in touch with another brilliant scholar of decoloniality, Ms Sumita Ambasta, who introduced me to literature that shed light on colonial language policies, and the writings of Arturo Escobar whose perspectives on the relationship between coloniality and 'development' is a must-read for development professionals in Bharat.

In my exploration of the subject, I learnt that 'coloniality', as first conceptualised by Latin-American scholar Aníbal Quijano, informed the European coloniser's use of power and was the very basis and justification for the exploitation of the world. Coloniality was the fount of European colonialism, which in turn was rooted in the coloniser's religious beliefs that gave birth to his sense of racial superiority that placed the Christian White European coloniser at the top of the world order. It was this sense of superiority, which the European coloniser treated as both a divinely ordained right and scientific fact, that led to the creation of racial hierarchies the world over. Coloniality reshaped the very concept of history and time through the creation of constructs as 'modernity' and 'rationality', terms which are loosely used in contemporary everyday conversations without the knowledge of their colonial origins. This colonial matrix of power, to which both modernity and rationality were integral, had the effect of negating the cultural experience and subjectivities of colonised societies, so much so that according to the coloniser, their histories began only upon his advent.

The literature taught me that 'decoloniality' was the response to coloniality and the Eurocentric/Western-normative framework introduced in colonised societies by the European coloniser. The goal of decoloniality was to unshackle hitherto colonised societies from the totalising universalisms of European colonialism and its current-day successor, Western imperialism, in order to restore agency and dignity to their consciousness.

The more I read the literature on coloniality, the more I realised that there was a clear and inadvertent handshake between such literature and the works of Dr. Balagangadhara and Dr. De Roover on colonial consciousness. This told me that at the very least the framework merited serious consideration, whether or not it held all the answers to consciousness-related questions faced by contemporary Bharat. Also, the framework gave me the opportunity to call out the double standards that were being applied to decolonial movements in other decolonised societies on the one hand, and the Indic movement for cultural decolonisation and reclamation of its civilisational identity on the other. While the former has received serious and positive attention, the latter has been branded illiberal, xenophobic and lacking in historical basis. This hypocrisy needed to be called out.

By the first week of May 2020, I began writing a Friday column, 'Indic Views', in *The Daily Guardian* on the interplay between civilisation and the Constitution, approached through the lens of decoloniality. The column received positive feedback for its take on a new approach to constitutionalism. By early September 2020, after writing close to 18 pieces under the column, I knew I was ready to write a book on the convergence between coloniality, civilisation and the Constitution, by no stretch of the imagination as an expert but as a genuine and committed learner. The hope was that it would start fresh, timely and nuanced conversations in and about Bharat on these issues. And so, in the second week of October 2020, I started writing this book.

This book is the first of the Bharat trilogy that explores the influence of European colonial consciousness/coloniality, in particular its religious and racial roots, on Bharat as the successor State to the Indic civilisation and the origins of the Indian Constitution. It lays the foundation for its sequels by covering the period between the Age of Discovery, marked by Christopher Columbus' expedition in 1492, and the reshaping of Bharat through a British-made constitution— the Government of India Act of 1919.

The book is split into three sections—Coloniality, Civilisation, and Constitution—with the third section as the ultimate object of my attention. The canvas is global in the first section and moves towards Bharat-centric analysis of coloniality/colonial consciousness in the second and third with greater specificity.

Given the abundance of stand-alone literature on the subjects of the first two sections, I have limited the scope of the discussion only to the extent it serves as the foundation for my examination of the Constitution for coloniality/colonial consciousness in the third section of this book and its sequels.

In the first section, citing the literature on coloniality, I broadly discuss the genesis of a Eurocentric/Western-normative framework starting from the Age of Discovery, which began with Christopher Columbus' expedition in 1492, its religious inspiration and racial underpinning, its relationship with modernity and rationality, its impact on colonised societies and the rise of decoloniality as a response. In particular, I have focused on the impact of coloniality on nature, religion, language, knowledge, education and law, and the Westphalian origin of a 'nation-state'. I have also taken the position that, owing to its Latin-American origins, decolonial scholarship focusses primarily on European coloniality and, therefore, its vision of decoloniality is limited to the same. This means that every society should identify the forms of colonisation it has been subjected to and outline for itself the contours of its decoloniality.

In the second section of the book, in the backdrop of the global experience with European coloniality, I have discussed its impact on Bharat primarily in the realms of religion, caste, tribe, education and political infrastructure covering the period between 1600 and 1853. This section also traces the origins of seemingly universal constructs, such as 'toleration', 'secularism' and 'humanism', to Christian political theology. Their subsequent role in subverting the indigenous Indic consciousness through a secularised and universalised Reformation is examined. I have also put forth the concept of Middle Eastern coloniality since Middle Eastern colonisation of Bharat preceded the European variant; the underlying idea being that Bharat's version of decoloniality must address both forms of colonialities to preserve its civilisational character in light of its history and continuing contemporary challenges. Further, I have explained why postcolonialism in Bharat has served to entrench both forms of colonialities and must, therefore, give way to decoloniality.

The third section is effectively an extension of the second but with a greater focus on Bharat's colonial constitutional journey. This section covers the period between 1858, when the British Crown directly took charge of Bharat, and 1919, when the first British-made Constitution for India, that is, the Government of India Act of 1919, was passed. This includes international developments leading to the founding of the League of Nations by the Western powers that tangibly impacted this journey. The object of this section is to demonstrate that the 'civilising' and evangelising tendency of the European coloniser, which emanates from his coloniality, impacted the politico-legal infrastructure established by him in Bharat, including a constitutional form of government. The other important object is to underscore the use of international law by European colonising nations to universalise their evangelical mission. The discussion in this section of the book serves as the foundation for the sequels. The first sequel will cover the crucial period between 1920 and 1951, when the Constitution of independent Bharat was framed and adopted, and amended for the first time in 1951. The second sequel will tentatively cover the period between 1952 and 1977.

I must caveat this endeavour by stating clearly that by no means is this analysis of the Constitution comprehensive; however, it is certainly intended to be a starting point from a decolonial perspective so that Indic consciousness can replace colonial consciousness. The attempt has been to share my learnings in the hope that they trigger a much-needed round of fresh and honest conversations not just among the specialists, but even, and especially, among the non-specialists who seek to make sense of all the noise being made around the identity of Bharat and its Constitution. In the process, I have tried my best to let facts speak for themselves and have attempted to draw only those inferences and conclusions that are reasonably supported by literature. Whether or not I have succeeded in this exercise is, of course, for the readers and posterity to judge, *applying a decolonial lens*. As for the tautness and the rigidity that have crept into my writing over the years, these are occupational hazards of being a litigator. On the overall quality of the exercise, I leave it to the readers to decide if the book reflects my commitment to my journey as a learner.

Section I

COLONIALITY

Colonisation, Colonialism, Coloniality and Decoloniality: Language Matters

The First Voyage

The First Voyage, chromolithograph by L. Prang & Co., published by the Prang Educational Co., Boston, 1893. A scene of Christopher Columbus bidding farewell to the Queen of Spain on his departure for the New World, 3 August 1492.

In July 2018, the arguments I submitted on behalf of the female devotees of Swami Ayyappa before a Constitution Bench of the Supreme Court, supporting the religious practice of the Sabarimala Ayyappa Temple, were widely reported by the national media.[1] Based on the tone and tenor of the reportage, it seemed to me that the reason the arguments received nationwide traction was due to my emphasis on the fundamental rights of the Deity as:

1. a 'person' within the meaning of Article 25(1) of the Constitution; and
2. the very fount of the religious practices observed by and in the Sabarimala Temple, which lent the temple a denominational/'sampradayic'[2] character within the Dharmic fold under Article 26.

In my view, I presented a fairly clear, reasonable and constitutionally rooted argument in support of the temple's practice, especially on the rights of the Deity, which was the product of the creative and untiring efforts of a dedicated team that blended the religious with the constitutional. To date, I stand by my legal submissions and see no reason to change my position whatsoever. I say this from a position of clarity and conviction, especially in light of the subsequent endorsement of the juristic character of a Deity by a Constitution Bench of the Supreme Court in the Shri Ram Janmabhoomi verdict delivered on 9 November 2019.[3]

Not surprisingly, given the breathless nature of the news cycle and the terminal decline of facts and nuance in public discourse, very few media outlets made an honest attempt to understand or unbundle that multilayered argument. Instead, sensationalism defined the headlines as well as the contents of news reports with few honourable exceptions. Public reactions to the arguments too were mostly in the extreme with almost no room for a middle ground, which perhaps says a lot about the times we live in than my own arguments. The more predictable jibes like 'patriarchal' and the like did not pique my attention much given the nature of the matter and the dramatis personae involved, apart from the sloganeering hue such words have acquired over the years instead of standing for the genuine concerns and issues they were meant to represent in the first place.

What I found most interesting was that those who disagreed with me used words such as 'orthodox', 'traditional', 'anti-rational' and 'anti-modern' to caricature my position.[4] To be clear, I was intrigued not by the criticism itself, which was expected, but by the use of such words as pejoratives to criticise a position that supported a religious institution. After all, I asked myself, was not a religious institution's commitment first and foremost to the object of its establishment, and in the case of a temple to the object of its consecration and worship, namely the Deity and the associated practices and traditions? If yes, why was 'traditional' being hurled as a pejorative if adherence to tradition was hardly surprising given the religious nature of the institution? Did that mean that the word had acquired a secondary significance that needed to be unpacked and understood better? During the course of several public debates after my arguments, I attempted to pull this particular thread based on my intuitive understanding of the colonial assumptions underlying the use of such words as pejoratives.

In fact, in a public debate on the topic 'A Tug of War Between Constitution and Faith' held at the Chennai International Centre on 7 September 2018, I specifically spoke of the need to remove the colonial lens while trying to assess and evaluate the constitutionality of indigenous and Indic religious practices, such as the one followed by the Sabarimala Ayyappa Temple.[5] That said, it was only after I started reading the literature on coloniality/colonial consciousness that I understood the root cause better from the standpoint of an articulable and articulated framework that underscored the relationship between coloniality, modernity and rationality.[6] For the first time, I understood, based on the literature on the subject, that terms such as 'modern' and 'rational', which we use casually and, dare I say, unthinkingly in our daily conversations about the contemporary relevance of Indic social and religious practices as well as in relation to the societal structures of Bharat, had deeper meanings that could be traced to their European colonial origins.[7] The judgment and sanctimony inherent in the use of such terms became apparent to me after my exposure to coloniality. But then, what exactly is coloniality, and how is it different from or related to colonialism and colonisation? What is the specific historical context in which these terms must be located, and is their use limited by and to such context?

Colonisation, as understood by scholars, refers to a process or phenomenon by which people belonging to a nation establish colonies in other societies while retaining their bonds with the parent nation, and exploit the colonised societies to benefit the parent nation and themselves. Simply put, the process of establishing colonies is called colonisation and the policy of using colonisation to increase one's footprint is called colonialism. At least four forms of colonialism are recognised, namely exploitation colonialism, settler colonialism, surrogate colonialism and internal colonialism, the first two being the most well-known. In exploitation colonialism, the colonising group treats the colonised territory primarily as a resource to further its economic growth and increase the dominion under its control without actually settling in the colony. In settler colonialism, the colonisers not only retain their bonds with their parent nation but also settle in large numbers in the colony and take over all aspects of the colonised society, thereby reducing the natives to a secondary status.

'Coloniality' refers to the fundamental eleme t or thought process that informs the policy of colonialism and advances the subtler end goal of colonisation, namely colonisation of the mind through complete domination of the culture and worldview of the colonised society. In short, coloniality is the fount of the policy of colonialism that results in colonisation, whose ultimate objective is to mould the subjugated society in the image of the coloniser. Therefore, implicit in the use of coloniality is 'cultural coloniality', which represents its all-encompassing character. This process of culturally dominating the colonised society may be termed 'colonialisation', which is different from the overt process of colonisation. Although the world has seen other forms of colonisation (and hence, coloniality) prior to the European version, which the literature on coloniality acknowledges, the use of the term 'coloniality' in the literature is primarily with reference to European colonisation. In other words, unless indicated otherwise, 'coloniality' means not just 'cultural coloniality' but 'European cultural coloniality', while the response of erstwhile colonised societies (primarily, Latin American) to European cultural coloniality in order to reclaim their agency over their consciousness and subjectivities has been termed 'decoloniality'.

Scholars agree that every society has the right to define coloniality and, therefore, decoloniality for itself based on its own history and experience.[8] However, the general consensus appears to be that of all the sources and forms of colonialism and coloniality the world has witnessed, none equals the European version (specifically Western European colonialism) in its reach, omnipresence and recorded longevity, which continues to affect both erstwhile colonised societies and the rest of the world.[9] To be clear, in discussing European colonialism and coloniality, the literature includes Western imperialism since the latter is seen as the descendant of and the successor to European colonialism. Consequently, scholars have directed their energies at understanding the coloniality of European colonialism as well as its successor, Western imperialism, both of which have been collectively referred to as Eurocentrism or Western-centrism or Western-normativism or 'North Atlantic abstract universal fictionalism'.[10]

The origins of Eurocentrism spawned by European colonialism and coloniality have been traced to what has been referred to as 'the Age of Discovery/Exploration' in the fifteenth century when Christopher Columbus set out in 1492 to 'discover' the 'New World', namely the non-Christian world.[11] Columbus' voyage marked the beginning of European colonisation and heralded a new chapter in European history, which led to the emergence of new conceptions of time, space and subjectivity that had tectonic implications for that continent and, most importantly, for 'others', that is, the rest of the world. In fact, the investigative spirit of 'The Renaissance', which is believed to have started in the fourteenth century, is credited to have laid the foundations for the Age of Discovery. The Age of Discovery significantly overlapped with The Renaissance, which was followed by 'The Reformation', leading to the Treaty of Westphalia in 1648, which was, in turn, followed by what is treated as the zenith of European civilisation—'The Age of Enlightenment/Reason' and 'The Industrial Revolution'.

The use of 'The' for each of these essentially European milestones by Europeans and the rest of the world is significant since it demonstrates the universalisation of European history as the history of humanity, in particular its 'modern' history. Specifically, the period between the fifteenth and nineteenth centuries is believed to have given birth to 'modernity' and several 'modern' concepts and ideas that are unconsciously accepted not only by Europe but also the rest of the world, including erstwhile colonised societies, which proudly, albeit unfortunately, base their contemporary discourse on such 'modern' ideas. These 'modern' ideas have significantly affected and altered conceptions of nature, universe, human agency, religion, race, language, political organisation of societies, the nature of State, its relationship with religion, conceptions of law and human rights, treatment of genders, science, notions of development and more across the globe. During the period of colonisation, European provincialism on each of these facets of life was introduced, rather imposed, and universalised in colonised societies, thereby replacing indigenous worldviews. Since all of this has been traced by scholars to Columbus' expedition of 1492, the expedition and its significance for world history has engendered a raging debate.

One school of thought, the 'modern' school, believes that Columbus' voyage was and must be seen as a 'glorious and heroic achievement' that marked the beginning of the Christian West's 'destiny' to 'liberate' non-Christian indigenous societies from their wretched existence.[12] The second school of thought, the 'postmodern' school, is seen as a response to Europe's claims over modernity and rejects the grand narratives woven around it. However, this school's opposition to modernism is largely in the realm of culture.

The third school, namely the 'postcolonial' school, which enjoys a significant overlap with postmodern thought and even draws from it, too rejects the universalising claims of Eurocentrism albeit in the political realm; however, it uses the very same tools as the coloniser instead of deconstructing and questioning colonial presumptions.[13] For instance, while the postcolonial school focuses on the local, it tries to universalise the local, thereby falling prey to the same universalising tendency of colonialism. In other words, the postcolonial school certainly changes the *content* of the discussion but not the *terms of engagement* or the *framework* of the discussion, having imbibed the European penchant for universalisation.[14] The limitations of the postcolonial school, among other things, lie in its inability to see and comprehend the continued contemporary impact of colonial structures even after decolonisation.

The fourth school, namely the 'decolonial' school, akin to postcolonialism, challenges European universalisms, particularly in the political realm. It too believes that Columbus' voyage marked the beginning of one of the most repressive, bloody, racist and genocidal chapters ever witnessed in human history that led to the extinction of several cultures and, critically, wreaked havoc on nature on an unprecedented scale. However, where the decolonial school differs from postcolonial thought is its identification of the element of 'coloniality', which, according to it, informed European colonisation that began with the Age of Discovery.

According to decolonial thought, European coloniality gave birth to the 'cultural complex' of 'modernity' and 'rationality', apart from the 'modern' categories of religion and race. Importantly, according to the decolonial school, 'postcolonialism' gives the impression that the colonial mindset or consciousness ended with decolonisation, when, in fact, it has survived decolonisation and continues to impact decolonised/'independent' societies.

Also, the decolonial school rejects the totalising universalist claims of Europeanism in a much more balanced fashion. That is, instead of treating the European position as the sole universal benchmark, decoloniality prefers to treat it as but one of the options or subjectivities within the global pool of thought. Therefore, it rejects Europe's monopoly over time, space and subjectivity. It is important to understand these critical distinctions because it is easy to conflate and confuse the decolonial position with the postcolonial. Decolonial scholars have gone a step further to claim that while postcolonialism is a state of affairs, decoloniality is a *state of mind* just as coloniality is. These finer aspects will be discussed in some detail in the ensuing portions of this section of the book after the examination of coloniality as conceptualised and understood by the decolonial school.

According to the decolonial school, the celebration of the Age of Discovery by proponents of Europeanism, that is, European supremacism, is understandable because the period was preceded by the Dark Ages for a millennium *for Europe*. However, since the rest of the world did *not* live in the Dark Ages prior to the fifteenth century, the celebration of the Age of Discovery by several erstwhile colonised societies is truly tragic and naïve. This is because it shows that such societies have not even scratched the surface to understand the racial and religious supremacist character of the Age of Discovery and the European milestones that followed it, including the Enlightenment. They are oblivious to the impact of the Enlightenment on their ability to evaluate their own histories and cultures sans the shame, judgment and sanctimony induced by it. Decoloniality, therefore, seeks to restore the dignity of indigeneities and their subjectivities by unshackling them from the absolutism of European coloniality. These are the broad premises that inform decolonial scholarship which must be borne in mind even while discussing region- or country-specific experiences with European colonialism and coloniality. It is these foundational premises of the decolonial school that warrant attention and make its understanding imperative for decolonised societies which are still grappling with coloniality.

Interestingly, decolonial scholarship seems to have emanated from Latin America, which has contributed significantly to the understanding of coloniality and the response to it. In fact, the better part of the scholarship largely revolves around the Americas, which includes North America, South/Latin America and the Caribbean, followed by Africa. One would have expected Asian countries to lead the charge on this front given that the continent is home to living civilisations and indigenous cultural systems that have survived several forms of colonialism, not just the European variant. In fact, the continued survival of these living civilisations makes them the prime targets of coloniality in its present form, namely Western imperialism, and this makes the Asian voice all the more important from the standpoint of currency. And yet, Asia is not at the forefront of decolonial scholarship, which could indicate a deep-seated, continuing and unconscious coloniality in Asian societies, notwithstanding the survival of their cultural systems. This, as we shall see, is attributable to the predominance of postcolonial thought in Asia and the Middle East, especially Bharat and Palestine.

Also, the literature that exists on Asia in relation to coloniality from a decolonial perspective, even where it presents a subjective and contextual view of the Asian experience with coloniality, appears to imitate the works on the Americas and Africa. It is true that there are broad similarities in the colonial experience across continents, given the near-identical aims, actions and

underlying coloniality of European colonisers regardless of their
nationalities. However, this should not have limited voices from
Asia or voices that discuss Asia from capturing the diversity and
peculiarity of their colonial experience better so as to contribute
to the still-nascent pool of decolonial thought. Such an endeavour
is overdue and would, in fact, be consistent with decolonial
thought since a universalising approach to decoloniality would
defeat its stated objective. In other words, decoloniality, by
definition, accepts and underscores the need for subjectivity,
contextuality and local resistance to abstract universal definitions.
This is precisely why societies and civilisations of Asia can and
must craft for themselves their own definitions of coloniality
and decoloniality without being fettered or limited in any manner
by the experience and conclusions of the Americas and Africa.

One of the reasons I believe that the Asian experience could
impact the way colonialism, coloniality and decoloniality are
perceived is because, while almost the entirety of the Americas
and close to half of Africa have been converted to the religion
of the European coloniser (and about 40 per cent to Islam), this
is not the case with vast swathes of Asia. In stark contrast, the
practise of precolonial faith systems by quite a few countries
of Asia, such as Bharat, makes them 'living indigenous
civilisations' to a significant extent. This makes a critical
difference since decolonial scholarship, while being aware of
the theological origins of European coloniality, appears to
focus primarily on its racial aspects. This could be because
in the geography of origin of decolonial thought, namely the
Americas, colonised societies have become almost entirely
Christian. In other words, the preoccupation of decolonial
scholarship with race and its reluctance to address religion
with the same degree of candour may be attributed to the fact
that the regions that have produced much of the scholarship
on coloniality so far, follow the religion of the coloniser,
namely Christianity. Their demographic reality, perhaps,

offers an explanation as to their gaze being more alive to race than to religion, since reclaiming their indigenous religious identities may seem impossible despite having embarked on their decolonial journeys. Given the huge Christian settler colonial populations in the Americas in particular, the numbers may not even be conducive for indigenous peoples even if they wanted to revert to the faith of their ancestors. And if this were not enough, pragmatic considerations, such as the highly organised and evangelical nature of Christianity and its status as a global majority, have a direct and real bearing on the ability of any erstwhile non-Christian colonised society to reclaim and return to its roots.

These complex realities may explain the predominant focus of decolonial scholarship on race, as opposed to both religion and race. In my view, the Critical Theory of Race (popularly acronymised as CRT for Critical Race Theory), in some ways, may be treated as the precursor to decolonial thought.[15] This could explain the reasons for the scholarship on coloniality being centred on race, which continues to shine a spotlight on the race consciousness of the coloniser, its direct impact on the nature of colonial power, the manner of its exercise and its myriad all-pervasive manifestations. This is not to deny the existence of some stellar growing scholarship on coloniality that expressly brings religion, specifically Christianity, within its ambit, thereby acknowledging its role in European colonisation and in engendering race consciousness. That said, subject to correction, to the extent I have read the literature on coloniality, a significant cross-section of the scholarship continues to speak around the issue of religion, barring a handful of scholars, which could be a hangover from the religion-reticent legacy of CRT.

To be fair, this could also be because decolonial thought is relatively recent and, therefore, the Asian perspective, in particular the Indian perspective, could do a lot to address this reticence of the existing scholarship on coloniality in relation to religion without being dissuaded by it. This is because, unlike the Americas and Africa, since Asia has managed to preserve its non-Christian character to a considerable degree, its contemporary everyday encounters with coloniality are, in a way, representative of European coloniality's unfinished business in Asia. In fact, the active local resistance offered by the indigenous faith systems of Asia, in particular Bharat, to coloniality and its underlying evangelical motivations makes the study of coloniality all the more relevant and critical to their existence and survival.

Notwithstanding the reluctance of decolonial scholarship to discuss the role of religion—a reluctance that is hopefully diminishing—I believe that the societies of Asia and the rest of the world do have a lot to learn from the American and African experience with coloniality. After all, the aims and modus operandi of European colonisation were similar and were tempered only by the local conditions and the degree of resistance offered by different indigenous societies. This could at least present contemporary Asian societies with a decent starting point in their respective *original* decolonial journeys. It is also important that the Asians ask themselves whether the decolonial approach is the better approach for them in comparison to the postcolonial approach. As stated earlier, this question will be discussed in some detail in this section after discussing the various facets of coloniality, including its OET and racial foundations.

The Discovery of Coloniality and the Birth of Decoloniality

Destruction of the Indies, 1552

Depiction of Christopher Columbus' soldiers chopping the hands off of Arawak Indians who failed to meet the mining quota in Bartolomé de Las Casas' - *Brevisima relación de la destrucción de las Indias*. The print was made by two Flemish artists (who did not actually witness these atrocities)—Joos van Winghe was the designer and Theodor de Bry, the engraver.

At the turn of the twentieth century, after close to five centuries of European colonialism, thanks to the ebb and flow of history, the native elites of colonised societies began asserting themselves. From seeking political autonomy as dominions within colonising empires, they gradually progressed to demanding freedom as sovereign and independent 'nation-states' that could write their own destinies just as colonising nations could. The aspiration of the colonised to be sovereign nation-states on European lines has been attributed to European coloniality[1], owing to close to two centuries of unbroken colonialism. Scholars are of the view that coloniality was entrenched in colonised societies through the politico-legal infrastructure of European colonisers as well as the education system introduced by them, which shaped the thinking of the native elites. In fact, the early introduction of colonial education systems in colonised societies and the replacement of indigenous epistemologies and their structures ensured that coloniality informed their present, shaped their ideas of the future and, critically, coloured their visions of the past.[2] Depending on the inherent vitality and resilience of colonised cultures, the extent of internalisation of coloniality in the consciousness of dominated societies became truly evident when even their quests for political independence from the coloniser were based on the very framework introduced by him.

Most colonised societies did not realise that their entire worldview had changed, for they could not see beyond political independence and aspired for freedom to govern themselves, albeit using the same values and institutions they had 'inherited' from the European coloniser. In other words, owing to coloniality, the vision of independence of most native elites was limited to the politico-economic sphere, namely decolonisation, but did not include decolonialisation because they accepted the European worldview on the all-important cultural front as well.[3] Therefore, all that the colonialised native elites sought by way of 'independence' was the agency to be able to write their own futures but using the ideas, rules, tools and institutions of the erstwhile coloniser, which were designed for top-down imposition on a conquered and subjugated people in order to 'civilise' them.[4]

While coloniality is a fairly plausible explanation for the quest of nation-statehood of colonised societies, a more pragmatic way of looking at it could be that the global presence of European colonising empires, and therefore, the global spread of colonial politico-economic ideas and institutions, may have made it inconceivable and infeasible for colonised societies to revert to their precolonial forms of political and social organisation.[5] They may have been genuinely apprehensive of being isolated in a largely Europeanised and integrated world if they reverted to their precolonial political institutions. In today's telecom parlance, this can be compared with the situation of a mobile network operator, who, in the interest of interoperability, must comply with the technological standards laid down by the European Telecommunications Standards Institute (ETSI), failing which, the former's mobile phone users cannot interact with the users of other telecom operators that comply with the ETSI standards. Crudely speaking, similar considerations would have weighed on most colonised societies upon achieving political independence since the world's economy revolved around the West.

Therefore, given the omnipresence of European politico-economic and cultural coloniality, perhaps the only viable option available to the newly decolonised societies was to embrace the political structures, institutions and lexicon left behind by the coloniser to avoid the prospect of disintegration, annexation, anarchy and global isolation. However, broadly speaking, decolonised societies fell into two categories. In the first category, those societies that had a strong sense of indigenous consciousness, or whatever remained of it after centuries of colonialism, sought to compensate for continuing with European political legacy by infusing the edifice with ideas drawn from their cultures or by customising European definitions to suit their cultural palate. In the second category, those societies that were helmed by colonialised native elites became crucibles for a constant struggle between such elites and the native masses that had been relegated to the status of 'subalterns' and pushed to the margins of the process of nation-building. In this category of societies, on the one hand, the colonialised Europeanised native elites had stepped into the shoes of the coloniser to recast the native masses and the society in the European mould; on the other hand, the native masses were torn between the aspiration projected by the rulers to 'catch up' with the West and the opportunity history had finally presented them with to reclaim their roots, consciousness and identity. It was in the latter category of societies that coloniality manifested itself in all its glory, especially in the spheres of political thought, environment, language, religion, law, gender, economics, production of knowledge, education and even popular culture.[6]

To add to the woes of decolonised societies, while the era of colonialism was over, its place was occupied by an even more worthy successor—Western imperialism—which inherited and expanded the legacy of coloniality. As scholars have pointed out, Western imperialism has proved to be a much more effective derivative of colonialism since it extended the territorial reach and depth of coloniality. Not only is the relationship of Western imperialism with other cultures the same as that of colonialism, namely 'colonisation of the imagination of the dominated', it has also proved to be vastly more successful than colonialism in creating well-networked global power structures and totalising sub-frameworks that have sustained and advanced coloniality.[7] This is in stark contrast to colonialism which was much more territorial.

From the standpoint of preserving the continuity of coloniality, the Western-normative framework has delivered all the benefits of colonialism and more, without having to assume the same degree of burden and responsibility as colonialism, and with the added benefit of plausible deniability. While colonialism was more visible and direct because it required the subjugation of a population, the subterranean nature of Western imperialism has ensured that the dominated society aspires to become part of the erstwhile coloniser's social fabric *after* decolonisation. As a consequence, scholars agree that coloniality remains the most prevalent and powerful form of domination in the world. This could not have become possible without sufficient investment by the coloniser in the political, religious, knowledge and legal systems of colonised societies, which were carried forward by decolonised societies.

Until the end of the Cold War in the late 1980s, that is, even after close to four decades of decolonisation, there was not enough rigorous scholarship that made sense of the nature of colonial power and its continuing impact on the life and polity of decolonised nations. The Cold War had demonstrated that despite decolonisation, erstwhile colonies were caught in the crossfire between superpowers who sought to dominate the world. Even those who claimed to be non-aligned, could not remain uninfluenced by the Cold War and its dynamics. It was during this period in the late 1980s that Peruvian sociologist Aníbal Quijano presented the concept of coloniality of power, specifically European power, which he distinguished from colonialism, as the very fount of colonialism. In other words, colonisation is the process, colonialism is the policy and coloniality is the mindset or the thought that underpins or drives colonialism.

Coloniality, according to Quijano, is the totalising thought behind colonialism, which monopolises time, space and subjectivity, and makes all of them the exclusive preserve of the European coloniser. Quijano and other scholars, such as Sylvia Wynter, Walter D. Mignolo, Catherine E. Walsh, Nelson Maldonado-Torres and Ramón Grosfoguel, have contributed to the scholarship on the pathology of coloniality, its universalist claims and its all-pervasive character. Not only did they analyse the problem, they also offered an option/alternative, namely decoloniality, which moved away from the model presented by the postmodern and postcolonial schools. Decoloniality has been described as the movement for reclamation and restoration of indigeneity and its subjectivities. In hindsight, it could be said that the existence of omnipresent coloniality and the constantly shrinking space for indigeneity meant that at some point indigeneity would resist and talk back to coloniality, and seek to reclaim its consciousness and space. However, since it took several decades after decolonisation for the natives to find their voice and speak the language of decoloniality, it is important to understand the true nature of coloniality, its motivations, underpinnings, invisible yet ever-present devices and its impact on the entirety of indigenous worldviews. Not only would this help us understand the 'why' of decoloniality, it would also help us make sense of the 'how', rather a plurality of them.

On this front, Quijano's work represents the early pioneering years of the scholarship on coloniality when its primary focus was the colonial character of European power. Quijano was of the view that race was central to European coloniality and that there was an inextricable link between European/Western coloniality and modernity/rationality. He consciously used Europe and the West interchangeably owing to the European foundations of the Western worldview and civilisation. His diagnosis was that race consciousness and the introduction of the 'cultural complex' of modernity/rationality were the twin pillars of European coloniality or simply coloniality. These observations and propositions were based on his critical examination of the impact of European colonialism and coloniality on the societies and cultures of what is known as Latin America today. He identified that the relationship between European colonisers and the colonised societies of Latin America was one of 'direct political, social and cultural domination', which he called 'Eurocentered colonialism'. The European coloniser consciously believed in the 'biological and structural superiority' of his race, which, in the mind of the coloniser, distinguished him from the colonised. This belief, which was the premise of the colonial power structure and a figment of the coloniser's self-important worldview, was legitimised as being 'objective' or 'scientific' or 'rational', and therefore, 'natural'. This evidences the use of scientism by the coloniser to perpetuate, normalise and legitimise stereotypes about the colonised in order to justify discrimination. In fact, the 'scientific' racial consciousness of the coloniser led to race-based stratification of colonised populations across the world, and created specific forms of discrimination which remained in those societies long after decolonisation.

As part of the larger aim of stratification of the colonised society, the coloniser subtly co-opted dominant groups or the elite from the colonised society into the colonial power structure to gradually wean them away from the rest of their people. This was done by inventing pseudo-scientific racial theories to create fissures in the social structures of the native society, while simultaneously teaching them the ways of European culture. Quijano's seminal contribution was his acute observation that the dominant elites of colonised native societies were acculturated not just into the colonial power structure but also the European worldview through the introduction of the cultural complex, namely 'European modernity/rationality', that is, imputing Europeanness to anything that is new or novel or contemporary or relevant and rational. Modernity and rationality, as introduced and employed by the European coloniser, therefore, represented (and still represent) the weaponisation of time and appropriation of the very idea of 'reason' by the European coloniser and his successor, the Western imperialist, who negate and deny the histories and the lived experiences of entire civilisations from the moment of their arrival.[8] This gave birth to the process of cultural colonisation and the phenomenon or state of mind known as 'cultural coloniality'. In a nutshell, coloniality refers to a meta phenomenon that affects the mental constitution of the colonised society and reorients its entire worldview to bring it in line with the coloniser's by distorting, stereotyping, eliminating or acculturating the indigenous worldview.

The effect of the introduction of the modernity/rationality complex into the culture of colonised societies was that the entirety of native worldviews, especially their ontological, theological and epistemological systems, were 'otherised'. That is, the indigenous worldview became the 'other' to the 'modern and rational mainstream' and had to prove itself on the judgmental anvils of the latter. The native worldview could never succeed at proving its 'modern' relevance because the coloniality/modernity/rationality complex was *designed* either to exclude indigenous perspectives or acculturate it in case it happened to be of value, without crediting the indigenous perspective. According to Quijano, this is where the true genius of the European coloniser lay—not in the brutal economic and political repression of the native, but in successfully projecting his way of life as the aspirational ideal. The blanket consumption of this idea by the dominant native elites served to alienate them from the rest of the colonised society. As a consequence, if a fault line existed in the colonised society prior to the arrival of the European coloniser, the active co-option of the elites in the dominating power structure as well as the worldview of the coloniser only served to deepen the fault line. If a fault line did not exist hitherto, it was consciously created. In either case, the fault lines remained even after decolonisation as the legacy of colonialism.

That said, the coloniser was not content with the co-option of only the dominant elites among the natives but was interested in converting the entire native society to his way of life. To this end, Quijano pointed out that while the coloniser saw the colonised society as an economic resource to feed on, he also indulged in the systematic and extensive repression of indigenous ideas, beliefs, images and knowledge, including the systems of production of knowledge. This deprived the colonised society of its ability to respond culturally, even if it did not have the wherewithal to resist politically or militarily. Since most native elites that were at the helm of the centres of culture and production of knowledge had surrendered their agency over the indigenous worldview, the masses too gradually followed suit. The cumulative effect was the deep embedding of coloniality in the consciousness of the colonised society, so much so that it started believing that it had been defeated *because* of its cultural moorings. To the colonised and now *colonialised* native, it seemed that the only way to regain dignity was by adopting European culture and thought processes, which included the European way of achieving economic prosperity, that is, by exploiting nature. This disruption of the critical relationship between indigenous societies and nature came to affect the entire world.

Apart from the disastrous impact on nature, the universalisation of European culture made it *the* benchmark against which all other cultures had to judge their self-worth. In the process, the modernity/rationality complex was entrenched in every colonised society and reinforced in the colonising society as well.[9] The direct and intended consequence of coloniality and the introduction of the modernity/rationality complex was the creation of supposedly universal standards for morals, ethics, religion, language, knowledge, scientific temper, political organisation, nationhood, individual rights and more—in short, culture and civilisation.[10]

This complex did not die with decolonisation but remains alive and kicking even today, just as coloniality is. After all, as scholars have identified, coloniality goes hand in hand with modernity/rationality and vice versa. As long as coloniality is alive, despite its outward proclamations of open-mindedness, dialogue and diversity, the colonial DNA of modernity and rationality will continue to actively resist and oust indigeneity. It will staunchly refuse to accord indigeneity the respect of an equal and will continue to use time and 'reason' as weapons to question the very relevance of the indigenous point of view, because the underlying premise—indigeneity is racially inferior—has not changed. The successful universalisation of the modernity/rationality complex is further evidenced by the fact that neither word is prefaced with 'European' anymore despite the entire edifice being Eurocentric.

Interestingly, in her paper titled 'Early Modernity: The History of a Word', Patricia Seed, who specialises in early modern and colonial European eras, traced the origins of the word 'modern' to the sixth century CE, when it was first used in northern Italy.[11] This was when the Roman Empire still existed but northern Italy was conquered and ruled by Germanic Ostrogoths. According to Seed, the word 'modern' made its debut in the context of architecture when the Ostrogothic ruler of northern Italy encouraged wealthy Roman families to undertake reconstruction of public buildings at their private expense. The outcome was that the new buildings had a different architectural style that distinguished them from those built under Roman imperial rule. Praising the contribution of one particular family for its reconstruction of the Theatre of Pompey, the scribe of the Ostrogothic ruler called the family 'a careful imitator of antiquity and the noblest founder of modern works' (translation). In this context, according to Seed, the word modern simply meant 'different' without any value being imputed to it, neither positive nor negative.

Subsequently, for a brief period, the word doubled as a synonym for 'new', thereby bringing in the element of time. In other words, the word 'modern' was not only a reference to the time that something belonged to, it was also importantly a reference to the period it did *not* belong to. Seed revealed that around the early fourteenth century, 'modern' was significantly used in Dante's *The Divine Comedy*, wherein it was a synonym for 'contemporary'. It was used to compare the present with the past, with the present faring poorly, making the use of 'modern' a veiled criticism of the present. According to Seed, it was only almost a century later, around the 1430s, that 'modern' was used in Southern Romance languages to show the past in poor light and congratulate the present.

As for English, Scottish poet William Dunbar is credited for using it first in his poems, wherein 'modern' was used to portray the present in a positive light while remaining tight-lipped about the past. The adversarial pitting of the past and the present with the balance tilting in favour of the latter occurred in English in the sixteenth century when 'modern' meant 'someone who takes part in the tastes and cares of his age, and is opposed to all conservatism'. In a nutshell, positive connotations, such as open-mindedness, newness and relevance, were imputed to 'modern', and negative stereotypes, such as parochiality, outdatedness and rigidity, were associated with 'conservative/traditional'. That this imputation coincided with the period around which European powers had established colonies across the globe was no coincidence. This is evidenced by the established nexus between coloniality and 'modernity', both of which are undergirded by notions of anthropological superiority, as articulated by Quijano.

Quijano identified that the process of classification of the world on racial lines by the European coloniser led to sub-humanisation and dehumanisation of several communities depending on their perceived worth in the eyes of the coloniser. The ramifications of such a classification included geographic identities acquiring racial connotations, specific skin tones being associated with the respective races of the coloniser and the colonised, and the creation of a new structure of division of labour and resources. Each of these strands ultimately contributed to the creation of serfdom and slavery, notions of master (or superior) and slave (inferior) races, and notions of the 'manifest destiny' of some to rule over others and the fate of others to be perpetually ruled. Lines were drawn between the West and the East, the 'civilised' and the 'primitive', the scientific and the superstitious, the rational and the irrational, modern and traditional, historical and mythological—essentially, European and non-European. Even where the coloniser ('the Occident') begrudgingly admitted that there was indeed culture and civilisation outside of Europe, he resorted to stereotyping and exotification by calling it 'the Orient'.

This racial classification of the entirety of humanity to subserve colonial interests forms the foundation of the Eurocentric world order. In fact, Quijano highlighted the relationship between European colonialism and globalisation that resulted in Western hegemony over all of human experience. Critically, this included control over all forms of subjectivity, culture and production of knowledge. Quijano did not mince words in calling the phenomenon of globalisation the 'culmination of a process that began with the constitution of America and colonial/modern Eurocentered capitalism as a new global power'. Race and, therefore, coloniality remain as relevant today as they were in the colonial era, notwithstanding globalisation's professed love for the concept of a 'global village'. Simply put, globalisation, contrary to popular perception, is not a friend of diversity, nor is it a melting pot of cultures. On the contrary, it denotes the gradual and unconscious eradication of heterogeneity, more particularly, the diversity of indigeneity, and is proof of the existence of common denominators of culture and civilisation for the entire world, which are distinctly Western-normative in character.

Quijano also argued that any attempts to obfuscate history by taking the position that modernity was not European but was merely a reference to newness of ideas would be tantamount to turning a blind eye to the colonialism of the last five centuries, which had lent specific meanings to modernity and rationality that are distinctly European in nature. In other words, the totalising effect of European colonisation since the Age of Discovery has given the word 'modernity' a distinct historical connotation that is impossible to ignore given the continuing presence of coloniality.[12] Critically, Quijano acknowledged that while colonialism may have existed in different parts of the world in different forms prior to European colonisation, none of them compared to European colonialism's vision of global domination. This is because European coloniality required the entire world to share a common perspective on the entirety of human history and experience.

It is precisely for this reason that it is impossible to limit the impact of European colonialism to any one particular facet of life. The intended goal of European colonialism and the outcome was global cultural hegemony, which includes a subject that has become a sensitive one to broach due to deeply ingrained unconscious coloniality—the religious origins and impact of European colonialism on indigenous onto-epistemological structures and processes, simply put, their spirituality and faith. Given the catch-all use of 'culture' in the literature on coloniality, there is a tendency to assume that colonialism was driven only by race, economics and hunger for power. Fortunately, and refreshingly, despite the extensive focus on race due to the legacy of the Critical Theory of Race, there exists literature that discusses the religious motivations that spurred race-based colonialism and its impact on indigenous onto-epistemological systems. This facet of colonialism is especially relevant to those decolonised societies that have not been fully converted to the European coloniser's faith and, therefore, continue to face and resist coloniality's expansionist advances even today.

In his work on race and coloniality, Quijano did touch upon the ways in which colonised societies were forced to learn and adopt the culture of the coloniser so as to aid the process of colonisation, which included learning both the material and metaphysical, specifically Judeo-Christian religious traditions. That said, in my view, the Christian character of Christopher Columbus' expansionist voyage of 'discovery' was dealt with more explicitly by Jamaican writer and cultural theorist Sylvia Wynter, Walter D. Mignolo (Argentine semiotician and professor at Duke University, North Carolina), Nelson Maldonado-Torres (a professor of Latino and Caribbean Studies) and others,[13] who have contributed to the understanding of the direct role of the Christian religion in European colonisation and its effect on the race consciousness of the coloniser.

Wynter drew attention to the reconceptualisation of geography and the very meaning of 'humanity' triggered by the Age of Discovery.[14] She argued that since the Age of Discovery altered conceptions of time, space and subjectivity, it also altered notions of empathy for the 'other' since humans have always used time, space and subjectivity to make sense of themselves and their surroundings. This meant that the Age of Discovery also led to new conceptions of life and death, and legal agency over them. In a nutshell, European coloniality/modernity affected not just ontology, theology, epistemology and anthropology, it also birthed new notions of ethics (and therefore, affected education), and defined both politics and policy.

Wynter was also forthright in her view that the Age of Discovery, evangelisation and colonisation went hand in hand, and credited that period with 'secularisation of the key elements of the Christian episteme', which meant that what was valid within the Christian worldview was deemed 'good' for the entire world, and those that did not conform had to convert or perish. Her views are certainly supported by the fact that a papal bull called *Inter Caetera* was issued by Pope Alexander VI in 1493, which authorised Spain and Portugal to colonise, convert and enslave non-Christians. Following are the contents of the bull, which make for an eye-opening read:

Alexander, bishop, servant of the servants of God, to the illustrious sovereigns, our very dear son in Christ, Ferdinand, king, and our very dear daughter in Christ, Isabella, queen of Castile, Leon, Aragon, Sicily, and Granada, health and apostolic benediction. Among other works well pleasing to the Divine Majesty and cherished of our heart, this assuredly ranks highest, that in our times especially the Catholic faith and the Christian religion be exalted and be everywhere increased and spread, that the health of souls be cared for and that barbarous nations be overthrown and brought to the faith itself. Wherefore inasmuch as by the favor of divine clemency, we, though of insufficient merits, have been called to this Holy See of Peter, recognizing that as true Catholic kings and princes, such as we have known you always to be, and as your illustrious deeds already known to almost the whole world declare, you not only eagerly desire but with every effort, zeal, and diligence, without regard to hardships, expenses, dangers, with the shedding even of your blood, are laboring to that end; recognizing also that you have long since dedicated to this purpose your whole soul and all your endeavors—as witnessed in these times with so much glory to the Divine Name in your recovery of the kingdom of Granada from the yoke of the Saracens—*we therefore are rightly led, and hold it as our duty, to grant you even of our own accord and in your favor those things whereby with effort each day more hearty you may be enabled for the honor of God himself and the spread of the Christian rule to carry forward your holy and praiseworthy purpose so pleasing to immortal God.*

We have indeed learned that you, who for a long time had intended to seek out and discover certain islands and mainlands remote and unknown and not hitherto discovered by others, to the end that you might bring to the worship of our Redeemer and the profession of the Catholic faith their residents and inhabitants, having been up to the present time greatly engaged in the siege and recovery of the kingdom itself of Granada were unable to accomplish this holy and praiseworthy purpose; *but the said kingdom having at length been regained, as was pleasing to the Lord, you, with the wish to fulfill your desire, chose our beloved son, Christopher Columbus, a man assuredly worthy and of the highest recommendations and fitted for so great an undertaking, whom you furnished with ships and men equipped for like designs, not without the greatest hardships, dangers, and expenses, to make diligent quest for these remote and unknown mainlands and islands through the sea, where hitherto no one had sailed;* and they at length, with divine aid and with the utmost diligence sailing in the ocean sea, discovered certain very remote islands and even mainlands that hitherto had not been discovered by others; wherein dwell very many peoples living in peace, and, as reported, going unclothed, and not eating flesh. Moreover, as your aforesaid envoys are of opinion, these very peoples living in the said islands and countries believe in one God, the Creator in heaven, and seem sufficiently disposed to embrace the Catholic faith and be trained in good morals.

And it is hoped that, were they instructed, the name of the Savior, our Lord Jesus Christ, would easily be introduced into the said countries and islands. Also, on one of the chief of these aforesaid islands the said Christopher has already caused to be put together and built a fortress fairly equipped, wherein he has stationed as garrison certain Christians, companions of his, who are to make search for other remote and unknown islands and mainlands. In the islands and countries already discovered are found gold, spices, and very many other precious things of divers kinds and qualities.

Wherefore, as becomes Catholic kings and princes, after earnest consideration of all matters, especially of the rise and spread of the Catholic faith, as was the fashion of your ancestors, kings of renowned memory, you have purposed with the favor of divine clemency to bring under your sway the said mainlands and islands with their residents and inhabitants and to bring them to the Catholic faith. Hence, heartily commending in the Lord this your holy and praiseworthy purpose, and desirous that it be duly accomplished, and that the name of our Savior be carried into those regions, we exhort you very earnestly in the Lord and by your reception of holy baptism, whereby you are bound to our apostolic commands, and by the bowels of the mercy of our Lord Jesus Christ, enjoin strictly, that inasmuch as with eager zeal for the true faith you design to equip and despatch this expedition, you purpose also, as is your duty, to lead the peoples dwelling in those islands and countries to embrace the Christian religion; nor at any time let dangers or hardships deter you therefrom, with the stout hope and trust in your hearts that Almighty God will further your undertakings.

And, in order that you may enter upon so great an undertaking with greater readiness and heartiness endowed with the benefit of our apostolic favor, we, of our own accord, not at your instance nor the request of anyone else in your regard, but of our own sole largess and certain knowledge and out of the fullness of our apostolic power, by the authority of Almighty God conferred upon us in blessed Peter and of the vicarship of Jesus Christ, which we hold on earth, do by tenor of these presents, should any of said islands have been found by your envoys and captains, give, grant, and assign to you and your heirs and successors, kings of Castile and Leon, forever, together with all their dominions, cities, camps, places, and villages, and all rights, jurisdictions, and appurtenances, all islands and mainlands found and to be found, discovered and to be discovered towards the west and south, by drawing and establishing a line from the Arctic pole, namely the north, to the Antarctic pole, namely the south, *no matter whether the said mainlands and islands are found and to be found in the direction of India or towards any other quarter, the said line to be distant one hundred leagues towards the west and south from any of the islands commonly known as the Azores and Cape Verde.*

With this proviso however that none of the islands and mainlands, found and to be found, discovered and to be discovered, beyond that said line towards the west and south, be in the actual possession of any Christian king or prince up to the birthday of our Lord Jesus Christ just past from which the present year one thousand four hundred and ninety-three begins. And we make, appoint, and depute you and your said heirs and successors lords of them with full and free power, authority, and jurisdiction of every kind; with this proviso however, that by this our gift, grant, and assignment no right acquired by any Christian prince, who may be in actual possession of said islands and mainlands prior to the said birthday of our Lord Jesus Christ, is hereby to be understood to be withdrawn or taken away.

Moreover we command you in virtue of holy obedience that, employing all due diligence in the premises, as you also promise—nor do we doubt your compliance therein in accordance with your loyalty and royal greatness of spirit— you should appoint to the aforesaid mainlands and islands worthy, God-fearing, learned, skilled, and experienced men, in order to instruct the aforesaid inhabitants and residents in the Catholic faith and train them in good morals. Furthermore, under penalty of excommunication late sententie *to be incurred ipso facto, should anyone thus contravene, we strictly forbid all persons of whatsoever rank, even imperial and royal, or of whatsoever estate, degree, order, or condition, to dare, without your special permit or that of your aforesaid heirs and successors, to go for the purpose of trade or any other reason to the islands or* mainlands, found and to be found, discovered and to be discovered, towards the west and south, by drawing and establishing a line from the Arctic pole to the Antarctic pole, no matter whether the mainlands and islands, found and to be found, lie in the direction of India or toward any other quarter whatsoever, the said line to be distant one hundred leagues towards the west and south, as is aforesaid, from any of the islands commonly known as the Azores and Cape Verde; apostolic constitutions and ordinances and other decrees whatsoever to the contrary notwithstanding.

We trust in Him from whom empires and governments and all good things proceed, that, should you, with the Lord's guidance, pursue this holy and praiseworthy undertaking, in a short while your hardships and endeavors will attain the most felicitous result, to the happiness and glory of all Christendom. But inasmuch as it would be difficult to have these present letters sent to all places where desirable, we wish, and with similar accord and knowledge do decree, that to copies of them, signed by the hand of a public notary commissioned therefor, and sealed with the seal of any ecclesiastical officer or ecclesiastical court, the same respect is to be shown in court and outside as well as anywhere else as would be given to these presents should they thus be exhibited or shown. Let no one, therefore, infringe, or with rash boldness contravene, this our recommendation, exhortation, requisition, gift, grant, assignment, constitution, deputation, decree, mandate, prohibition, and will. Should anyone presume to attempt this, be it known to him that he will incur the wrath of Almighty God and of the blessed apostles Peter and Paul. Given at Rome, at St. Peter's, in the year of the incarnation of our Lord one thousand four hundred and ninety-three, the fourth of May, and the first year of our pontificate.

Gratis by order of our most holy lord, the pope.

Alexander

May 4, 1493[15] [emphasis added]

The Christian command to convert non-Christians could not have been more explicit. Importantly, the reference to India in the bull was of direct consequence to the European colonisation of Bharat as we shall see later in Chapter 8. While the bull was issued after Columbus' expedition of 1492, as is evident from the bull, Christian injunctions undergirded both the expedition and the subsequent voyages to the New World. According to Wynter, the treatment of 'pagan polytheistic peoples' as 'idolators' by Columbus was traceable to the Judeo-Christian perception of the world's population being divided into:

1. Christians (who had heard and accepted the new Word of the gospel),
2. infidels like the Muslims and Jews, who, although they were monotheists, had refused the Word, and
3. those pagan polytheistic peoples who had either ignored or had not yet been preached the Word.

Wynter was of the view that the religious term 'idolator' informed the meaning of secular terms, such as 'Indios' or 'Indians', which led to the religion-induced racial othering of non-Christian idol-worshipping communities encountered by Columbus. The encounter of the Christian European coloniser with non-Christian idol-worshipping societies, in turn, led to the justification of 'liberation' and 'civilisation' being offered for the colonisation of a religiously and, hence, racially inferior people. This ultimately paved the way for institutionalised slavery and an economy based on it.[16] Mignolo too echoed these thoughts in his paper titled 'Racism as We Sense It Today' in which he charted the Christian OET-driven origins of the European coloniser's obsession with race/ethnicity.[17]

Building on the works of Quijano and Wynter, Nelson Maldonado-Torres suggested that religion as an anthropological category and race as an organising principle of human identification and social organisation were the products of European colonialism, which only expanded with the growth of Western modernity.[18] According to him, both religion and race were constituted together and became two of the most central categories that altered global history at every level. Therefore, the critical theory of religion was highly relevant to understanding the critical theory of race, and both were relevant to understanding the evolution of ethics. In essence, any understanding of coloniality/modernity was incomplete without applying the twin lenses of religion and race, and the only way to present an alternative foundation for ethics was to adopt a decolonial approach, given the near-complete hegemony of coloniality and modernity on contemporary ideas of ethics.

According to Torres, the Age of Discovery necessitated the broadening of the understanding of European conceptions of religion when the Christian European coloniser came into contact with non-Christian indigenous societies of the New World. Citing the work of Guy Stroumsa, an Israeli scholar of religious studies, Torres took the view that the Age of Discovery prompted a new approach to religion in view of Christianity's encounter with Amerindians; this is what makes the Age of Discovery relevant for understanding the emergence of the modern categories of religion and race. According to him, this was a major 'epistemic revolution' in its own right. He also felt that the link between race and religion was better understood by taking into account Christianity's theological conceptions of Judaism, given its attempts to sever itself from its Jewish racial roots, as well as its perceptions of Islam. For a more comprehensive understanding of the race–religion interplay, he suggested the inclusion of perceptions of blackness (namely the perceived link between race, colour and the existence of a soul) and indigeneity as well.

On the issue of broadening of conceptions of religion upon Christianity's encounter with indigenous societies, Torres' interpretation of Columbus' encounter with the native peoples of Americas differed from Wynter's. He was of the view that since Christianity recognised only three categories— Christians, infidels and idolators—Columbus initially struggled to place the natives of the Americas in any of the three, and, therefore, assumed that they were not people from a 'wrong' or 'false' religion, but were simply without religion. The absence of religion was perceived as the absence of a soul in Christian thought, with the soul being a condition precedent for a human to establish a connection with the divine. This divide between those with a soul and without, according to Torres, led to race consciousness in the European coloniser because the coloniser saw the coloured native people as 'non-souls'. This converted religion into an anthropological category because it had become a marker of race.

That the European Christian coloniser was White and the native peoples were 'Black' (or of colour) was not lost on the former. The White Christian became the one with a soul, and therefore fully human, while the Black native was without a soul, and therefore not fully human, or simply non-human.

Owing to this crucible of religion, race and colour, the soulless non-Christian Black natives were subjected to religion-induced dehumanisation, which justified and facilitated their treatment as slaves, or at the very least, as those upon whom the light of Christianity, Europeanness and civilisation had to be shone.

Entire continents and societies were associated with soullessness, requiring either enslavement or conversion, since adopting Christianity was believed to infuse a soul into the dark soulless native. In other words, in the eyes of the Christian European coloniser, he was not merely 'saving' the soul of a non-Christian infidel or idolator but was breathing soul into a Satan-worshipping subhuman, an animal, through his Christianising and civilising European touch. If this healing touch was resisted, the subhuman had to be put down ruthlessly like a beast. What is important to note is that whether approached from the perspective of Wynter, where natives were seen as idolators by Columbus, or from the point of view of Torres, that Columbus considered them soulless, both views emanated from Christian OET as it existed then and shared a common purpose—native non-Christian communities had to convert or die.

Initially, native Americans were welcoming of Europeans, as evidenced by the alteration of their Creation lore to accommodate the existence of the 'White man'. However, as contact and trade increased between the two groups, the native gradually saw his land being lost to the European to cover the debts incurred in the course of trade,[19] and as the coloniser's greed for native land increased, conversion to Christianity did too. At the very least, serious efforts were invested by Christian European missionaries to map local traditions and deities onto Christianity to reconcile the two and gradually ease the native into the coloniser's religion. Conversion to Christianity was also projected to the native as a way of gaining social respectability, acceptance into the circles of the coloniser and access to European education being offered by missionaries. This meant that Christianity satisfied the practical needs of the native peoples, needs which were created by the coloniser, instead of fulfilling their spiritual needs.

In her paper 'The Impact of Colonial Contact on the Cultural Heritage of Native American Indian People', Nassima Dalal suggested that evangelical attempts to convert indigenous populations had more than one objective. The first was, of course, to spread the word of the Gospel and the second was to acquire the land of indigenous populations.[20] Some would say it was the other way around and that religion was used as a means to an end,[21] the end being the integration of native peoples into European culture and complete elimination of the native culture.[22] This was achieved through several means, one of which was to massacre vast numbers of the community, and to ensure that the rest of the community fell in line, they were forced onto reservations with minimal resources. In some cases, diseases, such as smallpox and the plague, were introduced with the knowledge that the indigenous community was not immune to them.

There are recorded instances of 'voluntary conversion' by indigenous peoples when the threat of confrontation with the coloniser loomed large. The hope was that such conversions to Christianity would prevent violence and start a dialogue between the communities. Clearly, such conversion was seen as the only alternative to annihilation. Notwithstanding such attempts to make peace with the 'civilised' Christian coloniser, literature tells us that just about 10 per cent of the native population survived European diseases, massacres, displacement and assimilation[23] which wiped out most of its bearers of tradition and knowledge.[24] In contemporary discourse, it is sometimes argued that the little that survives of indigenous tradition is proof of the coloniser's accommodative nature, when, on the contrary, it is proof of the determination of the community to keep its identity alive.

The Europeanisation and Christianisation of native populations was accelerated and cemented by the fact that the coloniser actively wielded both the stick and the carrot. A once thriving and vibrant society with its own centres of production of culture and knowledge was physically and culturally exterminated and reduced to a colonised human mass of illiterate peasants, thereby creating the infamous 'White Man's Burden'. On the other hand, the yawning void so created was filled by offering European culture as the way to climb the social ladder. In other words, the demand for European culture was created and met by the European coloniser, not just for the present but for all time to come. This the European coloniser passed off as his benevolence for he was saving the heathen native's soul from the latter's own ignorance, superstition and savagery. Had it not been for archaeological and ethnological studies, it would have been next to impossible to reconstruct native life as it existed in precolonial times or the genocides perpetrated by the coloniser. But for this evidence, European coloniality would have successfully justified and explained the civilising effect of colonisation and convinced us all that its culture, religion and way of life were globalised through peaceful means.[25]

This explains the present Christian character of the Americas and large parts of Africa, which should come as no surprise. Given the complete cultural domination colonised societies in Latin America were subjected to by the European coloniser, it was only human on the part of the dominated to latch onto the closest living culture (including religion) available to them, namely that of the coloniser, which they wore as a badge of honour with the zeal of a new convert. The adoption of the coloniser's culture was clearly not a matter of choice but a sheer human reaction and perhaps even a necessity, thanks to the atrocious and inhuman conditions created by the coloniser.

It was only a matter of time before the new convert to European culture and religion not only disowned his previous identity but also spewed venom against it because he associated his past and heritage with weakness, superstition and defeatism, thus completing the process of severing ties with his roots. To use a pop culture reference, coloniality was a form of 'inception' performed on the minds of the colonised so that colonialism and colonisation were no more external to their consciousness, but became internal to it. Importantly, be it the Americas or Africa or Asia, the replacement or dilution of indigenous faith systems by the European coloniser's religion had an adverse bearing on the sacred relationship between indigenous societies and their land, and consequently with nature. This, in turn, severely affected indigenous onto-epistemology and culture, as shall be seen in the next chapter.

3

Coloniality, Indigenous Faiths, Nature and Knowledge

Christians Destroy Irminsul, the World Tree

The destruction of Irminsul by Charlemagne (1882) by Heinrich Leutemann. In the 770s, a holy wood at Eresburg, also sacred to the Saxons, was taken in battle by Charlemagne. The victorious Christian forces destroyed the holy Irminsul, a tall pillar in the wood representing the world tree Yggdrasil. Surviving Saxon boys were carried off to be indoctrinated and trained as missionaries.

Most studies on European colonialism are typically centred around its impact on the political independence of colonised native societies, the immense economic harm caused to them and the consequent 'illiteracy' and impoverishment of these societies. In my opinion, this in itself is proof of coloniality since quite a few native societies are yet to understand the true impact of colonialism, namely the loss of an original indigenous perspective, which does not even seem to figure in their list of things to reclaim.

To restate, if a colonised society assesses even the loss it has suffered on account of colonialism on the anvils of 'development' as defined by the European coloniser, it only proves the entrenchment of coloniality. In fact, it firmly establishes the extent of internalisation of the colonial worldview deep within the native society's consciousness, so much so that it is oblivious to the loss of its own agency over such consciousness. After all, how can one feel the loss of a thing whose existence one has become unconscious to? While it is easy to dismiss this as the elitism of the well-fed, the exhortation is not about obsessing over the loss of high culture while the masses are left to deal with soul-crushing poverty. Instead, it is about restoring something as fundamental as dignity to the native perspective so that the indigenous society can rebuild itself using its own ideals and tools instead of those of the coloniser.

Fortunately, there exists scholarship which avoids the predictable, superficial and mercantile lines of enquiry in relation to the impact of European colonialism, and delves deeper by examining the very character of economic growth which has been universalised by the European coloniser at the expense of nature. Scholars agree that apart from wiping out entire civilisations, restructuring economies and redrawing the map of the world, European colonialism's deadliest consequence for the entire world has been its fundamental conceptual alteration of the relationship between human beings and nature.[1] In short, the introduction of 'humanism' and its relationship with 'materialism' and 'consumerism' can be traced to European coloniality. In stark contrast to the benevolent connotations imputed to humanism, the literature reveals, as we shall see, that it has the direct effect of placing humans over and above nature, which is the product of coloniality. This monumental shift in the approach to nature affected indigenous societies the most, since prior to European colonisation, the entirety of their culture was inextricably linked to and revolved around nature, including their faith systems, sense of community, systems of production and dissemination of knowledge, and economy.[2]

For instance, the Native Americans believed that life emerged from the interior of the earth and that the earth resembled the womb of a mother in which she nurtured life.[3] Prior to the advent of the European coloniser, this belief formed the basis of fraternal relations between various tribes as well as between communities and their respective geographies. The end result or, perhaps, the objective was to preserve respect for nature and its balance. That a fraternal bond existed between diverse communities, which are often lumped together as 'indigenous peoples', is clear from the fact that when the European coloniser arrived in North America, there were close to 2,000 cultural groups that had their own lifestyles, languages, beliefs and customs. Notwithstanding territorial conflicts, which may be attributed to human nature, their coexistence has been attributed to their 'human-to-land' ethic and their belief that they were all citizens of nature.[4] This ability to think as a species that is not removed from nature, and to simultaneously preserve and celebrate the cultural diversity within, is of immense relevance to several contemporary debates where discussions around social cohesion and 'unity' are loaded with an overbearing penchant for homogenisation and standardisation.

In his book *The Spiritual Legacy of the American Indian*, Joseph Epes Brown,[5] a scholar of Native American traditions, observed that despite their diversity, the Amerindian peoples lived 'a metaphysic of nature', wherein each group spelt out in great detail the roles and responsibilities of the members of the community. This enumeration of roles was based on the realisation of the 'vast web of humankind's cyclical interrelationships with the elements, the earth and all that lives upon the land'.[6] Their relationship with the earth was one of 'reciprocal appropriation', that is, to give and receive, 'in which humans participate[d] in the landscape while at the same time they incorporate[d] the landscape and its inhabitants into the most fundamental human experience and understanding'.[7] To them, nature was never meant to be isolated from humans and studied in a silo. As opposed to being an object of a clinical study, it was meant to be lived with in harmony. This 'environmental morality' instilled humility and informed both inter-community relations as well as their collective relationship with nature.[8] This ethical relationship with nature was based on the fundamental belief that there was a spiritual dimension to the earth, of which humans too were a part (but only a part), and it was believed that upsetting the balance of nature would not go unpunished by it.

The natives' respect for nature gave rise to their faith, and the symbols or icons used were inspired by animals and landforms, thereby putting nature at the centre of their lives. Connections among members of the community were forged through specific traditions.[9] Even their epistemology revolved around nature and communal harmony. It was this deeply spiritual relationship, embedded in traditional practices and oral knowledge of tribe elders that constituted their 'religion', thus tying together nature, faith and knowledge.[10]

On a related note, perhaps followers of certain Indic schools of philosophy can relate to the beliefs of the Siouan culture as depicted by Brown in his book *The Sacred Pipe*.[11] The Siouan people believed that the whole of creation was essentially one and that all parts within the whole were related. What was particularly interesting was the way the Sioux referred to each other in relational terms. For instance, an old woman would be addressed as 'mother' and a much older woman as 'grandmother'. Such an approach to human relations is a direct corollary of the community's spiritual attitude to nature. All of this changed when Columbus' Christian expeditionary party landed on the shores of America with an intention to colonise it.

When the European coloniser set foot on the American soil, he was staunchly rooted in the Christian belief that humans were above other creatures since humans (read the White Christian) were 'beings' because they possessed souls and the rest were 'non-beings' because they had no souls. Christianity placed the 'human being', preferably the Christian White European, above the rest of creation, thereby furthering the belief that nature existed solely for the 'pursuit of his happiness' and his 'manifest destiny'. The difference in the attitudes of the Native Americans and the coloniser towards nature could not have been starker. One worshipped nature and saw himself as a part of it, while the other put himself above nature and sought to enjoy its plenty as a matter of divinely ordained right. It is no surprise then that 'humanism' and 'materialism' are the direct consequences of the coloniser's OET, which, among other things, gave birth to a Cartesian dualistic approach, whose distinction between subject/mind and object/body placed human beings above nature. This explains the coloniser's approach to 'development' as well. Simply put, coloniality objectified nature apart from dehumanising vast swathes of humanity.[12]

Interestingly, while the Enlightenment is celebrated for ushering in the Age of Reason through its supposed challenge to Christian dogma, it is the Enlightenment whose emphasis on Christianity's Cartesian dualistic approach to humans and nature that advanced the idea of superiority of the 'rational human mind' over 'non-rational nature'. This paved the way for the conquest of nature by the 'superior' human.[13] Nature was reduced to a commodity, the knowledge of which was necessary not to live with or in it, but for the utilisation of 'natural resources'.[14] Richard Drayton, in *Nature's Government*, argued that the commodification of nature was the driving force behind imperialism and colonialism, which gave birth to capitalism and universalist developmentalism.[15] This is because, to the Christian European coloniser, the rest of the world represented 'wildness' and so he took it upon himself to 'civilise' populations and subdue nature by introducing them to 'rationality' and 'order'. This civilising mission took the form of aggressive industrialisation and spawned the development discourse which dominated the twentieth century and continues to have contemporary purchase in several decolonised countries that are still trying to 'catch up' with the West.[16] Critically, despite the diversity of human experiences and natural conditions encountered by the coloniser in different parts of the world, he was convinced beyond doubt that the same model of economic growth, industrialisation and development could be replicated uniformly across the world without exception. This once again reflects the homogenising intent and effect of the modernity/rationality complex of European coloniality.

Raymond Murphy went so far as to say that control over nature and its utilisation as a resource may have even shaped the European coloniser's ideas on government, empire and economics since the goal was to govern all of nature. It has been posited that the very idea of rationality and its dimensions may have been the consequence of the intention to explore, exploit and govern nature in a systematic fashion, so much so that colonialism has been called the 'outworking of bureaucratic rationalisation'. Murphy argued that four dimensions of rationality became the central features of colonial States, which have been identified as follows[17]:

1. The development of science and technology, which has been defined as 'the calculated, systematic expansion of the means to understand and manipulate nature', and the scientific worldview's 'belief in the mastery of nature and of humans through increased scientific and technical knowledge';

2. The expansion of the capitalist economy with its rationally organised and, in turn, organising market;
3. Formal hierarchical organisation, namely the creation of executive government, translating social action into rationally organised action; and
4. The elaboration of a formal legal system to manage social conflict and promote the predictability and calculability of the consequences of social action.

To these four dimensions, I would add two more: (5) rejection of any onto-epistemological system that worships nature instead of conquering and harnessing it which led to either Christianity being imposed on the natives, or in some cases, Christianising the native faith; and (6) replacement of indigenous education systems, and systems of production of knowledge with a Christian European model of education which embedded the first five dimensions deep within the native citizens of a colonialised future and shaped their entire worldview.

Murphy laid the blame for the 'radical uncoupling of the cultural and the social from nature'[18] at the doors of the Enlightenment which, he believed, spurred the colonial project of reordering nature to serve human needs. This perhaps explains why the colonised territory was primarily viewed as a resource for exploitation, with its inhabitants being treated as subhuman, dark, idol-worshipping, soulless, heathen irritants who obstructed the coloniser's unhindered use of nature. Naturally, such an approach wreaked havoc on indigenous lands, so much so that even the coloniser was alarmed and had to start thinking about 'conservation' of nature. However, since the coloniser's mind was the very fount of coloniality, his approach to conservation too was colonial because the silo-based approach to human beings and nature continued to plague his new mission of conserving nature. The 'modern', 'rational', 'scientific' Christian European coloniser could not get himself to acknowledge that the lived experience and traditional knowledge of native societies gathered over millennia could teach him more than a thing or two about living in harmony with nature as opposed to merely salvaging what remained of it in the name of 'sustainable' development. It took him ages to even concede that there was something seriously amiss in his attitude to nature, by which time nature had started reacting to the plunder and devastation it had been subjected to.

Apart from wreaking unprecedented havoc on nature and wiping out native faith systems, the presence of the coloniser also had a direct bearing on native knowledge traditions because as stated earlier, such traditions were tied to the native faith, which was in turn rooted in nature. Native knowledge traditions were largely passed on through the generations orally, employing storytelling as a means of transmitting knowledge.[19] One of its objectives was to keep the knowledge within the community, so that it was accessible only to those who understood both its meaning and, importantly, its sanctity. This obviated the need for written records. However, the fundamental differences in their ontologies, coupled with the absence of written records, the importance given to the written word by the Christian coloniser and the consequent treatment of oral traditions as apocryphal and 'mythical', may collectively explain the coloniser's attitudes to indigenous onto-epistemological systems.

For all its expression of iconoclasm towards polytheistic and idol-worshipping indigenous communities, the religion of the European coloniser deifies its central scripture as the 'Word of God', given its revelatory treatment. Therefore, only that which was contained in their scripture or the Book was deemed to be true, making the colonisers the People of the Book. The expectation that every religion must have a 'book' as its sole authority that captured its tenets was essentially a Christian expectation, which was imposed on the onto-epistemological systems of native communities in order to delegitimise or Christianise their faiths. The absence of a 'book' not only rendered their faiths but also their entire history legendary and mythical in the eyes of the coloniser. Simply put, if the proof of the object of faith did not exist in writing, the object did not exist. The result was that instead of faith being treated as an experiential path to the divine, its validity had to be established in the eyes of a coloniser who was intent on judging indigenous faith systems on Christian European anvils of modernity and rationality.

The absence of written records made it more convenient for the coloniser to erase native histories after destroying or appropriating their sacred spaces. In an age prior to globalisation, since the rest of the world did not know much about native culture before the advent of the Christian European coloniser, thenceforth their story would be the one written by the coloniser. In any case, given that close to 90 per cent of the native population was wiped out in several colonised societies, such as the Americas, it had a direct impact on the continuity of their onto-epistemological traditions and systems. This only added to the apocryphal aura that European colonialism had enveloped native cultures in.

Apart from the calculated use of violence, the coloniser introduced linguistic and education policies intended to ensure that the native population that survived genocide was recast in the colonial mould. The Christian coloniser was acutely alive to the fact that language captured a culture's journey and reflected it through its stories, idioms, proverbs and usages, which connected the speaker with the collective past. To remove traces of the past in the language of the future, native children were forbidden from speaking in their languages,[20] a practice that continues in English-medium schools to this day. Children were separated from their families and placed in boarding schools to eliminate the influence of parents and their culture. This way, a 'modern' Christian education created an entire generation of colonialised Native Americans divorced from their heritage, with no sense of belonging to their roots or even their family. Critically, a cultural divide had been created within members of the same family and community, and the only culture the future of the community was exposed to was that of the coloniser.[21]

The locations of these boarding schools were chosen to further the goal of cultural distancing by situating them as far away as possible from the cultural centres of the native society, and the medium of instruction was the language of the coloniser— either Portuguese, Spanish, French or English. Unfortunately for the coloniser, traces of the native culture survived, albeit in the coloniser's language, but with that, the essence and the lived experience of the culture was altered forever.[22] While some scholars have interpreted the use of the coloniser's language to keep the native culture alive as a form of 'creative resistance' on the part of indigenous colonised communities,[23] in my view, such an interpretation is, at best, human optimism at work. Until natives fully reclaim their agency, which includes linguistic agency, there is no escaping the fact that they lead incomplete, inchoate and incoherent lives, individually and collectively.

The colonial intent behind linguistic policies was equally reflective of the entire system of colonial education. Colonial education was offered not as an alternative to pre-existing indigenous forms of education but with the specific objective of gradually erasing their existence. The literature on the African experience with colonial education introduced by the British, especially in South Africa, tells us that colonial investment in 'educating' the colonised population had several motivations, religious not excluded, wherein the modernity/rationality complex played a significant role.[24] The coloniser's perceived sense of religious and racial superiority meant that he felt obligated to 'civilise' and 'educate' the indigenous population and 'liberate' indigenous souls from the ignorance and superstition that possessed them. In this sense, colonial education was a form of exorcism performed on the heathen native by the Christian coloniser. That apart, the more mundane and practical consideration that was couched in loftier otherworldly objectives was the need to cultivate loyalty towards the colonising empire in the short term and lay the foundations for long-term co-option and assimilation of the natives into the European way of life, albeit as second-grade human beings. Therefore, education was perhaps one of the most potent tools for cultural Europeanisation of indigenous peoples.

There was no attempt on the part of the colonial government to even hide the stated goals of colonial education, namely social engineering. Education was expressly employed to 'shape the political, social, cultural, and economic direction of the colonies'[25] and was designed to reinforce and reproduce racist structures. In short, it was an investment in a colonial future. There even exist recorded instances of European legislators in colonial South Africa exhorting the South African government to 'win the fight against the non-White in the classroom instead of losing it in the battlefield'.[26] So much for all the vaunted liberation and civilisation being benevolently offered by the coloniser through his education.

In Africa, even schools were not spared racial segregation, and it goes without saying that the schools meant for European students were better than those for African children. Expenditures and budgetary outlay for the education of White students were generally ten times higher than those for Black students.[27] Importantly, the goal of social engineering and subservience of the native society was embedded in the curriculum since the coloniser was aware of its power to 'shape the economic, social and political futures of students'.[28] Clearly, any system of colonial education was but a way of maintaining political control over the production of knowledge and social discourse.[29] While colonial education was offered as a means to climb the social ladder with acceptance by the European being its ultimate destination, there were glass ceilings firmly in place which ensured that native students were always kept below the European.[30]

The colonial curriculum was often imported from either Britain or North America and was designed to produce Africans who would always consider themselves inferior in their interactions with Europeans and would take pride in serving the interests of the White man. It was formulated to prepare native children for taking up subordinate roles and to protect the interests of the coloniser at the expense of those of the colonised community.[31] Impressionable young Africans were being taught that a 'civilised' African was one who assimilated into European culture. Even teachers were trained in such a manner so as to ensure that African and European children in British colonies did not receive the same education.[32] The entire stated goal of colonial education was to preserve and maintain the 'unquestioned superiority and supremacy' of the Whites, which has been summarised by scholars as follows:

> The brown workman would always have to work under a European and therefore there would be no conflict. The cast of mind of the Native is such that he could rarely take charge. His lack of inventiveness and of ingenuity in mechanical work would make him inferior to the European as a trained workman, and at no time would he compete with the European.[33]

One 'scientific' reason that was offered to explain the disparity in curricula was the coloniser's perception of a given colonised community's aptitude for knowledge based on race, the pecking order being Whites, Indians, Coloureds and Black Africans.[34] The premise of this racial stratification was that Africans could not master 'bookish subjects' and therefore, even if given an opportunity, were incapable of competing with Europeans. Accordingly, they were offered only vocational or industrial training. On the rare occasion that 'exceptional' African students were offered access to an 'academic curriculum', the medium of instruction was English, proficiency in which was integral to academic success.[35] That said, even the academic curriculum would be centred on Europe and North America, which were portrayed as 'modern' and 'developed', while African countries were shown as being 'traditional' and 'backward'. The policy of racial segregation was not limited to academics but extended to extracurricular activities as well. Those sports with higher earning potential, such as cricket, rugby, tennis, hockey and polo, were reserved for White students, whereas soccer, netball, volleyball, track and field events were open to all, including the 'others'.

Commenting on the objective of colonial education in Africa, Nelson Mandela remarked thus[36]:

> The educated Englishman was our model; what we aspired to be were 'black Englishmen'. We were taught—and believed—that the best ideas were English ideas, the best government was English government, and the best men were Englishmen.

Mandela was acutely aware of the fact that the purpose of colonial education in educating people like him was to create a new 'Black elite' in Africa that looked up to the coloniser and his way of life. Clearly, as some scholars on colonial education in Africa have pointed out, non-European and European children in British colonies did not receive the same education: while one was taught to serve, the other to rule, which was the vision of the coloniser—to colonialise the colonised society.[37]

To assume that this goal was limited to the education introduced by colonial governments would be factually incorrect. In Africa—which was divided up between the European colonisers, such as Britain, France, Germany and Belgium, through the 1884 Berlin Conference—education was taken up by missionaries, merchants and colonial governments. Missionaries were much more candid than colonial governments about their objective of educating Africans—evangelisation.[38] Literature reveals that the intent behind sending Christian missionaries to Native American societies too was the same.[39] The transgenerational trauma inflicted by Christian missionaries who accompanied the coloniser and who were responsible for running colonial schools was immeasurable.

While some societies in Africa completely succumbed to European education, others resisted and turned schools into centres of revolutionary protests, thereby birthing liberation movements.[40] However, by and large, the overall impact of colonial education was that the colonised were left with a limited sense of their past and their indigenous traditions were gradually pushed towards extinction. To cut a long story short, colonial education annihilated a society's belief in itself. It made the colonised people see their past as one vast wasteland of non-achievement; it made them desirous of distancing themselves from that wasteland and instead identify with an entity that was furthest removed from them—European culture. Not only did it push the colonialised natives further away from their heritage but it also undermined their self-confidence at an individual level.

All in all, this much is clear: European coloniality was directly responsible for disrupting the sacred relationship between indigenous peoples and nature, the destruction of their faith, language, political and societal structures and knowledge—in short, their entire culture. This led to what the scholars have termed 'psychocultural marginality'[41], wherein loss of cultural identity results in social and individual disorganisation which manifests as 'low self-esteem, extreme poverty, oppression, depression, loss of identity, substance abuse, violence, lower life expectancy, low educational attainment, limited employment, poor housing and ill health'.[42] It is a continuing state of limbo wherein the natives are neither capable of subscribing to the culture of the coloniser nor going back to their own roots, since they do not exist as a whole any longer. This transgenerational trauma is 'cumulative, unresolved, historic, and ongoing'[43] as long as coloniality is alive and kicking. It was to the credit of the determination of native peoples which kept alive whatever remained of their culture. It was this determination that gave colonised societies the strength and confidence needed to aspire for political independence, which was also partly a consequence of colonial education backfiring on the coloniser.

However, as we shall see in the next chapter, the deep entrenchment of the coloniality of the Christian European coloniser through the establishment of his political, legal and educational infrastructure impacted even the freedom struggles of colonised societies. So much so that their political aspirations—starting from the manner in which they defined freedom, to the political institutions they hoped to set up after independence, including their vision for the decolonised society—were all influenced by coloniality. While the impact of coloniality on freedom movements could not have been and was not uniform, there is no denying the fact that coloniality influenced them to varying degrees. As we shall see, the manifestation of 'secularised' coloniality remains most rampant in the political, legal and religious spheres, which reflects in the misplaced sense of pride that several decolonised nations draw as inheritors of a 'common law tradition', or being part of the 'commonwealth of civilised nations' or as the 'beneficiaries of the Magna Carta'. This includes internalisation of that most fundamental of European political conceptions, 'nation-statehood' and its attendant trappings.

4

Entrenchment of Coloniality through European Political Structures

Protestant Reformation of Martin Luther

Martin Luther burning the papal bull of excommunication, with vignettes from Luther's life and portraits of Hus, Savonarola, Wycliffe, Cruciger, Melanchton, Bugenhagen, Gustav Adolf and Bernhard, Duke of Saxe-Weimar.

Based on the discussion undertaken thus far on the nature and origins of European coloniality, it is possible to reasonably posit the following:

1. The European colonial project, which started with Columbus' expedition in 1492, did indeed have a clear Christian inspiration that viewed nature as well as the non-Christian New World through its Cartesian dualist/humanist prism; and

2. This dualist approach gave birth to the European coloniser's sense of superiority over the rest of nature, including non-Christian idolatrous and nature-worshipping indigenous peoples. It led to the reshaping of nature to suit the material goals of the European coloniser, thereby giving rise to modern notions of development, and his sense of anthropological superiority created a race consciousness that spawned the global imperial exercise to civilise the soulless heathen natives by replacing the entirety of their cultures with the European's. The cumulative effect was a colonial remapping of geographies/boundaries and a distinctly religion-inspired, race-driven reallocation of labour and resources, culminating in the creation of the modern economy as well as its political institutions.

Naturally, the political, religious, legal and educational infrastructure set up by the coloniser was geared towards meeting the end goals of the said global project. However, the extent of investment and settlement in indigenous lands by the European coloniser depended on the opportunity they represented and their hospitability, both physical and social. According to Patrick Ziltener, where conditions were conducive for settlement, including for political consolidation, it led to settler colonialism, and therefore greater institutional investment in the colonised society.[1] For instance, after setting up the administrative and legal apparatus which ensured that the reins of the colonised society were firmly in the hands of the coloniser, educational institutions were established primarily in those colonies where the coloniser settled.[2] In contrast, in those lands which were not conducive for settlement but were rich in resources, institutions that facilitated the process of rent-seeking and expropriation of resources through the purchased or coerced aid of local rulers were set up.

Importantly, the manner in which natives were recruited into the colonial power structure was yet another proof of the European coloniser's deeply ingrained ethno-religious consciousness. Soldiers and mercenaries were recruited from those sections of the native society that were identified as 'martial races', which was developed into a full-fledged doctrine and also applied in India.[3] The British Indian army was organised on religious and caste lines, again pointing to the coloniser's racial approach not just to religion but also to caste. The after-effects of such an approach to indigenous social structures are being felt even today in our understanding of the idea of caste and the way it has been portrayed in India studies within Bharat and the rest of the world. A similar approach to army recruitment based on ethnicity was employed in British Borneo, Burma and the British areas of Africa. The Dutch were no different in their recruitment strategies in the Dutch East Indies.

Apart from the army, this policy of recruitment was extended to civil services as well wherein native elites, who had bought into the idea of the European Way being the pinnacle of civilisation, were given preferential access to European education so that they could occupy posts of 'prestige' in the colonial administrative structure. Those that converted to Christianity clearly enjoyed greater representation in the colonial administration, such as in the case of the Christian Sinhalese in British Ceylon. Further, communities and groups were pitted against one another through preferential treatment which created animosities. Similarly, on the economic front, stereotypes relating to occupational specialisations were reinforced and made further rigid through colonial policies, thereby interfering with the organic flow of the native society's sociocultural dynamics.

The political structure established by the Christian European coloniser in the colonies not only furthered the goal of economic exploitation but also served to consciously keep the native society in a constantly fragmented state while consolidating the European's political and territorial hold over it. This strategy ensured that for a long time, native voices would not unite to oppose the coloniser's presence; instead, they would entirely depend on the coloniser, his ideas and his institutions for continuity of life. The extent of dependence was evidenced by the fact that even the native elites, or perhaps especially the elites, began to subscribe to the coloniser's view that the native society would fall into disarray and utter confusion if the coloniser were to pack his bags and leave. In the mind of the native, the success of the coloniser in keeping the native society under his thumb was attributed to his overall cultural superiority (race included) and specifically, to the most visible aspect of the colonial apparatus, namely the administrative and legal systems imposed on the colonised societies. Naturally, the political and legal theories underlying the edifice found significant purchase among native elites, thanks to their participation in the colonial administration as well as through colonial education, both of which covered the praxis and theory of colonial political thought.

It needs to be appreciated that by the mid-nineteenth century, thanks to the continued global presence of the coloniser for over a century, the Christian European vision for civilising the rest of the world had been significantly secularised and universalised, consciously and otherwise. This meant that colonised societies that looked up to the edifice of the coloniser were no more alive, if they ever were, to the Christian onto-episteme that informed the colonial worldview. Consequently, the premises and pillars of the colonial political, administrative and legal ecosystems were accepted as the universal norm by the native elites. Critically, European ideas and institutions were deemed to be equally valid for a decolonised future that was 'independent' of the coloniser, and this independence too was defined in European terms. An independent 'nation-state' modelled on European lines was the decolonised future towards which native aspirations were generally oriented.[4] It is in this context that it becomes imperative to understand some of the key ideas and their entirely unsecular origins that informed the colonial political structure. The objective of this decolonial exercise is to be able to understand the impact that these ideas, including secularism and constitutionalism, had on freedom movements in colonised societies and their culmination in the creation of nation-states built on the colonial legacy.

One might ask, so what if the political edifice of the European coloniser was informed by a non-secular and patently religious framework if ultimately it has been secularised? Why obsess over the coloniser's religion? Such a question misses the entire point of the analysis, namely to identify the theological foundations of the colonial infrastructure since it has no legs to stand on independent of them, and therefore, their identification is necessary to outline and define a decolonial approach. In this regard, based on my reading of Dr. Jakob De Roover's work on the history of secularism, it needs to be underscored that the secularisation of the Christian onto-episteme is the consequence of obscuring the source of a certain thought and focusing exclusively on its outward expression.[5] This outward expression must be examined for its undergirding because those who do not subscribe to that OET, which is the fount of that particular thought, have the right to know of its origins and reject its imposition. This would be consistent with the right of every society to wish to be governed by its own values which are derived from its own culture. Only *after* being apprised of its source, it is for the society to decide whether to embrace a thought, notwithstanding its foreign theological inspiration.

In other words, the society has the right to prior informed consent before the imposition of an alien principle. To pixelate and deny the origins of a thought, in my view, is plain deception. This argument acquires greater validity and legitimacy in the context of imposition of the coloniser's politico-economic worldview on dominated societies, where the power balance was obviously skewed in favour of the coloniser and remained so for centuries. Therefore, an examination of such worldview through the prism of coloniality necessarily requires us to question whether a specific foreign theological framework was at play, notwithstanding all the attempts at secularising and universalising it because universalisation of a particular way of life was the very object of coloniality. Simply put, despite the discomfort such examination is bound to cause, which too is attributable to ingrained coloniality, it is indispensable and inevitable if indigenous societies are to reclaim their right to agency at the most fundamental level.

The Protestant Reformation, the Doctrine of Two Kingdoms, Secularism and the Nation-State

There is a general consensus among most scholars that the concept of a nation-state, as has been understood since the late nineteenth and early twentieth centuries, may be traced to the Peace of Westphalia entered into on 24 October 1648, which ended the Thirty Years' War in Europe after five years of negotiations.[6] But what was the Thirty Years' War all about? What led to it? Was it a secular war or did it have a distinctly and predominantly religious hue? If yes, which religion? How did the Peace of Westphalia lead or contribute to colonialism and coloniality?

Prior to the advent of the Westphalian State, the Christian Commonwealth or the Christian Republic (*Res publica Christiana*) or simply 'Christendom' existed in Europe wherein power was distributed between the pope, the bishops, the Holy Roman Emperor, princes of States and nobles who thought of themselves as being part of the Christian civilisation. Pertinently, while there were States and rulers, they operated under the umbrella of the pope and the emperor, which for all practical purposes, made them feudal principalities. Starting from at least 1517 CE, that is, over 100 years before the Peace of Westphalia, resistance to the Catholic Church led by pastor-theologians Martin Luther (German) and John Calvin (French)—known as the Protestant Reformation—had begun, owing to the abuse of papal authority and the absolute control of the Catholic priesthood over Christianity. The nature of the challenge posed to papal authority needs to be understood at a deeper level in order to appreciate the true impact of Protestant OET on the Peace of Westphalia and the Westphalian nation-state system with its attendant trappings that were later imposed upon colonised societies. The nature of the Protestant Reformation warrants understanding, especially from the perspective of Bharat, for yet another critical reason—its anti-clericalism was exported by the coloniser to the colonised indigenous societies as well. In other words, all the ills, real and perceived, associated by the Protestant Reformation with the Roman Catholic Church were subsequently projected onto those classes of people in the colonised societies who, according to the Reformed coloniser, occupied the same position as the Catholic Church. In the case of Bharat (as we shall see in the second section of the book), Brahmins and 'Brahminism' were the subject of this Reformative approach. Therefore, the ensuing portion, which deals with the thought behind the Protestant Reformation, must be paid attention to for more reasons than one.

On this subject, Dr. Jakob De Roover's book *Europe, India, and the Limits of Secularism* is deeply educative. But before I go into the details of his work, I will digress a little to address something that affects the larger issue of openness to scholarship that questions the so-called secular and neutral premise of contemporary institutions. De Roover's work is piercing and rigorous in this regard, and yet has unfortunately not received the kind of attention in Bharat that it ought to have, given that the subject of his scholarship is the specific impact of European 'secularism' on Bharat. What makes his work a must-read is his examination of the theological underpinnings of both the Reformation and the Enlightenment. The tendency to ignore his work and that of other scholars who share his position, in my opinion, is indicative of the larger unspoken stifling of decolonial thought and scholarship in Bharat because it has the potential to upset the status quo on several fronts in favour of the Indic civilisational perspective (an issue I address in greater detail in the second section). Therefore, wherever I believe a certain work has not received its due in Bharat despite its manifest relevance, I have consciously chosen to discuss it at length, as opposed to merely referencing it, in the hope of greater dissemination of important decolonial scholarship, such as that of De Roover.

Coming to his book, De Roover sheds light on the Protestant politico-theological framework behind the distinction that the 'modern' nation-states (including those formerly colonised) make between the spiritual and the temporal or secular. According to him, this distinction significantly informed the Protestant Reformation which started in the sixteenth century. His view is that the liberal model of religious toleration and secularism, which continues to have purchase in the West and in decolonised States, is based on the specific theological framework that was conceptually conceived of during the Protestant Reformation. He calls it the 'crystallization of the political theology of Christian freedom and the two Kingdoms'. His insights on this subject and the nexus that he unearths between the political theology arising from the Protestant Reformation and the very definition of what it means to be a Christian are profound and extremely relevant for decolonised societies that have inherited the European political structure. His work is an essential reading in my opinion, especially for indigenous societies, for them to become aware of the patently non-secular context of the modern distinction between the 'spiritual' and the 'secular' because it calls out the claim of neutral application of values, such as secularism, which have been inherited from the coloniser.

According to De Roover, to appreciate the true nature of 'secularisation' of Christianity achieved by and through the Protestant Reformation, one must understand what the specific object of 'reformation' was. This requires us to delve briefly into Roman Catholic OET prior to the Protestant Reformation, and more specifically into the process of 'Conversion'. Today, while conversion in the context of Christianity is synonymous with proselytisation of non-Christians in order to bring them into the Christian fold, the very first people who underwent 'conversion' were the Christians themselves. The process of Conversion, however, refers to a structured spiritual regimen that was evolved in the medieval age by Christian monks in monasteries (who were distinct from the clergy) to achieve a true Christian life of absolute submission to God. Submission to the Creator meant obedience and sacrificing individual purpose at the altar of the divine purpose. The specific goal of the process was to 're-form' man in the image of God, for which he must overcome the original sin that stood in the way of such 'reformation'.[7]

In practice, the process of conversion divided both human beings and the world into two realms, namely the spiritual and the temporal. The temporal world was given a shelf life until the second coming of Christ, whereas the spiritual was eternal. Until the second coming, the obligation of a true Christian was to constantly work towards overcoming the desires of the flesh so as to make the spirit and body more spiritual.[8] This meant that the process of conversion towards the object of reformation was a never-ending one for two reasons: first, the 'original sin' was too seductive to overcome and therefore, human beings would assuredly fail, thereby reinforcing their status as wretched sinners; and second, this process had to continue until the second coming.

The silver lining, if any, of this never-ending process of conversion was that the degree of conversion achieved in this world would determine the extent of freedom conferred in the next world. Importantly, those who had submitted themselves fully to God were beyond the reach of human authorities and hence, free from their control. Not only were they free from the restrictions imposed by any earthly authority, their submission to God also gave them the ability to resist the desires of the flesh. However, in order to achieve complete submission to God and total freedom from secular authorities, faith in Christ was the only way since Christ had received divine grace. Without such grace, humans were themselves incapable of resisting the seductive lure of sin. Simply put, according to Catholic belief, for all humans, Christ was the only way to reach God.

In the medieval age, various Christian monastic orders that revolved around the institutionalisation of this process of conversion influenced the Church significantly. Since these Christian monastic orders had dedicated their entire lives to the achievement of this divine purpose through rigorous practice, their supposedly exalted spiritual position, according to them, also gave them power over the earthly society and secular authority in order to convert them. The Church, being alive to the austerities of monks, absorbed them as bishops or elevated them to positions of leadership within the Church. The consequence of this nexus between monastic orders and the Church was the pursuit of reformation of the society in the image of the monastic community. De Roover has referred to this milestone as 'the monasticisation of the Church' and, therefore, Christendom itself. Given the proliferation of monastic orders, their rules and practices, and their manifest impact on the reform of the Church between the tenth and twelfth centuries, the rules followed within various monasteries were rationalised in the interest of uniformity and preserving the rigour of the process of conversion for reformation.

The next phase was the division of the spiritual realm between the monks and the priests of the Church since monastic orders had not fully merged with the Church. However, the influence of the monastic orders on the Church led to the morphing of priesthood to mirror the rigours of a monastic life, which involved the four-stage process of vocation, reform, conversion and purification. Since monks and their way of life were exemplified as truly Christian by the Church, a hierarchy of sorts was created among the subjects of God, with monks occupying the top position followed by the clergy, the 'earthly secular' rulers and finally, the laity (lay believers). The order was a function of submission to God—the greater and more complete the submission, the greater the freedom from earthly authority and the higher the station occupied on Earth as well as in the next world. Critically, there was an allocation of worlds between the monks and the clergy; the monks would lead the rest of the 'flock' in the other world, the Church and its clergy would lead the flock, including the rulers, in the earthly world akin to shepherds.[9] In effect, the priests became conduits to salvation and God since they were the true servants of God. This is the essence of the Christian doctrine *extra ecclesiam nulla salus*— all salvation is through Christ and Christ can be reached only through the Church, and therefore there is no salvation outside the Church.

Given its penultimate station in the spiritual hierarchy in the earthly world, the Church was regarded as the 'soul', while kings were the 'body'. Naturally, the Church, the soul which was deemed superior to the body, took it upon itself to preserve order in the earthly world and assumed an advisory role to the body, that is, the earthly rulers, on all matters both religious and secular. This effectively turned Christianity into a religion of the priests and the entirety of Christendom into the fiefdom of the Church, which freed the Church from the scrutiny of any form of earthly authority and secured for it, overlordship over earthly authority. The other less lofty objective was to secure complete proprietorial ownership of the Church, which was the property of the temporal rulers/kings until the eleventh century.

According to De Roover, what helped the Church in making a case for its freedom from all forms of secular dominion was the fact that the separation of the spiritual and the secular 'was essential to Christianity itself and its understanding of human existence from the very beginning'. In fact, the distinction was traceable to a combined reading of specific chapters and verses of the King James Bible, namely John 18:36 ('My kingdom is not of this world'), Luke 20:20 and Mark 12:17 ('Render to Caesar the things that are Caesar's, and to God the things that are God's'). What is to be discerned from this history is that the distinction between the secular and the spiritual was drawn from *within* the Christian framework and not outside of it. The sum and substance of the distinction was elaborated as follows by Hugh of Saint Victor in *De Sacramentis Christinae Fidei*:

> There are two lives, one earthly, the other heavenly, one corporeal, the other spiritual. By one the body lives from the soul, by the other the soul lives from God. Each has its own good by which it is invigorated and nourished so that it can subsist. The earthly life is nourished with earthly goods, the spiritual life with spiritual goods. To the earthly life belong all things that are earthly, to the spiritual life all goods that are spiritual.... Among laymen, to whose zeal and forethought the things that are necessary for earthly life pertain, the power is earthly. Among the clergy, to whose office the goods of the spiritual life belong, the power is divine. The one power is therefore called secular, the other spiritual.[10]

Clearly, the divide between the spiritual and the secular was not outside the scope of Christian OET.[11] In fact, De Roover categorically states that 'without the support of a cluster of Christian-theological notions—soul and body, the earthly and spiritual life, divine power and the kingdom of Christ, and so on—this distinction would dissolve into thin air'[12]. Consequently, neither term, spiritual nor secular, when used in the context of contemporary nation-states must be divorced from the Christian origins in which they are embedded.[13] De

Roover goes as far as to say that the metes and bounds of the spiritual and secular realms were determined on the basis of Christian OET over which the Roman Catholic Church had the final word.

Given that the freedom enjoyed by the Church translated to freedom to prevail over earthly rulers as well, it expectedly led to strained relations between the Roman Catholic Church headed by the pope and earthly authorities. Even the common people, the lowest in the spiritual hierarchy of Christianity, resented the sanctimonious intervention of a hierarchically organised Catholic Church in all facets of life. The constant sermons to overcome sin and to repent for it contributed to a general distrust of the Christian clergy, while their own ability to rise above the very sin they preached against was called into question. Ironically, this did not translate to loss of faith in Christianity; instead, the lay believers organised themselves in private groups to circumvent the overarching influence of the Church and drew inspiration instead from the monastic orders that had influenced the Church itself. However, since it was impossible for the lay believer to observe all the rigours of a monastic life, the process of conversion, for which monastic orders had been created, spilled over into the society and acquired a life of its own, thereby inching towards the Protestant Reformation. De Roover calls it the 'monasticisation of daily life', which prepared the ground for a confrontation with the Roman Catholic Church. After all, the Church's monopoly over sin and penitence was being seriously undermined owing to the secularisation, rather de-Churchification, of conversion and reform, the very pillars of Christian belief—the raison d'être of the Church.

What made matters worse for the Church was the fact that people were willing to believe the accounts and stories of lecherous priests, and the Church itself began to be seen as the biggest obstacle to the practise of true Christian faith. No longer were the Church and its clergy seen as the sole conduits to God, nor were they treated as exclusive or special beneficiaries of divine grace. This empowered the lay believer's ability to pursue his or her own faith through individual and direct submission to God without any form of ecclesiastical intercession. This was the bedrock of the approach of the Protestant Reformation to Christianity. To digress on a related note, those who are familiar with the origins of anti-Brahmin attitudes in Bharat after the arrival of the European coloniser, would be able to draw parallels between the Protestant Reformation's grievances with the Roman Catholic Church and the projection of similar grievances onto institutions, practices and groups in Bharat that were seen as 'Brahminical'. As we shall see in the next section, the Protestant lens led the Christian European coloniser to treat 'Buddhism', 'Jainism' and 'Sikhism' as Reformative movements that challenged 'Brahminism'. In other words, even the history of indigenous religious developments within the Dharmic fold was reimagined on Protestant lines and presented as historical facts.

Contributing to the Protestant Reformation through their writings, Martin Luther and John Calvin democratised the spiritual process of conversion beyond the monastic and papal echelons. In 1520, Luther wrote in *The Freedom of a Christian* that faith alone was sufficient for salvation and faith made the believer free from human laws and obligations. Luther and other Reformers argued that faith in the divine itself was the result of the will of God acting through the Holy Spirit without the need for channels like the Church, its clergy or the monks. The Reformers opposed 'the tyranny of papacy' and its monopoly over conversion and freedom from laws. Consequently, according to the Reformers, no one was a priest and everyone was a priest, which led to deeper percolation of Christianity in society.

The Reformers went a step further and argued that if submission to God made monks and priests free from earthly rulers and laws, the same principle would apply to lay believers as well if they too could achieve spiritual conversion to the same degree as monks and priests. However, perhaps they realised that this could put them in direct confrontation with the authority of secular rulers, apart from plunging the society into anarchy and chaos. Therefore, the theory of two kingdoms was formulated, with Biblical support of course, by both Luther and Calvin, who struck a distinction between Christ's spiritual Kingdom and the temporal Kingdom of Earth where secular authorities held sway. It was postulated that Christians enjoyed freedom in the spiritual sphere while being required to obey the secular laws of temporal rulers to the extent that the latter did not encroach upon their faith. The caveat to this position was that true Christians were free from all human laws, similar to the view held by monks and priests, except that this freedom was previously limited under the Catholic position to those belonging to the spiritual estate, namely the monks and the priests themselves. In contrast, since the Reformers rejected the authority of the Catholic Church, its clergy and the monks, all true Christians were entitled to freedom from human laws if the process of conversion was complete and submission to God was undiluted.

Further, the Reformers rejected all the spiritual laws laid down by the Roman Catholic Church as 'false religion', designed to oppress the lay believers. The bottom line was that, according to the Reformers, no human had the power to lay down spiritual laws since even they were ultimately human laws with nothing 'spiritual' about them. Specifically, Calvin claimed that the Kingdom of Christ was invaded by the so-called spiritual laws created by the Roman Catholic Church which oppressed the freedom given by Christ to the conscience of the believers. Here, it is hard to miss the reference to the 'freedom of conscience', which has become part of the discourse on religious freedom in 'civilised nations', namely the colonising as well as the colonialised nations.

The theory of two kingdoms was, in several ways, the precursor to the present-day doctrine of separation of the Church and the State since both Luther and Calvin put forth the view that temporal authority could extend only to the affairs of the earth and never enter the spiritual sphere, which was the exclusive preserve of God, the fount of all things spiritual. However, contrary to the contemporary assumptions of the 'modern' State being a 'secular' entity, Protestant Reformers were of the clear view that the State too was a divine order whose existence was necessary to prevent people from following an immoral path, since as sinners they were fundamentally prone to depravity without an external check. In other words, the apparatus of the State was a Christian necessity to enforce Christian morality through the instrumentality of the law, with the Church and the State working together to fulfil their respective Biblically ordained Christian obligations.

What this proves is that the irreligious or 'secular' nature that is imputed to a 'modern' nation-state owing to its observance of the policy of separation of the Church and State is completely ahistorical and baseless. This is because the history of the Protestant Reformation is clear in that the political theology of the two kingdoms upon which the policy is based was strongly rooted in Christian beliefs and functioned entirely within the Christian framework. It was a conversation happening *within* the Christian society, and therefore any present-day discussion on separation of the Church and the State is incapable of being supported by assumptions outside the fold of Christianity. De Roover makes it abundantly clear that a secular government in terms of the Protestant Reformation is nothing but a *Christian* secular government without any conflict or logical inconsistency, given its clear Christian origins.[14] Former colonies, the current-day decolonised nations, must bear this in mind before parroting the secularised received Christian wisdom behind secularism.

Coming back to the Protestant Reformation, thanks to direct attacks by the Reformers on the Roman Catholic Church, its legal idolatry, corruption and the abuse of power, the Edict of Worms was issued in 1521 by the Holy Roman Emperor, Charles V, at the behest of Pope Leo X. The edict banned the propagation of Lutheran ideas, condemned its followers and excommunicated Luther himself as a notorious heretic. Naturally, this disturbed the uneasy peace of the previous years and the next few decades saw the spread of the Reformation, particularly Radical Reformation, across Europe with increasingly armed reactions from the Catholic Church. However, apart from the antipathy between Catholicism and the Reformation movement, the relationship between Lutherans and Calvinists too was schismatic.

After over three decades of the edict, in 1555, when both the Lutheran and Calvinist forms of Protestantism held sway over vast swathes of Europe, the Peace of Augsburg or the Augsburg Settlement was entered into between the Catholic and Lutheran sides, which resulted in the permanent recognition of Lutheranism as a valid Christian denomination alongside Roman Catholicism.[15] This gave the rulers/princes of States within the Holy Roman Empire the freedom to choose one of the two denominations under the principle of 'cuius regio, eius religio', which translated to 'whose realm, his religion'. Effectively, the Augsburg Settlement had the historic consequence of allowing each State within the empire to determine its Christian denominational identity, which laid the foundation for sovereign States in Europe, and marked the beginning of the decline of the Holy Roman Empire. However, Calvinism was still not recognised by the Augsburg Settlement, which made the Peace of Augsburg a shaky one and sowed the seeds for the coming strife, namely the Thirty Years' War.

It must be appreciated that prior to the advent of the Protestant Reformation, religion—specifically that of the Catholic Church, the papal authority and the Holy Status of the Roman Emperor— bound the Christian empire together despite differences in political and economic goals of the principalities within the empire. While the Reformation may have loosened their bonds to the Catholic Church and the Holy Roman Empire, contrary to popular perception, their bonds to Christianity were not broken. In fact, the Peace of Augsburg is proof of freedom of religion *within* the Christian fold with each State/principality within the empire claiming for itself a State denomination of Christianity, namely either Roman Catholicism or Lutheranism.

However, matters precipitated when in 1608, the Protestant Union was set up after the Imperial Diet, the deliberative body of the Holy Roman Empire, failed to formally confirm the Peace of Augsburg. In response to the Protestant Union, the Catholic League was formed in 1609, gradually moving towards a large-scale European conflagration, namely the Thirty Years' War, with Christian denominational freedom at the heart of the conflict, among other things. The commencement of the war is traced to 1618, which ended in 1648 with the signing of the Peace of Westphalia.[16] The salient terms of the Peace of Westphalia, which are relevant for our discussion, are as follows:

1. The Peace of Augsburg of 1555 along with the principle of 'cuius regio, eius religio' was recognised, strengthening the concept of religion-defined State sovereignty, with a defined territory having an official Christian denomination being identified as the realm of a particular State over which princes/rulers held dominion. Thenceforth, princes would have the right to determine the official Christian denomination of their States without interference from the Roman Catholic Church or what remained of the Holy Roman Empire after the war. What needs to be appreciated is that the Peace of Westphalia did not result in the creation of 'secular' sovereign States as we understand them today, that is, States without an official religion. On the contrary, the war itself was fought for the right to have an official State religion, more specifically, to choose a State denomination within the Christian religion without having to dance to the writ of the Roman Catholic Church;

2. These sovereign States had exclusive rights over their subjects on both secular and religious matters without having to suffer the interference of the empire or other sovereign States. This allowed them to levy taxes and raise armies of their own, which became a priority, especially after the experience of the Thirty Years' War, notwithstanding the precedent of diplomatic negotiations to resolve disputes and conflicts set by the Peace of Westphalia. In short, the importance of preservation of the balance of power was understood. Also, these States could enter into alliances with each other with the exception of alliances against the Empire;

3. Those Christian citizens whose denominational affiliation was different from that of the State were guaranteed the freedom of conscience to practise in private and limited rights to practise in public. In other words, religious 'minorities' in this context were denominational minorities from *within* the same religion, namely Christianity, and their ability to practise their denominational faith in public was contingent upon the goodwill of the State and therefore, the majority denomination; and

4. Calvinism, which was previously not recognised as one of the permanent denominations of Christianity under the Peace of Augsburg of 1555, was included as the third official permanent denomination.

Given the drastic truncation, if not complete elimination, of both the papacy and the overlordship of the Holy Roman Empire, Pope Innocent X issued a papal bull, *Zel Domus*, which declared the Westphalian Peace treaties 'null, void, invalid, iniquitous, unjust, damnable, reprobate, inane, empty of meaning and effect for all time'.[17] Anticipating this papal tantrum, the Peace of Westphalia contained a clause that pre-emptively stated that the pope's protests would not render the treaties void.

That the Christian Peace of Westphalia laid the foundation for sovereign nation-states is evident from the definition of the State in the Montevideo Convention on the Rights and Duties of States (1933).[18] Article 1 of the said convention reads as under:

> The state as a person of international law should possess the following qualifications: (*a*) a permanent population; (*b*) a defined territory; (*c*) government; and (*d*) capacity to enter into relations with the other states.

The purpose of the preceding not-so-brief historical discussion was to demonstrate and advance the point that the Peace of Westphalia was distinctly Christian in nature, which has been secularised over time.[19] In fact, while it is true that the Peace of Westphalia resulted in a transition of hegemony from the Habsburg Empire to sovereign States, parties to the peace saw themselves as 'the Senate of Christian Europe'. Thanks to their newfound status as States with greater sovereignty, if not complete independence from the Holy Roman Empire, European States were at greater liberty to assert and develop their respective 'national identities' based on ethnicity, language and religious denomination as well as to pursue their respective religious, economic and political goals. The freedom from the vice-like grip of the Roman Catholic Church allowed the people to develop a closer connection with their States and their national identities, paving the way for greater crystallisation of nation-statehood and the beginnings of European nationalism.

In addition, since these States saw themselves as defenders of the Christian faith owing to the loss of the Habsburg Empire's monopoly over *the* faith, they developed their own competitive 'national systems of morality' within and drawing from Christian OET, and set their sights on acquiring greater resources to further their respective competing visions.

Therefore, while Columbus' expedition began in 1492 and colonisation by the Spaniards and the Portuguese had already taken root, the creation of sovereign States by the Westphalian Peace meant that there were more European States in the fray who now competed for the resources of the New World. Consequently, it came as no surprise that the new States followed the Spanish and the Portuguese policies of establishing colonies with papal benedictions.

This spurred on the race for competitive nationalism and colonialism while remaining firmly within the Christian fold, a point which needs to be emphasised given the excruciatingly embarrassing contemporary tendency to secularise history. There is sufficient basis to conclude that these States were driven by inter-denominational competitiveness, triggered by the Protestant Reformation and the Peace of Westphalia. The New World or the non-Christian world became the battleground for this aggressive rivalry for wealth, territory, resources and ultimately, national cum denominational supremacy.

These zealous colonising ventures of the European States were funded by wealthy aristocrats in alliance with the ruling elite to preserve their positions within the States as well as to benefit from the expansionist colonising vision of the 'Christian secular' monarchs. That the alliance between wealthy aristocrats and the governing class gave rise to mercantilism, nationalism and, perhaps, nationalistic mercantilism would not be an unsubstantiated statement to make.[20] Some scholars believe that these alliances contributed to the rise of capitalism, which is still a visible feature of the Westphalian nation-state system, where those with capital work with those in power to preserve and advance 'national interest'. Critically, there is a demonstrable nexus between the Westphalian State system and the 'standard of civilisation' as set by international law, which needs to be understood in order to appreciate its specific local manifestations in the political thought of former European colonies.

The Coloniality of 'Civilised Nations' under International Law: A Westphalian Legacy

The legacy of the Peace of Westphalia was not limited to the creation of nation-states but also extended to universalisation of the Westphalian or European experience through the instrumentality of 'international law' using the 'standard of civilisation' as a legal benchmark to judge societies. This is evident from Articles 9 and 38(1) of the Statute of the International Court of Justice which was established in 1945, that is, almost three centuries after the Peace of Westphalia. The said provisions read as under[21]:

Article 9: At every election, the electors shall bear in mind not only that the persons to be elected should individually possess the qualifications required, but also that in the body as a whole the representation of the *main forms of civilization* and of the principal legal systems of the world should be assured.

Article 38: 1. The Court, whose function is to decide in accordance with international law such disputes as are submitted to it, shall apply:
a.   international conventions, whether general or particular, establishing rules expressly recognized by the contesting states;
b.   international custom, as evidence of a general practice accepted as law;
c.   the general principles of law recognized by *civilized nations*;
d.   subject to the provisions of Article 59, judicial decisions and the teachings of the most highly qualified publicists of the various nations, as subsidiary means for the determination of rules of law.

2.   This provision shall not prejudice the power of the Court to decide a case ex aequo et bono, if the parties agree thereto. [emphasis added]

While Article 9 uses the words 'main forms of civilization', Article 38(1)(c) uses the term 'civilized nations'. Given that these terms have been used in the context of an international legal instrument that applies to an international court set up under the aegis of the United Nations, these terms must be attributed specific meanings and cannot be used or interpreted loosely. Article 38 has been typically understood as enumerating the 'sources' of international law. However, scholars agree that these 'sources' themselves are the product of the Western civilisation. In fact, they believe that international law is 'a living artifact' of the Western civilisation, or more specifically the 'Westphalian civilisation', since this politico-theological framework of civilisation was universalised through its imposition on the rest of the world by Europe and the United States under the garb of 'international law'.[22] Therefore, it can be reasonably contended that international law itself is a denouement as well as a tool of coloniality since colonies were faced with no other option but to adopt Eurocentric/Western ideas, norms and institutions.

Scholars agree that the sources alluded to in Article 38(1) were the result of the application of the 'Standard of Civilization' (SOC) by the West to bestow upon societies the status of 'civilised nations', which were expected to observe and abide by the rules laid down as 'international law'.[23] Importantly, the more practical and less lofty reason for the growth of international law was Europe's need to transact with non-European societies wherein the SOC was employed as an organising principle. It ensured that business was conducted within a Eurocentric framework in order to protect the citizens of the West and Western ideas of 'universal rights/ freedoms'. Those that agreed to comply with the framework by recognising the said rights and freedoms were deemed worthy of being accorded the status of 'civilised nations'. Interestingly, the expectation was not limited to the application of the SOC framework to Westerners in the non-West; instead, non-Western societies were expected to re-order themselves on the same lines as European Westphalian States, which meant that the change was not merely external but also deeply internal to the non-West. The following were some of the specific changes expected of the non-West by the West[24]:

1. Those rights and freedoms that were guaranteed to citizens of the West in their nation-states were expected to be recognised and available to them in the non-West;

2. Non-Western societies were expected to adopt the same forms of government as the West so as to protect the freedoms and property of Western nationals within their territories. This effectively meant the gradual universalisation of the idea of a constitutional form of government with three identified organs, namely the legislature, the executive and the judiciary, whose metes and bounds were determined by the doctrine of separation of powers. The theoretical foundations of the same were provided by Enlightenment thinkers, such as Baron de Montesquieu and John Locke, in the eighteenth century. As part of this expectation, codification of laws, which could be administered by courts set up on the same lines as courts in the West, was deemed mandatory so as to protect the property rights of Western nationals. This had the Lockean influence written all over it;

3. Non-Western societies were expected to reorganise themselves in a manner beneficial to the individual freedoms of Western nationals, although such nationals were immune to the application of domestic civil and criminal laws, being answerable exclusively to the consulates of Western governments. The basis for this position was distinctly supremacist and racist, that is, non-Western nations were not 'civilised', and therefore Western nationals could not be subjected to the 'uncivilised' political and legal systems of the non-West;

4. Non-Western societies were expected to have the capacity to defend their borders/territories against external

aggression apart from subscribing to the Westphalian model of international diplomacy and State sovereignty, which included non-interference in the domestic affairs of other nation-states; and

5. Not only were non-Western societies expected to abide by the principles of 'international law' and become 'nation-states' that subscribed to 'the rule of law' with regard to Western nationals, they were also expected to conform domestically to the norms, mores and customs recognised in and by Western societies.

Effectively, European imperial powers gained extraterritorial jurisdiction over non-Western societies through the application of international law, which was nothing but the enforcement of Protestant Reformation-inspired Westphalian principles.[25] In the third section of this book, which relates to Bharat's constitutional journey, this subject is addressed in greater detail to demonstrate the application of the SOC as a legal requirement for membership to international bodies, such as the League of Nations. The point being made is that 'harmonisation' of both economic and legal systems as a consequence of the application of international law, that is, internationalised European/Western law, was inevitable. To anyone who follows contemporary discussions surrounding international trade relations or human rights, it must be fairly evident that the situation has not changed. If anything, post decolonisation, the normalisation of European coloniality through the use of international law has only been further entrenched, owing to the economic dependency of former colonies on the West.

To digress a bit, it is important to remember that in the middle of the twentieth century, when several colonised societies attained 'independence', the focus of the 'civilised world' suddenly fell on the 'poverty' of the 'Third World'. It was conveniently forgotten that this impoverished situation of the Third World was a direct consequence of centuries of colonisation. Instead, decolonisation engendered a new talking point, namely that the newly formed 'nation-states' must 'catch up' with the West by focusing on 'development' the European way.[26] Viewed in this light, the impact of the 'economic aid' extended by the erstwhile colonisers to Third World countries on the shaping of the discourse surrounding 'rights' and 'development' warrants deeper examination by experts from the perspective of entrenchment of coloniality using the economic needs of the former colonies as a bargaining tool.

Coming back to the use of the SOC, it clearly served as a litmus test for 'civilisation' and international interactions, which led to the elimination of 'pluriversalism' and civilisational diversity, only to be replaced by Western-normative universalism and a 'liberal' globalised Westphalian civilisation. While on the one hand, the Westphalian system emphasised State sovereignty and non-interference in the domestic affairs of nation-states, it hypocritically interfered with the domestic affairs and the fundamental consciousness of non-Western societies. Simply put, the concept of State sovereignty was selectively applied to Christian European nation-states while the rest of the world was fair game for undue interference. This completely eviscerates the claim of the Peace of Westphalia being a secular, liberal and egalitarian milestone that ushered in an era of respect among nations as equals. Members of the Christian civilisation that subscribed to Westphalian principles were equals, but those outside of it, namely the non-Christian indigenous societies of the New World, were lesser and unevolved, who needed to be 'civilised' and 'reformed' through the instrumentality of international law.

Scholars believe that the 'liberal' globalised civilisation is, in fact, merely a secularised version of the Westphalian civilisation whose secularisation is largely attributed to the nature of the Enlightenment itself. Therefore, it is important to examine the Christian secular nature of the Enlightenment and its coloniality. On this subject, the work of Dr. S.N. Balagangadhara and Dr. De Roover is incisive and critical.[27]

Christianity, Enlightenment and Coloniality

It is often assumed that the Enlightenment represented the predominance of reason over faith not just for Europe but also for the rest of the world. That non-European civilisations had their own respective journeys and subjectivities is often lost in this simultaneously deliberate and unconscious Europeanisation of world history. Colonised indigenous societies have suffered the most as a consequence of this approach since their journeys of millennia, their lived experiences, their onto-epistemological systems, their individual and collective identities and their right to agency all have been casually and superciliously dismissed as legends, myths and superstitions. That this 'Enlightened' attitude continues to date through the colonialised native establishment makes it imperative for us to understand the so-called secular character of the Enlightenment. While it is relatively easy to discern the direct nexus between the Protestant Reformation and the Peace of Westphalia, which demonstrates the latter's Christian character, the Enlightenment could be mistaken for a break from religion, more specifically from Christianity, towards a more 'liberal' and 'secular' outlook owing to the claim that it marked the beginning of the 'Age of Reason'. Therefore, this claim needs to be examined in order to understand whether the Enlightenment and the values that stemmed from it were secular, as in truly irreligious, or 'Christian secular'. Its impact on the politico-theological framework of the European coloniser needs to be examined as well.

While discussing the Enlightenment, De Roover starts with a dissection of the idea of religious toleration, which is often treated as a value that arose out of the Enlightenment. This makes the value as well as the Enlightenment itself seem secular and non-Christian because after all, why would a Christian movement preach toleration for other faith systems when proselytisation remains one of the cornerstones of that faith? But did toleration truly have a non-religious origin? Also, did toleration mean the ability to practise one's conscience without being judged or without having to apprehend proselytisation? These are the questions that De Roover addresses with scintillating clarity.

To start with, De Roover examines the views of one of the central figures of the Enlightenment, the English philosopher John Locke, who contributed significantly to the development of liberalism with his views on religious toleration, equality and the concept of rights. De Roover compares and contrasts two schools of thought—the first which interprets Locke's views as liberal and hence secular, and the second that sees the Protestant framework clearly at play behind Locke's positions,[28] divorced from which theological framework and its premises, several of his claims would be 'simply unintelligible'. De Roover explains the relevance of this examination especially for non-Christian societies because a liberal model of toleration that draws significantly from the Protestant framework is bound to interfere with the course of such societies, unless they share the same underlying ontological and theological premises, which cannot be said of most indigenous societies. If anything, as discussed in the previous chapters, the Christian understanding of the relationship between 'God', human beings and nature is as divergent as it can get from those cultures that venerate nature and see themselves as part of nature and not outside of it. This effectively undermines any semblance of a common ground between the worldview of indigenous societies and that of Christian Europe.

Does this mean that it is not possible to base liberalism on purely secular values? To answer this, Jeremy Waldron, professor of law and philosophy, says that while it may be possible to build the edifice of liberalism and equality on non-Christian foundations, as a matter of 'ethical history' it must be acknowledged that the 'modern' thought around equality has been shaped by religion, specifically Christianity.[29] He suspects that the contemporary notion of equality among human beings might fall apart without the underlying Christian premise. In other words, contemporary equality and liberalism are, in fact, secularised versions of Christian equality and Christian liberalism. Given the global presence of European coloniality, Waldron's position may indeed be historically accurate. What this means is that equality per se as a notion was not unknown to non-Christian societies prior to the advent of the Christian coloniser; however, every society has the right to define equality according to its cultural experience sans the judgment induced by Christian coloniality. Further, to fashion a universal definition of equality, if at all it is desirable and possible, it must equally consider non-Christian positions on equality, which has not been the case thus far.

Coming back to Locke, De Roover reviews Locke's division of society into two spheres, namely the civil and the religious based on his writings in *A Letter Concerning Toleration*, and highlights the stark similarities between the Lockean position and the Christian political theology of two kingdoms and the idea of Christian liberty. The Lockean premise of the need for civil authority is that humans are designed to prey on the fruits of others' labour, and therefore need civil authority in the non-religious sphere, which is kept distinct from the religious sphere. De Roover demonstrates that this is but a secularised replication of the Christian assumption that humans are stained by sin and are fundamentally depraved, therefore needing a regnal authority to rein them in. What is evidently common to the Protestant and Lockean positions is that the separation of the civil/temporal and the religious/spiritual is based on Christian OET. Critically, De Roover recognises that this distinction may not hold good for non-Christian societies whose conception of the relationship between temporal and secular authorities may be very different, assuming that they even subscribe to such a distinction in the first place. The limits of Locke's religious toleration are thrown into sharp relief when Catholicism and atheism stand excluded from his idea of toleration, which demonstrates that his views were clearly informed by the Protestant conception of true and false religions.

However, the question still remains as to why the toleration of other faiths and non-faiths would be preached if the Protestant framework accepted that faith in Christ and the Christian conception of God were indispensable for salvation. While Catholics and atheists were excluded from Locke's notions of toleration, other thinkers argued for toleration of Catholics, Jews, Muslims and even pagan 'devil worshippers'—contrary to our expectations from a Christian-derived idea. The answer to this lies in the concept of 'toleration' itself, its source and end goal. First, the concept of true and false religions, and heresy are embedded in the Christian understanding of toleration, with toleration here not being the same as acceptance, mutual respect or pluralism. Second, toleration of false religions and heretics was not the product of secular liberal thinking but was the restatement of the will of God, the Christian God, that no conscience should be coerced even if it desecrated the will of God. Third, while the 'sword of coercion' was forbidden by God, the 'Sword of God's spirit', namely the Word of God or the gospel was certainly permissible. The gospel was believed to be 'soul-piercing' and 'soul-saving', and therefore, the alternative to coercion was proselytisation, which was deemed benign, biblically sanctioned and even mandated. Thus, even here, it was Christian liberty at play with the end goal being the realisation of God's will on earth. In light of this, there is no escaping the fact that the Enlightenment's 'toleration' was a secularised fulfilment of a true Christian's obligation, namely conversion for reformation of both Christians and non-Christians. The political theology of the Protestant Reformation could not have been written clearer on the walls of the Enlightenment project.

It is precisely for these reasons that De Roover calls both secularism and liberalism secularised versions of Christian onto-epistemology, obscured by the employment of secularism itself as a filter to understand history. De Roover is not alone in holding this view. There are others, such as Carl L. Becker, S.J. Barnett and Elizabeth S. Hurd, who believe that at the very least the evidence to support the common assumption that the Enlightenment was a move away from Christianity towards secular reason is as far as it can get from being conclusive. That the secularisation of the Enlightenment is perhaps the consequence of a retrospective approach to history appears to be the more plausible argument. This is because several of the leading Enlightenment thinkers were pious Christians in a society heavily committed to Christianity, whose philosophies were significantly more influenced by Christian thought than they were comfortable admitting. This may be because 'orthodoxy' was passé and it was more acceptable to speak out against orthodoxy in favour of the new, the 'modern', even in the context of Christianity, which only proves that even the challenge to Christian orthodoxy was a conversation *within* Christianity and not outside of it.[30] In fact, scholars believe that the views of such thinkers were effectively a manifestation of their desire for a 'different kind of Church in a different kind of society', which strengthens the case in favour of the Enlightenment's Christian character.[31] Another strong case in point are the views of the German philosopher Immanuel Kant, whose theories and positions on morality were primarily a generic form of Christianity devoid of the sectarian divide that defined the times he lived in.[32] His contribution was the individualisation of morality while retaining the distinct qualities of Christianity.

If the Church was seen as an indispensable institution for acceptable social peace by even the most radical Enlightenment thinkers, surely it did not indicate a departure from a Christian past, but only a much more secularised approach to Christianity itself, which is the legacy of the Protestant Reformation. Therefore, the conclusion that the most 'secular' milestone of European history, namely the Enlightenment, was informed by the political theology of Protestantism, is a fairly reasonable one to arrive at given the source of its thought, and its inability to remain intelligible and consistent when divorced from its Christian moorings. The Enlightenment represented the second wave of progressive secularisation of Protestant Christian OET, which served to advance the political theology of the Reformation, thereby strengthening the idea of 'a true religion'. This idea had a hierarchy of religions, and hence cultures, embedded in it. Therefore, there is no reason to avoid the reasonable conclusion that these very same Enlightened ideas and values informed the European colonisers, and continue to inform contemporary Western thought, whose Christian premise both the secularised West and colonialised former colonies desperately try to deny despite the evidence stacked against them.

After all, there is no proof that the effect of the Enlightenment was to question, let alone impede, the march of European colonialism. If anything, the sanctimony underlying the notion of true religion, which did not spare even Catholicism, provided the added impetus to the religiously inspired, race-driven 'civilising' mission of the colonial project. There is also no evidence to suggest that the Enlightenment altered the fundamental Christian understanding of 'man's' relationship with nature or those who were outside 'the light of Christianity', such as indigenous communities. If the idea of toleration is sought to be invoked to canvas the secular, liberal and broad-minded vision of the Enlightenment, the very writings of the leading thinkers of this movement only prove the contrary, that is, whether intentional or otherwise, toleration was a means to an end—to save the soul of those outside the true religion, with the Word of God acting as the soul-piercing sword.

Further, the 'scientific temper' that arose out of the Enlightenment may have actually provided 'scientific' justifications for the race consciousness and perceived superiority of the White Christian European coloniser, as distilled from the writings of Kant himself. There is enough literature to suggest that at least until 1795, when Kant completed the manuscript of *Toward Perpetual Peace* at the age of 71, he consciously and openly believed in the hierarchy of races, and in particular, the superiority of the Whites over the non-Whites. In 1788, he was of the view that people from Africa and India lacked the drive to activity, and hence lacked the mental capacities to be self-motivated and successful in northern climates.[33] To him, the Native Americans were weak, inert, incapable of any culture and occupied the lowest rung of the racial hierarchy. For someone who is credited with the formulation of a universalist moral theory, until the age of 71, Kant's belief that the Whites represented the perfection of humanity was writ large in his writings. At the very least, it calls into question the views expressed by Kant during this period on a host of topics, such as equality and morality, when he published some of his most seminal works, such as the *Critique of Pure Reason* (1781).

In fact, Kant's views on race were consistent from 1764, when he was 40 years of age, until 1795. In *Observations on the Feeling of the Beautiful and Sublime* (1764), he wrote that the black colour of a 'negro carpenter' proved the stupidity of whatever he said and that the difference in the mental faculties of the Whites and Blacks was as large as the difference in their colours.[34] On the Hindus, he was of the view that they were superior to the 'Negroes' because they could be educated but only in the arts and not in the sciences and other subjects that required powers of abstraction. Of course, there are those who believe that his subdued approach on race post 1795, after a lifetime of belief in a racial hierarchy and White superiority as a scientific fact, was proof of a change of heart.[35] What such apologists fail to understand is that the brunt of Kant's race-driven morality during his prime years and those of other Enlightenment thinkers was borne by indigenous societies because the best minds of the Enlightenment were comfortable offering pearls of wisdom to the entire world on morality and equality while openly wearing their White Christian supremacy on their sleeves. Obviously, this casual Janusian approach reflected in the conduct of the colonisers as well in their attitudes towards the non-White, non-Christian, colonised, indigenous societies because they drew inspiration from their own leading Enlightened thinkers who normalised such glaring moral inconsistency and hypocrisy in the most eloquent and 'scientific' of manners.

Another important aspect of the Enlightenment is its manifold enhancement of the universalising and totalising tendency of the political theology of the Protestant Reformation by providing supposedly secular, liberal, scientific and, hence, universalist justifications for it, which fit well with the one-size-fits-all approach of the European coloniser. One could go a step further and state that the utter conviction of the Enlightenment thinkers in their universalist and inflexible approach to questions of morality and values, without any regard for the peculiar experiences and conditions of each culture/civilisation, may have inspired the colonialists further and bolstered their inherent coloniality.[36] In this regard, it must be borne in mind that the attitude of such thinkers was distinctly Christian because the idea of one God and/or one universal morality for all peoples was at the heart of this thought notwithstanding the secular and liberal labels they may have congratulated themselves with. Therefore, the temporal overlap between the Enlightenment and the prime years of colonialism, including the very birth of contemporary notions of modernity, cannot be dismissed as a mere coincidence.[37]

Even if one were to take into account the fact that a few Enlightenment thinkers may have objected to the cruel treatment of indigenous peoples at the hands of the White Christian European coloniser, two aspects undermine such apologia: first, the objection was perhaps limited to the treatment of colonised peoples but not to the colonisation project itself, because 'civilising' the non-Christian lesser mortal was part of their 'toleration' project; and second, the so-called secular liberal thinkers of that period did not deem it fit to take into account indigenous views on morality and ethics in formulating their universalist theories. That they never felt the need to offer indigenous views an equal place at the high-table of human thought as a matter of right, and not privilege, is proof enough of their patronising approach to indigenous worldviews. Surely it cannot be argued on their behalf that their egalitarianism can be presumed despite an express absence of dialogue with the indigenous peoples in the formulation of universalist theories which treated Europe and its civilisation as the centre of the universe. Clearly, there is a need for more honest conversations around the dark side of the Enlightenment, particularly from the perspective of formerly colonised societies, most of which have suffered irreversible all-round harm.

The contemporary and practical relevance of such conversations from an indigenous perspective is the urgent need to acknowledge the Protestant-inspired, race-conscious coloniality of the political structure established by the European coloniser in colonies. The second critical takeaway, in my opinion and in which I am supported by the work of De Roover and others including Mignolo,[38] is that the presumptions of secularity, liberality, neutrality, equality and universality—which are imputed to the Enlightenment and its values—are seriously rebuttable, circumspect and, dare I say, even baseless. As stated earlier, extending such presumptions would be downright dishonest in the context of the relationship between the coloniser and the colonised. Third, in light of the first two conclusions, surviving indigenous civilisations that were formerly colonised have the right to reclaim their worldviews and draw from them to redefine their political landscapes, which impact all aspects of their lives, in particular their right to practise their ways of life without having to prove themselves on the anvils of European values and benchmarks. One cannot underscore enough the importance of this form of agency since despite attaining 'political independence', former colonies that became new entrants to the club of nation-states were expected to be mere 'passive participants' in the Eurocentric world order.

In this club, concepts, such as nation-statehood and sovereignty, were predefined with no scope for indigenous contribution. Those who did not play by these rules were treated as outliers to the 'world order' and subjected to constant judgment stemming from never-ending Reformation-style sanctimony and virtue-signalling, which remains the position till date. Indigenous societies with varied forms of precolonial social and political organisation were expected to rearrange themselves to conform to the definition of nation-statehood, which required the domination of one particular ethno-linguistic or religious group over all others so as to become a largely homogenous 'nation' with safe spaces created for 'minorities'.

To say that this triggered a competitive tussle for identification/creation of ethnicities and ethnic domination in indigenous societies would be an understatement. The ones to suffer the most were plural and diverse civilisational societies, such as Bharat, that were linked internally by millennia of coexistence wherein no single marker, such as ethnicity or language or the Christian concept of religion, could be used to make sense of their oneness, which was more a lived reality. In such societies, owing to the pressure of nation-statehood, every marker of identity, real or artificial, became the foundation for identifying the in-group and the out-group, thereby creating multiple centrifugal forces that led to competitive nationalism. This is not to say that the idea of in- and out-groups was absent prior to the advent of the European coloniser. However, indigenous societies had certainly evolved processes and mechanisms through traditions developed over ages to retain diverse individual as well as group identities, and yet coexist with others in relative harmony. The expectations that came with the imposition of a nation-statehood posed a unique challenge to their own conceptions of political unity, which they could not avoid or overcome given the Europeanised world they now existed in.

To overcome the fissiparous tendencies created by the imposition of nation-statehood, colonies upon achieving independence were forced to adopt legal mechanisms to preserve their integrity, the foremost of which was a constitution that was populated by Enlightened Europeanism. Naturally, over time, the constitution, which was initially intended to be a means to forge a nation-state and was a product of necessity, was elevated to the status of a religious document. In short, the means became an end in itself and, to make matters worse, thanks to the colonial values subscribed to by the constitutions of decolonised societies, the space for indigenous ways of life started shrinking once again. The only difference was that this time the political structure was helmed not by the European coloniser but by the colonialised native who was a new convert to constitutionalism, constitutional morality and ultimately Europeanism/Western-normativism. It is precisely for these reasons that constitutionalism and its coloniality warrant a closer look.

Coloniality/Modernity and 'Enlightened' Constitutionalism: The New True Religion of Former Colonies

From the history of the Protestant Reformation, the genesis and globalisation of the Westphalian civilisation, and the Enlightenment discussed thus far, it is evident that these European milestones distinctly shaped and strengthened European coloniality, which, in turn, reflected in the political structures established in the colonies. Therefore, it should come as no surprise that the ideas and values of these milestones formed the basis of the constitutions introduced in the colonies by the coloniser. Among them, the most cardinal is the conception of colonised societies as nation-states—the *grundnorm* of Western political organisation.

When European nation-states emerged following the Peace of Westphalia, they were still a part of Christian Europe, with the three Christian denominations vying for the status of the true religion. Therefore, notwithstanding the internal fissures, conversations and debates, they were united in their stated goal of the expansion of the boundaries of Christianity through conquest of the New World. In other words, Christian nation-states were acutely alive to the religious-cum-territorial canvas they were located within, which means that their nation-statehood was Christian in nature with a clear focus on demarcating their respective territories *within* Christian Europe. To impute secular nation-statehood to such States reflects wishful thinking on the part of those that view history with rose-tinted glasses.

In stark contrast to the 'Christian secular' character of European nation-states, the secularised model of nation-statehood that was exported to the colonies required the natives to abandon their consciousness and start on a clean slate on the assumption that their identities began only with the arrival of the coloniser to whom the only acceptable form of political organisation was that of a nation-state. As a consequence, most colonies embraced nationalism of the territorial kind, which altered their priorities significantly. The deprivation of a cultural or civilisational anchor to their 'modern' identities meant that their visions of the past, present and future were limited to merely preserving territorial integrity while constantly ceding space on civilisational integrity to coloniality. Thenceforth, civilisational consciousness and integrity would be the exclusive preserve of Western imperialism, while the rest of the world was expected to abandon its roots, reduced to a mere source of primary data for the West to analyse, thereby handing them the power to theorise and formulate abstract universals even after decolonisation.

Along with the internalisation of nation-statehood, concepts, such as separation of the Church and the State ('secularism'), separation of powers, 'toleration', 'liberty' and notions of rights and duties, were secularised with a view to universalise them. These 'secular' values found their way into 'national' constitutions, with the colonised natives being oblivious to the underlying Protestant origins of the Eurocentric abstract universals. In effect, national constitutions became the codified fount of coloniality and morphed into secular yet sacred instrumentalities through which Eurocentrism could be amplified and perpetuated in colonies.[39] In light of this, it can be argued that colonial constitutionalism represents the third wave of secularisation and universalisation of Protestantism as well as the institutionalisation of the coloniality/modernity/rationality matrix, whose contours were fleshed out by the Enlightenment, the so-called Age of Reason. Naturally, the never-ending process of conversion and its end goal, namely reformation, were given a pride of place in an ostensibly secular legal instrument, namely constitution, whose claim of neutrality in relation to indigenous worldviews was as true as a modern-day politician's promise.

While the adoption of national constitutions facilitated the creation of political entities which could now be called nation-states, this was largely a product of colonial imposition through 'international law' as discussed earlier, and not necessarily reflective of the irrelevance of other forms of political organisation. The irony of the situation was that on the one hand, former colonies had to rely on their past to stake a claim for their nation-statehood, and on the other hand, to be accepted into the 'commonwealth of civilised States', they had to embrace modernity and sever ties with their past. Naturally, these tensions affected the making of their constitutions, with coloniality more often than not having the upper hand. Consequently, under constitutions imbued with coloniality and a strained relationship with the past, the colonialised nation-states donned the robes of a contemporary Martin Luther, holding forth from the bully pulpit and calling for the reform of the native under the authority of the new Bible, namely the constitution. Even today, in such societies, each arm of the State competes with the other to modernise and reform the native under the authority conferred by the constitution, which has become the source of Statist morality that is to be enforced top-down with no meaningful participation from or dialogue with the native. For all their claims of having transitioned to a republican and democratic form of government, nation-states in most former colonies have retained hegemony over questions of morals, ethics, faith and in general OET systems, much akin to the ecclesiastical approach.

Ironically, under this structure of government in decolonised societies, the judiciary in particular has gradually come to occupy a similar position as the Roman Catholic Church, wielding the same impervious authority while dispensing Protestant and Enlightenment values on both secular and religious matters. In that sense, instead of decentralising morality and allowing the society's indigenous cultural moorings to inform law and policy, blind and unthinking constitutionalism has effectively contributed to the concentration of totalising powers over morality and worldview in the hands of unelected institutions and individuals. While the monasticised Roman Catholic Church served the true God, the true religion and Christ, and advanced the process of conversion towards reformation of man in the image of God, modern-day constitutional institutions serve colonial constitutionalism and advance the cause of reformation of the native society in the image of the European civilisation, perhaps under the belief that the native society's salvation lies in Westernisation.

This process of constitutional conversion of the indigenous society takes the shape of 'transformative constitutionalism' or 'progressive constitutionalism', both of which suffer from varying degrees of coloniality. One is alive to the fact that transformative constitutionalism may land differently in different jurisdictions depending on their respective histories and socio-economic conditions. For instance, in South Africa, transformative constitutionalism represents the transition from an apartheid State to a democratic society, which has even facilitated decolonialisation, and hence the Africanisation of legal education.[40] In contrast, in countries like Bharat, transformative constitutionalism has led to the severing of ties between the civilisational ethos of Bharat and the evolution of constitutional jurisprudence. This is attributable to the fundamental differences in historical premise and end goals that inform such transformative constitutionalism. If the premise is rooted in colonialised versions of indigenous history, it is but natural that transformative constitutionalism constantly sees the need to reform the native out of his/her identity. On the contrary, if the historical premise is the recognition of deep-seated coloniality in every aspect of the society, which is sought to be addressed, transformative constitutionalism could lead to shifting the locus of onto-epistemology and consciousness from the West to the indigenous society.

Having said this, the fact remains that the politico-legal structures of several 'independent' former colonies under the auspices of national constitutions present a curious incongruity wherein Catholicised institutions advance secularised and Enlightened Protestant OET, with the consequence being that the indigenous worldview invariably gets the rough end of the stick. This is borne out by the fact that in order to avail of the 'fundamental rights' guaranteed by constitutions, indigenous OET systems have had to conform to colonial definitions of 'religion', 'religious denomination' and the like, which are clearly rooted in Christian OET. Therefore, indigenous OETs developed over several millennia have had to approximate and truncate themselves to conform to a political theology that is barely half a millennium old and whose approach to those outside its fold is one of 'toleration' until the Word of God pierces and saves the native soul. Further, indigenous beliefs are expected to pass muster on the evidentiary anvils inspired by two sources: the first is the Christian need for a written scripture or the indigenous equivalent of the Word of God, and the second is that indigenous practices, traditions and beliefs have had to satisfy the all-important condition precedent of 'reason', that is, secularised, Protestant OET.

Those practices which fail to acquit themselves on these benchmarks and standards are branded 'orthodox', 'traditional' and 'anachronistic', gradually leading to Protestantisation of indigenous OET systems. Naturally, the colonial constitutional framework in most former colonies, while promising equality, has been loaded with values that are more conducive to the Christian worldview. In societies that still have surviving non-Christian populations, the indigenous worldview finds itself constantly on the backfoot, torn between its commitment to keep its way of life alive and the constitutional expectation to validate itself in order to stave off legally sanctioned extinction.

For instance, it is a documented fact that despite the American Indian Religious Freedom Act of 1978, which expressly acknowledges and guarantees the right of Native Americans to practise their indigenous forms of spirituality and worship, they have frequently found themselves in court in an effort to protect their rights. Despite putting faith in the legal process and the promise of equality enshrined in the American Constitution, their sacred sites have been destroyed to build roads in the name of development.[41] To assume that such treatment is limited to countries where the natives do not enjoy numerical strength is to underestimate and misunderstand the entrenchment of coloniality.

Even in societies that are still predominantly non-Christian, such as Bharat, the indigenous identity (barring a few pockets) has largely been 'secularised', which means that the situation of the practitioners of indigenous faith systems in Bharat is not vastly different from that of the Native Americans. Apart from having to constitutionally validate themselves, practitioners of indigenous OET systems have had to suffer exotification, misrepresentation, appropriation, stereotyping and exploitation in the very lands of their origin thanks to, among other things, 'tourism' and 'development', which have gradually pushed them into ever-shrinking enclaves where they can only hope to practise whatever remains of their way of life without interference or ridicule or 'modern scrutiny'. In fact, since such practitioners have to contend with the colonialised from among their own community as well as the State establishment, their ordeal is much more arduous but they have fewer sympathisers because they are supposedly part of the 'majority'. The harsh reality, however, is that such practitioners are a minority within a numerical majority, with the numerical majority itself being a colonialised global minority. This makes the practitioners of indigenous ways of life a micro-minority, who may perhaps be the last surviving members of their cultures and civilisations.

To add to it, in order to demonstrate their 'tolerance' by virtue of being the 'majority', surviving indigenous global minorities are expected to remain mum about their histories. This is one of the lesser appreciated ramifications of modern constitutionalism, given its propensity to secularise history, which has a direct impact on education policy in general, and specifically on shaping of the curriculum. Not only is the past secularised to ostensibly further constitutional goals and morality, indigenous peoples are expected to silently accommodate the proselytising overtures of colonising OET systems in the present. The constitutional fiction that requires such accommodation on the part of indigenous peoples to their own detriment is that all OET systems are the same in their make-up and therefore, deserve equal treatment under the law. The net result is that non-Christian indigenous societies are left with no option but to subscribe to a secular identity and offer equal opportunity and space to the coloniser's faith in order to demonstrate their commitment to liberal constitutional values. Clearly, the notions of a 'level playing field' are, to put it mildly, examples of dark legal fictions in view of the history of at least the last five centuries, ever since the dice was loaded against indigenous worldviews.

What makes matters worse is the sense of religiosity with which constitutions are approached in former colonies, almost as if to prove with vengeance their modern, secular and liberal bona fides to their erstwhile colonial masters, and to earn their validation as 'civilised nations of laws'. In short, the message that is being conveyed by the colonialised native is that 'we are no less European/Western/modern/rational and therefore, your equals' instead of saying 'we do not wish to be European/Western, for we are comfortable in our skin and our subjectivities'. It is this deep-seated coloniality and sense of cultural/civilisational inferiority among colonialised natives that has given rise to bizarre concepts such as 'constitutional patriotism'. Professing allegiance to constitutionalism is understandable; however, it is a reflection of coloniality when constitutional patriots lose sight of what ought to have been or perhaps is the very object of the constitution's protection, namely preservation and perpetuation of indigeneity and its right to agency.

In short, it is a textbook case of missing the forest for the trees, since such constitutional patriotism has no sense of history or consciousness that is rooted in indigeneity. This makes it detrimental to the indigenous worldview since the colonialised constitutional patriot has already bought into Eurocentrism/ Western-normativism either consciously or otherwise, thereby turning into an ambassador and evangelist for the coloniality/ modernity/rationality complex. That their identity as a member of the indigenous community has been weaponised to act against indigenous consciousness is lost in the incoherent and self-absorbed din of modernity, rationality and constitutional patriotism.

Given that in contemporary nation-states, constitutions as documents create multiplier effects by serving as launchpads for mass enforcement of ideas not just on the politico-economic front but also on the larger civilisational canvas, the priority of former colonies must be to first decolonialise this document so that indigeneity finds its rightful place first within its own territory of origin before it can hope to take its rightful place as an equal at the global high table. After all, there is no denying the fact that the effect of contemporary constitutionalism, at least in former colonies, has become such that it is all-pervasive, which is a reflection of its totalising nature given its entrenched coloniality.

Therefore, the constitution—the supreme law, the fount of constitutional morality, the document which contains the original intent—must be the primary subject of decolonial scholarship and efforts in indigenous societies while they still have the power to restore their agency over their consciousness and accord indigeneity its rightful place. After all, if indigeneity has no respect in the land of its birth in the context of law and policymaking and is relegated to a mere ornamental talking point, it cannot hope to be taken seriously in a colonialised modern world.

While thus far the discussion has revolved around the origins and character of coloniality, modernity and rationality, it is equally important to understand the response, namely decoloniality, indigeneity, subjectivity and relationality. It is also imperative to understand what they do *not* stand for because it is easy to mistake them as codes for 'xenophobia', 'ethnonationalism' and several other cognate pejoratives that are typically used to label and, hence, stigmatise the indigenous perspective. Accordingly, in the next chapter, I will unpack decoloniality, indigeneity, subjectivity and relationality which shall set the tone for the next two sections of this book.

Decoloniality, Indigeneity, Subjectivity and Relationality

Native Americans Worshipping the Sun

Depiction of the Native Americans worshipping the Sun with a harvest offering. The skin of a large stag was stuffed with vegetables and carried to a clearing in the forest on the first day of spring. It was mounted on a pole and prayers would be offered to the Sun for a bountiful harvest (courtesy of the University of South Florida).

In the first chapter, I had undertaken a brief and broad discussion on four schools of thought, namely:

1. the modernist school, which puts stock in Eurocentric universalism and believes in its continued relevance;

2. the postmodern school, which rejects this universalist claim predominantly in the realm of culture;

3. the postcolonial school, which is in the neighbourhood of the postmodern school and critiques colonialism and its Eurocentrism primarily in the political realm, albeit without deconstructing its fundamentals; and

4. the decolonial school, which goes beyond the postcolonial school by identifying the existence of European coloniality even after decolonisation, dissects its OET foundations and seeks to unshackle indigeneity from the universal fictions of coloniality.

For the purposes of the discussion here, I have consciously limited the scope primarily to understanding the areas of intersection and exclusion between the postcolonial and decolonial schools as the former already has a strong base in Bharat and the latter is yet to be fully tapped into as an alternative. To this end, I am interested in bringing out the inherent limitations of postcolonialism (and its offspring, subaltern studies)[1] in addressing the OET framework underlying the colonial legacy, apart from failing to empower the indigenous voice. In fact, from what I have read, postcolonialism has reinforced colonial stereotypes of the indigenous worldview, which is precisely why the viability of decoloniality as an alternative must be seriously considered. While in the second section of the book, I will attempt to make a Bharat-specific case for the application of decoloniality, in this chapter, I will generally lay out the reasons for taking this position.

'De'colonial, Not 'Post'colonial

Be it an individual or a society, neither must cede nor surrender the inherent and fundamental right to self-definition or self-determination to an external entity. To give up this most intimate form of agency is to externalise the locus of one's consciousness and its most tangible outward manifestation—identity. This alienation then takes a life of its own and is extremely difficult to reverse and reclaim. However, no matter how arduous the process of reclamation, no self-respecting society has the option of lacking or losing the will to take back its right to define the self. What would be worse is for a society to believe that it is better off living in the yawning shadow of a contemptuously overwritten version of its self by another. This is because it would signify a complete and utter failure to not only understand the value of the right to self-definition but also everything else of value that emanates from it.

From the point of view of former colonies, the framework that facilitates a more rounded and complete reclamation of their agency over their consciousness sans coloniality is the one that is most suited for their re-emergence. It is for this reason that the decolonial school merits consideration since the identification of coloniality by Aníbal Quijano represents one of the most significant contributions to understanding the cause underlying the cause, namely European coloniality and its continuing after-effects. In other words, decolonial thought appears to have understood the motivation underlying European colonialism better than other schools of thought, as reflected by the discussion undertaken in the previous chapters. The idea of coloniality is what distinguishes the decolonial from the older postcolonial school because it encapsulates a grand unified theory of sorts within itself that explains the mental constitution of the coloniser. It necessarily leads to a line of enquiry that examines the very OET framework upon which the colonial edifice rested, and allows us to follow the pattern of thought which manifested itself consistently regardless of the nationality of the European coloniser or the geography of colonisation. Critically, it enables us to see through the coloniality of contemporary structures. Having recognised the tendency of the coloniser to obsessively universalise the European provincial worldview through secularization,[2] decoloniality steers clear of the same mistakes and instead believes in a pluriversal approach, thereby enabling the coexistence of diverse subjectivities.

In contrast, postcolonial thought does not engage in the deconstruction of the coloniser's colonial consciousness, but merely questions the fairness of the coloniser's treatment of indigenous societies and registers its objection to the imposition of Eurocentrism on the colonised.[3] While the postmodern foundations of postcolonialism translate to an irreverent challenge to Eurocentric modernity, both the language and terms of challenge are rooted in Europeanism.[4] Starting from an understanding of time and history, postcolonial thought, while rejecting the claims of the coloniser, draws liberally from his OET to view indigenous histories and succumbs to the Christian European trait of universalisation of a particular worldview.[5] In other words, postcolonialism is oblivious to its subliminal acceptance of coloniality through its own version of coloniality, which results in what is at best a critical study of the atrocities and impact of colonialism, but not an examination of its undergirding. While it challenges colonial authority, it falls significantly short of providing an alternative rooted in indigeneity that can facilitate its reclamation.[6] Also, postcolonialism fails to recognise the omnipresence of coloniality in contemporary structures and relationships, which explains its 'post' as well as highlights its limitation in empowering indigeneity.[7] After all, how can it offer a solution to a problem it is oblivious to?

In terms of timelines, while postcolonialism focusses mostly on the eighteenth century and thereafter, that is, from the Enlightenment onwards, decoloniality pushes it further back to the fifteenth century, starting with Columbus' expedition of 1492, which it believes to be the beginning of the Age of Discovery and therefore, of colonisation and evangelisation. Postcolonial critique is typically associated with Bharat[8] and Palestine, whereas decoloniality is traced to Latin America.[9] Postcolonialism unconsciously accepts the West's conception and monopolisation of time and subjectivity, whereas decoloniality rejects this monopoly because it explicitly believes in the coexistence of multiple subjectivities. The former is unable to see, which the latter does, that Western imperialism flows from the same fount of coloniality. It is for these reasons that scholars believe that postcolonial critique is itself in dire need of a decolonial approach.

Decoloniality, according to Walter D. Mignolo, is a political project which recognises that coloniality, modernity and rationality are inseparable and therefore, the relevance of decoloniality is determined by the presence or absence of coloniality.[10] Its response to the modernity/rationality complex is indigeneity, subjectivity and relationality. The primary goal of decoloniality, according to Quijano, is 'epistemological decolonisation' to enable a new form of intercultural communication.[11] Simply put, it seeks to release production of knowledge from the stranglehold of the West, which could lead to greater diversity of thought and subjectivity, in particular, resurgence and re-existence of indigenous perspectives which Quijano[12] and Mignolo[13] also refer to as 'epistemic reconstitution'[14]. This translates to relocation of the geography and biography of knowledge to native peoples who are best placed to address their own vulnerabilities instead of having to operate within the Eurocentric universalist lines painted by the coloniser. Among other things, this requires indigenous societies to question the European paradigm of rationality that is predicated on Cartesian dualism since it informs perhaps the most important aspect of Western civilisation, namely its approach to nature, and hence, to non-Christian cultures. This subject–object lens of Cartesian dualism has affected the crucial disciplines of anthropology and ethnology, thereby reducing the people of the non-West to the status of objects of study.

While recognising the totalising and totalitarian nature of coloniality, decoloniality does not reject the idea of totality in its entirety; instead, it posits that the scope of colonial totality must be restricted to the European community with the intent of liberating the production of knowledge in the rest of the world from the European complex.[15] This is because it recognises that every culture's vision includes a perspective of totality. However, what distinguishes indigenous perspectives from the European is that the former's vision accommodates and acknowledges the desirability of heterogeneity and diversity, whereas the latter insists on homogeneity, which is traceable to its Christian OET. This insatiable need of the European coloniser to homogenise and standardise, inspired by religious and hence racial supremacism, even distinguishes European colonialism from pre-Christian Roman imperialism, which brings out in stark relief the coloniality of European Christian colonisation. In other words, diversity of thought and experience perhaps found greater acceptance under pre-Christian Roman imperialism than under European colonialism, which is attributable to the latter's Christian character.

What makes decoloniality more appealing as an option compared to postcolonial critique is that it draws its strength and vitality from the fact that unlike coloniality, it is not bound by one universal definition. This fundamental character of decoloniality is underscored by scholars, such as Catherine E. Walsh and Mignolo, who acknowledge that decoloniality is meant to be subjective and contextual and, therefore, to provide abstract universals may go against its very grain.[16] Their stated claim and object of interest is relationality, that is, opening up conversations between different local histories and practices of decoloniality so that the 'politico-epistemic violence of modernity' can be contested everywhere. Their emphasis on relationality is precisely to drive home the point that there is no one way to 'do and conceive decoloniality', which also means that each society has the right to define what constitutes coloniality in its context. Importantly, to ensure that decoloniality is not relegated to the ivory towers of academia, they underscore that decoloniality is 'a way, an option, a standpoint, an analytic, a project, practice, and praxis'. It rejects the tendency to compartmentalise theory and praxis, and insists that since coloniality is primarily a state of mind, to challenge colonial thought by presenting the decolonial perspective is as much praxis as it is theory.

Walsh and Mignolo categorically assert that a decolonial world cannot be and, might I add, *must not* be built using the conceptual tools of the Renaissance and the Enlightenment. Other scholars, such as Ramón Grosfoguel, also subscribe to this position because they believe that the non-West is responding to Eurocentrism with Eurocentric solutions, which explains the rise of European-style nationalism in former colonies instead of responses that are more rooted in their own cultures and civilisations.[17] As opposed to questioning the European expectation and benchmark of 'civilised nations' using indigenous thought, former colonies seem more eager to join the club of civilised nation-states to prove that they are not 'savages' anymore. That this generates a form of internal coloniality that strengthens the European worldview, especially in the political realm, is lost sight of. The other extreme of the non-West's response is to reject the validity of everything that has emanated from Europe without realising that some of the so-called European contributions may, in fact, be products of acculturation that the coloniser may have misappropriated from indigenous cultures without attribution.

In light of the above, a middle path has been proposed, which insists on greater dialogue between the West and the non-West with the clear acknowledgement by the West of the skewed power relations and the coloniality of the system as it exists. The decolonial approach gives the non-West the option of not playing by the rules of the West, especially in the political realm, which allows them to think outside the Westphalian box. In this sense, decoloniality is a form of measured 'epistemic disobedience', which is not limited in its application to a particular sphere. Such an approach has been described as a move towards a 'decolonialised transmodern world' which presents two options to indigenous

societies: the first allows them to fully re-inscribe indigenous
OET by reconceptualising values and institutions; and should
that not be possible or feasible, the second envisages formulation
of creative alternative definitions based on indigenous onto-
epistemologies for so-called European values.[18] Depending on
an indigenous society's conviction and taking into consideration
the integrated nature of the contemporary world, it may choose
between the two. From a practical standpoint, what this means is
that a decolonialised indigenous society can choose to completely
overhaul its political structure based on its indigenous traditions, or
retain the skeletal structure inherited from the coloniser and infuse
it with the indigenous spirit by defining the role of the State and the
concept of rights and duties based on its native onto-episteme. This
also means either doing away with the imported ideological divides
of the Left, the Right and the Centre, or redefining them based on
indigenous intellectual traditions and experience.

Interestingly, scholars of decoloniality acknowledge and
agree that the Eurocentric colonialities of such ideological
divides in every jurisdiction, especially in the non-West, must be
confronted. In fact, of pertinence to Bharat is the view of scholars,
such as Ramón Grosfoguel, that the Left's underestimation of the
coloniality ingrained within contemporary structures is responsible
for the second-class treatment of indigenous populations in the
non-West, though under ostensibly indigenous governments.[19]
Such treatment of indigenous masses in decolonised societies
by colonialised native elites in the political and intellectual
establishments inherited from the coloniser, with the support
of the international Left, has caused significant disillusionment
with the international Left's so-called commitment to truth and
justice.

The other critical aspect that emerges from the decolonial
approach is its primary focus on resuscitation of indigenous onto-
epistemologies (knowledge) as opposed to being exclusively
mired in exclusionary ethnocentrism (race), which has informed
colonialism and afflicts postcolonialism as well. In other words,

decoloniality cannot be conflated with or accused of defending 'identity politics' the way it is currently understood.[20] Instead, it approaches the question of 'consciousness', and not merely identity (there being a clear distinction between the two), from an OET perspective for two reasons: first, most contemporary national and intra-national or sub-national identities are the products of colonial remapping of geographies and creation of identities and, therefore, cannot form the basis of a decolonial approach; and second, a purely ethnocentric approach to culture is characteristic of coloniality which decoloniality seeks to counter.[21] Simply stated, a North American-style ethnocentric blood quantum-based approach to issues of culture, consciousness and indigeneity have been largely steered clear of by the decolonial school since it uses the OET of a society as its primary marker. This is in contradistinction to coloniality's embedded Christian-inspired race consciousness, which is projected on to every indigenous movement, whether or not ethnic consciousness is material to it. Therefore, decoloniality's attempts at de-racialisation of indigeneity to the extent permitted by indigenous worldviews pre-empts labels, such as ethnonationalism and xenophobia, which are often used to undermine the legitimacy of indigenous movements.

It is important to clarify that decoloniality does not turn a blind eye to issues of ethnicity, including historic realities, where ethnicity has formed the basis of discrimination by the coloniser. However, its prism of enquiry is largely, if not exclusively, based on the 'culture is a way of life' approach which recognises that a culture or a civilisation is the product of several influences. Further, decoloniality seeks to rid both 'culture' and 'civilisation' of its colonial code, an exercise integral to the freeing of indigenous societies from the burden of having to demonstrate their cultured and civilised status on Western-normative benchmarks.

One of the reasons ethnicity is perhaps but one of the components of a decolonial approach, as opposed to being the sole, is the recognition that an exclusively ethnocentric approach can be a slippery slope, given the constant migration or invasion or intermingling of peoples in history. It is for this reason that decoloniality pays more attention to the relationship between an OET framework which informs consciousness, and a culture or a civilisation. The corollary to and consequence of this OET-based approach to consciousness is that it accommodates and is alive to the fact that just as there are colonialised natives who subscribe to the European worldview despite not sharing the race of the coloniser, so are there decolonialised non-natives who are committed to protecting indigenous OETs despite not sharing the native ethnicity. After all, if coloniality is a state of mind that cuts across ethnicities, so should decoloniality, which too is a state of mind.

At this juncture, it is also important to address another aspect of indigenous societies, namely hereditary social structures, which have been burdened with ethnocentrism without basis as a consequence of the coloniser's race-conscious approach to colonised societies. In other words, indigenous societies and their traditional social structures have been unfairly saddled with the West's new-found guilt complex in respect of its race consciousness. In this regard, the decolonial approach should be to understand such structures through the indigenous lens sans colonial biases, and it must be left to each indigenous society to determine the contemporary purchase of such structures based on its OET without being burdened by the guilt-racked conscience of the West. This would be consistent with decoloniality's commitment to diversity. This point shall be explained better in the context of discussions surrounding 'caste' and 'tribe' in and about Bharat in the next section of the book.

The sum and substance of the preceding discussion is that, wherever possible, without doing injustice to indigenous worldviews, a decolonial approach to indigeneity with an intent to preserve indigenous consciousness will be able to better navigate the seemingly uncomfortable yet inescapable realities, such as identifying the in-group and out-group, to the indigenous worldview. Unfortunately, the very suggestion to identify in- and out-groups is bound to ruffle quite a few feathers and invite criticisms of 'parochiality', 'narrow-mindedness' and so on and so forth, but the fact is that even in the contemporary 'modern' and 'liberal' world, these are the very issues that public discourse, law and policymaking revolve around, especially when questions of heritage, identity and access to resources are involved. Neither modernity nor liberalism has been able to do away with 'identity politics'. If anything, their innate coloniality has pushed such discussions further into the arms of ethnocentrism, particularly in indigenous societies like Bharat. Consequently, since othering is a reality of life that cannot be avoided, it is better to do so on the basis of consciousness as opposed to 'identity'. Accordingly, from a decolonial perspective, it would help to define indigeneity on the basis of consciousness instead of identity.

Having said this, throughout the discussion undertaken thus far, I have used 'indigenous/indigeneity' to distinguish the coloniser from the colonised. I have also attempted to explain that decoloniality's approach to indigeneity is primarily OET-centric as opposed to being purely ethnocentric since ethnocentrism and race-consciousness are central to coloniality. In the interest of honesty, conceptual clarity and consistency, and given the centrality of indigeneity to decoloniality, it is important to unpack the concept of indigeneity in further detail to bring out its assumptions and layers.

The Decolonial Evolution from 'Indigenous Peoples' to 'Indigeneity'

Before I proceed to discuss the use of 'indigenous peoples' and 'indigeneity' in decolonial literature, it must be appreciated that the need for identification of indigenous peoples and making sense of indigeneity has arisen as a result of colonization, which has irreparably devastated the ways of life of the colonised. Therefore, the identification of the self in this case has been necessitated by the domination of the self by the other to whom othering was central to his worldview as opposed to being a mere part. Thanks to coloniality, othering has occupied centre stage, notwithstanding the current-day professions of universalism, globalism and cosmopolitanism, all of which rest on the colonial foundations of universalisation of Western provincial thought.

In the ensuing portions, I shall first discuss international law that deals with 'indigenous peoples' before discussing the position of decolonial scholarship on indigeneity. While there are at least a dozen international instruments that deal with various rights of indigenous peoples,[22] this legal prelude is limited to the assessment of whether discussions on law and policymaking in relation to 'indigenous peoples' are informed by coloniality and, therefore, warrant a decolonial review. As part of this, I shall also examine if the law recognises the distinction between indigenous peoples and indigeneity.

Among the earliest organisations to work on issues relating to 'indigenous peoples' was the International Labour Organization (ILO), which adopted the Indigenous and Tribal Populations Convention in 1957.[23] Although this Convention does not contain a specific definition for indigenous peoples, Article 1 enumerates the scope of the Convention's application as follows:

1.   This Convention applies to:
     (a)   members of *tribal or semi-tribal* populations in independent countries whose social and economic conditions are at a less advanced stage than the stage reached by the other sections of the national community, and whose status is regulated wholly or partially by their own customs or traditions or by special laws or regulations;
     (b)   members of *tribal or semi-tribal* populations in independent countries which are regarded as indigenous on account of their descent from the populations which inhabited the country, or a

geographical region to which the country belongs,
at the time of conquest or colonisation and which,
irrespective of their legal status, live more in
conformity with the social, economic and cultural
institutions of that time than with the institutions
of the nation to which they belong.

2.   For the purposes of this Convention, *the term semi-
tribal includes groups and persons who, although they are in
the process of losing their tribal characteristics, are not yet
integrated into the national community.*

3.   The indigenous and other tribal or semi-tribal
populations mentioned in paragraphs 1 and 2 of this
Article are referred to hereinafter as 'the populations
concerned'. [emphasis added]

A second Convention on Indigenous and Tribal Populations
was adopted by the ILO in 1989, in which a similar approach to
those who were the intended beneficiaries was taken, which is
set out below[24]:

Article 1
1.   This Convention applies to:
      (a)   *tribal peoples* in independent countries whose social,
             cultural and economic conditions distinguish them
             from other sections of the *national community*, and
             whose status is regulated wholly or partially by
             their own customs or traditions or by special laws
             or regulations;
      (b)   peoples in independent countries *who are regarded
             as indigenous* on account of their descent from
             the populations which inhabited the country, or a
             geographical region to which the country belongs,
             at the time of conquest or colonisation or the
             establishment of present state boundaries and
             who, irrespective of their legal status, retain some

       or all of their own social, economic, cultural and political institutions.

2.   Self-identification as *indigenous or tribal* shall be regarded as a fundamental criterion for determining the groups to which the provisions of this Convention apply.

3.   The use of the term peoples in this Convention shall not be construed as having any implications as regards the rights which may attach to the term under international law. [emphasis added]

From these provisions of the 1957 and 1989 Conventions, it is evident that both use terms such as 'tribe' and 'indigenous peoples' or 'indigenous populations' interchangeably to distinguish them from the 'national communities' of former colonies. Such an ethnocentric distinction makes sense in the context of those colonies that experienced European settler colonialism and continue to have significant settler populations. But given the breadth of the definition, it appears that the distinction is equally applied to those former colonies, such as Bharat, where the European settler population is not considerable. As a consequence of this, the distinction between 'dominant national communities' and 'indigenous/tribal peoples' when applied to countries like Bharat introduces internal coloniality *within* the native population by treating 'minority tribal communities' as being racially and culturally distinct from 'majority national communities', which has no basis in the native worldview. In other words, a permanent fault line or division is created through an international instrument that manufactures an artificial power hierarchy between 'national communities' and indigenous populations or tribes while treating majority national communities as colonisers and less indigenous than the tribes. Putting such national communities in the same category as the European coloniser is as mischievous as it can get because it makes them the successors of the legacy of European colonialism and treats them as pre-European colonisers of indigenous lands. The origin of this categorisation can be traced to the creation of a 'tribal' identity by the European coloniser in colonised societies for the purpose of creating ethnic fissures that could simultaneously facilitate co-option of the influential cultural elites, and conversion of 'indigenous tribal groups' through evangelical activity. This factum of creation of 'tribe' as a colonial category for colonised peoples has been dealt with in the second section of the book in the context of Bharat. What this proves is that the framework of the ILO Conventions strikes a distinction between 'national communities' and 'tribes' *because* they are based on the colonial creation called 'tribe'.

This colonial classification was subsequently taken forward by subaltern studies, which emanates from postcolonial thought since postcolonialism views indigenous history through a Eurocentric lens and assumes that the 'majority national community' exhibited the same behavioural pattern as that of the a European coloniser.[25] Further, as opposed to recognising the right of former colonies to craft their own definitions of indigenous peoples and what constitutes indigeneity, the internationalisation of the issue through international legal instruments effectively allows the West to interfere with the social dynamics and history of former colonies, thereby diluting their sovereignty as well as their agency over their cultural experience. This proves my earlier point on international law being an instrumentality of coloniality. Further, the focus of both ILO definitions is on 'identity' as opposed to 'consciousness', wherein the former focusses on who are 'indigenous peoples' as opposed to also asking what constitutes or makes up 'indigeneity'.

In this regard, the other important legal literature that merits examination is the 'Study on the Problem of Discrimination against Indigenous Populations' commissioned by the United Nations in 1972. The Study was authored by the Special Rapporteur of the Sub-Commission on Prevention of Discrimination and Protection of Minorities, Jose R. Martinez Cobo,[26] and came to be known as the Martinez Cobo Study. This exercise, which was completed in 1987, is considered one of the most comprehensive works on the subject. A working definition of who and what constitutes 'indigenous' was provided in it, which is as follows:

Indigenous communities, peoples and nations are those which, having a *historical continuity with pre-invasion and pre-colonial societies* that developed on their territories, consider themselves distinct from other sectors of the societies now prevailing on those territories, or parts of them. They form at present *non-dominant sectors* of society and are determined to preserve, develop and transmit to future generations their ancestral territories, and their ethnic identity, as the basis of their continued existence as peoples, in accordance with their own cultural patterns, social institutions, and legal system.

This historical continuity may consist of the continuation, for an extended period reaching into the present of one or more of the following factors:
a.   Occupation of ancestral lands, or at least of part of them;
b.   Common ancestry with the original occupants of these lands;
c.   Culture in general, or in specific manifestations (such as religion, living under a tribal system, membership of an indigenous community, dress, means of livelihood, life-style, etc.);
d.   Language (whether used as the only language, as mother-tongue, as the habitual means of communication at home or in the family, or as the main, preferred, habitual, general or normal language);
e.   Residence in certain parts of the country, or in certain regions of the world;
f.   Other relevant factors.

On an individual basis, an indigenous person is one who belongs to these indigenous populations through self-identification as indigenous (group consciousness) and is recognized and accepted by these populations as one of its members (acceptance by the group).

This preserves for these communities the sovereign right and power to decide who belongs to them, without external interference. [emphasis added]

As is evident, this working definition contains quite a few agreeable aspects since it combines elements of who are indigenous peoples and what makes them indigenous, which goes beyond ethnic considerations. That said, this definition too is better applicable to those countries with significant European settler populations, such as the Americas, New Zealand and Australia, since it is based on the premise that such indigenous groups are in a position of relative non-dominance. Application of this definition to countries like Bharat with negligible European settler population results in the same pitfalls as the ILO definitions. Effectively, it passes on the European coloniser's guilt as a legacy to the native 'dominant'/'majority national communities' of Bharat.

Further, in Bharat, this distinction based on dominant/ 'majority' national groups and marginalised/'minority' indigenous/tribal groups has only worked to the detriment of the native society since 'tribal' groups have been incongruously arrayed alongside 'religious minorities' and pitted against the rest of the 'majority' population of which they have been an organic part for millennia. While I will build more on this point in the second section of the book as part of my discussion on creation of tribal identities by the coloniser in Bharat, the working definition of the Martinez Cobo Study, among other things, has the effect of negating the precolonial histories of countries like Bharat. Given that Cobo's definition was formulated in 1986-1987, that is, before Quijano's formulation of coloniality (in 1989), the application of the decolonial option to Cobo's definition is imperative. Critically, international instruments on indigenous peoples and their issues continue to build on the

Cartesian subject–object relationship by treating 'indigenous peoples' and 'dominant majority populations' as communities that are destined to live in walled gardens for eternity with the 'indigenous tribes' forming the objects of study.

This silo-based colonial approach to indigeneity has not changed despite the adoption of the United Nations Declaration of the Rights of Indigenous Peoples (UNDRIP)[27] by 144 countries in September 2007, which was voted against by the United States of America, Canada, Australia and New Zealand, and abstained from by 11 countries, namely Azerbaijan, Bangladesh, Bhutan, Burundi, Colombia, Georgia, Kenya, Nigeria, the Russian Federation, Samoa and Ukraine. The rights enumerated in the declaration 'constitute the minimum standards for the survival, dignity and well-being of the Indigenous Peoples of the world'.[28] Ostensibly, the declaration protects both collective rights and individual rights of indigenous peoples in matters of self-government, land, education, employment, health and other areas, which is essentially a Europeanisation of indigenous issues because the central issue of mainstreaming the indigenous consciousness remains untouched. However, the silver lining is that the declaration does not define indigenous peoples or spell out the parameters for their identification, giving former colonies the chance to break from colonial stereotypes and metrics. In other words, the absence of a universal definition, although unintentionally decolonial, provides a pluriversal window to former colonies to address issues of indigeneity.

Then again, the declaration also makes it clear that there is significant room for 'international' intervention so that member States are 'encouraged to comply with and effectively implement all their obligations as they apply to indigenous peoples under international instruments'. It says: '[The] rights affirmed in treaties, agreements and other constructive arrangements between States and indigenous peoples are, in some situations, matters of international concern, interest, responsibility and character.' Clearly, these instruments act as tools to undermine the sovereignty of former colonies, with the 'international' community or the West acting as the Big Brother.

Interestingly, none of these instruments addresses the thorny subject of evangelical attempts to convert 'tribal' populations to Christianity, which ought to have been fairly obvious given the history of the Americas and other regions. Ironically, while the 'dominant' national majorities are expected to respect the identities of 'indigenous peoples', there is no international commitment to prevent external actors, such as missionary groups, from interfering with the course of indigenous life in the name of 'educating' or 'civilising' them. This proves that the coloniality of international law itself needs to be revisited before reviewing instruments that relate to the rights of indigenous peoples. None of this is to take away from the fact that the declaration does indeed attempt to legitimise and ensure equal treatment of indigenous peoples. However, that it limits the scope of its vision exclusively to the creation of safe spaces for 'indigenous peoples or the indigenous identity' (a category which in itself warrants serious revision), as opposed to delinking their destinies from coloniality altogether, remains a fundamental limitation that overshadows incremental recognition of all other rights.

Having discussed the pith and marrow of the legal position on indigenous peoples, it becomes important to understand the colonial and modern nature of 'development', which is one of the most powerful social, cultural and political forces in the world today that affects indigenous ways of life. This is especially relevant to former colonies which were categorised as 'under-developed' or 'developing' following decolonisation.[29] The work of Colombian-American anthropologist Arturo Escobar in this regard is particularly arresting because he highlights the fact that this convenient categorisation by the West succeeded in creating the impression that former colonies were always 'backward' while the 'West' has always been a beacon of reason, progress and scientific temper.[30] The irony of former colonies becoming 'recipient countries' and the colonisers—the 'developed', 'modern' Western imperialists—becoming 'donor countries' is not lost on him. From positions on respect for nature to the rights of indigenous peoples to practising their ways of life, everything is affected by modern conceptions of 'development' in former colonies that aspire to Westernisation instead of identifying their own goals based on indigenous frameworks.[31] Therefore, 'development' warrants a brief unpacking to understand its impact on indigeneity. [32]

While the 2007 Declaration is said to be the most comprehensive document on indigenous rights, it in itself treats 'development' as the universal set in which the indigenous way of life is but a subset, an island, a safe space carved out, thereby tragically failing to understand the very concept of indigeneity and address the coloniality underlying contemporary notions of development. Not only is development laced with modernity as defined by the West, the manner in which such development must be pursued and attained is also dictated by the West ever since the grant of 'development aid' was made contingent on reshaping 'independent' former colonies in the mould of the West. As a result, the pursuit of such yardsticks of development has been adopted as the national goal of several former colonies. All aspects of life—from laws to 'religion' to the production of knowledge and education—have been reoriented towards the achievement of Western-style development. Therefore, until 'development' is itself subjected to a decolonial filter, it will single-handedly propel indigenous peoples towards a Westernised future because it first and foremost affects a community's relationship with nature, which percolates right down to the individual. Clearly, at the heart of it, the tussle is between the colonial perception of humankind's centrality to nature on the one hand, and its actual place within nature on the other, which informs indigeneity and, hence, decoloniality.

Coming to decolonial scholarship on 'indigeneity', in contrast to the ILO definitions that are heavily ethnocentric and are subscribed to by the postcolonial school, decoloniality focusses on indigenous consciousness owing to its recognition that the 'tribal' identity was invented by the European coloniser to advance the goals of colonialism. Decolonial thought takes a multipronged approach to 'indigeneity' by distilling the building blocks that constitute the 'state of being indigenous' beyond the superficial plane of 'identity'.[33] This is also because decolonial thought is aware of the Latin origins of 'indigenous', which is derived from the Latin term 'indigenes', meaning 'born in the country'. Such a purely birth-based approach could have the automatic effect of treating even the settler coloniser's progeny as indigenous, which would be absurd from a consciousness perspective. In any case, assumptions of ethnic purity to retain the status of being indigenous must necessarily subscribe to certain ahistorical and perhaps even unscientific approximations.

Also, if ethnicity or birth were to be accepted as the sole or primary metrics for indigeneity, it would fail to address those situations where ethnicity remains the same and the entire OET framework is altered owing to evangelisation. Therefore, a strictly birth-based or ethnocentric approach to indigeneity, which is a consequence of present-day rules for the acquisition of citizenship being retrofitted to a much more complex construct, misses the entire point of indigeneity. Since contemporary laws of acquisition of nationality operate within a legal framework that is colonial, they cannot and must not be used to understand indigeneity that challenges the foundations of the system as it exists.

Finally, several decolonised societies, despite not having converted to the religion of the coloniser, have moved on from their precolonial pasts because they have embraced secularised coloniality, namely 'modernity'. This means that those who retain their indigenous consciousness by subscribing to the indigenous way of life ('indigeneity') are dwindling in number while the indigenous 'identity' has become merely an external legal marker. Simply put, the former is a state or condition of the mind, while the latter is a legal status. Since one of the objects of decoloniality is to revive and preserve the former as a response to coloniality, the term indigeneity, that is, the state of being indigenous and retaining indigenous consciousness, is preferred to 'indigenous peoples'.

At this juncture, it also needs to be pointed out that scholars, such as Mignolo, while recognising that re-emergence of indigeneity results in decolonial delinking of the Western imperialist's control over lives all over the world, take the position that decoloniality 'does not equal indigenous struggle' and that it is 'not an ethnic, national or religious identification project'.[34] In my opinion, the goal of decoloniality may be to limit the universalist claim of the modernity/rationality complex of coloniality; however, what must replace coloniality and what must be the priority of indigeneity should be determined not by scholars of decoloniality, but by decolonialised indigenous societies, even if it takes the shape of an ethnic or religious identification project based on their respective histories.

What does this translate to in practical application? In the context of Latin America, scholars of decoloniality take the position that indigeneity is defined as the state of indigenous societies as they existed prior to 1492, that is, before Columbus' expedition. But non-Latin American societies, which have experienced pre-European forms of colonising aggression, such as Middle Eastern colonialism, have the right to identify their own respective 'cut-off' periods to define indigeneity. This is consistent with decoloniality's rejection of formulation of abstract universals and commitment to contextuality. Therefore, every society has the right to identify and define coloniality and decoloniality based on its own unique history and experience.

The Relational Land Ontology of Indigeneity

Having said the above, the next issue that needs to be addressed is the relationship between indigeneity and nature, given the paradigm shift triggered by coloniality's approach to nature. From the perspective of the Christian European coloniser, the forced transaction with indigenous peoples that took the shape of colonisation was only incidental to his true objective—the acquisition of territory for the imposition of his worldview and subjugation through conversion or elimination of those who stood in the way. The coloniser had no use for indigenous peoples because they were impediments to his divine right and duty to establish his dominion over any non-Christian territory. The only divine purpose fulfilled by the indigenous peoples was to present the coloniser with the opportunity to fulfil his evangelical obligations. In other words, the relationship between coloniality and nature/land/geography was one of ownership for the purposes of enjoyment, which is the product of its dualist undergirding and the specific Christian OET behind humanism.

In contrast to the proprietorial approach of coloniality, indigeneity's attitude to land/nature is based on 'relationality'.[35] The use of relationality here is different from its use earlier in the context of facilitating intercultural communication. Here, relationality means seeing humans as being part of nature and not outside of it. This translates to obligations towards nature, including 'reciprocal obligations between humans and the other-than-human'. Such relationality not only informs the relationship between indigenous communities and nature, it also shapes their epistemologies and faiths as we saw earlier.[36] Specific rituals and traditions are evolved that give primacy to the geography and elevate the relationship to a sacred status, a relationship that people of Bharat can relate to. Such an approach cannot be compared to the clinically proprietorial and territorial attitude of the coloniser.

Thanks to the territoriality of the coloniser's approach to land, the nationalism of the coloniser too is territorial. In stark contrast, the spiritual character of the relationship between indigeneity and nature is an emotion that the coloniser can at best exoticise but can never relate to. I use the word spiritual not in a bohemian mystical sense but to refer to the OET embedded therein, which is the product of the lived experience of millennia, handed down through generations to preserve the same respect for nature. Clearly, there is a marked difference in the land ontologies of the European Christian coloniser and the non-Christian precolonial non-West. This does not mean that there is no element of territoriality in the indigenous approach to land; however, what underpins the territoriality, namely relationality, forms the substratum of its land ontology.[37] Having said that, I realise that this could be a gross generalisation since the true position is best answered by each indigenous society or representatives of indigeneity in former colonies. Therefore, in keeping with decoloniality's commitment to pluriversality and subjectivity, and its justified reticence to universalising provincialism of any kind, I will undertake a Bharat-specific discussion in the next section.

It is possible to arrive at the facile and typically postcolonial conclusion that ultimately both coloniality and indigeneity are about establishing ownership over land, resources and labour, but this would be drawing a false symmetry, apart from missing the point entirely. Coloniality as a phenomenon has opened up issues that include but extend beyond dominion over geography. It raises questions of agency to practise a way of life that is associated with a geography owing to the relational dynamic between the indigenous worldview and the geography it is contained in. This also explains why indigenous epistemology sees its people as custodians of a sacred geography, whereas European nationalism perceives territory as an external object of possession and ownership. Therefore, at the heart of the transformation called for by decoloniality is the re-inscription of relationality into the indigenous approach to nature in order for indigeneity to take root, which is bound to have a direct bearing on all other aspects of life and civilisation. This would begin as well as complete the process of delinking the indigenous consciousness from coloniality and a colonial universe.

From the discussion undertaken in this section, a few questions may arise. For instance, how practical is the decolonial option? After all, if coloniality is omnipresent by design and has resulted in a globalised and heavily integrated world that places the West (the Global North) at the top and the rest at the bottom as the Global South, how does decoloniality hope to upset the established global order? Also, what is decoloniality's vision of the future, assuming it has the wherewithal to achieve its goals? First, in order to answer these questions, it may help to understand that 500 years is nothing from the standpoint of human history and therefore, there is no reason to assume that the history of the last five centuries shall remain the history even for the next hundred years. After all, the West is not what it was even half a century ago. Second, while different commentators and authorities on the subject of decoloniality may have differing views, from what I have understood, it seems to me that the goal is to regain the space for indigeneities to breathe, which allows them to compete in the supposedly free market of ideas by letting them tell their own stories in their own languages.

Some believe the world has changed forever by virtue of European colonialism and there is no going back to precolonial ways of life, which makes indigenous societies eternal victims. However, ever since the offshoots of coloniality, namely globalisation and unconscientious mercantilism, have begun to expose the utterly destructive impact of coloniality on nature placing the world in a crisis, the cautious hope is that the world will begin its quest for alternatives that respect nature as being central to civilisation as opposed to relegating it to the category of a mere resource. This endeavour could possibly bring the world to the doorstep of indigenous knowledge systems, which could, in turn, lead to the resurgence of a relational association with nature, which is perhaps the intended outcome of decoloniality.

In other words, it is this window of global introspection on the treatment of nature that is capable of enabling the re-inscription of indigeneities in their respective spheres of influence/geographies, thereby exposing the provincial validity of Europeanism and its false claim of universalism. The idea is to show that the rest of the world was not living in the Dark Ages before Pax Europaea or European Peace, and will certainly not plunge into ignorance and darkness after the demise of Pax Europaea. Therefore, it is time to discard the idea that the rest of the world is the Christian White man's burden.

To be clear, while decoloniality may not result in the extinction of Europeanism, it may certainly limit Europeanism to the borders of its origin, and allow indigeneities to re-exist, albeit in a hybrid form. This could have implications for Europeanism even within Europe in the sense that it may introspect and revisit its pre-Christian past, which could re-establish the centrality of nature in the mothership of Christian Cartesian dualism. But again, I am getting ahead of myself. At this point, if in the foreseeable future, indigeneities can rid themselves of their colonial strings and find respectability and acceptance in their own geographies, it would be a good start by all accounts.

With these lessons drawn from the literature on coloniality and the nature of decolonial thought, the next section will examine the impact of coloniality on Bharat's indigenous consciousness.

Section II

CIVILISATION

Bharat, Coloniality and Colonial Consciousness

Sir Thomas Stood Before the Mogul

Sir Thomas Roe began his diplomatic career in India as an ambassador to the court of the Mughal Emperor Jahangir. In his four years of duty (1614–1618) there, he furthered the fortunes of the English East India Company. Roe's primary role was to obtain protection for the East India Company's factory at Surat.

In the previous section, I presented a summary of my understanding of coloniality and decoloniality in order to evaluate their relevance for and applicability to Bharat from the perspective of reclaiming its indigenous consciousness. To this end, I have formulated the following Bharat-specific questions:

1. In view of the literature on European colonialism and coloniality, and Bharat's long tryst with it, is it possible to assume that the European coloniser's intentions and conduct towards Bharat were any different from his treatment of other colonised societies, or that Bharat's consciousness remained unaffected by it?

2. If Bharat's consciousness was indeed affected by coloniality, has it actively impeded Bharat from candidly acknowledging and discussing a pre-European form of coloniality it has been subjected to, which continues to affect its consciousness?

3. If Bharat's indigenous consciousness is weighed down by both European and pre-European colonialities, is decoloniality the better framework for Bharat in order to reclaim its indigenous consciousness/indigeneity as opposed to the postcolonial critique?

4. If yes, and if the decolonial framework were to be applied to Bharat, what is its conception of itself? Is it a civilisation or a nation or a synthetic product of colonisation? Also, what constitutes Bharat's indigeneity and how does one etch its contours?

5. Applying the decolonial framework specifically to Bharat's political institutions as viewed through the prism of the Constitution, is the Constitution informed by Bharat's indigeneity? Does the history of the movement towards constitutionalism bear this out?

6. If the history of the Constitution is consistent with Bharat's indigeneity, what explains the current view among a vast cross-section of people that Bharat's Constitution is at loggerheads with its indigeneity?

7. Alternatively, if Bharat's Constitution is a product of coloniality, what would a decolonial revisitation of the document look like?

Out of these issues, the first four fall within the realm of experts trained in the relevant fields of humanities. Therefore, I will address them briefly in this section, as a learner, based on the literature. Also, given the nature of the said issues and their overlap, it may not be possible or even desirable to address them in a linear fashion, and so a fair degree of non-linearity must be expected. As for the last three issues, which I am in some position to address given my training as a lawyer and my first-hand application of constitutional law and history in matters of civilisational significance, I will address them in this section and the next. These sections span the founding of the English East India Company in 1600 until 1919, when the League of Nations was established and the first British-made Constitution for Bharat was passed, namely the Government of India Act of 1919. The period subsequent to that, including the adoption of independent Bharat's Constitution on 26 January 1950 and the first amendment to the Constitution in 1951, shall be addressed in the sequel to this book. Therefore, whether independent Bharat's Constitution suffers from coloniality, and if so, to what degree, will be addressed in the sequel, the foundation for which will be laid in this section and the next.

In the previous section, we saw that decolonial literature traces the origins of European colonialism to the fifteenth century, specifically to 1492, when the Age of Discovery began with Christopher Columbus' expedition in search of 'India', which instead, took him to the Americas, resulting in their colonisation. Therefore, the 'discovery' of Bharat in 1492 was delayed, albeit only for a short period, since Vasco da Gama's arrival by the end of the same century marked the advent of the Portuguese, followed by others including the Dutch, the British and the French. While trade was the ostensible purpose of Christian European arrival in Bharat, the *Inter Caetera* of 1493 issued by

Pope Alexander VI authorising Spain and Portugal to colonise, convert and enslave indigenous peoples is proof enough of the European's colonising and evangelising objectives regardless of his 'nationality'.

If the *Inter Caetera* is treated as proof of intent with papal benediction or even inspiration, the experience of colonised societies with colonialism and coloniality bears out the actualisation of that intent. The replacement of the indigenous worldview with a Christian European one in the Americas, the Caribbean, Africa, Australia and other parts of the world is a matter of fact, and not subjective opinion, notwithstanding the profession of toleration on the part of the European coloniser. In fact, as discussed earlier, the Christian character of toleration too has been demonstrated by scholars. Further, in view of the domination of almost the entire world by European colonisers for at least five centuries, European coloniality was globalised, which explains its omnipresence. To use a pop culture reference, European coloniality is like the 'Matrix'. One just needs to become aware of it, after which it is impossible to unsee, especially in matters of religion, polity, education, economics and the law.

Given this, and the fact that Bharat was the original destination of Columbus' expedition, what explains the prevalent superficial assumption in Bharat that the European coloniser's actions were driven solely by racism and his lust for power and wealth? What explains this tendency to 'secularise' the manifestly unsecular intent and conduct of the Christian coloniser? It could be attributed to ingrained coloniality, which results in an insular approach to the history of European colonisation of Bharat, instead of seeing it as part of the colonisation of the New World by the Christian coloniser.

What is also ironic is that, despite the experience of other indigenous societies whose precolonial religious identities have been either annihilated or reduced to a minority by the coloniser, in Bharat, the failure of the very same coloniser to significantly convert the indigenous population to his faith is interpreted as proof of his secular and purely mercantile intent. As opposed to crediting the inherent strength of the indigenous OET for resisting the coloniser's evangelising overtures, the benefit of benevolence or tolerance is extended to the coloniser, who consciously operated under a distinct sense of anthropological superiority that stemmed from his religious beliefs. It is this blinkered approach that gives rise to ill-informed questions, such as 'is colonisation not proof of Bharat's inherent weakness?' Such an ahistorical, secularised and self-defeating approach to the intent and conduct of the Christian coloniser is clear proof of entrenched coloniality in contemporary Bharat's consciousness. As a consequence, Bharat's analysis of colonialism revolves around race and economics, while the Christian OET of the coloniser gets a free pass even in the most withering analysis of his rule of close to 200 years. Ironically, indigenous OET systems are scrutinised more than the coloniser's OET thanks to this coloniality.

It is precisely for this reason that the European coloniser's track record in the rest of the world, which screams religious *and hence* racial supremacism, ought to be understood better even if one's interest is limited to Bharat. How else can one hope to make sense of a global phenomenon? Unfortunately, barring the work of a handful of scholars, this aspect has not received the kind of rigorous and serious scrutiny in Bharat that it should have. The result being that the deep and innate strength of Bharat's consciousness—which has resisted the tsunami of coloniality with a greater degree of success than most other indigenous societies whose cultures, civilisations and consciousness were nearly wiped out—is never recognised and acknowledged. This is not to deny that European coloniality did indeed make deep inroads even in Bharat, which is evident from the latter's present tendency to secularise facts. This tendency has put to sleep a society that is in dire need of awareness of its own strength and consciousness to deal with the continued presence of coloniality of more than one kind.

To cut a long story short, it is my considered position that in the absence of any hard evidence to the contrary, the most plausible and reasonable inference that may be drawn based on the global experience with European coloniality is that Bharat too was approached with the same colonial lens, and one need not even delve into Bharat-specific literature to make this point. That said, Bharat-specific literature needs to be delved into to understand the local/contextual manifestations of coloniality and its continuing effects. The object of this exercise is to prove the core premise of decolonial thought, which distinguishes it from postcolonial critique, that is, that coloniality did not cease to exist with the decolonisation of Bharat but has successfully continued in 'independent' Bharat, having been secularised, modernised and internalised—either due to complete ignorance or deliberate negation of history.

The internalisation of European coloniality in Bharat is evident from the constant refrain of its elites that had it not been for the British—who had apparently stitched together a single country out of disparate entities with nothing in common— Bharat would not have been a single political unit or a 'nation'; and that Bharat would have lacked infrastructure, such as trains, post, telegraph and the like, but for 'investment' by the coloniser in Bharat. In short, the very idea of Bharat, its civilisational unity, its relationship with time and its subjectivity have been tied to the advent of the coloniser, independent of whom it is assumed that Bharat had no consciousness of its own. This is glaring evidence of an abysmal understanding of the global history and nature of colonialism.

The clearest proof, of course, is the fact that the 'independent' Indian State tests its standing on the global stage not on its ability to reclaim its consciousness and live by its own values, but on the basis of its position in the 'global order' (read the West) as a 'civilised nation'. There does not appear to be a conscious attempt on the part of the Indian State to break free from the universalised fictions and illusions created by coloniality.

Therefore, a decolonial approach to rid Bharat of coloniality is imperative.

This is not possible without challenging the predominance of postcolonialism in Bharat given its role in perpetuating coloniality. To this end, it is important to understand the specific manifestations of coloniality in Bharat, especially the following, which have altered its consciousness in the most fundamental of ways:

1. The impact of the Christian European coloniser's conceptions of 'religion' on Indic OET systems and the attendant alienation of nature;

2. The application of the coloniser's racial lens to Bharat's societal structures, which gave rise to what we understand today as 'caste' and 'tribe';

3. The introduction of the coloniser's education system at the expense of indigenous knowledge production and education systems;

4. The imposition of the Westphalian nation-state model on a diverse civilisational society; and

5. The impact of the coloniser's notion of 'development'.

Surprisingly, each of these is abundantly supported by the literature except that the underlying cause, namely coloniality, which is common, has not been paid attention to.

Before I am misunderstood and labelled a revisionist, let me clarify that I do not mean that prior to the advent of the European coloniser there were no stratifications or hierarchies in Bharatiya society. However, it is certainly my case, based on the literature on coloniality and its impact on societal structures of other colonised societies, that the manner in which religion, caste and tribe are understood in contemporary Bharat bears a distinct colonial stamp. The influence of both secularised and non-secularised Protestant Reformation-informed Christian OET is inescapable. Therefore, if at all we wish to judge Bharat's contemporary social structures or their past, a decolonial approach would require that they be understood *minus* the judgment and sanctimony induced by Reformed and Enlightened European coloniality. By 'understood', I do not mean glorified, I simply mean made sense of for what they were before the coloniser's evangelising and civilising influence afflicted them and their characterisation.

I am supported in these views by the stellar work of several scholars, such as Dr. S.N. Balagangadhara, Dr. Jakob De Roover and Nicholas B. Dirks. This is not a call to authority, instead it is my position that the work of these scholars is consistent with the central theme of the decolonial school, that is, the existence of coloniality is a fact. The corollary being that any work that fails to or deliberately ignores the impact of coloniality on Indic societal structures and dynamics perpetuates coloniality. To explain this position in greater detail, as in the first section, I will use this opportunity to discuss material that, in my opinion, deserves wider dissemination and whose relevance alongside, if not within, the framework of decoloniality is evident to me.

In this regard, the works of Dr. Balagangadhara and Dr. De Roover are particularly important since they are closer to the decolonial school owing to their recognition of the existence of 'colonial consciousness', which is similar to Quijano's recognition of coloniality.[1] Based on what I have read thus far, I was, in fact, surprised at the lack of a direct and express handshake between the scholarship on decoloniality, which focusses predominantly on the Americas, and the scholarship on colonial consciousness, whose primary focus is Bharat. Therefore, before I proceed to examine the literature on the impact of coloniality on religion, caste, tribe and political thought in the context of Bharat, it is important to understand the nature of 'colonial consciousness' as formulated by Balagangadhara and De Roover, with particular attention to Bharat.

Colonial Consciousness, Postcolonialism and the Native's Options

Balagandhara and De Roover highlight that apart from being malleable and fluid over time, labels such as 'the Left' and 'the

Right', 'liberal' and 'conservative', are located within the same worldview, namely the colonial worldview. This, according to them, is a product of 'colonial consciousness', which they believe has not been understood well enough in Bharat since the postcolonial school in the country has only focussed on the external manifestations of colonialism and its effects. As stated earlier, this puts the position of both scholars in the neighbourhood of the decolonial school.

Further, they believe, as do decolonial scholars, that colonial consciousness is not a thing of the past, given its continued presence in contemporary structures and attitudes. In its erstwhile form as colonialism and in its current form as Western imperialism, colonial consciousness, according to both scholars, is aimed at establishing and projecting the civilisational superiority of the West. They too agree that colonial consciousness takes away from a colonised people their agency over their cultural experiences and permits them to describe such experiences only using the framework and lexicon prescribed by the coloniser. Such consciousness creates a set of attitudes and feelings that serve to preserve colonial legacy in indigenous societies including 'the feeling of shame about their own culture, the conviction that they are backward, the desire to learn from the coloniser' and so on, which are cemented through the application of 'scientism'. That is to say that the claimed physiological and religious superiority of the coloniser are treated as scientific facts to explain and justify the factum of colonisation and simultaneously prove the weakness of colonised societies.

Each of these thoughts clearly echoes the decolonial school's dissection of coloniality and its impact, which is the deprivation of indigenous subjectivities and the universalisation of Eurocentric subjectivity through imposition. It is this alienation from one's own cultural experience that makes colonialism and colonial consciousness immoral according to Balagangadhara and De Roover. Both call colonialism an 'educational project' in the sense that, akin to education, it acts as a filter that alters human experience through the introduction of a particular framework. This is evident from the coloniser's belief that he was merely discharging his moral and binding obligation to 'educate' and 'civilise' the native, which flowed from his Christian OET that mandated that devil-worshipping heathens had to be 'saved' from their 'false religions' and their own immorality.

Given that Bharat was (and remains) the land of heathendom in the eyes of the Christian coloniser, it was axiomatic that false religion abounded and immorality prospered. This laid the foundations of the colonial stereotype that the indigenous idol-worshipping Hindu was 'untrustworthy, immoral, corrupt and cowardly' and compared poorly to the 'unyielding Muslim' who, though he rejected the gospel, was closer to the Christian worldview, being 'of the book'. These stereotypes continue to find purchase long after the British have left, proving the continued existence of colonial consciousness. In other words, the continuity between the 'fundamental and structural descriptions' of Bharat by the British and the manner in which 'independent' generations have viewed Bharat's past and present are evidence of colonial consciousness being alive and kicking. While this continuity of thought is laid at the doors of Bharat's indigeneity by the postcolonial school, given the latter's perception of Bharat as an inherently weak and servile civilisation, according to Balagangadhara and De Roover, colonial consciousness must be held responsible for such continuity of thought.

They identify the presence of such continuity in the critical realm of faith that led to 'Buddhism' and 'Jainism' being reshaped and reimagined as rebellions against 'Brahminical hegemony'; this reimagination was evidently inspired by the anti-clericalism of the Protestant Reformation. Further, the project of 'reforming' native faith systems and practices, which found enthusiastic native takers during the colonial period and spawned several 'reformist' movements, continues to find purchase in contemporary Bharat regardless of political or ideological labels, such as the Left or the Right.

This is not to contend that but for the impact of coloniality/ colonial consciousness, Bharat's society was without the need for forward movement. That is an entirely different line of enquiry altogether which cannot be embarked upon until there is a decolonialised understanding of precolonial Bharat's indigenous culture and society. The point being advanced is that the framework of our discussions, conversations and debates, and its undergirding are predominantly colonial and until that lens is replaced with the indigenous lens, there is no scope for an honest discussion on the need for 'reform'.

In this regard, Balagangadhara and De Roover are of the view that replacement of colonial consciousness with native/ Indic consciousness cannot translate to going back to the precolonial ways of life since colonialism may have changed the universe of the colonised forever. What, then, is the purpose of identification of colonial consciousness? According to them, acknowledgement of moral responsibility is the first step by both the coloniser and the colonised for their respective roles in perpetuating colonial consciousness. The erstwhile coloniser and his successor, the Western imperialist, must take responsibility for actively inserting colonial consciousness into colonised societies while the colonised must take responsibility for advancing the same even after decolonisation. Simply put, the treatment of the European experience and view of the Indic society as 'fact' is a textbook case of the colonised being complicit in advancing and nurturing colonial consciousness because it feeds off of the unquestioning acceptance of the Western worldview. This position is similar to the one taken by Mignolo and Walsh as seen in the last section.

Second, from the point of view of relevance, they take the position that colonised societies, such as Bharat, must take cognisance of the Protestant Christian OET behind the emergence of concepts, such as secularism, which significantly inform their criticism of their own culture and societal structures.[2] The ignorance of formerly colonised societies of the specific religious and cultural backdrop that gave birth to the so-called 'modern' ideas, such as 'secularism', makes them culpable for perpetuating colonial consciousness.

Third, awareness of coloniality or colonial consciousness will awaken formerly colonised societies to the 'hybridity' that defines their existence and their tendency to look at their own cultures as mere variants of the Western civilisation. This highlights another critical point of departure between the decolonial and the postcolonial schools—decolonial thought refuses to celebrate this hybridity because it relegates the formerly colonised to the eternal status of the 'other', of the 'Occident', which forms the basis of Orientalism. On the other hand, postcolonial thought sees value in and celebrates hybridity as a form of 'cultural resistance' to the West since it supposedly subverts Western civilisation through imitation and, therefore, 'contaminates' what belongs to the West. But Balagangadhara and De Roover are of the view that hybridity and deliberate contamination of Western thought, even if employed as strategies of resistance, reduce the formerly colonised to the status of 'immoral' creatures because their 'moral cowardice' is writ large in the forgery and mimicry they employ while challenging Western thought.

In any case, to hope to subvert Western thought by operating within its framework is to fail to recognise that it only serves to further and legitimise the framework as a whole along with its claims of universal validity. The net result is the same—while the coloniser's coloniality painted the native as fundamentally untrustworthy due to the immorality ingrained in his 'false' religion, postcolonial thought's endorsement of hybridity and mimicry as tools of subversion internalises this immorality and doublespeak, thereby validating the untrustworthiness of the native. Therefore, according to postcolonial thought, there is only one way to live, one worldview, one 'option'—the colonial option. As a consequence, postcolonialism becomes the unpaid, or perhaps the paid, champion of coloniality/colonial consciousness. Even if its original intent was the subversion of Western hegemony, its unintended consequences, at least in the case of Bharat, are: the reinforcement, entrenchment and secularisation of colonialism (whose origins are not secular), the alienation of the native's own cultural experience, the stifling and suppression of indigenous consciousness and its replacement with self-loathing.

Middle Eastern Coloniality, Postcolonial Thought and Marxism

There is yet another aspect of the postcolonial approach that needs to be dealt with so that the choice between the decolonial and the postcolonial schools becomes obvious. The postcolonial school, while on the one hand challenging European colonialism and the latter's monopoly over truth and subjectivity, takes a curiously inconsistent position with respect to the colonisation of Bharat by imperialists professing Islam—'Middle Eastern colonialism'—which had a similar integral and indispensable ethno-religious sense of superiority as European coloniality.[3] Since quite a few of the colonisers professing Islam arrived from Central Asia, the use of Middle Eastern colonialism may be deemed geographically inaccurate. But I stand by the use of the term because the identity and aims of colonialism are defined by the geographical locus of the consciousness from which it draws its inspiration and to which it owes its allegiance. Therefore, the reference to the 'Middle East' is to a certain form of consciousness that inspired the colonisers regardless of their ethnicity or geographical origins.[4] In other words, just as 'the West' is more a state of mind and not a mere geography, 'the Middle East' too is a state of mind.

The dichotomous approach of postcolonial thought to European colonialism and Middle Eastern colonialism may be attributable to the influence of its Palestinian connection, or the fact that Middle Eastern consciousness and Indic consciousness are lumped together under the category of the Oriental and are seen as equal victims of European colonialism. In that sense, Orientalism has had the effect of pixelating from public scrutiny the motivations, conduct and impact of Middle Eastern colonialism on the Indic civilisation and its consciousness. It also needs to be said that the attempt to give the impression that Middle Eastern consciousness is native to the Indic civilisational fabric is dishonest and without basis in history. However, that discussion, which requires a deeper examination by experts, is beyond the scope of this book.

For the purposes of the current discussion, what is certainly relevant and sufficient is the recognition that the postcolonial school, while rejecting the tall claims of European colonialism, actively obstructs any honest analysis of Middle Eastern colonialism and its coloniality, thereby allowing it to thrive in Bharat.[5] Given the manifest and significant similarities in the OET frameworks between European and Middle Eastern colonialities, at the very least, postcolonial thought ought to have challenged the latter's untenable claim of being the final repository of the truth in the same manner and to the same degree as its challenge to the former's claim of universal validity. After all, both forms of colonialities are significantly inspired by their respective OETs, which enjoin them to colonise, enslave and evangelise idol-worshipping indigenous societies.[6]

Both proceed on the axiomatic presumption that prior to their advent, colonised societies were consumed by darkness and ignorance (called 'Jahilliya' in the case of Middle Eastern coloniality), which requires them to spread the 'light' of their respective OETs either through force or inducement or both.[7] In fact, their attitudes towards their own respective pre-Christian and pre-Muslim histories are one of contempt and condescension, which are directed at the rest of the world, after their own respective conversions to the 'true faiths'. As a corollary, both believe in the concept of 'the true faith' and heathendom, which 'others' and dehumanises the rest of the world at the outset. Both view the lands of the infidel or the heathen, as the case may be, as objects of conquest, an attitude that persists even after settling in conquered lands since both owe their allegiances to OETs that have their origins outside of the conquered lands.

Further, their attitude towards nature is similar, which makes it impossible for them to relate to the veneration of nature and codification of knowledge through tradition by indigenous societies, such as Bharat. In so far as Bharat is concerned, both forms of colonialities are non-indigenous since the OETs they are inspired by are not only outside the civilisational weave of Bharat but are also positively at loggerheads with Indic OET systems. In a nutshell, Bharat and its indigenous values represent nothing more than a territory and people to be conquered, converted or annihilated by either of the colonialities until one of them attains a position of relative strength and supremacy over the other. The common adversary is, of course, the indigenous worldview, which must be annihilated at any cost by any means necessary and by colluding with any ally available. This explains the cosy relationship of both forms of coloniality with Marxism in Bharat, which I will come to shortly.

In view of this, since Bharat as a civilisation has been at the receiving end of both forms of colonialism and coloniality, unlike the Americas, it need not and cannot afford to limit the scope of its enquiry only to European colonialism. If anything, the partition of Bharat in 1947 on religious/civilisational lines[8] and the continuing tensions within Bharat, such as in Kashmir, Bengal, Kerala and other parts of the country, warrant the examination of Middle Eastern coloniality from a decolonial perspective just as much as European coloniality. Therefore, Bharat's version of coloniality, and hence decoloniality, must encompass both forms of colonialism and colonialities.

This position is justified in my view since contemporary decolonial scholarship concerns itself predominantly with the impact of European settler colonialism, and Bharat has experienced Middle Eastern settler colonialism longer than it has experienced the European variant. Critically, the living embodiments of Middle Eastern coloniality, *regardless of the faith they subscribe to*, presently thrive within Bharat's boundaries as well as in its immediate neighbourhood, which were carved out of its civilisational geography through force. In other words, while the former colonies to the west of the Atlantic associate settler coloniality primarily with Europe, from the perspective of Bharat, Europeanism is perhaps, at best, a much more sophisticated and systematic version of Middle Eastern coloniality.

I consciously use the words 'sophisticated' and 'systematic', since Middle Eastern colonialism's predominant use of force inspired a similar response, which made it possible for Bharat's indigeneity to offer fierce resistance and survive where other cultures and civilisations were wiped out for eternity. The expression of contempt and the intention to annihilate the other was worn on the sleeve by Middle Eastern coloniality, and therefore, the other (Bharat's indigeneity) was acutely aware of the need to defend itself. On the contrary, European coloniality's use of institutional mechanisms to co-opt the indigenous society and project Europeanism as the aspirational goal, lulled the indigenous consciousness into a false sense of comfort that coexistence was possible. The indigenous society seemed to have bought into the stated policy of 'toleration' of the European coloniser whose end goal it was oblivious to. And yet, the postcolonial school actively obstructs scrutiny of either coloniality, forget calling them out, despite the fact that both forms of colonialities are alive and kicking within contemporary Bharat at the expense of the indigenous consciousness.

Further, notwithstanding its self-image and professions of challenging coloniality's monopoly over time and subjectivity, the fact remains that postcolonial thought's characterisation of who or what constitutes 'subaltern' in

Bharat itself is loaded with coloniality since it is informed by colonial assumptions of the native society and its societal structures, specifically the 'caste system'. In addition to this, at least insofar as Bharat is concerned, the postcolonial and the Marxist schools have forged a collaborative partnership, in the sense that both advance European and Middle Eastern colonialities in their own ways by creating divisions within the indigenous consciousness or by digesting it, 'subalternism' being a case in point.

This may not be surprising given Marx's own Eurocentrism and avowed belief that British colonialism was good for Bharat.[9] Marx believed that England had to fulfil 'a double mission in India', namely the annihilation of the old Asiatic society and the laying of the material foundations of Western society in Asia.[10] These were his views despite his own knowledge of the selfish nature of British colonisation of Bharat, best captured by his statement that 'whatever may have been the crimes of England she was the unconscious tool of history in bringing about that revolution', that is, in laying the foundations for 'the material basis of the new world'. The entrenchment of the Marxist view of colonialism in Bharat is illustratively reflected by the fact that contemporary colonialised elites in Bharat share Marx's view that European colonialism was good for Bharat since it resulted in 'development', evidenced by the introduction of the railway system. The underlying assumption that is advanced in citing this example is that, according to the Marxist school, had it not been for British colonialism, the concept of scientific temper, progress and 'development' were and would have remained unknown to Bharat.[11] In that sense, Marxism shares the Eurocentric belief that science is the monopoly of the West, and 'rationality', although universal, owes its origins to Europe.

Further, Marxism's attitudes to European colonialism and Middle Eastern colonialism in the context of Bharat have given rise to creatures, such as Christian Marxism[12] and Islamic Marxism[13], wherein Marxism serves as a convenient vehicle to further European and Middle Eastern colonialities. While Marxism masquerades as an independent ideology elsewhere, in Bharat, it has effectively acted as the perfect foil for colonising mindsets whose attitudes towards indigenous consciousness have been one of contempt and condescension, neither of which allows for peaceful coexistence.

The larger point being made is that given the ethically and morally suspect alliance between the postcolonial and Marxist schools in Bharat and their willingness to act as conduits to two forms of colonialities that have no love lost for Bharat's indigenous consciousness, neither school presents itself as the better option for Bharat in its quest for reclamation of its indigeneity. Even in the world of scholarship, those such as Sitaram Goel, Ram Swarup, Dharampal, Dr. Koenraad Elst, Dr. Balagangadhara and Dr. De Roover, whether 'indigenous' or otherwise, who have attempted to rigorously examine the history of both Middle Eastern and European colonisations of Bharat, have been branded 'extremist' or 'far right' by both the postcolonial and Marxist schools. Sadly, these scholars have received a similar treatment even by those who, although claim to root for indigenous consciousness, operate under the mistaken belief that such consciousness can regain its rightful place without being vocal about its legitimate expectations or its opposition to both forms of colonialities.

In the process, both the postcolonial and Marxist schools have arrogated to themselves the status of self-appointed guardians of 'India Studies', now 'South Asia Studies', which gives them monopoly over Bharat's subjectivity, history and, therefore, its future. This is one of the reasons for my conscious decision to place Bharat-specific literature on colonial consciousness alongside global literature on decoloniality to demonstrate that while the latter is celebrated in the context of the Americas, the former is relentlessly maligned despite seeking to achieve a similar goal as decoloniality—to stand up for Indic indigenous consciousness which is surrounded by an ocean of proselytising and expansionist colonialities. Clearly, even if postcolonial and Marxist schools have advanced the cause of indigeneities outside Bharat, the principle of harm suggests that both schools have harmed Bharat's indigenous consciousness more than empowering it.

It is for the above-mentioned reasons that the decolonial school merits serious consideration.[14] The decolonial option gives the indigenous consciousness a voice it sorely needs to speak out against both forms of continuing colonialities.[15] Decoloniality, to my mind, serves as a better lens because it clips the universalising tendency of both by awakening people to the presence of such colonialities and enables movement towards their own cultural experience. Whether this movement towards indigenous consciousness ultimately translates to the retention of colonial consciousness or embracing of indigeneity or formulation of a decolonial yet hybrid framework that is different from the hybridity celebrated by postcolonial thought, remains a matter of analysis by domain experts. After all, such choices are significantly contingent on the 'practicality' and 'pragmatism' of replacement of colonial consciousness with indigenous consciousness.

From the perspective of ascertaining a 'cut-off' period to determine Bharat's indigeneity by expanding Bharat's version of colonialities to include both forms, one may tentatively arrive at the eighth century when the first wave of recorded Muslim Arab invasions of Bharat began. This is similar to European colonialism being traced by the decolonial school to the fifteenth century when the Age of Discovery began. While the period between the twelfth and sixteenth centuries is typically associated with a more consistent and frequent wave of Islamic invasions of Bharat, the eighth century certainly marked its beginning. Perhaps scholars trained in history may disagree with me with regard to the exact time period, but the underlying principle I seek to advance is similar to the position of decolonial scholars with respect to indigeneity in the context of Latin America. To not do so would be to display rank intellectual inconsistency and dishonesty, thereby proving coloniality, in this case Middle Eastern coloniality.

In this regard, I place limited reliance on Dr. B.R. Ambedkar's views wherein he suggested a continuum of thought between the Islamic OET-inspired invasions of Bharat in the eighth century and the ultimate demand for the creation of Pakistan by the leading lights of the Pakistan movement, citing the Two-Nation Theory. Following are a few relevant extracts from his book *Pakistan or the Partition of India* wherein Dr. Ambedkar charts the Islamic invasion of Bharat on a timeline beginning from the invasion of Sindh by Muhammad Bin Qasim in 711 CE (close to 80 years after the Islamic Prophet's passing) to the Third Battle of Panipat between Ahmad Shah Abdali and the Maratha Empire in 1761[16]:

These Muslim invasions were not undertaken merely out of lust for loot or conquest. There was another object behind them. The expedition against Sind by Mahommad bin Qasim was of a punitive character and was undertaken to punish Raja Dahir of Sind who had refused to make restitution for the seizure of an Arab ship at Debul, one of the sea-port towns of Sind. But, there is no doubt that striking a blow at the idolatry and polytheism of Hindus and establishing Islam in India was also one of the aims of this expedition....

...All this was not the result of mere caprice or moral perversion. On the other hand, what was done was in accordance with the ruling ideas of the leaders of Islam in the broadest aspects. These ideas were well expressed by the Kazi in reply to a question put by Sultan Ala-ud-Din wanting to know the legal position of the Hindus under Muslim law. The Kazi said:

'They are called payers of tribute, and when the revenue officer demands silver from them they should without question, and with all humility and respect, tender gold. If the officer throws dirt in their mouths, they must without reluctance open their mouths wide to receive it. . . . The due subordination of the Dhimmi is exhibited in this humble payment, and by this throwing of dirt into their mouths. The glorification of Islam is a duty, and contempt for religion is vain. God holds them in contempt, for he says, "Keep them in subjection." To keep the Hindus in abasement is especially a religious duty, because they are the most inveterate enemies of the Prophet, and because the Prophet has commanded us to slay them, plunder them, and make them captive, saying, "Convert them to Islam or kill them, and make them slaves, and spoil their wealth and [property]." No doctor but the great doctor (Hanifah), to whose school we belong, has assented to the imposition of jizya on Hindus; doctors of other schools allow no other alternative but "Death or Islam."'

The reason I specifically quote Dr. Ambedkar and place limited reliance on his views on this subject in the context of Middle Eastern colonialism is to make the point that Dr. Ambedkar, the chairman of the Drafting Committee of the Indian Constitution, was of the view that the Two-Nation Theory was a reality that the indigenous society of Bharat must accept instead of squeamishly denying. Here are his views after his summary of the history of Muslim invasions of Bharat[17]:

How far is it open to the Hindus to say that Northern India is part of Aryavarta? How far is it open to the Hindus to say because once it belonged to them, therefore, it must remain for ever an integral part of India? Those who oppose separation and hold to the 'historic sentiment' arising out of an ancient fact that Northern India including Afghanistan was once part of India and that the people of that area were either Buddhist or Hindus, must be asked whether the events of these 762 years of incessant Muslim invasions, the object with which they were launched and the methods adopted by

these invaders to give effect to their object, are to be treated
as though they were matters of no account?

Apart from other consequences which have flowed from
them these invasions have, in my opinion, so profoundly
altered the culture and character of the northern areas, which
it is now proposed to be included in a Pakistan, that there is
not only no unity between that area and the rest of India but
that there is as a matter of fact a real antipathy between the
two.

The first consequence of these invasions was the breaking
up of the unity of Northern India with the rest of India.
After his conquest of Northern India, Muhammad of Ghazni
detached it from India and ruled it from Ghazni. When
Mahommed Ghori came in the field as a conqueror, he again
attached it to India and ruled it from Lahore and then from
Delhi. Hakim, the brother of Akbar, detached Kabul and
Kandahar from Northern India. Akbar again attached it to
Northern India. They were again detached by Nadirshah
in 1738 and the whole of Northern India would have been
severed from India had it not been for the check provided
by the rise of the Sikhs. Northern India, therefore, has been
like a wagon in a train, which can be coupled or uncoupled
according to the circumstances of the moment. If analogy is
wanted, the case of Alsace-Lorraine could be cited. Alsace-
Lorraine was originally part of Germany, like the rest of
Switzerland and the Low Countries. It continued to be so
till 1680, when it was taken by France and incorporated into
French territory. It belonged to France till 1871, when it was
detached by Germany and made part of her territory. In
1918, it was again detached from Germany and made part of
France. In 1940, it was detached from France and made part
of Germany.

The methods adopted by the invaders have left behind
them their aftermath. One aftermath is the bitterness between
the Hindus and the Muslims which they have caused. This

bitterness between the two is so deep-seated that a century of political life has neither succeeded in assuaging it, nor in making people forget it. As the invasions were accompanied with destruction of temples and forced conversions, with spoliation of property, with slaughter, enslavement and abasement of men, women and children, what wonder if the memory of these invasions has ever remained green, as a source of pride to the Muslims and as a source of shame to the Hindus? But these things apart, this north-west corner of India has been a theatre in which a stern drama has been played. Muslim hordes, in wave after wave, have surged down into this area and from thence scattered themselves in spray over the rest of India. These reached the rest of India in thin currents. In time, they also receded from their farthest limits; while they lasted, they left a deep deposit of Islamic culture over the original Aryan culture in this north-west corner of India which has given it a totally different colour, both in religious and political outlook.

The Muslim invaders, no doubt, came to India singing a hymn of hate against the Hindus. But, they did not merely sing their hymn of hate and go back burning a few temples on the way. That would have been a blessing. They were not content with so negative a result. They did a positive act, namely, to plant the seed of Islam. The growth of this plant is remarkable. It is not a summer sapling. It is as great and as strong as an oak. Its growth is the thickest in Northern India. The successive invasions have deposited their 'silt' more there than anywhere else, and have served as watering exercises of devoted gardeners. Its growth is so thick in Northern India that the remnants of Hindu and Buddhist culture are just shrubs. Even the Sikh axe could not fell this oak. Sikhs, no doubt, became the political masters of Northern India, but they did not gain back Northern India to that spiritual and cultural unity by which it was bound to the rest of India before Hsuan Tsang. The Sikhs coupled it back to India.

Still, it remains like Alsace-Lorraine politically detachable and spiritually alien so far as the rest of India is concerned. It is only an unimaginative person who could fail to take notice of these facts or insist in the face of them that Pakistan means breaking up into two what is one whole.

What is the unity the Hindu sees between Pakistan and Hindustan? If it is geographical unity, then that is no unity. Geographical unity is unity intended by nature. In building up a nationality on geographical unity, it must be remembered that it is a case where Nature proposes and Man disposes. If it is unity in external things, such as ways and habits of life, that is no unity. Such unity is the result of exposure to a common environment. If it is administrative unity, that again is no unity. The instance of Burma is in point. Arakan and Tenasserim were annexed in 1826 by the treaty of Yendabu. Pegu and Martaban were annexed in 1852. Upper Burma was annexed in 1886. The administrative unity between India and Burma was forged in 1826. For over 110 years that administrative unity continued to exist. In 1937, the knot that tied the two together was cut asunder and nobody shed a tear over it. The unity between India and Burma was not less fundamental. If unity is to be of an abiding character, it must be founded on a sense of kinship, in the feeling of being kindred. In short, it must be spiritual. Judged in the light of these considerations, the unity between Pakistan and Hindustan is a myth. Indeed, there is more spiritual unity between Hindustan and Burma than there is between Pakistan and Hindustan. And if the Hindus did not object to the severance of Burma from India, it is difficult to understand how the Hindus can object to the severance of an area like Pakistan, which, to repeat, is politically detachable from, socially hostile and spiritually alien to, the rest of India.

For the sake of clarity, I repeat that my reliance on Dr. Ambedkar's views on the subject is limited to the extent of demonstrating that the recognition of Middle Eastern coloniality is imperative in the context of Bharat alongside European coloniality. I am alive to Dr. Ambedkar's views on Indic OETs, in particular on the caste system; however, given the undeniable existence of European coloniality during his life and times and his own colonial education, it is imperative to revisit his views on caste applying the filter of decoloniality *without* denying his experience or those of others. What is important for the present discussion is that notwithstanding Dr. Ambedkar's views on native OETs, he did *not* lose sight of the fact that Middle Eastern colonialism had its origins in OETs that lay outside the pale of the Indic civilisational fabric.

Critically, Dr. Ambedkar was clear that if the remnants of a culture were to be wiped out from a certain territory, the culture's connection with the territory and any claim it may have over it were weakened. While his observations were in the context of the creation of Pakistan, we would do well to remember that what constitutes Pakistan today was part of Bharat once and, therefore, if Bharat's indigeneity does not realise the imperative of a decolonialising exercise, it is bound to witness yet another cession of civilisational space, not just 'territory'. After all, the creation of Pakistan is not too far back in time and the event has not put an end to Middle Eastern colonialism; instead, it has only provided a firm launch pad for the systematic advancement of Middle Eastern colonialism through the instrumentality of a State that was expressly created for the attainment of the said goal. Venkat Dhulipala's work in this regard on the founding and organising principles of Pakistan is an example of stellar scholarship that only bolsters this position.

In his book *Creating a New Medina: State Power, Islam, and the Quest for Pakistan in Late Colonial North India*, Dhulipala demonstrates, based on research surrounding the ideation and eventual creation of Pakistan, that it was conceived of as the 'New Medina'.[18] To support this position, Dhulipala cites the statements and efforts of proponents of Pakistan, such as Maulana Shabbir

Ahmad Usmani, one of the founding members of Jamia Millia Islamia University and the founder of the pro-Pakistan political party Jamiat Ulema-e-Islam. Dhulipala cites Usmani's speech delivered in Lahore in 1946 wherein the latter declared thus:

> [Just] as Medina had provided a base for the eventual victory of Islam in Arabia, Pakistan would pave the way for the triumphal return of Islam as the ruling power over the entire subcontinent. The whole of Hindustan would thus be turned into Pakistan just as the Prophet himself had turned all of Arabia into Pakistan.

Usmani went so far as to make a Quranic case for the Two-Nation Theory based on the distinction struck between the *momin* (believer) and the *kafir* (infidel) by the Islamic Prophet. The sequitur to this distinction, according to Usmani, was that Indian Muslims constituted a separate nation and any claim of the composite nationality of Indians was 'false and anti-Islamic'. Therefore, a concrete Islamic theological justification was offered for the creation of Pakistan as an Islamic State. It is clear that the creation of Pakistan was envisaged as an end as well as the means to the end, namely the return of Islam to the Asian subcontinent.[19] Post its creation and the partition of Bharat, we must ask ourselves whether Middle Eastern colonialism and coloniality has waxed or waned, especially in view of the number of political and violent movements and causes that have surfaced within and surrounding Bharat in the name of Middle Eastern OET. Given the clear and express belief of the proponents of Middle Eastern coloniality that their consciousness is mandated and enjoined by the scripture they believe in, it is certainly not unreasonable or baseless to conclude that Indic consciousness has as much incentive to protect itself from Middle Eastern coloniality as it does from European coloniality.[20] Rather, it has an existential disincentive to not protect itself from either. This cannot be branded as fear-mongering given the irrefutable history of both colonialities in this part of the world. After all, facts cannot be replaced with wishful secularised thinking.

In view of this, it is possible to justifiably contend that Bharat's definitions of coloniality and decoloniality must include European and Middle Eastern colonialities, in that order, since the former protects the latter and the latter rides on the former's coattails to legitimise itself. The continuing existential threat posed by both colonialities to Bharat's indigeneity makes decoloniality not just an 'option' but a civilisational imperative, which can no longer be delayed. However, I am in no position to universalise this argument as my vision in this regard is limited to Bharat.

Also, I recognise that decoloniality may not be the silver bullet to all of Bharat's civilisational challenges, that it may not have all the answers to the questions that stare at Bharat's indigenous consciousness; but it certainly has the potential to serve as a lens for Bharat to be better equipped to square up to its past and make sense of its own journey by applying its own frameworks instead of using frameworks that subtly or overtly exert an imperial colonialising influence.

One of the important premises of the preceding discussion is that Bharat is a 'civilisation' with an Indic consciousness whose agency was interfered with by European coloniality in ways that have resulted in the internalisation of the European worldview as the benchmark to be lived up to. Therefore, before I proceed to discuss the impact of European coloniality on Bharat's consciousness, in the next chapter I will attempt to make good the assumption that Bharat was and remains a civilisation, at least at the level of the society, which has implications for the formulation of policies and lawmaking. This can offer clarity on what makes a society a civilisation and why Bharat must be treated as one, so as to better understand (*a*) the true impact of the European coloniser's nation-state project on Bharat, and (b) whether Bharat's journey towards constitutionalism reflects its self-understanding as a civilisation.

Bharat as a Civilisation

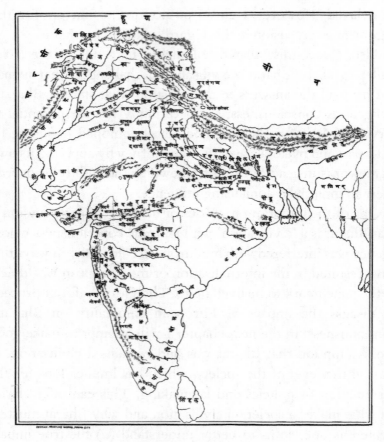

Mahabharata: Bharatvarsh

Names of places in India associated with the Mahabharata (courtesy of US Library of Congress: Geography and Map Division).

Ever since British author and columnist Martin Jacques[1] proposed about a decade ago that China was a 'civilisation-state' which Europe could not relate to given the latter's nation-state-based worldview,[2] similar assertions have been made about Bharat being a civilisation-state. In 2014, Dr. Koenraad Elst wrote a piece on his blog titled 'India as a civilisation-state' wherein, citing Zhang Weiwei's book *The China Wave: Rise of a Civilizational State*,[3] he contended that Bharat too must make a similar case for itself.[4] Dr. Elst's position was based on his view that Bharat's 'self-understanding' supported its case of being or becoming a civilisation-state. Subsequently, this position has been echoed by others, including the current National Security Advisor Shri Ajit Doval.[5] In my opinion, such a position must be examined and made good from both a conceptual and practical perspective if the purpose is to give effect to that position at the level of law and policymaking, failing which, it would be reduced to just another fashionable buzzword or a mere talking point.

The claim that Bharat is a civilisation-state requires us to address the following layers at the very least, including those which inhere in them:

1. What are the ingredients that constitute a nation and a civilisation, and what distinguishes the two?
2. What separates a civilisation-state from a nation-state?
3. What makes Bharat a civilisation, if at all?
4. Independent of how the Constitution treats Bharat, what is the basis for the view that a civilisation-state model suits Bharat better than the nation-state model?
5. If Bharat is a civilisation, does the Constitution's treatment do justice to its nature?

I will try and address each of these questions as organically as possible with primary reliance being placed on Indic and pro-Indic voices (broadly, 'Indic scholars'), who have taken the considered position that Bharat is indeed a civilisation, based on their knowledge of its history and consciousness. While I leave it to the experts to comment on the merits of the scholarship, the scope of my enquiry for the purposes of the discussion at hand is limited to assessing their positions for consensus on Bharat's status as a civilisation and their basis for holding such a view.

My other objective, as stated previously, is to draw the attention of the reader to Indic scholars whose works have either been systematically sidelined or completely pixelated on the ground that they championed 'Hindu nationalism' and sought to exclude non-Hindu identities from the journey of Bharat. These labels were expectedly hurled at such scholars by the postcolonial and Marxist schools, which have normalised such labels in mainstream discourse, largely due to the monopoly enjoyed by them in the realms of education, journalism, culture and policymaking. Instead of engaging with Indic scholars on the merits of their position, the approach of the postcolonial and Marxist schools has been to impute anti-minority and hyper-nationalist motives to the views of such scholars in order to pre-empt them from reaching a wider audience.

Clearly, the dark legacy of European nationalism and its destructive tendencies have been foisted on genuine Indic decolonial attempts in order to silence the voice of the native. As stated earlier, the Eurocentric criticism and stifling of indigenous efforts to regain agency over native consciousness is writ large on the conduct of the postcolonial and Marxist schools. To push back against this, keeping with the spirit of decoloniality, through the ensuing discussion I have attempted to showcase the views of a few early Indic scholars, namely Har Bilas Sarda, Radha Kumud Mookerji, Jadunath Sarkar and R.C. Majumdar, who collectively lend support to the position that Bharat is indeed a civilisation and must be treated as such.

These scholars, to me, represent the beginnings of an Indic Renaissance in the realm of history, starting in the second half of the nineteenth century when Bharat's aspirations of self-determination were being called into question on the ground that Bharat had never been 'one nation' and, therefore, could not aspire to independent statehood. It is in response to this colonial position that such Indic voices started generating rigorous scholarship that reinforced the unity of Bharat as a civilisation, and went to the extent of confidently asserting that (*a*) Bharat's indigenous identity must be traced to a period before the Islamic invasions (Middle Eastern colonialism) and European colonisation, and (*b*) 'the Hindu religion' was the glue that bound this civilisation. Their caveat, however, was that Indic OET systems must not be understood through the prism of the faith of the European coloniser despite using the word 'religion' to crudely refer to them for colonial consumption. It is important to appreciate that while some of these works were published in English and also cited or quoted the views of Europeans on the subject, they endeavoured at talking back to the European coloniser and reclaiming the agency of indigenous consciousness to speak for and about itself.

Through their scholarship, these stalwarts successfully refuted the self-serving claim of the White European Christian coloniser that it was his civilising benevolence that led to disparate and unrelated communities being stitched into one political unit. That such Indic voices stood up for the native at a time when European colonialism was perhaps at its zenith speaks volumes of their conviction in the strength and relevance of Indic consciousness. Even if the works of such scholars suffered from colonial consciousness to a certain degree, I am willing to overlook it given the times such scholars lived in, the resources at their disposal and their leonine attempts at speaking truth to a global colonising, enslaving and evangelising power. To my mind, such Indic scholars bravely pursued the goals of decoloniality whilst living under the yoke of the coloniser. This is in stark contrast to the deeply entrenched coloniality that one witnesses in a supposedly independent contemporary 'India' in every discussion where Bharat's past is subject to scrutiny with unadulterated hindsight bias, sanctimony and judgment.

Among the earliest Indic scholars was Har Bilas Sarda, whose book *Hindu Superiority: An Attempt to Determine the Position of the Hindu Race in the Scale of Nations*, which was published in 1906, apart from being relevant to his times, was way ahead of its time when seen through a decolonial lens.[6] Throughout the book, Sarda uses the term 'Hindu civilisation' while referring to 'ancient India'. In his discussion on the defining feature of the Hindu/Indic civilisation, Sarda underscores the integral and indispensable role of nature in the schema of 'ancient Indians', which formed the basis of Hindu laws and institutions. This brings out two significant aspects: (*a*) that the native identity of Bharat being the Indic/Hindu identity never appeared to be a matter of contestation in Sarda's discussion, and (*b*) that a harmonious relationship with nature defines the Hindu/Indic consciousness, from which emanates its worldview and institutions.

In etching the arc of the Hindu civilisation, what is astounding in hindsight is that Sarda treats the end of the Mahabharata War, the beginning of Kali Yuga, as the turning point in the history of Bharat—an approach consistent with that of Indic epistemological systems. Now, barely 115 years after Sarda's book was published, anyone who believes in the historicity of the Mahabharata War or the concept of a Kali Yuga, would be ridiculed for putting stock in 'myth' and 'fiction'. This demonstrates the manner in which the agency of the Indic consciousness over time and its subjectivity has become entirely subservient to the totalising nature of the casual coloniality we encounter in Bharat today. Ironically, the very same servile colonialised Indian mind would have no qualms accepting the historicity of the founder of the White European Christian coloniser's faith as a given.

While undertaking an exercise that panoramically surveys Bharat's history, consciousness and civilisation, Sarda posits that religion is *one* of the tests of civilisation. In the case of Bharat, according to him, *gnana* or knowledge is the true religion of Bharat, which was made possible only due to the 'pre-eminence

of morals, philosophy, literature, science and general culture'.
While making a case for respecting the Indic consciousness,
Sarda cautions against judging the past through the lens of the
present given that the present is a far cry from the past.

Sarda defines the Hindu religion as an anthology of eternal
truths as follows:

> The Hindu religion is the knowledge and comprehension of
> those eternal principles which govern nature and man, those
> immutable laws which in one sphere are called 'science', in
> another, 'true philosophy'. It concerns itself not with things
> true under certain conditions or at certain times: its precepts
> are ever true, true in the past, true in the present, true in
> the future. True knowledge being one, it takes, without
> any distinction, into its fold, Indians, Arabs, Europeans,
> Americans, Africans and Chinese. Its principles circumscribe
> the globe and govern all humanity.

When the construct of 'religion' is reconsidered in light of this
description, it is evident that the term does not do justice to
Sanatana Dharma, exposing the problem of applying colonial
Christian OET and linguistics to Bharat's indigenous systems that
are rooted in an onto-epistemology which is vastly different from
that of the coloniser's. Naturally, the White European Christian
coloniser could not wrap his head around it and presumed that
ethnicity and religion were as related in the Indic 'religion' as
they were in his faith and worldview, which led to ethnocentric
representations of Indic OET as well as its societal structures.

Starting in 1912, another scholar who wrote extensively
on various aspects of the Indic civilisation spanning over
four decades was Radha Kumud Mookerji. In the context of
establishing the civilisational character of Bharat, five of his
works are particularly helpful: *The Fundamental Unity of India*
(1914), *Nationalism in Hindu Culture* (1921), *Hindu Civilization:
From the Earliest Times up to the Establishment of the Maurya*

Empire (1936 and 1950),[7] *A New Approach to the Communal Problem* (1943)[8] and *Akhand Bharat* (1945),[9] with the leitmotif of Mookerji's work being captured in the first two.

In *The Fundamental Unity of India*, Mookerji marshals evidence from sources that are central to the Indic OET to make a case for its civilisational oneness through the unification of its geography despite the diversity that meets the eye.[10] Mookerji takes the clear position that this unity antedates the arrival of the British coloniser by millennia and, therefore, the coloniser cannot remotely claim to have unified and created 'India'. The premise of Mookerji's position is that in order for a group identity to take shape as a nation or a civilisation, 'the fundamental and indispensable factor is the possession of a common country, a fixed, definite abode'.

He compares the necessity for a fixed geography for the blossoming of a national or civilisational identity to a body through which the spirit operates. It is the place, the geography, the territory that enables the feeling of community, which leads to broader identities, such as national or civilisational. The development of an independent and identifiable cultural identity, which includes language, OET, literature and culture, is itself a function of the place and its characteristics. In the case of a diverse society, such as Bharat, according to Mookerji, an 'expanded geographical consciousness' is a condition precedent to the creation of a political unit that acts as one. To make his case for a common expanded Indic geographical consciousness, Mookerji first draws attention to the British coloniser's treatment of Bharat as not one but a 'collection of countries' and cites this Eurocentric perception as an impediment in making sense of Bharat. That such a perception is based on European conceptions of nation-statehood is evident to Mookerji since he specifically cites the scepticism of Anglo-Indian authorities, such as John Strachey, who were of the view that 'there is not and never was an India, or even any country of India, possessing, according to European ideas, any sort of unity, physical, political'.[11] It is remarkable that similar sceptical opinions of Bharat's consciousness and its history are echoed even in contemporary Bharat, which is proof of continued coloniality.

To rebut the coloniser's contention that Bharat did not exist as a single unit, whether political or geographical, Mookerji cites authorities on Bharat's geography, such as Vincent Arthur Smith and George Chisholm, who were of the following view[12]:

> India, encircled as she is by seas and mountains, is indisputably a geographical unit, and as such is rightly designated by one name. ...
>
> There is no part of the world better marked out by Nature as a region by itself than India, exclusive of Burma. It is a region indeed full of contrasts in physical features and in climate, but the features that divide it as a whole from surrounding regions are too clear to be overlooked.

Notwithstanding the clear identification of Bharat's natural borders, the sheer human diversity contained within it is bound to confound any observer who superficially attempts to apply the yardsticks of a 'nation' to Bharat. It is evident that the monochromatic concept of a nation does not do justice to Bharat, and therefore as opposed to cutting the head to fit the hat, a different yardstick must be applied, which is that of a civilisation, given that diversity and scale are two of the central requirements of a civilisation. However, that would still require us to demonstrate that despite the scale and variety, there is something that binds this vast land and its ocean of humanity. What is the unity that binds this diversity for it to stake a legitimate claim as one civilisation?

One may be tempted to draw parallels with the idea of a 'Christian civilisation' or 'Islamic civilisation' wherein people belonging to different races, speaking different languages, are seen as being part of one civilisation; however, given that Christianity and Islam impose a common faith and practices that unify the members from within and also explicitly identify the out-group, it is possible to entertain the idea of Christian and Islamic civilisations. This cannot be said of the 'Indic civilisation' since 'religion', as understood in the Abrahamic sense, does not apply to Indic OET, as a consequence of which it may not be possible to distil visible commonalities with the same ease as in Christianity or Islam. In fact, that temptation must be avoided since even the attempt to define a fundamental concept, such as unity in the Abrahamic sense, is proof of unconscious Abrahamic coloniality at work, which defeats the very object of undertaking a decolonial approach to defining an Indic civilisational identity.

Mookerji addresses the question of civilisational unity and quotes Vincent Arthur Smith on the subject, who wrote extensively on Bharat between 1893 and 1919[13]:

> [The civilisation of India] has many features which differentiate it from that of all other regions of the world, while they are common to the whole country, or rather continent, in a degree sufficient to justify its treatment as a unit in the history of human, social, and intellectual development.

Building on this thought and to demonstrate that such evolution and existence as a single unit with vast internal diversity was a matter of antiquity with no role played by the European coloniser, Mookerji cites the use of names, such as 'Jambudvipa' and 'Bharatavarsha', to identify this vast geography both by its people and outsiders. He clarifies that while Jambudvipa is a geographical reference, Bharatavarsha is a political reference, both of which demonstrate a unified geographical and political consciousness much before the idea of a British identity was even born. The underlying premise behind Mookerji's argument is that if a landmass with immense variety, natural and human, is given a common name, it is proof of unity in diversity with clear historical and political significance.

The unification of this land by Emperor Bharata after whom Bharatavarsha is named, just as Rome is derived from its founder

Romulus, is the argument advanced by Mookerji to establish Bharat's civilisational unity. He marshals evidence from the *Aitareya Brahmana* of the *Rig Veda* to support his argument. While I am in no position to refute or accept this argument as someone who is not formally trained in the Vedas, I understand Mookerji's reliance on the Vedas given their centrality to Indic OET and their treatment as documents of historicity. Coloniality would result in the Vedas being dismissed as embellished and exaggerated myths, while decoloniality would require us to respect them as primary sources of indigenous OET, and therefore not apply colonial benchmarks to what indigeneity has to say about the journey of this land and its civilisation.

At this point, I must admit that Mookerji's work appears to be premised on the existence of an Aryan identity, which remains the subject of intense debate even to date, with the evidence perhaps going against the Aryan Invasion Theory (AIT). In fact, the treatment of AIT as a colonial invention driven by the European coloniser's race-driven consciousness shall be dealt with briefly in Chapter 9. In any case, since this issue is for better-qualified people and domain experts to comment on, I will limit myself to the position that the spread of a common culture and civilisation through the efforts of Emperor Bharata, from whom the name Bharat is derived, is attested to by Indic sources. According to Mookerji, such efforts resulted in establishing cultural unity within a 'federation' of 'different creeds, cults and cultures with liberty to each to preserve its own special features and genius and contribute its own quota to enrich the central culture'.[14] In that sense, Bharat's civilisation may be understood as a federal civilisation with multiple sub-identities that are free to retain their identities but have remained culturally and politically bound for millennia. This is evidenced by the fact that this land has a recorded history of being politically referred to as 'Bharatavarsha' or 'Bharat' without interruption notwithstanding the Islamic invasions or European colonisation. Simply put, Bharat's self-understanding as a single cultural, civilisational and political unit has not changed and its internal diversity has not come in the way of such unity in the least. The European worldview, which puts stock in the domination of 'one nation' or 'one people' over others at the expense of the identity of others or their very existence, naturally, cannot seem to fathom what keeps Bharat together despite its diversity.

Apart from citing the use of a common name to identify this part of the world as a single civilisational unit, Mookerji explains the nature of Indic land ontology, the understanding of which, according to me, is critical to distinguish it from the European coloniser's territorial approach. Mookerji explains that the connection of the Indic civilisation with Bharat rests on its veneration of the land, quite literally, since She is worshipped as the vast Mother who is a living Deity with Her geographical attributes, such as the land and its rivers, being woven in hymns and prayers to simultaneously evoke shared feelings of devotion, unity and patriotism. This deification of the land itself, the blending of faith and patriotism, is proof of the inseparable and most fundamental connect between the land and its civilisation. The gradual expansion of this civilisation's geographical consciousness went hand in hand with the expansion of its presence and is reflected in the accommodation of a larger geography over time in the hymns of the Vedas. As opposed to being the subject of conquest and dominion, Bharat is treated as an object of worship, with respect for its geographical attributes being richly reflected in the hymns. This brings out the fundamental divergence between the attitudes of Middle Eastern and European colonialities to Bharat and nature on the one hand, and the attitude of the indigenous Indic consciousness towards its sacred geography on the other. On this, Mookerji has the following to say[15]:

The perennial beauty of the Himalayas has captivated the national imagination and has made them the refuge of holy men, drawing unending streams of pilgrims. Indeed, the Hindu's pilgrimages are always to the glacier-clad mountain, the palm-clad seashore or ocean-isle, or the almost impenetrable depths of hill and jungle, where the tread of the generations of Man has scarcely been heard, and Nature left free to exercise her healing and healthful influence. Thus, the Indian treats the beauty of place in a peculiar way, foreign to the West: his method of appreciating and celebrating it is quite different. A spot of beauty is no place for social enjoyment or self-indulgence; it is the place for self-restraint, for solitary meditation which leads the mind from nature up to Nature's God.

Had Niagara been situated on the Ganges, how different would have been its valuation by humanity. Instead of occasional picnics and railway pleasure trips, the perennial pilgrimage of worshipping crowds. Instead of parks, asramas. Instead of hotels, temples. Instead of ostentatious excess, simple austerity. Instead of the desire to harness its mighty forces to the chariot of human utility, an absorbing subjectivity, a complete detachment from the body and the outward world to feed the life of the spirit!

Thus, the institution of pilgrimage is undeniably a most powerful instrument for developing the geographical sense in the people which enables them to think and feel that India is not a mere congeries of geographical fragments, but a single, though immense, organism, filled with the tide of one strong pulsating life from end to end. The visit to holy places as an imperative religious duty has made wide travelling a national habit in India in all ages of life, with young and old alike, and travelling in ages preceding the era of steam and mechanical transport could not but promote a deep knowledge of the tracts traversed which is easily escaped by modern globe-trotters. It was this supremely Indian institution in fact which served in the past in place of the modern railway and facilities for travel to promote popular movements from place to place and intercommunication between parts producing a perception of the whole. It allowed no parochial, provincial sense to grow up which might interfere with the growth of the idea of the geographical unity of the mighty motherland; allowed no sense of physical comforts to stand in the way of the sacred duty of intimately knowing one's mother country; and softened the severities of old world travelling by breaking the pilgrim's route by a holy halting place at short intervals. It is difficult indeed to count up the innumerable sacred spots which an overflowing religious feeling has planted throughout India.

This excerpt captures the essence of my deliberations in the previous section on the vast differences in the land ontology of the European coloniser and indigenous societies. From its mountains to its rivers, almost every geographical feature of Bharat is treated as a place of pilgrimage, which brings out the triple matrix of nature, faith and patriotism that was used to forge cultural unity while keeping the diversity alive. In fact, according to Mookerji, the institution of pilgrimage not only sanctified the parts but also mandated reverence of the whole. For instance, worship of the seven rivers, the seven mountains, the seven cities, the four abodes of pilgrimage and the like created and strengthened the idea of Bharat as a sacred geography. As a consequence, the people were not merely encouraged but also enjoined to see themselves as citizens of a living civilisation whose territorial metes and bounds were deeply embedded in popular memory through traditions, prayers and rituals. The network of shrines spread across the length and breadth of the land naturally triggered a movement of people so that their allegiance to vibrant regional identities did not submerge or prevail over the civilisational identity. Simply put, from the Vedic period to the time of Adi Shankaracharya, the establishment of a network of pilgrimages in the extremities of the land has served to reinforce respect for nature and the fundamental unity of this land and its people as the inheritors of one civilisation with federal components contained within its bosom. Mookerji supports this central assertion in the book with multiple references from what he calls 'Hindu Sources' and what we may call Indic OET in the context of our discussion.

While these sources served as positive proof of an identified landmass being associated with a specific culture, the negative proof, according to Mookerji, lay in the fact that all these objects of veneration, that is, the foci and loci of religious and cultural identities were located within the same geography as opposed to in a distant land. He substantially reiterates this position in his work *Nationalism in Hindu Culture* (1921)[16]; however, what takes the discussion forward is his view that the principal sects of Hinduism not only advanced Indic spiritual thought but also strengthened the bonds of their followers to this land by not limiting themselves to any particular part of the country. According to Mookerji[17]:

All the subordinate sects of Hinduism stand on the common platform of a larger outlook, an imperial conception of the geographical integrity and individuality of the mighty motherland; all the creeds have a common catholicity so far as a devotion to the motherland, a sense of its complete sacredness, are concerned the sacredness not merely of the whole, but of each and all of its parts....

... Thus if one is a Saiva, the Sastras present before him the necessity of his cultivation of the conception of the totality of that vast area throughout which are scattered the various places consecrated to the worship of the great God Siva. If he wants to be a genuine devotee of his God, he must visit all these various places, each of which has been exalted into a holy place for its association with one out of the innumerable aspects of the deity....

... Similarly for the Vaishnava are singled out innumerable sacred places distributed throughout the country in all its four quarters, so that he may be trained in a wider geographical consciousness and made to identify himself with the interests of a much larger country transcending the narrow limitations of his original place of birth....

... Thus, whether the Hindu is a Saiva, or a Vaishnava, or a Sakta in his choice of the special mode of his spiritual culture, he is bound to cultivate in common with all his co-religionists the sense of an expanded geographical consciousness, which alone can contribute to the expansion of his mind and soul. Indeed, it has been rightly assumed and asserted that the physical geography of India has partially influenced her history and shaped and moulded the course of her culture and civilisation.

It is evident that the objective of establishing such networks even for individual sects was to prevent any sense of regional parochialism from informing the faith of the worshipper, apart from, of course, seeking to disseminate their philosophy in the entirety of Bharat. Consequently, the deities and the devout belong to all of Bharat and all of Bharat belongs to the deities and the devout. This firm territorial connection between Indic OET systems and Bharat is what makes the Indic OET native to this land and, as a corollary, also explains why the OETs that inspire and drive Middle Eastern and European colonialities are not native to it. This is not a matter of subjective opinion or expression of xenophobia of any kind but is a statement of fact.

The other important layer that needs to be peeled away is that while the term 'nationalism' has indeed been used by scholars, such as Mookerji, to make a case for Indian nationalism based on Hindu nationalism, their use of 'nationalism' was meant to signify Bharat acting as a single political unit without taking away the civilisational character of Bharat. In that sense, Mookerji's reference is to 'civilisational nationalism', that is, a living federal civilisation that acts as one insofar as the rest of the world is concerned. This is obviously very different from the European conception of a nation whose condition precedent is internal homogeneity.

At this juncture, before I proceed to discuss Mookerji's views further on Bharat's civilisation and his prescriptions for its politico-legal and social infrastructure, a relevant digression is warranted to credibly demonstrate the manner in which the sum and substance of Mookerji's cogitation resonated with the framers of the Indian Constitution. While in the next section of this book and the sequels to this book I will examine if Bharat's movement towards a constitution and the Constitution itself are informed by coloniality/colonial consciousness, there is indeed credible material that reasonably establishes the following:

1. The framers of the Constitution acknowledged the umbilical cord that connects independent Bharat with its civilisational history; and
2. The presence of 'India, that is Bharat' in Article 1 of the Constitution is the consequence of civilisationally conscious suggestions that were put forth by several members of the Constituent Assembly, which were ultimately accepted.

In support of the first point, I will place reliance on the Objectives Resolution adopted by the Constituent Assembly on 22 January 1947, which is as follows[18]:

(1) This Constituent Assembly declares its firm and solemn resolve to proclaim India as an Independent Sovereign Republic and to draw up for her future governance a Constitution:
(2) WHEREIN the territories that now comprise British India, the territories that now form the Indian States, and such other parts of India as are outside British India and the States as well as such other territories as are willing to be constituted into the Independent Sovereign India, shall be a Union of them all; and

(3) WHEREIN the said territories, whether with their present boundaries or with such others as may be determined by the Constituent Assembly and thereafter according to law of the Constitution, shall possess and retain the status of autonomous units, together with residuary powers, and exercise all powers and functions of government and administration, save and except such powers and functions as are vested in or assigned to the Union, or as are inherent or implied in the Union or resulting therefrom, and

(4) WHEREIN all power and authority of the Sovereign Independent India, its constituent parts and organs of government, are derived from the people; and

(5) WHEREIN shall be guaranteed and secured to all the people of India justice, social, economic, and political; equality of status, of opportunity, and before the law; freedom of thought, expression, belief, faith, worship, vocation, association and action, subject to law and public morality; and

(6) WHEREIN adequate safeguards shall be provided for minorities, backward and tribal areas, and depressed and other backward classes; and

(7) WHEREBY shall be maintained the integrity of the territory of the Republic and its sovereign rights on land, sea and air according to justice and the law of civilised nations; and

(8) this *ancient land* attains its rightful and honoured place in the world and make its full and willing contribution to the promotion of world peace and the welfare of mankind. [emphasis added]

Clearly, the framers of the Constitution expressly acknowledged that they were not founding a hitherto non-existent country, but were, in fact, putting together a statist apparatus for an ancient civilisation of which they were descendants. In fact, there is nothing in the Constituent Assembly debates that suggests that the framers of the Constitution operated under the belief that Bharat was a synthetic product of colonial efforts or that

Bharat owed its very existence to the Constitution. In other words, there is no basis for the colonialised myth that Bharat was created by the British coloniser prior to which it lacked a sense of self and history.

With regard to the use of 'India, that is Bharat' in Article 1 of the Constitution, for the limited purposes of the specific discussion at hand, let us start from the point where the Draft Constitution prepared by the Drafting Committee[19] was taken up for a clause-by-clause debate by the Constituent Assembly for the first time on 15 November 1948, after the Draft Constitution was presented to the Assembly on 4 November 1948. The Draft Article 1 of the Draft Constitution read as follows:

1.   (1)   *India* shall be a Union of States.

      (2)   The States shall mean the States for the time being specified in Parts I, II and III of the First Schedule.

      (3)   The territory of India shall comprise-

          (a)   The territories of the States;

          (b)   The territories for the time being specified in Part IV of the First Schedule; and

          (c)   Such other territories as may be acquired. [emphasis added]

The said Article was considered and debated in the Constituent Assembly on 15 November 1948, 17 November 1948, 17 September 1949 and 18 September 1949. From the debates of 15 November 1948, following are the relevant excerpts on the amendments proposed to the Draft Article 1 on the issue of the naming of the country[20]:

ARTICLE 1.

Shri M. Ananthasyanam Ayyangar (Madras: General): Sir, I submit that amendments Nos. 83 to 96, both inclusive, may kindly be allowed to stand over. They relate to the alternative names, or rather the substitution of names—BHARAT,

BHARAT VARSHA, HINDUSTAN—for the word INDIA, in Article 1, clause (1).

It requires some consideration. Through you I am requesting the Assembly to kindly pass over these items and allow these amendments to stand over for some time. A few days later when we come to the Preamble these amendments might be then taken up. I am referring to amendments Nos. 83 to 96, both inclusive, and also amendment No. 97 which reads:

'That in clause (1) of article 1, for the word "India" the word "Bharat (India)" and for the word "States" the word "Provinces" be substituted.'

So I would like all these to stand over.

Mr. Vice-President: Is that agreed to by the House?

Honourable Members: Yes.

Shri Lokanath Misra (Orissa: General): Of course I would have no objection, Sir, if you defer consideration of these amendments for two or three days, but I beg to bring to your notice that amendment No. 85, which stands in my name, does not only mean to change the name of India into 'Bharatavarsha', but it means something more and I am afraid if you hold over this amendment those things would be inappropriate at a later stage. I am submitting that I may be allowed to move this amendment, of course without committing myself to the change of the name of India to 'Bharatavarsha' or otherwise. Though I am not insisting on the change of name just now, I ask that I may be allowed to move the other part of my amendment.

Shri M. Ananthasayanam Ayyangar: My request was that amendments relating only to the name may stand over and in his case on the understanding that the word 'India' be changed to some other name, he may move his amendment. I am not asking that the other portion of this amendment may not be moved.

Mr. Vice-President: So the Honourable Member may take the opportunity of moving the second part of his amendment at the proper place.

In addition to the above-proposed amendments with respect to constitutionally naming the country as Bharat, the insertion of Part I-A to the Constitution after Part I was proposed by Shibban Lal Saksena. Following is the relevant portion of the amendment proposed by him:

Prof. Shibban Lal Saksena (United Provinces: General): Mr. Vice-President, Sir, the amendment moved by Mr. Tyagi is a very important amendment. I have myself given notice of a similar amendment (No. 189) which runs as follows:

'That the following new Part be inserted after Part I and the subsequent Parts and articles be renumbered accordingly:-

Part I-A General Principles

6. The name of the Union shall be BHARAT.

7. Bharat shall be a sovereign, independent, democratic, socialist Republic.

8. All powers of government, legislative, executive and judicial, shall be derived from the people, and shall be exercisable only by or on the authority of the organs of the government established by this Constitution.

9. The National Flag of Bharat shall be the tricolour of saffron, white and green of pure hand-spun and hand-woven Khadi cloth, with the Dharmachakra of Asoka inscribed in blue in the centre in the middle stripe, the ratio between the width and breath being 2:1.

10. Hindi written in the Devanagri script shall be the National language of Bharat:

Provided that each State in the Union shall have the right to choose its own regional language as its State language in addition to Hindi for use inside that particular State.

11. English shall be the second official language of Bharat during the transition period of the first five years of the inauguration of this Constitution.

12. The National Anthem of Bharat shall be the "Vandemataram" which is reproduced in the Second Scheduled.

[Note:- The subsequent Schedules be renumbered accordingly.]

13. The Arms of Bharat consist of the Three Lions above the pedestal and the Dharmachakra, as are depicted on the top of the Asoka pillar at Sarnath.

14. The capital of Bharat is the City of Delhi.'

Since the question of naming of the country was agreed to be adjourned to another date, it was taken up on 17 November 1948.[21] However, on the said date, Pandit Govind Ballabh Pant wanted it deferred on the ground that the members of the Assembly had 'not been able to reach unanimity on this important point'. Another member, Seth Govind Das, in support of the substitution of India with Bharat, was also of the view that the decision must be taken unanimously since it related to the very naming of the country and affected how the rest of the world perceived the country. Dr. Ambedkar too threw his weight behind the decision to defer the issue once again, and accordingly, the matter was postponed for future consideration. Following are the relevant excerpts of the debate of 17 November 1948:

Mr. Vice-President: I find that so far as item No. 85 is concerned the first part of it may be moved as the other portion has been disposed of already. I therefore call upon Mr. Lokanath Misra to move the first part.

The Honourable Pandit Govind Ballabh Pant (United Provinces: General): Sir, I move that we now pass on the Article 2 and postpone discussion on the remaining amendments to Article 1. So far we have not been able to reach unanimity on this important point. I am not without hope that if the discussion is postponed, it may be possible to find some solution that may be acceptable to all. So, nothing will be lost. After all we have to take the decision, today, tomorrow or the day after: nobody will suffer thereby, but if we can find something that satisfies everybody, I think the House will feel all the stronger for facing the tasks that lie ahead of it. I hope there will be no difference of opinion on this point and I do not see why there should be any opposition from any quarter. After all, we will take the decision. Nobody else is going to add to or diminish the strength of any section or of any group here, and we are not here as sections or groups. Every one of us is here to make the best contribution towards the solution of these most intricate, complicated and difficult problems and if we handle them with a little patience, I hope we will be able to settle them more satisfactorily than we would otherwise. So, I suggest that the discussion on the rest of the amendments to Article 1 be postponed.

Shri H.V. Kamath (C.P. and Berar: General): Mr. Vice-President, Sir, I appreciate the arguments that have been advanced by my honourable Friend, Pandit Govind Ballabh Pant. I only wish to know from you, Sir, for how long a time these amendments Nos. 85 to 96 both inclusive are going to be held over. It will create, I submit, Sir, a very bad impression in the outside world and in our own country, if we go on postponing the consideration of the amendments dealing with the very first word in the very first clause.

Honourable Members: No, no.

Shri H.V. Kamath: And if we go on postponing the consideration of these amendments indefinitely, it would certainly create a bad impression. I want to know, therefore, for how long I will be held over.

Shri R.K. Sidhwa (C.P. and Berar: General): Sir, I am rather surprised at the argument advanced by my honourable Friend, Mr. Kamath that if we postpone this matter indefinitely the outside world will be rather surprised. On the contrary, if we come to a satisfactory solution and a unanimous decision on this matter, the outside world will have really a very high opinion of this House. I feel, therefore, that the suggestion made by my honourable Friend Pandit Pant should certainly be accepted unanimously. I am rather surprised that of all persons Mr. Kamath should have come forward to speak in this manner. What Pandit Pant stated was really a very fine solution and I was expecting from this House that instead of creating any kind of dissension, if we really come to a unanimous decision, it will be really a record in the history of this Constitution. I therefore, very heartily and strongly support the motion moved by my honourable friend, Pandit Pant.

The Honourable Dr. B.R. Ambedkar: I support the suggestion made by Pandit Govind Ballabh Pant.

Seth Govind Das (C.P. and Berar: General): Sir, I wholeheartedly support Pandit Pant's proposition. The House very well knows how clear I am for naming our country BHARAT, but at the same time, we must try to bring unanimity of every group in this House. Of course, if that is not possible, we can go our own ways; but up to the time there was any possibility of reaching a unanimous decision by any compromise, that effort must be made. Sir, I Support this proposition, and I hope that by the efforts of our leaders, there will not be any division on fundamental points like this, and not only this proposition, but other propositions also, like that our national language, national script etc., we shall be able to carry unanimously. I, therefore, support the views just expressed by the Honourable Pandit Pant.

Shri H.V. Kamath: I only wanted to know for how long the amendments will be held over.

An Honourable Member: It may be a day, a week or a fortnight.

Mr. Vice-President: I hold that a discussion of these few clauses should be held over till sufficient time has been given for arriving at some sort of understanding. This will be to the best interests of the House and of the country at large.

The next time the issue was taken up for significant discussion by the Assembly was on 17 September 1949, that is, after close to a year of its introduction. Dr. Ambedkar brought up the Draft Article 1 at the fag end of the session on the said date as follows[22]:

> Mr. President: There is one more article, article 1.
>
> The Honourable Dr. B.R. Ambedkar: Sir, I propose to move amendment No. 130 and incorporate in it my amendment No. 197 which makes a little verbal change in sub-clause (2).
>
> Sir, I move:
>
> 'That for clauses (1) and (2) of article 1, the following clauses be substituted:-
>
> (1) India, that is, Bharat shall be a Union of States.
>
> (2) The States and the territories thereof shall be the States and their territories for the time being specified in Parts 1, 11 and 111 of the First Schedule.'

It bears noting that the language of Draft Article 1, as originally contained in the Draft Constitution in November 1948 presented to the Assembly by Dr. Ambedkar, did not contain 'Bharat' in it. In contrast, when Draft Article 1 was taken up for discussion on 17 September 1949, the version moved by Dr. Ambedkar replaced the original Draft version with 'India, that is, Bharat'. It may be reasonably inferred that Dr. Ambedkar agreed, in principle, with the amendments proposed by Lokanath Misra and Shibban Lal Saksena. However, this time Maulana Hasrat Mohani wanted the discussion to be adjourned to the next day citing paucity of time to discuss such a cardinal provision. That said, his primary objection was *not* to the insertion of Bharat in Draft Article 1, but was with respect to the use of 'Union of States' since he favoured the concept of a republic as opposed to a Union of States. After a

lot of back and forth on the issue of adjournment, the matter
was finally adjourned to another date. This effectively meant
that the question of the naming of the country was taken up
meaningfully only on 18 September 1949, which was the date
on which the Article was finally adopted.[23]

On 18 September, when the issue was finally taken up,
H.V. Kamath proposed Bharat and Hind as alternatives to India.
Following is the relevant excerpt of the debate, which also
showcases Dr. Ambedkar's brusqueness in hearing out other
members of the Assembly on such an important issue:

Mr. President: The House will now take up article 1. I think
Mr. Kamath has moved amendment 220 and finished his speech.

Shri H.V. Kamath: I have not finished my speech, Sir.

Mr. President: Then, go ahead.

Shri H.V. Kamath: I move

'That in amendment No. 130 of List IV (Eighth Week),
for the proposed clause (1) of article 1, the following be
substituted:-

"(1) Bharat or, in the English language, India, shall be a
Union of States."'

or, alternatively, 'That in amendment No. 130 of List IV
(Eighth Week), for the proposed clause (1) of article 1, the
following be substituted:

"(1) Hind, or, in the English language, India, shall be a
Union of States."'

...Taking my first amendment first, amendment No. 220,
it is customary among most peoples of the world to have
what is called a *Namakaran* or a naming ceremony for the
new-born. India as a Republic is going to be born very
shortly and naturally there has been a movement in the
country among many sections—almost all sections—of
the people that this birth of the new Republic should be
accompanied by a *Namakaran* ceremony as well. There are
various suggestions put forward as to the proper name which

should be given to this new baby of the Indian Republic. The prominent suggestions have been Bharat, Hindustan, Hind and Bharatbhumi or Bharatvarsh and names of that kind. At this stage it would be desirable and perhaps profitable also to go into the question as to what name is best suited to this occasion of the birth of the new baby—the Indian Republic. Some say, why name the baby at all? India will suffice. Well and good. If there was no need for a *Namakaran* ceremony we could have continued India, but if we grant this point that there must be a new name to this baby, then of course the question arises as to what name should be given.

Now, those who argue for Bharat or Bharatvarsh or Bharatbhumi, take their stand on the fact that this is the most ancient name of this land. Historians and philologists have delved deep into this matter of the name of this country, especially the origin of this name Bharat. All of them are not agreed as to the genesis of this name Bharat. Some ascribe it to the son of Dushyant and Shakuntala who was also known as 'Sarvadamana' or all-conqueror and who established his suzerainty and kingdom in this ancient land. After him this land came to be known as Bharat. Another school of research scholars hold that Bharat dates back to Vedic...

The Honourable Dr. B.R. Ambedkar (Bombay: General): Is it necessary to trace all this? I do not understand the purpose of it. It may be well Interesting in some other place. My Friend accepts the word 'Bharat'. The only thing is that he has got an alternative. I am very sorry but there ought to be some sense of proportion, in view of the limited time before the House.

Shri H.V. Kamath: I hope it is not for Dr. Ambedkar to regulate the business of the House.

On being pressed by the President of the Assembly to choose between Bharat and Hind, Kamath chose Bharat and objected to the phrase 'India, that is, Bharat' as proposed by

Dr. Ambedkar since he felt it was 'clumsy' for use in the Constitution. To support his position, Kamath referred to the fourth Article of the Irish Constitution which read as follows:

The name of the State is Eire, or, in the English language, Ireland.

Apart from Kamath, Brajeshwar Prasad too moved an amendment to Draft Article 1 which contained Bharat. The said amendment read as follows:

(1) India, that is, Bharat is one integral unit.

Seth Govind Das preferred Bharat to India and relied on the Vedas, the Upanishads, the *Vishnu Purana*, the *Brahma Purana* and the works of the Chinese monk and traveller Hiuen Tsang to make his case for Bharat. Kallur Subba Rao supported Das citing the *Rig Veda* and the *Vayu Purana*, with the geographical metes and bounds of Bharat being identified as follows:

It means that land that is to the south of the Himalayas and north of the (Southern ocean) Samundras is called Bharat.

B.M. Gupta, Ram Sahai and Kamalapathi Tripathi too favoured the use of Bharat and insisted that Bharat be used before India in Article 1 if Dr. Ambedkar insisted on retaining India in Article 1. Tripathi's contentions in this regard are in perfect sync with the spirit of decoloniality and the reclamation of self-identity. Following are a few relevant excerpts:

Sir, I am enamoured of the historic name of 'Bharat'. Even the mere uttering of this word conjures before us by a stroke of magic the picture of cultured life of the centuries that have gone by. In my opinion, there is no other country in the world which has such a history, such a culture, and such a name, whose age is counted in millenniums as our country has. There is no country in the world which has been able to preserve its name and its genius even after undergoing the amount of repression, the insults and prolonged slavery which our country had to pass through. Even after thousands of years, our country is still known as 'Bharat'. Since Vedic times, this name has been appearing in our literature. Our Puranas have all through eulogised the name of Bharat. The gods have been remembering the name of this country in the heavens.

The gods have a keen desire to be born in the sacred land of Bharat and to achieve their supreme goal after passing their lives here. For us, this name is full of sacred remembrances. The moment we pronounce this name, the pictures of our ancient history and ancient glory and our ancient culture come to our minds. We are reminded that this is the country where in past ages great men and great Maharishis gave birth to a great culture. That culture not only spread over all the different areas of this land, but crossing its borders, reached every corner of the Far East too. We are reminded that on the one hand, this culture reached the Mediterranean and on the other it touched the shores of the Pacific. We are reminded that thousands of years ago, the leaders and thinkers of this country moulded a great nation and extended their culture to all the four corners of the world and achieved for themselves a position of prestige. When we pronounce, this word, we are reminded of the Mantras of the Rig Veda uttered by our *Maharishis* in which they have described the vision of truth and soul-experience. When we pronounce this word, we are reminded of those brave words of the Upanishads which urged humanity to awake, to arise, and to achieve its goal. When we pronounce this word, we are reminded of those words of Lord Krishna through which he taught a practical philosophy to the people of this country—the philosophy which can enable humanity even to lay to achieve its goal of peace and bless. When we pronounce this word, we are reminded of Lord Buddha, who had boldly told men all over the world that greatest good of the greatest number, greatest happiness of the largest number and the welfare of humanity should be the watch-words of their lives and that they should awake and arise to promote the welfare of mortals and gods and to show to the world the path of knowledge. When we pronounce this word, we are reminded of Shankaracharya, who gave a new vision to the world. When we pronounce this word, we are reminded of the mighty arms of Bhagwan Rama which by twanging the chord of the bow sent echoes through the Himalayas, the seas around this land and the heavens. When we pronounce this word, we are reminded of the wheel of Lord Krishna which destroyed the terrible, Imperialism of Kshatriyas from India and relieved this land of its burden.

Hargovind Pant was in favour of using 'Bharatvarsha' and was keen on doing away with India altogether since he felt that clinging to India was proof of a colonialised mindset. Extracted below are his views on the subject:

Shri Hargovind Pant: (United Provinces: General): Mr. President, during the early sittings of the Assembly I had moved an amendment to the effect that for the name of the country, we should have the word 'Bharat' or 'Bharat Varsha' in place of 'India'. I am gratified to see that some change in the name has at last been accepted. I, however, fail to understand why the word 'Bharat Varsha' is not acceptable to the House when the importance and glory of this word is being admitted by all here. I do not want to repeat what the other Members have said in regard to the acceptance of this glorious word, but I would make only a few observations in respect of this word.

The word 'Bharat' or 'Bharat Varsha' is used by us in our daily religious duties while reciting the Sankalpa. Even at the time of taking our bath we say in Sanskrit:

'Jamboo Dwipay, Bharata Varshe, Bharat Khande, Aryavartay, etc.'

It means that I so and so, of Aryavart in Bharat Khand, etc. ...

The most celebrated and world-famous poet Kalidasa has used this word in his immortal work depicting the story of his two great characters—King Dushyanta and his queen Shakuntala. The son born of them was named 'Bharat' and his Kingdom was known as 'Bharat'. There are many fascinating descriptions of the heroism of Bharat in our ancient books. It is said that in his childhood he used to play with lion cubs and overpowered them. We are well acquainted with the story of Bharat. I fail to understand, in view of all this, why we are reluctant to accept, from the core of our heart the word 'Bharat Varsha' as the name of our country.

So far as the word 'India' is concerned, the Members seem to have, and really I fail to understand why, some attachment for it. We must know that this name was given to our country by foreigners who having heard of the riches of this land were tempted towards it and had robbed us of our freedom in order to acquire the wealth of our country. If we, even then, cling to the word 'India', it would only show that we are not ashamed of having this insulting word which has been imposed on us by alien rulers. Really, I do not understand why we are accepting this word.

'Bharat' or 'Bharat Varsha' is and has been the name of our country for ages according to our ancient history and tradition and in fact this word inspires enthusiasm and courage... I would, therefore, submit that we should have no hesitation at all in accepting this word. It will be a matter of great shame for us if we do not accept this word and have some other word for the name of our country. I represent the people of the Northern part of India where sacred places like Shri Badrinath, Shri Kedarnath, Shri Bageshwar and Manasarovar are situated. I am placing before you the wishes of the people of this part. I may be permitted to state, Sir, that the people of this area want that the name of our country should be 'Bharat Varsha' and nothing else.

After such detailed discussions, Dr. Ambedkar's amendment, 'India, that is, Bharat', was adopted in Article 1. Notwithstanding the adoption of Dr. Ambedkar's version, which had both India and Bharat in it, it is abundantly clear from the debates that the members of the Constituent Assembly were acutely aware of the civilisational significance of the use of 'Bharat', its identity and its geographical extent as evidenced by Bharat's indigenous epistemology. By adopting a name that harkens back to a civilisational identity that antedates the arrival of both Middle Eastern and European colonialities, the framers of the Constitution cemented the position that independent Bharat is indeed the successor State to the Indic civilisation. This is consistent with my position in the previous chapter wherein I had identified the 'cut-off' period of the eighth century to define Bharat's indigeneity. In this regard, both the framers and Indic scholars, such as Mookerji, are on the same page even with regard to the use of Indic sources to arrive at the same conclusions. Having said that, it could be argued that the use of both India and Bharat represents a dual persona with some identifying more with India and others with Bharat.[24] Decoloniality would require that the name Bharat alone be retained and the tendency to view Bharat through the lens of India must be addressed and rectified in the fields of history, production of knowledge, education and the law.

That said, merely because Bharat is a living civilisation in the realm of society, it does not translate to Bharat being a civilisation-state. In other words, a State that presides over a civilisation is not a civilisation-state; instead, a State that is conscious of the civilisational character of its society and structures itself on civilisational lines is a civilisation-state. Therefore, one needs to go beyond the name Bharat to understand if the manner in which the Indian State has been structured and functions is alive to the fact that the society it presides over is a federal civilisation and not a nation in the European sense. Specifically, for the Indian State to be treated as an Indic civilisation-state, we would need to examine whether the State has been built on the fundamental building blocks of this civilisation and whether its political and social infrastructure viewed through the prism of its Constitution is designed to replace the colonial consciousness with Indic consciousness.

This takes us back to Mookerji's *The Fundamental Unity of India*, where he spells out what has been and must be the framework of Bharat as a civilisation-state as well as the principles for harmonious coexistence between sovereign nations based on Bharat's internal experience. The civilisational treatment of Bharat is again implicit in the latter approach for it treats Bharat as the microcosm of the world, not because of some divine mandate but because its sheer diversity and existence as a single civilisational unit for millennia are treated as exemplars for the rest of the world.

Given that Mookerji's conclusion has several layers that warrant unpacking in the context of multiple current-day debates surrounding Bharat's handling of consciousness and identity-related issues, I have reproduced a significant portion of it below to pull each of the threads it touches upon:

> Where the country is more a cultural than a material possession, it appeals less to the instinct of appropriation. There is more of disinterested sharing, more of community of life and enjoyment. India thus early became the happy home of many races, cults, and cultures, coexisting in concord, without seeking overlordship or mutual extermination. With this high and complex initial responsibility India becomes the land of composite systems in respect of race, language, civil and personal law, social structure, and religious cult. Other national systems exclude the possibility of such radical diversities, and break down in the attempt to unify them.

Federation and Imperialism have perhaps been born too late for their task.

Such composite systems are built up necessarily on the basis of an extended unit of society. Here the social and political composition is based on the group, and not the individual, as the unit: e.g. the family, the village community, the caste, and various other similar corporations, of which a special study is made in another work of mine entitled *Local Government in Ancient India* (Clarendon Press, Oxford, 2nd ed., 1920). Such a principle of social construction minimises the friction and collision of atomic units and helps to harmonise the parts in and through the whole. Biologically speaking, such constructions correspond to the more developed forms of organic life which, in their nervous interconnections, show a greater power of integration than the looser and more incoherent organisms lower down in the evolutionary series.

Accordingly, it should be further noted, it is the quasi-instinctive postulates and conventions of group-life which come to be formulated as law, and not the mandate, command, or decree of a single, central authority in the State. Law, under these conditions, is not an artifice, but a natural growth of consensus and communal life. Thus, ever new social and political constructions arise by the original and direct action of the groups and communities in the State, and not by the intervention of the absolute sovereign power and its creative fiats, as under all centralised constitutions. The nationality formed on such principles is a composite nationality, and not one of the rigid, unitary type.

The relation of the State to its constituent groups becomes, under this scheme, one of copartnership, each maintaining the others in their place. It is not the State that, by its sanction or charter, creates its own constituent bodies or corporations, but, on the other hand, the groups establish, and are established by, the State. The genius of the Hindus has adhered firmly to this fundamental principle of political organisation amidst the most trying and adverse conditions in the course of their history. Even when the State ceased to be a national or organic one (as under the Mahomedan rule, for instance) they fell back upon the resources and possibilities of that ultimate political creed to work out the necessary adjustments and adaptations to the new situation as means of their self-preservation as a people. They clung fast to their time-honoured and confirmed conception of the State, which was based upon a respect for the original and primary rights of group-life, for the sanctity of natural groupings, the inviolability of the vital modes of human association, to which a full scope was, accordingly, never denied. And thus, the Hindu State came naturally to be associated, and indeed very largely identified, with a multitude of institutions and corporations of diverse types, structures, and functions, in and through which the many-sided genius of the race expressed itself. It was these intermediate bodies between the individual and the State which mattered most to the life of the people, to the conservation of their culture, as the real seats and centres of national activity.

Accordingly, when a State of this complex composition and structure happens to pass under foreign control, the nation can maintain the freedom of its life and culture by means of that larger and more vital part of the State which is not amenable to foreign control, and is, by design, independent of the central authority. An elaborately devised machinery of social and economic self-government amply safeguards the interests of national life and culture. What is lost is but an inferior and insignificant limb of the body politic: its more vital organs are quite intact. It is as if the mere outwork has fallen the main stronghold of national life stands firm and entire against the onslaughts of alien aggression, protected by a deep and wide gulf of separation and aloofness from the domain of central authority, which can find no points of substantial contact with the life of the people and no means of controlling the institutions expressing and moulding that life. It is thus that Hindu culture has had a continuous history uninterrupted by the foreign domination to which a national culture would otherwise succumb.

A complete exposition of this composite type of nationality and polity, such as stands to the credit of India as her special achievement, must wait for another opportunity and occasion. But, in passing, we may as well broadly indicate the lines of its actual operation, and also of its possibilities as an instrument for the unification of the human race or the federation of man. The principles of the Indian political constructions tend naturally, as a closer analysis will show, to reconcile the conflicting claims, and ideals of Nationalism and Internationalism in a stable synthesis towards which the League of Nations is hopelessly striving. The relations obtaining within the State between the central authority and the constituent groups on which depend so largely its internal order and peace, form the plan and pattern of its external relations also. Comparative politics, indeed, point to a kind of correspondence between the principles governing the internal constitution of States and the principles governing their external expansion. The intra-State and the inter-State relations are fundamentally of the same type. The State that is of a central type, and thus absorbs the original and originating groups in its own unitary life, will also exhibit the same militarist spirit of domination and aggression in its movement of expansion by absorbing other States. Similarly, the expansion or extension of the Indian State will not be a process of absorption by assimilation or extermination of external States, neighbourly or rival, but will be governed by those principles, already referred to, which regulate the internal constitution of the State itself in relation to its constituent groups. Those are the principles of a generous comprehension that broaden the basis of an inter-State convention under which all subject peoples are established in their own conventions and all subject States in their own constitution or customary law.

The problems before the League of Nations, of reconciling the self-determination of individual sovereign States with the interests of the collective brotherhood of all the States, will defy solution under the militarist and unitary principles of political formation, such as we meet with in the West, but they are amenable to the other method of comprehension which has been explained as the basic principle of the Indian type of State in both its internal and external relations. It is hoped that the Indian experiment in Nationality which seeks, and is called upon, to unify different ethnic stocks and cultures, different systems of law and cult, different groups and corporations, in an all-embracing and all-comprehensive polity, will be found to be a much-needed guide in our progress towards that 'far-off divine event to which the whole creation moves,' peace on earth and goodwill among men.

This conclusion must be read over and over to truly appreciate Mookerji's deep and penetrative understanding of the nature of a civilisation and the role of the State in a civilisational society. Today, when the concept of a civilisation-state is being casually thrown around as a cosmetic talking point, Mookerji's views are an educative read from an application perspective.

First, when he calls Bharat more of a cultural possession than a material one, Mookerji strikes a clear distinction between the territorial nationalism of the European coloniser and the cultural veneration of the Indic native. It is this cultural veneration and a sense of relational custodianship, to put it in the language of decoloniality, as opposed to a sense of territorial ownership, that has made it possible for Bharat to be a melting pot of diverse sects that have coexisted *within* the Dharmic fold. This is precisely what separates the Indic civilisational worldview from those that drive Middle Eastern and European colonialities, which are founded on the firm belief of domination or annihilation of identities that do not conform to their own, and that they have been divinely ordained to expand territorially in the service of their respective belief systems.

As long as this divergence and incompatibility remain, Indic civilisational consciousness has no option but to approach both colonialities with a sense of justified circumspection and vigilance given their respective histories in Bharat and in the rest of the world. In fact, I would go to the extent of stating that since Bharat is the only natural homeland for the Indic consciousness, the Indian State has the civilisational duty to ensure that this space remains as such, and the accommodation of any other consciousness is contingent on (*a*) respect for the undeniable and inseparable relationship between Bharat and the Indic consciousness, and (*b*) giving up those tenets that dehumanise the Indic consciousness or call for its extermination, whether scripturally sanctioned or not.

Second, inherent in the treatment of Bharat as a cultural possession as opposed to a material one is the respect for, nay deification of its geographical features. The retention of this relational land ontology as part of Bharat's mindset is critical for the preservation of its indigenous consciousness. This affects its political approach to its geography and borders as much as it affects its approach to what constitutes 'development'. This would translate to the principle that no part of this sacred geography must be tested solely on the anvils of its utility as a natural resource. To this culturally rooted perspective, it does not make a difference whether 'even a blade of grass' grows or not, or whether a particular part of this geography is 'useless uninhabitable land'. That such words were used by the first prime minister of Bharat, Jawaharlal Nehru, in 1962 to describe a part of this sacred geography, and that too in the backdrop of Chinese aggression, is a reflection of how far removed Bharat was even in 1962 from its cultural spirit of veneration and deification of all parts of its geography to instead employ a cold, downright utilitarian and territorial approach. In my opinion, that every inch of this land is sacred and its sanctity is inviolable is a greater driving force in preserving its integrity than the mercantile territorial European approach that appears to have seeped into Bharat's consciousness over time.

This subversion of the Indic perspective is equally reflected in the manner in which Bharat treats its geography on issues of development. The civilisational logic behind the treatment of ecologically fragile or sensitive areas as sacred pilgrimage spots appears to have been completely lost on the 'modern' Indian State. This is because the State seems obsessed with 'religious tourism' and 'ecotourism', with diminishing respect for the fundamental matrix of nature, faith and patriotism that informs and makes this civilisation. Critically, this matrix includes respect for the rights of non-humans and their habitat. Bharat's civilisation is not one that reduces nature to just another branch of study, namely 'environmentalism', to be ticked off as just another box in an environmental impact assessment checklist. Instead, it puts nature right at the heart of its worldview and sees divinity in every aspect, form and manifestation of nature. From such lofty heights that directly affected ecological balance, and therefore survival, for this civilisation to now put development and nature in two different baskets with the former being treated as the priority is the clearest reflection of the pervasion of colonial consciousness. Pointing this out may invite labels, such as 'tree hugger', 'luddite' or being 'anti-development', but all of these are terms typically used in the West, thereby exposing the coloniality even in the reactions. In other words, neither is the contemporary position on development indigenous nor is the response to those who oppose colonialised development. The absence of indigeneity could not have been starker.

In my opinion, this attitude is not limited to any particular dispensation, notwithstanding public professions of commitment to the consciousness of this land, the difference being only in intent and degree. While one dispensation may actively promote coloniality because it sees nothing of value in the past and has effectively surrendered indigenous agency at the feet of either or both colonialities, the other may see some value in native consciousness and yet suffer from unconscious coloniality. Also, the degree of coloniality varies in different spheres depending on exposure, exigency and expediency. That said, it would be unfair to draw false symmetries between dispensations because the dispensation and the establishment that presided over the formative years of independent Bharat must necessarily assume the primary responsibility for the entrenched coloniality at the level of society. Critically, this entrenchment was facilitated by continuing with colonial education that has played a significant role in colonialising successive generations, and it is not an easy task by any standard to reverse the damage already done.

Further, apart from the apparatus of the State, the indigenous society of Bharat too must take some measure of responsibility for leaving matters of culture and civilisation entirely to the State, which goes against the grain of its civilisational thinking. In the process, over the decades, Bharat's indigenous society has ceded its institutional independence and capabilities at the feet of the State. As a consequence, it now finds itself deprived of the means of self-reliance and at the mercy of a State that, for the most part, has pandered to the very colonialities whose animus towards Indic consciousness is a matter of historical fact. Therefore, notwithstanding the time, effort and resources that may be required, decoloniality is an existential civilisational imperative that must be undertaken, at the very least in the critical realms of nature, knowledge and faith (which are interconnected), history, education, development and the law in order for the society to reflect its civilisational consciousness in its future electoral priorities, choices and policies.

Third, from the perspective of the treatment of various sub-identities that form part of the larger Indic civilisational fabric, recognition of the federal character of this civilisation is critical from the perspective of formulation of law and policy, which have a bearing on the sub-identities and their relationship with the whole. This is particularly relevant in the realms of faith, history, production of knowledge, education, language and preservation of ways of life, including personal laws. Therefore, when 'uniformity' in any realm, including and especially in civil law, is the subject of deliberation, the federal character of this civilisation and the reasons for its survival must be borne in mind before resorting to a European-style 'national' treatment of a federal civilisation. At least in the context of Bharat, the whole is as strong as its parts and the survival of the parts is contingent on the existence of the whole. Preserving this balance is easier said than done but as long as the State is committed to preserving this balance and is also *seen* as being committed to it, it would be keeping intact the civilisational, political and territorial integrity of Bharat by protecting it against centrifugal impulses, either homegrown or external.

To this end, Mookerji underscores two important aspects that are rarely understood in contemporary Bharat given its preoccupation with the rule of law as understood by the European coloniser. Mookerji makes it abundantly clear that one of the direct consequences of existing as a federal civilisation is the recognition that law must be significantly informed by the practices and experiences of the community that is the subject of a legislative measure. The realisation that custom and practice have more wisdom and utility in a society that is civilisationally diverse is the reason laws in ancient Bharat were not top-down impositions by the ruler, but were, more often than not, codifications of the collective experience of a society as long as relevant. In that sense, Mookerji alludes to the fact that perhaps the *Smritis* were more descriptive than prescriptive and a similar approach in contemporary Bharat may serve the cause of 'law and order'. This would also mean that sitting in judgment over the *Smritis* by treating them as prescriptive injunctions or mandates in the sense law is understood by the European makes very little sense since the colonial and Indic understanding of law is starkly different.

The decentralisation and federalisation of the process of lawmaking by turning it into a more organic process that has its pulse on society is one of the biggest takeaways from Mookerji's thoughts. His cautionary note against treating Bharat as a unitary nation-state stripped of its Dharmic federal character warrants serious consideration in the corridors of power regardless of who wields it and whatever their stated ideological persuasions may be.

Fourth, the existential importance of preserving this decentralised and bottom-up approach has been captured with scintillating clarity by Mookerji. Apart from the custom-based evolution of laws, he also highlights the fact that Bharat has typically put faith in the society's freedom and duty to establish institutions that are independent of the State in order to protect and preserve those values which the society holds dear. In other words, the State was expected to create conditions that were conducive to the establishment of institutions that could capably address the society's needs and defend its interests vis-à-vis the State. The creation of such institutions that maintained an arm's length distance from the State allowed the core of the Indic society to remain largely untouched by the disruption of the State apparatus due to repeated Islamic invasions or systematic European Christian colonisation. Unfortunately, these are the very same societal groupings, structures and institutions that have suffered the most in independent 'modern' India since both the Indian State and the indigenous society have taken forward the sanctimony and judgment of the European coloniser with the zeal of a new convert with respect to Bharat's past, resulting in the weakening or destruction of those structures that kept the Indic ways of life alive through the ravages of time and history.

The irony is that, as opposed to appreciating the value of such systems which were independent of the State, every such system (including civilisational nerve centres, such as places of worship) has been brought under the looming shadow of the State in 'modern' India. In the process, the Indic society has been left entirely dependent on the State for preservation of its core interests, while the State continues speeding down the path of greater colonialisation (not colonisation) while paying lip service to Bharat as a civilisational State. This poses a serious and existential challenge to the long-term survival of the Indic consciousness since those worldviews which have historically displayed a marked inability to peacefully coexist with the Indic consciousness have been afforded greater freedom to preserve their societal groupings and institutions with almost no interference by the Indian State, ostensibly in the name of advancement of the rights of 'minorities'. As a consequence, the Indic civilisational worldview finds itself disempowered in its own homeland despite decolonisation. Perhaps, no other country is in such dire need of decoloniality as Bharat given the stepmotherly treatment the Indian State metes out to the adherents of its native consciousness.

Fifth, and I expect to raise quite a few hackles with this point—in a civilisation-state, the core unit is *not* the individual, instead it is the group, rather groups. The logic behind this position is that a European-style nation-state is built on the premise of a 'nation', that is, people bound by one or more factors, such as language, faith or ethnicity. Given the internal homogeneity of a European nation-state, it makes sense and is perhaps more desirable to treat the individual as the core unit whose rights must be safeguarded against intrusion by the State and other individuals. However, in a civilisation-state, every group is rightly interested in protecting its own identity from encroachment by other groups as well as by the State. Such being the case, to claim on the one hand that Bharat is a civilisation-state and to argue on the other that individual rights must remain supreme in a civilisation-state are logically, historically and constitutionally incongruent assertions whose impracticality, coloniality and naiveté are writ large on the face of it. Only a mind thoroughly dyed in Eurocentric/Western-normative ideas on individual rights while paying lip service to Bharat being a civilisation-state, is capable of missing the whole point of a civilisation-state by light-years by treating the individual as the core of a civilisational society.

I must clarify that I do not mean for a moment that the individual has no rights in a civilisation-state, or that in all circumstances and in every conceivable situation the individual's right must give way to the group's interests. However, it is certainly my case that where the individual's whim is couched as a right and has the effect of adversely affecting the interests of the group, or the interests of other groups, or the civilisational interest, the individual's right must necessarily be traded off against the greater good. Even Europe and the West are beginning to see the light of this position given their ongoing tryst with 'multiculturalism' and its impact on European 'national' identities.

Apart from this, it is my considered position that in the context of Bharat, given its history, which has seen the Indic consciousness being subjected to subjugation at an unparalleled scale, the Indic civilisational worldview can only be protected by recognising its group identities and rights. This position is even more applicable in light of the continued demonisation of Bharat by both Middle Eastern and European colonialities, both within and outside Bharat. That this is a question of survival, is certainly not a far-fetched or remotely alarmist position to take since the history of the last 1,300 years speaks volumes for those who are willing to listen and act with honesty and integrity. If this position invites criticisms of being illiberal, it only demonstrates that liberalism has been weaponised to further the ends of coloniality or it is fundamentally colonial, which is perhaps the case. In either case, it is detrimental to indigenous identities. Therefore, decoloniality must confront it head-on since the goals of decoloniality are far more important for indigenous consciousness and, dare I say, the entire world, than the goals of liberalism.

Sixth, Mookerji holds up the Indic civilisational experience as a template worthy of emulation by the rest of the world, both from the perspective of inter- and intra-State relations since Bharat follows the path of accommodation as opposed to assimilation. The former is the approach of a civilisation whereas the latter is the approach of a Europeanised nation-state. That said, while Bharat has certainly accommodated cultures and OET systems whose centres of consciousness are outside its sacred geography, such accommodation has been contingent on such cultures not seeking to annihilate Bharat's indigenous civilisation. Simply put, as long as a non-Indic worldview is capable of coexistence with Bharat's indigenous worldview and does not seek to deny or sever the bonds that tie this land to its culture and its adherents, Bharat provides refuge and shelter to even such worldviews. After all, there are credible instances of groups whose OETs are diametrically opposite to that of Bharat's, and yet they have thrived in Bharat without persecution or loss of their individuality. This is attributable to the fact that they put aside some of their scriptural mandates in the larger interest of coexistence and with a spirit of gratitude towards Bharat's welcoming nature. This is evident from Bharat's provision of refuge to the Jews and Zoroastrians after they were driven out of their respective homelands by pre-Christian European imperialism and Middle Eastern colonialism respectively.

According to Mookerji, the lesson that Bharat's internal experience as a civilisation holds for the rest of the world is that no sovereign power must attempt to impose its values on others, despite its best intentions. So long as international politics is driven by Westphalian nation-state values that contain the seeds of secularised Christian European expansionism and a marked intolerant tolerance for other worldviews, no international body will succeed in securing peace for the world since international law and institutions rest on the universalisation of European provincialism. Conflict is writ large in such an approach. This is precisely why Mookerji was of the view that Bharat's lived experience as a federal civilisation may serve as a beacon of hope for the rest of the world.

And seventh, no part of Mookerji's views on Bharat's civilisational character or the reasons for its fundamental unity rest on the premise of ethnocentrism. In fact, the emphasis on cultural unity is a direct refutation of any accusation of ethnocentrism. Even in responding to the European coloniser's contention that Bharat was never a 'nation', Mookerji does not feel the need to prove that we are a nation bound by a single ethnicity or language or 'religion' in the Christian sense. Instead, his calm response is the rejection of European nationhood as a yardstick for Bharat to pass muster on, and the emphasis on federal civilisationalism as the appropriate lens to understand Bharat. While Mookerji managed to convince a good cross-section of Europeans of his time, the unfortunate contemporary reality is that colonialised Indians still subscribe to colonial assumptions about Bharat and conflate Bharat's cultural unity with ethnocentrism and xenophobia, which demonstrates the internalisation of colonial ethnocentrism and the acceptance of its universal validity. What is more is that Mookerji was not alone in his views; his position on the civilisational character of Bharat, its cultural unity and the causal factors for the same were echoed by yet another stalwart, Jadunath Sarkar, in his book *India Through the Ages* (1928).[25] Following are a few relevant extracts:

The Indian People form one common and distinct type
No careful student of our history can help being struck by one supreme vital characteristic of the Indian people. It is their vitality as a distinct type, with a distinct civilization of their own and a mind as active after centuries of foreign rule as ever in the past. The Indian people of to-day are no doubt a composite ethnical product; but whatever their different constituent elements may have been in origin, they have all acquired a common Indian stamp, and have all been contributing to a common culture and building up a common type of traditions, thought and literature. Even Sir

Herbert Risley, who is so sceptical about the Indians' claim to be considered as one people, has been forced to admit that 'Beneath the manifold diversity of physical and social type, language, custom and religion, which strikes the observer in India, there can still be discerned a certain "underlying uniformity of life from the Himalayas to Cape Comorin". There is in fact an Indian character, a general Indian personality, which we cannot resolve into its component elements.' (*People of India*, 2nd ed., p. 299).

This common Indian type has stood the test of time, it has outlived the shock of dynastic revolutions, foreign invasions, religious conflicts, and widespread natural disasters. Its best right to live is the vital power displayed by it through many thousand years of cataclysmic change in our land.

Sarkar further identifies the 'agencies' that united Bharat despite its physical and human diversities and led to the evolution of a common culture. According to him:

[From] early Hindu times, this internal isolation was often broken and a pan-Indian community of ideas, customs and culture was created by certain agencies. These were: (i) the pilgrim-student, (ii) the soldier of fortune, (iii) the imperial conqueror, and (iv) the son-in-law imported from the centres of blue blood (such as Kanauj or Prayag for Brahmans and Mewar and Marwar in the case of Kshatriyas) for the purpose of hypergamy or raising the social status of a rich man settled among lower castes in a far-off province.

The great holy cities of the different provinces were regarded as sources of sanctity by all Indians alike. They were, besides, seats of the highest Sanskrit learning, or universities of the type of the medieval university of Paris. Such were Benares and Nalanda, Mathura and Taxila, Ujjaini and Prayag, Kanchi and Madura, and to a lesser extent Navadwip in Bengal. The sacred streams and temples of the north were looked upon with veneration and lifelong yearning to visit them, by the men of the south, and in the same way, Puri and Kanchi, Setubandha and Sringeri, Dwaraka and Nasik were eagerly visited by devoted pilgrims from the north of India, in spite of the immense distances to be crossed. Furthermore, for the benefit of those who could not travel, some local rivers and cities of the south were named after those of the north and regarded as equally sanctifying. Thus, Madura is the southern Mathura, and the Godavari is the southern Ganges, Ganga Godavari. Great Sanskrit scholars and saints, like Shankaracharya and Chaitanya, have passed from one end of Hindu India to another, everywhere conquering their rivals in disputation, as Samudragupta and other kings bent on *dig-vijaya* did in arms. This presupposed cultural uniformity.

Not only do Sarkar's views on Bharat's civilisation broadly resonate with those of Mookerji, the views of both these scholars were also broadly reflected in *An Advanced History of India* (1946) jointly authored by R.C. Majumdar, H.C. Raychaudhuri and Kalikinkar Datta,[26] and again in Majumdar's *Ancient India* (1952).[27] It can be safely said on the authority of such scholars that around the time of the freedom movement, there was a significant chorus of Indic scholars proclaiming the civilisational status of Bharat to lay the foundations for its independent statehood. This could plausibly explain the reference to 'ancient land' in the Objectives Resolution passed by the Constituent Assembly as well as the adoption of Bharat in Article 1 of the Constitution.

To me, what is astounding is the dignity, poise and clarity with which scholars, such as Sarda, Mookerji, Sarkar and Majumdar, and their contemporaries, presented their views on the antiquity and achievements of the Indic civilisation in the face of colonial hubris. To illustrate the atmospherics of the period, one need not look beyond a 21-page paper titled 'The Origins of Indian Nationalism According to Native Writers' authored by Bruce T. McCully, an American professor of history, in 1935, which was published in *The Journal of Modern History*.[28] The stated object of the study was 'to determine the origins of Indian nationalism as indicated in the works of native writers'. However, McCully's Eurocentrism reveals itself through his language that reeks of sheer condescension and contempt for the works of Mookerji and other 'native' voices, and is best captured in his own words:

The attempt to interpret the unity of ancient India in terms of religion and culture, aside from the improbability of this theory in the light of historical research, appears to be more in the nature of a rationalisation to support the contention that India has always possessed certain of the component elements of nationality than an explanation of the origins of nationalism. ...

.... With their somewhat romantic attachment to the past glories of India in contrast to the despised present, these writers seem to invite criticism by their cavalier disregard for the evidences of history.... Far more weighty in number, diversity, and value are the writings which attribute the origins of Indian nationalism to the influences, on the whole beneficent, flowing into India as a consequence of British rule.

.... The evidence indicates that an overwhelming majority of the writings examined prefer the latter thesis, thereby inclining to admit that Indian nationalism is not of indigenous origin but exotic, implanted not by native but by foreign hands, and germinating only under conditions and influences supplied by a foreign nation and people. It is equally apparent that a majority of the writers believe that the British supplied not only environmental and other factors necessary to evoke a national consciousness in India, but also the germ in the form of the nation-idea which they acknowledge to have been originally entirely foreign to the Indian mind.

The evidence further demonstrates that at least a few of the writers have perceived the profound significance upon the origins of the movement of socialising agencies carried into the land by the British; it seems to suggest that in the course of time Indian writers and commentators will tend increasingly to emphasise the influence of the British-born institutions which have tended to bear upon every part of the social fabric, rather than those institutions having a strictly political character.

Sadly, McCully's prognosis of the future was prophetic since, to me, it certainly seems that in contemporary Bharat there are more voices, even among 'experts', which endorse and echo McCully's views on Bharat's history than those that subscribe to the Indic school of thought. Clearly, the study of history and its representation is not as neutral and objective as is often made out to be. The irony is that the colonial consciousness of the Indian mind is best captured by the fact that the very same views expressed by Sarda, Mookerji, Sarkar, Majumdar and others[29] on the civilisational character of Bharat[30] and its cultural unity[31] are welcomed and received with a lot more enthusiasm when a book titled *India: A Sacred Geography* is written by Diana L. Eck.[32] Perhaps, the colonial consciousness of the Indian mind is put at ease by the fact that a White Westerner, and that too a professor of comparative religion and Indian studies at Harvard University, has recognised the sacred nature of Bharat's geography and appropriately caveated her position with standard-issue expressions of the fear of her work feeding the 'fervor of an exclusive new Hindu nationalism'. Since all the right boxes have been ticked in the mind of the colonialised Indian, both the messenger and the message are kosher or halal.

In a nutshell, there are typically only two acceptable choices for those who wish to understand Bharat's history—they must either subscribe to that school of thought which denies Bharat's antiquity, unity and Indic consciousness, or accept the view which recognises the validity of Bharat's indigenous OET, with the caveat that 'Hindu nationalism' must be exorcised from the Indian mind. And preferably, voices belonging to either school must not be Indian, and if they are Indian or of Indian origin, their credentials must be certified and validated by Western academia. There is a dearth of schools of thought or voices, Indian or not, rooted in Bharat's indigenous OET that calmly assert the right of Indic consciousness to reclaim its space, both physical and mental, because they have the consequence of 'othering' Middle Eastern and European colonialities. That such assertion, crudely and simplistically dubbed as 'Hindu nationalism', is, in fact, an Indic civilisational and decolonial reawakening, somehow never occurs to those who crinkle their noses at it. Simply put, it is the expression of the decolonial urge of the silenced and long-silent native to reclaim and re-exist. When this expression is pejoratively and phobically caricatured as 'Hindu nationalism', the only logical inference that can be drawn is that every other culture and society has the right to exercise the decolonial option, except Bharat. In other words, if Bharat had converted to the religion of either coloniality, it would have been acceptable for it to bemoan its past applying primarily the racial filter like the Americas or Africa, but since it has clawed and retained its native OET systems, its attempts at decoloniality are conveniently labelled 'Hindu nationalism', which endangers the safety of 'national minorities'—spaces forcibly or fraudulently carved out by Middle Eastern and European colonialities at the expense of and to the detriment of Bharat's native consciousness.

If this is not a textbook case of furthering two expansionist colonialities to the detriment of Bharat's native consciousness, I do not know what is. This is precisely why I reiterate that it is my considered position that in the interest of its survival, Bharat *must* employ the decolonial option, failing which its history and consciousness will always be forced to seek the validation of the very same colonialities that have historically displayed a fundamental antipathy to the very existence of the Indic consciousness. If Bharat's native consciousness never gets to tell its story the way it has experienced it, not only will the world, including Bharatiyas, never know what Bharat has been subjected to, it will also amount to a monumental failure to memorialise its colonisation and colonialisation. This is the key to preventing similar or worse colonisation, whether ongoing or potential. After all, the survival of a consciousness is inextricably connected to its ability to remember the good, the bad and the ugly, and pass on that memory to future generations. Therefore, decoloniality in Bharat's context is not only an attempt to reclaim its fundamental right to the agency to define itself but also includes the right to transmit its lived experience on its own terms and using its own lexicon, in order to stave off a worse fate, which is reflected by the constantly shrinking size of its sacred geography.

Having discussed Bharat's federal civilisational character, its central constituents and broadly outlined the framework of a civilisation-state, in the next chapter I will place before the reader the coloniality manifest in the treatment of this civilisation and its indigeneity by the White European Christian coloniser, including the impact of the application of the standards of ethnocentric 'nationhood' on the Indic consciousness.

8

European Coloniality and the Indic Civilisation

Missionaries Travelling in India

'When the Missionaries in Heathen countries find that the people will not come to them to be taught, they go and look after the people. In this picture you see two Missionaries, who are travelling in India from place to place, where they think they shall find people to listen to their teaching.' - *The Wesleyan Juvenile Offering*, December 1860 (published by Wesleyan Methodist Missionary Society).

This chapter and the following one are intended to enable the reader to draw parallels between the global and the Indian experiences with coloniality, through an examination of the impact of coloniality on Bharat's indigenous OET systems and social structures. The objective is to broadly lay out the politico-legal, religious and social infrastructure established by the European coloniser in the backdrop of which Bharat's constitutional journey up until the year 1919 must be understood, so as to assess whether it was influenced by colonial perceptions of the Indic civilisation.

I must clarify that when I speak of the European coloniser, my focus is limited to the British, given that they had greater success than any other European nation in colonising Bharat in terms of the expanse of the territory under their control, the longevity of their colonisation, the institutions established, the fact that Bharat secured its independence from Britain, and their continuing impact on the consciousness of Bharat. Also, despite the distinct nationalities of European colonisers and the critical distinctions in their administration as well as their politico-legal theories, I have consciously proceeded on the established premise that European coloniality cut across European national identities.

Given these considered caveats on the scope and nature of my discussion, in this section, I will place before the reader the material drawn from watershed legislations enacted by the British Parliament in relation to Bharat until 1853, which include legislative debates that shed light on the coloniality that informed their understanding of Bharat and influenced their laws and policies. Alongside this legislative material, I will also present to the reader a snapshot of the scholarly work on the colonial reshaping of Bharat's indigenous OET systems, societal structures and social practices. As the material shall demonstrate, this colonial exercise resulted in either distortion of indigenous identities or creation of new ones by the coloniser to further his goals which were not purely political or 'secular' in character.

The Company, the Crown, Coloniality and Civilisation

On 31 December 1600, Queen Elizabeth I granted a Charter of incorporation to the Governor and Company of Merchants of London, better known to the world as the English East

India Company (the Company).¹ The Company was founded to establish direct trade relations with Bharat, which was necessitated, among other things, by the fear that if the English did not show the initiative, the Dutch would replace the stranglehold of the Spanish over trade in the East. In a way, the founding of the Company can be traced to the events triggered by the *Inter Caetera*, the papal bull of 1493 issued by Pope Alexander VI, which is referred to in Chapter 2.

Under the terms of the bull, which bound Spain and Portugal, Bharat fell within the non-Christian territories earmarked for colonisation, enslavement and evangelisation by Portugal. Subsequently, in 1580, the rights of Portugal over Indian territories were assigned to Spain as the latter's sovereignty extended to Portugal. However, since the Protestant Reformation had undermined the authority of the Catholic Church and the Pope, one of the consequences was the revolt of the Dutch against the Spanish, which resulted in the loss of Spain's monopoly over trade in the East, particularly in Java, between 1595 and 1599. Fearing a Dutch monopoly over eastern trade, the English East India Company was established. It is clear from this sequence of events that Bharat's colonisation by Europe was not uninfluenced by the Protestant Reformation.

Ostensibly, the Company was incorporated to establish trading posts in Bharat with the permission of the latter's local rulers and, therefore, the Company was not vested with sovereign powers. The Charter of 1600 issued by the British Crown to the Company, which gave the latter a juristic persona and commercial privileges, such as the exclusive right to trade in the territories identified therein, cloaked the Crown with jurisdiction over the Company and its members. The term of the Charter was originally 15 years, which was renewable at the prerogative of the Crown. The idea behind the grant of such exclusive rights to the Company was to equip it to better compete with other European nations without having to face internal competition from Britain. Effectively, the stage was set for a face-off between the English East India Company and the Dutch East Indies Company.[2] The torture and execution of employees of the English Company by the Dutch in 1623 in Java (known as the Amboyna Massacre), along with other factors, resulted in the presence of the English Company being largely limited to Bharat. This, in turn, led to the consolidation of the British presence in Bharat over the years—at first, it was trading posts, followed by the construction and ownership of forts for the security of the Company's factories and employees.[3]

While it is typically assumed that the Company, as a commercial entity, had no 'civilising' interest in aiding the spread of Christianity in Bharat, there is evidence to suggest the contrary. For instance, in 1614, the Company put in place measures 'for the recruitment of Indians for the propagation of the Gospel among their countrymen and for imparting to these missionaries such education, at the Company's expense, as would enable them to carry out effectively the purposes for which they were enlisted'[4]. Further, in 1659, the directors of the Company were clear that it was 'their earnest desire by all possible means to spread Christianity among the people of India', which led to missionaries being allowed to travel to Bharat on the Company's ships.[5]

With the cession of Bombay by Portugal to the British Crown in 1661 and the grant of authority over Bombay by the Crown to the Company in 1668, the Company gradually began to move beyond its commercial role towards the assumption of political authority. However, it would be a while before the British Parliament recognised this transition. This is notwithstanding the fact that by the 1680s, the Company was seen as an instrument for the creation of a British Empire in Bharat, which resulted in the Charter of 1683, giving the Company the complete powers to 'declare and make peace and war with any of the *heathen* [emphasis added] nations of Asia, Africa and America within the charter limits, to raise, arm, train, and muster such military forces as seemed requisite and necessary, and to execute martial law for the defence of their forts, places, and plantations against foreign invasion or domestic insurrection or rebellion'.[6]

The reference to 'heathen' nations, meaning non-Christian nations, is an indication of the religious consciousness of the British coloniser. Further, the Charter of 1683 made it clear that any sovereign powers that the Company may acquire over the territories of Asia, Africa and America was on behalf of the Crown. Critically, the Company was empowered to set up Admiralty Courts to enforce rights relatable to the Charter, which further deepened its roots. By 1686, the Company was permitted to frame a municipal constitution for Madras. Effectively, in less than 90 years of its entry into Bharat as a trading entity, the Company had managed to establish a framework that had the trappings of a sovereign power.[7]

That the Company was the product of coloniality and the Christian consciousness of the British Crown was established in judicial proceedings in 1683, when it brought an action against another English trader, Thomas Sandys, for directly trading with India in violation of the exclusive rights granted to it by the Crown under the Charter.[8] Among the reasons spelt out by the King's Bench of the England and Wales Court for upholding the legal validity of the Company's action against Sandys under the Charter, one was that the King, as a 'good Christian', ought to be and was deemed to be at war with 'infidels' forever, which applied equally to all his subjects. Therefore, as the defender of the Christian faith, it fell within the scope of his prerogative to relax this 'normal rule' for his subjects or for a class of them if he so deemed fit, and only such beneficiaries of the relaxation would be allowed to trade with the 'enemy', that is, the infidel.[9] It was not permissible for other subjects to trade with the enemy unless they were directly permitted by the King or were licensed to do so by the Company. Therefore, for all practical purposes, the Charter issued in favour of the Company had a distinct and express Christian colonial character, since it was bound by such rules of conduct regarding commerce with 'infidels'[10] that were consistent with those of the Christian faith.[11]

However, in the following years, there was a marked increase in the chorus of English traders who expressed serious displeasure at the exclusive munificence enjoyed by the Company. This, coupled with the Company's own arrogant attitude, led to the House of Commons passing a resolution to the effect that 'all the subjects of England have equal right to trade to the East Indies unless prohibited by Act of Parliament', which strengthened the position of the opponents of the Company. To cut a long story short, the opponents managed to secure permission for the establishment of a parallel company through the Charter of 5 September 1698, by the name of 'English Company Trading to the East Indies'[12], despite the existence of the earlier Charter in favour of the original entity. However, the original Company became the single largest shareholder in the new company and leveraged this position to negotiate terms of coexistence with the new one. These terms were captured in a tripartite agreement entered into by the two entities and the Queen in July 1702. Under this agreement, the original Company would surrender its exclusive rights by 1709, until which time both companies would trade in the name of the new amalgamated entity, renamed the 'United Company of Merchants of England Trading to the East Indies', whose affairs would be run jointly by representatives of both. The new entity would operate under the Charter of September 1698 for the remainder of the Charter's term. Thenceforth, all royal charters would be issued to the United Company, which became the new East India Company. Therefore, all references to the Company hereinafter are references to this entity.

For the purposes of the discussion here, the Charter of September 1698 is an important document, since it took forward the colonial evangelical intent of both the Company and the British Parliament in a limited yet concrete fashion by specifically inserting what came to be known as 'the Missionary Clause'. This Clause required the Company to maintain

Christian clergy at their Indian factories and to have chaplains on their ships which weighed 500 tons or more.[13] The clergy so appointed to reside in Bharat were required to learn Portuguese within a year of being sent to Bharat, and critically, were also obligated to learn the native language of the country where they shall reside 'to enable them to instruct the Gentoos that shall be the servants or slaves of the same Company or of their agents, in the Protestant religion'. In other words, at the very least, the Company was expected to spread the Gospel among its Indian employees, which, in my opinion, is proof of intent to 'civilise' the native and was a clear indication of what was to come in a more systematic fashion over the years.

By 1726, a royal charter was issued, which permitted the Company to establish mayor's courts in Madras, Bombay and Calcutta. Further, appeals could be preferred from the said courts to the governor and ultimately to the King, which marked the integration of the legal infrastructure between the colonies in India and the Crown. Between 1726 and 1773, thanks to victories of the Company in the Battles of Plassey (1757) and Buxar (1764), coupled with the brazen profiteering of the Company at the expense of the Indian population during the Bengal famine of 1770—when a fifth of Bengal's population perished under the governorship of Warren Hastings—it dawned upon the British Parliament that the Company had long moved away from being a mere commercial entity. The Company was seen for what it truly was or had become—an extension of British sovereignty in the East through delegation of powers reinforced by the nature of monopoly enjoyed by it under the Charter.

This, along with the Company's abysmal management of its fiscal affairs, forced it to seek a bailout from the British government, which provided the British Parliament with the window it sought to impose fiscal discipline on the Company and limit its political/sovereign powers. Accordingly, apart from granting a loan of £1,400,000 at 4 per cent to the Company along with a promise to suspend an outstanding debt of £400,000 until the repayment of the new loan, a ceiling of 6 per cent was imposed on the dividend that could be declared by the Company to its shareholders. Further, the Company was required to submit itself to half-yearly scrutiny by the Treasury. Critically, the Act 'for establishing certain Regulations for the better Management of the Affairs of the East India Company, as well in India as in Europe', also known as the 'Regulating Act of 1773' and later on as the East India Company Act, was passed by the British Parliament, which clipped the political wings of the Company and allowed the Crown to spread its own.[14] Apart from consolidating the power structure in Bharat through the creation of the office of Governor-General who would preside over British territories in Bharat, with Fort William in Bengal as the epicentre of British power, a Supreme Court of Judicature was also established in Fort William to primarily entertain legal actions against British subjects; Hastings was appointed as the first Governor-General.[15]

The East India Company Act of 1784, popularly known as Pitt's India Act, after the then British Prime Minister Willam Pitt, built on the changes made in the 1773 Act and introduced a dual system whereby the newly formed Board of Commissioners for the Affairs of India, also known as the Board of Control, would handle the non-commercial/public/political activities of the Company, whereas the directors of the Company would be limited to handling its commercial affairs. The Board consisted of the Chancellor of the Exchequer, a Secretary of State and four privy councillors appointed by the King and holding office at his pleasure. This effectively gave the British Parliament greater control and leverage over the Company's affairs, in particular those which could have political ramifications. Apart from this, the 1784 Act also introduced a raft of measures that rendered the Company subordinate to the Governor-General.

While the phrase 'British Territories in India' was not used in the title of the 1773 or the 1784 Acts, it was used in the 1793 Act, which was called—'An Act for continuing in the East-India Company, for a further term, the possession of the British Territories in India, together with their exclusive Trade, under certain limitations; for establishing further Regulations for the Government of the said Territories, and the better administration of Justice within the same; for appropriating to certain uses the Revenues and Profits of the said Company; and for making provision for the good order and government of the Towns of Calcutta, Madras and Bombay'. The provisions of the 1793 Act also clearly reflected the growing supremacy of the Crown over the Company in matters of polity and sovereignty compared with the previous Acts, which would reflect with greater vigour in the Government of India Act of 1800 that effectively proclaimed British sovereign control over territories in Bharat. Under this Act, a Supreme Court of Judicature was established in Fort Saint George in Madras on the same lines as the Court in Fort Saint William in Calcutta.

By 1813, in the East India Company Act of the same year, the Crown categorically spoke of its 'undoubted sovereignty' over the said territories and others. Critical to the discussion at hand on coloniality of the British coloniser are the provisions of the 1813 Act which related to 'religion', 'morals' and 'education'. Reproduced herein below are the relevant excerpts of Section 33 of the 1813 Act:

XXXIII: And whereas it is the duty of this country to promote the interest and happiness of the native inhabitants of the British dominions in India; and such measures ought to be adopted as may tend *to the introduction among them of useful knowledge, and of religious and moral improvement*: and in furtherance of the above objects, *sufficient facilities ought to be afforded by law to persons desirous of going to and remaining in India, for the purpose of accomplishing these benevolent designs, so as the authority of the local government respecting the intercourse of Europeans with the interior of the country to be preserved, and the principles of the British Government, on which the natives of India have hitherto relied for the free exercise of their*

religion, be inviolably maintained: and whereas it is expedient
to make provision for granting permission to persons desirous
of going to and remaining in India for the above purposes,
and also to persons desirous of going to and remaining there
for other lawful purposes;.... [emphasis added]

This extract succinctly captures the British Christian policy of
toleration as discussed in Chapter 4.[16] On the one hand, it paid
lip service to the right of the native inhabitants to practise 'their
religion' freely, while on the other, it spoke of the 'introduction'
of 'useful knowledge' to the natives and of their 'religious and
moral improvement'. Further, the provision spoke of extending
all facilities needed to 'persons going and remaining in India' for
the accomplishment of the 'benevolent designs' of the Christian
White European coloniser. The coloniality of the coloniser is
writ large in the express language of the provision itself which
envisaged the civilising of the native through 'religious and
moral improvement'.

The 'persons' who would remain in India for the achievement
of the said 'benevolent' designs were Christian missionaries, and
this becomes evident not only from the literature[17] but also from
other provisions of the Act. Sections 49–54 of the Act provided
an elaborate scheme for the creation of a church establishment
in the British Territories in India with the appointment of one
bishop and three archdeacons for Calcutta, Madras and Bombay.
Further, under Section 43, a sum of not less than a lakh of rupees
would be set apart annually 'for the revival and improvement
of literature, and the encouragement of the learned natives of
India, and *for the introduction and promotion of a knowledge of the
sciences among the inhabitants of the British Territories in India*'
[emphasis added], which underscores the colonial belief that
the sciences have European origins. Based on the provisions of
the 1813 Act, it could be reasonably inferred that the intent
of the Company as expressed in 1614 and 1659 to spread
Christianity among the people of Bharat, had formally crystallised

into the establishment of a Christian ecosystem in Bharat under the mandate of the Crown and the British Parliament.

The evangelical intent behind these provisions shines through the debates that took place in the British Parliament in relation to the 1813 Act, prior to its promulgation. In fact, according to the literature, the unequivocal provision of State support for the establishment and spread of Christianity in Bharat, as reflected in the 1813 Act, was a result of the persistent efforts of missionary groups for several years.[18] The conviction with which the case for Christianity in Bharat was pitched is evident from the fact that proponents of missionary work genuinely believed that the improvement of the condition of the people of Bharat was intimately bound to one essential prerequisite—conversion to Christianity. The resistance of the Company to increased missionary activity in Bharat until the 1813 Act did not spring from the well of religious neutrality or 'secularism' as some would like to believe, but was merely the product of mercantile pragmatism. There is no denying that the issue had multiple layers with several parties having divergent views and interests. That said, not a single one of the different strains of these views was remotely interested in non-interference with native faith systems out of respect for their beliefs and practices.

To add to this mix, the tussle between the Church of England, the official denomination of England, and Protestant Dissenters turned Bharat into yet another battleground for the conflict between Christian denominations.[19] The arrival of Dissenting Protestant Missionaries, such as William Carey[20] and John Thomas, in Bengal in 1793, made matters worse, and by 1811 it was feared even by the House of Lords that the rising number of Protestant denominations in England would render the Church of England a denominational minority. This led to competitive evangelism, wherein each group tried to win more converts for itself ('soul harvesting') to prove its commitment to the gospel, with both groups agreeing on the need for greater missionary activity in Bharat.[21] This was captured in the proposal put forth to the British Parliament in 1811 by William Wilberforce,[22] a British politician and Protestant Christian, which required the Company to finance missionary activities in its territories.[23] This proposal was defeated by both the Anglican Church and the Company for their own reasons, the former fearing the growth of Dissenting Protestantism and the latter being concerned about missionary activity interfering with commerce by alienating the native population. The Company's reluctance to institutionalise missionary activity was also partly owed to the experience of the Vellore Mutiny in 1806, which resulted in the death of 200 in a garrison of 370 due to a revolt of Indian soldiers against their officers.[24] The revolt was triggered by apprehensions among the soldiers that the Company was intent on converting them to Christianity by force. Therefore, the Company had its own reasons for partially staving off missionary activity at the levels sought by pro-mission groups.

However, between 1811 and 1813, the chorus for greater missionary activity in Bharat grew, and one of the reasons marshalled as the pretext for it was the inadequacy of the number of ministers of religion and chaplains in Bharat, which supposedly had led to 'grossly immoral behaviour' on the part of the Europeans. The blame for their immorality was, of course, conveniently laid at the doors of the native heathen population, which was deemed to be fundamentally and inherently immoral. Therefore, while the excuse cited was the growing European immorality in Bharat, the goal was ultimately the conversion of Indians, who had to be saved from their ignorance, darkness and devil-worshipping ways. To support their case of inherent immorality of the 'Hindoos', Hindu beliefs and practices were demonised, as evidenced by the propagandisation of the annual Shri Jagannath Rath Yatra at Puri (Odisha), as a 'dangerous cult' and the brazen exaggeration of the prevalence of Sati.[25] In this regard, the writings of Claudius Buchanan,[26] a Scottish clergyman and a missionary, were extremely popular in both England and America. In fact, he must be credited with the corruption of the word 'Jagannath' to 'juggernaut' and for using the Rath Yatra to portray Hinduism as a 'bloody, violent, superstitious and backward religious system', which had to be rendered extinct and replaced with the gospel. He made the case for the 'social reform' of Bharat to his audience in England which resonated greatly owing to the popularity of Protestantism.

As the date for the renewal of the Company's Charter in 1813 grew closer,[27] more efforts were invested by Buchanan and like-minded proponents to convince the British Parliament on the need for State support of Christian missionary efforts in Bharat. Buchanan managed to convince a sizeable section of the British public and lawmakers of the Company's profiteering tendencies, which contrasted against the Christian philanthropy of the missionaries.[28] Both Houses of the British Parliament received hundreds of petitions from British churches fervently appealing for the 'propagation of Christian knowledge in India'.[29]

Circumstances were now ripe for William Wilberforce to once again make his proposal; on 19 February 1813[30], he presented a Petition to the British Parliament from the Society in Scotland for propagating Christian knowledge, which read as follows:

That the society was incorporated in the year 1709, by a charter from her majesty queen Anne, *for the farther promoting of Christian knowledge and increase of piety and virtue within Scotland, especially in the Highlands, Islands, and remote [corners] thereof, and for propagating the same in Popish and infidel parts of the world* [sic]; and that since that time, in consequence of the donations and bequests of pious and benevolent persons, the funds of the society have increased to a considerable amount, and have been faithfully applied to the purposes of the charter, agreeably to the will of the donors; and that the labours of the society, by means of their teachers, catechists, and missionaries, have, it is well known, been attended with great success in the education of youth, in furthering the interests of religion and virtue, and in diffusing, both in Scotland and America, the blessings of civilisation and industry, subordination to lawful authority, and attachment to the constitution and government of the British empire; *and that it appears to the petitioners, that the exertions of the society can nowhere be employed more agreeably to the object of the royal charter, or with greater prospect of success, than in those territories and provinces in India which now form a part of his Majesty's dominions; and that, while the natives of those countries have long been and still continue in a state of deplorable ignorance, and addicted to various idolatrous and superstitious usages of the most degrading and horrible description, many of our own countrymen, members of the church of Scotland, employed in the different civil and military departments in India, are precluded from enjoying the ordinances of Christianity agreeably to the forms of the Church to which they are attached; and that, while the situation of India, destitute of the means of religious instruction, has long presented the most urgent claims to the humanity of Britons and of Christians, the restrictions to which the intercourse with those countries has hitherto been subjected, have prevented attempts for affording them the relief which the exigencies of their situation so imperiously required; and praying the House to take into consideration the facts which have been stated in this Petition, and to provide, in any Bill that may be passed for renewing the East India Company's charter, that it shall be lawful for the petitioners to impart the benefits of Christianity to the natives of India, and to afford the advantages of religious worship and instruction to our countrymen members of the church of Scotland, who may reside in that part of the British empire, subject always to such salutary regulations as parliament in its wisdom shall judge it necessary to establish.* [emphasis added]

The contents of the Petition must be read closely and carefully to understand the conviction of the petitioners and the number of layers it sheds light on that have contemporary relevance. The petition reinforces the deep-rooted Christian undergirding of European coloniality, a fact that was directly responsible for its unshakeable belief in its civilising global mission that has affected non-Christian systems across the world—in this case, Indic OET systems. It needs to be understood and acknowledged that the stereotypes about Hinduism that Buchanan gave birth to in the 1800s, which informed Wilberforce's Petition to make a case for missionary activity in Bharat, continue to relentlessly hound the followers of Sanatana Dharma, both in Bharat and in the West, though the West hypocritically preaches diversity and toleration to the rest of the world. Clearly, Christian OET has contributed substantially to the creation of the White man's saviour complex that has done more harm than good to the world.

Wilberforce's Petition is but an illustration of the dominant view of British society of the time, which ultimately led to the Company's Charter being renewed with the imposition of evangelical obligations. I use the word 'dominant' with basis, since the proposal to impose such obligations won with an overwhelming majority of 89 to 36 in the British Parliament, with the other important consequence being that the British government gained greater control over the affairs of the Company as well as over Bharat. Effectively, the insertion of the Missionary Clauses in the 1813 Act was a milestone that led to feverish missionary activity in Bharat. In the years that followed, both the Anglican Church and Protestant denominations gained greater access to Bharat with the patronage of the Company as mandated by the British Parliament and the Crown. Frankly, this alone obviates any need for further discussion on British 'secularism', since any government, especially a colonial one, which approaches a colonised society with a civilising mission based on a foreign theology that is premised on the supposed barbarism and immorality of the latter's faith and worldview, cannot reasonably expect to be deemed 'secular', that is, devoid of any religious identity or affiliation. On the contrary, its religious motivations could not have been clearer. Notwithstanding this, to prove the point further, just so that the 1813 Act is not dismissed as an aberration, I will place more material drawn from the subsequent Acts, legislative debates and the education cum language policies put in place by the British administration to further the manifestly Christian goals of European coloniality.

For instance, the State patronage of Christianity and its clergy in Bharat was made abundantly clear when the Indian bishops and Courts Act, 1823 was passed, which contained both 'secular' and 'non-secular/religious' aspects. Not only was this the legislation under which a Supreme Court of Judicature in Bombay was established, it also provided for payment of pensions to bishops and archdeacons who served in Bharat. A more incongruous mix of the religious and the secular cannot be found, but perhaps it did not appear incongruous to the British coloniser since his secularism was, after all, Christian secularism.

The impact of the Missionary Clause of the 1813 Act was the initiation of the evangelical project of 'reforming' Bharat, for which Buchanan's and other missionaries' work demonising Bharat, its faith systems, traditions and society in general, had laid the foundation.[31] The Bengal Sati Regulation of 1829 was a direct product of the movement for 'social reform'. In fact, Dr. Meenakshi Jain in her scholarly work *Sati: Evangelicals, Baptist Missionaries, and the Changing Colonial Discourse*[32] has brilliantly captured the direct nexus between the said law and the malicious representation of Hindu society using Sati as the soapbox to grandstand from in order to legitimise the civilising mission of the Christian White European coloniser. She demonstrates credibly in her book that the presence of Sati as a practice was nowhere close to being as rampant as it was made out to be by the missionaries to 'shock and motivate the British public and also garner funds at home for missionary work in India', apart from pushing for the inclusion of the Missionary Clause in the 1813 Act.

She underscores the fact that it could not have been a matter of mere coincidence that all the 'ills' of the Hindu society were to be found in the vicinity of Calcutta or in Bengal, which was the seat of British power and also that of the Bishop in India at the time. Jain rightly argues that it was possible for Sati to be addressed without demonising Hindus and Hinduism—as evidenced by the approach of the Tagore family[33]—and yet the goal of the missionaries in using Sati as the springboard for their attacks on the faith of the Indic heathen could not have been more obvious. I leave it to the reader to ask themselves whether the approach of the missionaries in the 1800s towards Hindu society, its faith, culture and institutions is mirrored in contemporary representations of Hindus and Hinduism, both *by Hindus themselves and others*. If the answer is in the affirmative, would it not be reasonable to conclude that this is due to ingrained coloniality and colonialised versions of Bharat's worldview by successive generations of 'natives'?

The next landmark legislation whose provisions as well as the surrounding legislative debates leave nothing to the imagination with respect to the evangelising nature of British colonisation is the Government of India Act of 1833 passed in August 1833, also known as the Charter Act of 1833.[34] This legislation officially cemented Britain's colonisation of Bharat as indicated by the following observations:

1. Under Section 1 of the Act, all British Indian territories would remain under the Company's government in India until 13 April 1854, and all property would be held by it as a trustee of the Crown;

2. Under Section 2, all privileges enjoyed by the Company would be in force only until April 1854;

3. Under Section 4, the Company was expected to expeditiously close its commercial business after 22 April 1854 and sell its properties;

4. Under Section 25, the Board of Control would thenceforth control all acts of the Company, which removed the distinction between the political and commercial activities of the Company;

5. Under Section 39, a provision was made for the Governor-General of India in Council, which would have both legislative and executive powers over all of British India. William Bentinck was the first to be appointed to the position of the Governor-General of India;

6. Under Section 45, all unrepealed laws would have the same force as any legislation passed by the British Parliament, and under Section 51, the power of the British Parliament to make laws for India was spelt out;

7. Under Section 53, the creation of a Law Commission was provided for, to enquire into existing laws, work on codification of laws for common applicability with due regard to local customs and usages and taking into account 'distinction of castes, difference of religion, and the manners and opinions prevailing among different races and in different parts of the said territories'. The use of the words 'caste' and 'races' in the Charter Act has immense significance, for it reflects the entry of both categories in the administrative and legal infrastructure of the coloniser's establishment. Further, it was the first pre-Independence Law Commission of 1834 under the Chairmanship of Thomas Babington Macaulay whose recommendations led to the Indian Penal Code of 1860, the original Code of Criminal Procedure of 1898, the Indian Evidence Act of 1872 and the Indian Contract Act of 1872;

8. Under Section 87, the entry of Indians into the colonial administrative structure was facilitated through the provision of a non-discrimination clause in favour of the natives. This was the precursor to the introduction of the civil services in Bharat; and

9. Under Section 89, two more bishops were appointed, one each for Madras and Bombay, who would be subject to the authority of the Bishop in Calcutta. Also, under Section 94, the Bishop of Calcutta was designated as the Metropolitan Bishop in India, to whom the other two bishops were

subordinate. The Bishop of Calcutta himself was subject to the superintendence of the Archbishop of Canterbury.

For all our contemporary understanding of the separation of the Church and the State, the provisions of the 1833 Charter Act themselves tell the story of the establishment of the Church by the State in Bharat by the Christian European coloniser. And if these provisions do not tell the story in its entirety, the parliamentary debates surrounding the passing of the 1833 Act speak volumes of the colonial and civilising mission of the British establishment in Bharat without a smidgen of equivocation or apologia for its intent or goals. From religion to education, the debates underscore the evangelical intent to 'reform' and convert Indians.

For instance, Charles Grey, who had held the office of the Chief Justice of the Supreme Court in India, had hoped that the diverse legal systems of Bharat would witness gradual consolidation with the increase in the number of 'native Christians, British and Colonial persons, and foreigners', 'a result which must gradually take place'. His views were quoted with approval on 13 June 1833[35] by Charles Grant, one of the leading proponents of Christian missionary activity and 'social reform and education' in Bharat in the British Parliament. He was a close like-minded associate of William Wilberforce, who believed in the marriage between evangelical Christianity and social reform. Following are the relevant extracts of Grant's views, quoted in second person from the debates that took place on the aforementioned date:

Under the influence of severe regulations, slowly and tardily relaxed, the number of Europeans in India had increased; and he proposed to increase the facilities for Europeans to settle in India. If he were asked whence arose the necessity for this change in the system under which British supremacy had grown up and been supported, he must advert to the singular change which had of late years taken place in the character of Indian society. There was nothing so remarkable in the history of India as the change which had of late years taken place in the dispositions and feelings of the natives, more particularly within the last fifteen years. The natives had become attached to European sciences and arts—they had learnt our language—they used our luxuries—and were making great strides towards adopting many of our habits. He would quote some admirable remarks made by Lord William Bentinck in a Minute drawn up on May 30, 1829. The right Honourable Gentleman read the following extract:- 'Recent events, and the occurrences now passing under our eyes, still more clearly justify the persuasion, that whatever change would be beneficial for our native subjects we may hope to see adopted, in part at least, at no distant period, if adequate means and motives be presented. I need scarcely mention the increasing demand which almost all who possess the means, evince for various articles of convenience and luxury purely European. It is in many cases very remarkable. Even in the celebration of their most sacred festivals, a great change is said to be perceptible in Calcutta. Much of what used, in old times, to be distributed among beggars and Brahmins, is now, in many instances, devoted to the ostentatious entertainment of Europeans; and generally the amount expended in useless alms is stated to have been greatly curtailed. *The complete and cordial co-operation of the native gentry in promoting education and in furthering other objects of public utility; the astonishing progress which a large body of Hindoo youth has made in the acquisition of the English language, literature, and science; the degree in which they have conquered prejudices that might otherwise have been deemed the most inveterate (the students in the medical class of the Hindoo College under Dr. Tytler, as well as in the medical native school under Dr. Breton, in which there are pupils of the highest castes, are said to dissect animals, and freely to handle the bones of a human skeleton); the freedom and the talent with which, in many of the essays we lately had exhibited to us, old customs are discussed; the anxiety evinced at Delhi, and at Agra, and elsewhere, for the means of instruction in the English language; the readiness everywhere shown to profit by such means of instruction as we have afforded; the facility with which the natives have adapted themselves to new rules and institutions; the extent to which they have entered into new speculations after the example of our countrymen; the spirit with which many are said to be now prosecuting that branch of manufacture (indigo) which has alone as yet been fully opened to British enterprise; the mutual confidence which Europeans and natives evince in their transactions as merchants and bankers; these, and other circumstances, leave in my mind no doubt that our native subjects would profit largely by a more general intercourse with intelligent and respectable Europeans, and would promptly recognise the advantage of it.* [emphasis added]

Following were the Resolutions moved by Grant:

1. That it is expedient that all his Majesty's subjects shall be at liberty to repair to the ports of the empire of China, and to trade in tea and in all other productions of the said empire; subject to such regulations as Parliament shall enact for the protection of the commercial and political interests of this country.
2. That it is expedient that, in case the East-India Company shall transfer to the Crown, on behalf of the Indian territory, all assets and claims of every description belonging to the said Company, the Crown, on behalf of the Indian territory, shall take on itself all the obligations of the said Company, of whatever description, and that the said Company shall receive from the revenues of the said territory such a sum, and paid in such a manner, and under such regulations, as Parliament shall enact.

3. That it is expedient that the Government of the British possessions in India be intrusted to the said Company, under such conditions and regulations as Parliament shall enact, for the purpose of extending the commerce of this country, *and of securing the good government and promoting the moral and religious improvement of the people of India.* [emphasis added]

These Resolutions were then communicated by the House of Commons on 17 June 1833 to the House of Lords for the latter's concurrence.[36] The debates that subsequently took place again in the House of Commons further reinforce Christian European coloniality. For instance, on 10 July 1833[37], the fact that the Company presided over a 'Christian government' was brought up several times to castigate it for its mercantilism and profiteering conduct despite its Christian character. Even in the most charitable of references to the 'Hindoo' society, which were meant to highlight their inhuman treatment by the Company and its greed, words such as superstition were used liberally. Sample the following extract from the submissions of James Silk Buckingham, the then member of the British Parliament from Sheffield:

He put it to the candour and the justice of the House, then, whether he had not adduced sufficient evidence to prove that even in their mercantile capacity they were wholly unable to manage their affairs advantageously for themselves? Nay, he would ask, whether the history of the world presented another instance of equal mismanagement to this? Where a Company, setting out with the means of importing the richest cargoes from the East without cost, and selling them without competition, had yet brought itself to a state of bankruptcy so complete as this? But, in addition to this, which for his own part he should deem sufficient ground for refusing to vest the government of India for another twenty years in the hands of such incapables, he would now advert to the condition to which they had brought the territory of India, by the grinding exactions to which they had subjected it; and show that in fiscal rapacity, they had gone beyond even the Mohammedans, to whose rule they had succeeded. *It was a maxim of the Mohammedan law, founded on the dictates of the Koran, that the lives and property of all conquered people were the absolute possession of the conquering power; and that it was perfectly just to exact from every estate the half of its gross produce, as the legitimate share of the Government, leaving to the cultivator the burthen of paying every charge of production, and subsisting as well as he could, out of the other half. But the Christian government of the India Company had refined upon this:* and, not content with this extravagant exaction of five-tenths of the gross produce of every estate in the country, as rent, (the Government claiming the right of absolute proprietorship in every acre of the soil) they had carried the superior fiscal knowledge which they possessed beyond the rapacity of their Mohammedan predecessors; and wrung out from the unhappy people subject to their dominion, more than the infidels or tyrants of the Mogul race, as they were called, had ever dreamed of exacting...

... Yet, with all this frugality of living, at an expense, perhaps, of less than 3d. per day, the unfortunate cultivators of Hindoostan had been unable to obtain, for their portion of the produce of the soil, sufficient for the barest subsistence that would keep men alive; and with all their attachment to their altars and their homes, they had been obliged by exaction and oppression, to leave both, and migrate into the territories of a native Indian prince, the Rajah of Mysore—there to find, *under the government of a heathen and an infidel,* that mercy which had been denied them *under the Christian government of the India Company,* to which we were nevertheless now called upon to consign over a hundred millions of these helpless people for a period of twenty years more! [emphasis added]

On how the Company, as a Christian government, was impeding the work of Christian missionaries in Bharat as opposed to aiding them, as was expected of a Christian government, the following was the criticism heaped by Buckingham in the House of Commons:

... Among the various pretexts on which the East-India Company grounded their claims to admiration, for the excellence of their rule, none was more frequently or powerfully insisted on than this: that, though they had conquered the country, they had always respected the religious usages of the people—*they were tolerant even of their abominations, and would not venture to disturb their most obscene or bloody rites*. But what was the real state of the case? It was this:- *Wherever no profit was to be made, by interfering with the native superstitions, there they permitted them to flourish, in all their rankness and deformity*. But wherever gain was to be acquired, they had no more scruple in violating the sanctity of their religion, than they had in overturning their thrones, in emptying their treasuries, in carrying off their wealth, or in violating their domestic hearths.

Let the testimony of others, however, prove this fact, rather than his own. He would cite the evidence of Colonel Phipps, an officer of the Bengal army, who, having been stationed at the great temple of the idol juggernaut, in command of the guard for preserving the peace, while the taxes were levied there, had the best means of arriving at the truth: and this was his statement, taken from a valuable work, entitled, 'India's Cries to British Humanity.' (The Honourable Member accordingly read a long passage, showing that the Government sanctioned the pilgrimage to Juggernaut, by taxing the pilgrims, and by adopting means in conjunction with the natives to make the tax easy of collection and productive, [*sic*] The conclusion was this: 'The Government at first authorised these people to collect at the barriers a fee from the pilgrims for their own benefit; but this privilege having been abused, it was resolved that the British Collector should levy, besides the tax for the State, an additional one, the amount of which he subsequently paid over to the Purharees and Pandas, in such proportions as they were entitled to, from the number of pilgrims, which each had succeeded in enticing to undertake the pilgrimage' p. 219.)

Here was an organised system of procuring pilgrims to the bloody shrine of the Indian Moloch. Here was a body of Idol Missionaries, far exceeding in number the whole of the Christian Missionaries in the East, going forth clothed with all the authority of the British name and power, paid by the Company's Government, and their zeal stimulated by a payment of a certain sum per head on every pilgrim brought to bow himself before the wooden god; and this too, when the Society for the Propagation of the Gospel in foreign parts, and the Society for Promoting Christian Knowledge, were each calling loudly for an increase to the number of the bishops in India. In the way of actual conversion, the bishops already sent had done nothing, though they were men of talent, learning, and zeal; and even the Christian missionaries had met with obstacles rather than encouragement from the India Company, and those holding authority under them; while the idol worshippers and pilgrim hunters, had made rapid progress, and were still increasing under the auspices of those honourable and Christian rulers, to whom we were again about to consign over India for their benefit. [emphasis added]

Just to be clear, the 'idol missionaries' referred to in the extract here were the Pandas/Brahmin Priests of the Shri Jagannath Temple and the 'wooden god' referred to was Lord Jagannath at Puri, Odisha. Once again, the Company was referred to as a 'Christian ruler', criticised for impeding the work of missionaries, apart from lamenting that the bishops that had already been sent to Bharat had done nothing by way of actual conversion and that 'idol worshippers' had made rapid progress under the auspices of 'Christian rulers'.

This was followed by a fairly detailed speech by Thomas Babington Macaulay on the same day, who touched upon a host of issues, including on the need for consolidation and codification of laws in Bharat, comparing its diversity with that of Europe. Apart from citing the need for uniformity in laws and legal outcomes, the approach to indigenous societal structures and the demonisation of the 'caste' system as well as Brahmins may be traced to Macaulay to a significant extent. Critically, he made no bones of the fact that the spread of European civilisation in the East would benefit Britain from the standpoint of governance since Europeanisation of the native population would bridge the cultural gap and make governance and assimilation less cumbersome. In addition to highlighting the practicality and commercial sense behind this approach, this position was couched in moral righteousness befitting the coloniser's coloniality. Following are a few relevant extracts from his speech that attest to this:

Having given to the Government supreme legislative power, we next propose to give to it for a time the assistance of a commission for the purpose of digesting and reforming the laws of India, so that those laws may, as soon as possible, be formed into a Code. *Gentleman of whom I wish to speak with the highest respect have expressed a doubt whether India be at present in a fit state to receive a benefit which is not yet enjoyed by this free and highly civilised country.* Sir, I can allow to this argument very little weight beyond that which it derives from the personal authority of those who use it. *For, in the first place, our freedom and our high civilisation make this improvement, desirable as it must always be, less indispensably necessary to us than to our Indian subjects; and in the next place, our freedom and civilisation, I fear, make it far more difficult for us to obtain this benefit for ourselves than to bestow it on them.*

I believe that no country ever stood so much in need of a code of laws as India; and I believe also that there never was a country in which the want might so easily be supplied. I said that there were many points of analogy between the state of that country after the fall of the Mogul power, and the state of Europe after the fall of the Roman empire. In one respect the analogy is very striking. As there were in Europe then, so there are in India now, several systems of law widely differing from each other, but coexisting and coequal. The indigenous population has its own laws. Each of the successive races of conquerors has brought with it its own peculiar jurisprudence: the Mussulman his Koran and the innumerable commentators on the Koran; the Englishman his Statute Book and his Term Reports. As there were established in Italy, at one and the same time, the Roman law, the Lombard law, the Ripuarian law, the Bavarian law, and the Salic law, so we have now in our Eastern empire Hindoo law, Mahometan law, Parsee law, English law, perpetually mingling with each other and disturbing each other, varying with the person, varying with the place. In one and the same cause the process and pleadings are in the fashion of one nation, the judgment is according to the laws of another. An issue is evolved according to the rules of Westminster, and decided according to those of Benares. The only Mahometan book in the nature of a code is the Koran; the only Hindoo book, the Institutes. Everybody who knows those books knows that they provide for a very small part of the cases which must arise in every community. All beyond them is comment and tradition. Our regulations in civil matters do not define rights, but merely establish remedies. If a point of Hindoo law arises, the Judge calls on the Pundit for an opinion. If a point of Mahometan law arises, the Judge applies to the Cauzee. What the integrity of these functionaries is, we may learn from Sir William Jones.

That eminent man declared that he could not answer it to his conscience to decide any point of law on the faith of a Hindoo expositor. Sir Thomas Strange confirms this declaration. Even if there were no suspicion of corruption on the part of the interpreters of the law, the science which they profess is in such a state of confusion that no reliance can be placed on their answers. Sir Francis Macnaghten tells us, that it is a delusion to fancy that there is any known and fixed law under which the Hindoo people live; that texts may be produced on any side of any question; that expositors equal in authority perpetually contradict each other: that the obsolete law is perpetually confounded with the law actually in force; and that the first lesson to be impressed on a functionary who has to administer Hindoo law is that it is vain to think of extracting certainty from the books of the jurist. The consequence is that in practice the decisions of the tribunals are altogether arbitrary. What is administered is not law, but a kind of rude and capricious equity. I asked an able and excellent judge lately returned from India how one of our Zillah Courts would decide several legal questions of great importance, questions not involving considerations of religion or of caste, mere questions of commercial law. He told me that it was a mere lottery. He knew how he should himself decide them. But he knew nothing more. I asked a most distinguished civil servant of the Company, with reference to the clause in this Bill on the subject of slavery, whether at present, if a dancing girl ran away from her master, the judge would force her to go back. 'Some judges,' he said, 'send a girl back. Others set her at liberty. The whole is a mere matter of chance. Everything depends on the temper of the individual judge.'

Even in this country we have had complaints of judge-made law; even in this country, where the standard of morality is higher than in almost any other part of the world; where, during several generations, not one depositary of our legal traditions has incurred the suspicion of personal corruption; where there are popular institutions; where every decision is watched by a shrewd and learned audience; where there is an intelligent and observant public; where every remarkable case is fully reported in a hundred newspapers; where, in short, there is everything which can mitigate the evils of such a system. But judge-made law, where there is an absolute government and a lax morality, where there is no bar and no public, is a curse and a scandal not to be endured. It is time that the magistrate should know what law he is to administer, that the subject should know under what law he is to live. We do not mean that all the people of India should live under the same law: far from it: there is not a word in the bill, there was not a word in my right honourable friend's speech, susceptible of such an interpretation. We know how desirable that object is; but we also know that it is unattainable. We know that respect must be paid to feelings generated by differences of religion, of nation, and of caste. Much, I am persuaded, may be done to assimilate the different systems of law without wounding those feelings. *But, whether we assimilate those systems or not, let us ascertain them; let us digest them. We propose no rash innovation; we wish to give no shock to the prejudices of any part of our subjects. Our principle is simply this; uniformity where you can have it: diversity where you must have it; but in all cases certainty.*

As I believe that India stands more in need of a code than any other country in the world, I believe also that there is no country on which that great benefit can more easily be conferred. A code is almost the only blessing, perhaps is the only blessing, which absolute governments are better fitted to confer on a nation than popular governments. The work of digesting a vast and artificial system of unwritten jurisprudence is far more easily performed, and far better performed, by few minds than by many, by a Napoleon than by a Chamber of Deputies and a Chamber of Peers, by a government like that of Prussia or Denmark than by a government like that of England. A quiet knot of two or three veteran jurists is an infinitely better machinery for such a purpose than a large popular assembly divided, as such assemblies almost always are, into adverse factions. This seems to me, therefore, to be precisely that point of time at which the advantage of a complete written code of laws may most easily be conferred on India. It is a work which cannot be well performed in an age of barbarism, which cannot without great difficulty be performed in an age of freedom. It is a work which especially belongs to a government like that of India, to an enlightened and paternal despotism.

I have detained the House so long, Sir, that I will defer what I had to say on some parts of this measure, important parts, indeed, but far less important, as I think, than those to which I have adverted, till we are in Committee. There is, however, one part of the bill on which, after what has recently passed elsewhere, I feel myself irresistibly impelled to say a few words. I allude to that wise, that benevolent, that noble clause which enacts that no native of our Indian empire shall, by reason of his colour, his descent, or his religion, be incapable of holding office. At the risk of being called by that nickname which is regarded as the most opprobrious of all nicknames by men of selfish hearts and contracted minds, at the risk of being called a philosopher, I must say that, to the last day of my life, I shall be proud of having been one of those who assisted in the framing of the bill which contains that clause. We are told that the time can never come when the natives of India can be admitted to high civil and military office. We are told that this is the condition on which we hold our power. We are told that we are bound to confer on our subjects every benefit— which they are capable of enjoying?—no;—which it is in our power to confer on them?—no;—but which we can confer on them without hazard to the perpetuity of our own domination. Against that proposition I solemnly protest as inconsistent alike with sound policy and sound morality.

I am far, very far, from wishing to proceed hastily in this most delicate matter. I feel that, for the good of India itself, the admission of natives to high office must be effected by slow degrees. But that, when the fulness of time is come, when the interest of India requires the change, we ought to refuse to make that change lest we should endanger our own power, this is a doctrine of which I cannot think without indignation. Governments, like men, may buy existence too dear. 'Propter vitam vivendi perdere causas,' is a despicable policy both in individuals and in states. In the present case, such a policy would be not only despicable, but absurd. The mere extent of empire is not necessarily an advantage. To many governments it has been cumbersome; to some it has been fatal. It will be allowed by every statesman of our time that the prosperity of a community is made up of the prosperity of those who compose the community, and that it is the most childish ambition to covet dominion which adds to no man's comfort or security. To the great trading nation, to the great manufacturing nation, no progress which any portion of the human race can make in knowledge, in taste for the conveniences of life, or in the wealth by which those conveniences are produced, can be matter of indifference. *It is scarcely possible to calculate the benefits which we might derive from the diffusion of European civilisation among the vast population of the East. It would be, on the most selfish view of the case, far better for us that the people of India were well governed and independent of us, than ill governed and subject to us; that they were ruled by their own kings, but wearing our broadcloth, and working with our cutlery, than that they were performing their salams to English collectors and English magistrates, but were too ignorant to value, or too poor to buy, English manufactures. To trade with civilised men is infinitely more profitable than to govern savages. That would, indeed, be a doting wisdom, which, in order that India might remain a dependency, would make it a useless and costly dependency, which would keep a hundred*

millions of men from being our customers in order that they might
continue to be our slaves.

It was, as Bernier tells us, the practice of the miserable
tyrants whom he found in India, when they dreaded the
capacity and spirit of some distinguished subject, and yet could
not venture to murder him, to administer to him a daily dose
of the pousta, a preparation of opium, the effect of which was
in a few months to destroy all the bodily and mental powers
of the wretch who was drugged with it, and to turn him into
a helpless idiot. The detestable artifice, more horrible than
assassination itself, was worthy of those who employed it. It
is no model for the English nation. We shall never consent
to administer the pousta to a whole community, to stupefy
and paralyse a great people whom God has committed to our
charge, for the wretched purpose of rendering them more
amenable to our control. *What is power worth if it is founded*
on vice, on ignorance, and on misery; if we can hold it only by
violating the most sacred duties which as governors we owe to
the governed, and which, as a people blessed with far more than
an ordinary measure of political liberty and of intellectual light,
we owe to a race debased by three thousand years of despotism
and priestcraft? We are free, we are civilised, to little purpose, if
we grudge to any portion of the human race an equal measure of
freedom and civilisation.

Are we to keep the people of India ignorant in order that
we may keep them submissive? Or do we think that we can
give them knowledge without awakening ambition? Or do
we mean to awaken ambition and to provide it with no
legitimate vent? Who will answer any of these questions
in the affirmative? Yet one of them must be answered
in the affirmative, by every person who maintains that
we ought permanently to exclude the natives from high
office. I have no fears. The path of duty is plain before us:
and it is also the path of wisdom, of national prosperity, of
national honour.

The destinies of our Indian empire are covered with thick darkness. It is difficult to form any conjecture as to the fate reserved for a state which resembles no other in history, and which forms by itself a separate class of political phenomena. The laws which regulate its growth and its decay are still unknown to us. *It may be that the public mind of India may expand under our system till it has outgrown that system; that by good government we may educate our subjects into a capacity for better government; that, having become instructed in European knowledge, they may, in some future age, demand European institutions. Whether such a day will ever come I know not. But never will I attempt to avert or to retard it. Whenever it comes, it will be the proudest day in English history. To have found a great people sunk in the lowest depths of slavery and superstition, to have so ruled them as to have made them desirous and capable of all the privileges of citizens, would indeed be a title to glory all our own. The sceptre may pass away from us. Unforeseen accidents may derange our most profound schemes of policy. Victory may be inconstant to our arms. But there are triumphs which are followed by no reverse. There is an empire exempt from all natural causes of decay. Those triumphs are the pacific triumphs of reason over barbarism; that empire is the imperishable empire of our arts and our morals, our literature and our laws.* [emphasis added]

Macaulay's speech captures the essence of colonial consciousness so thoroughly that I do not think I can improve upon it. On 19 July 1833[38], the ramping up of Church infrastructure in India was discussed in the House of Commons, with significant support for the proposal of Charles Grant, reflected in the debates as follows:

Mr. Finch—supported the clause, and contended, *that it was necessary for the advancement of religion that there should be an Established Church in India able to meet the increasing Christian population.*

Mr. O'Dwyer—opposed the clause, and said, that he could see no necessity for increasing the Episcopal Establishment in India. It would be moreover a precedent to extend the Church Establishment all over the British territory.

Mr. Ruthven—opposed the clause, at some length, and said, that it would be more fair if all denominations were placed on the same footing. He objected strongly to introducing a Church Establishment into India when this country was groaning under the weight of a Church Establishment.

Lord Morpeth—*When he compared the amount of service to be performed, and the extent of country and population over which it was spread, he did not think that three bishops were more than sufficient to perform those duties. The change did not propose any additional expense, and he thought the maintenance of an Established Church was a matter of national concern, and of the greatest importance to the British, as well as to the Pagan, or rather Semi Pagan inhabitants of India.*

Mr. Cutlar Fergusson—said, the only question before the House was, whether the Episcopal Establishment was to be increased or not? If the question had been whether the Episcopal Establishment was to be introduced into India, he should have voted differently. Two bishops might possibly be quite sufficient, and he did not pledge himself to the number. The bishops who had died in India so rapidly, had not died in consequence of excessive labour in their professional duties, but in consequence of the great precariousness of human life in that climate. ... Whether there should be two or three bishops, he did not mean to give an opinion; but there ought to be more than one. He did not think there was any hardship in compelling the inhabitants of India to pay not only for the Government which protects them, but also for the religion of that Government. With great submission to the Honourable Member for the University of Oxford, he must inform him that there was no dominant religion where the British flag was hoisted abroad. *In India as elsewhere, the Established Churches of England, Ireland, and that of Scotland, stood upon an equal footing*. He, therefore, concurred in this clause to the extent which he had mentioned, but no further, and without holding himself bound to any of the subsequent clauses relative to the Church in India. [emphasis added]

On 26 July 1833[39], when the Charter Bill was again taken up, on the question of Indians being expected to pay for the establishment of the Church in Bharat, Buckingham opposed this primarily on the grounds that (*a*) Indians must not be expected to pay for the establishment of a religion in Bharat which they believed to be false, and (*b*) Indians could be inspired to convert to Christianity if the Church establishment in Bharat conducted itself with Christian frugality, humility and piety. In other words, even those voices that appeared to speak for the rights of Indians were still convinced of the need to Christianise Bharat. Here are excerpts from his submissions to the House of Commons:

> But what would be said by us, if, in the event of a conquest of our country by Hindoos and Mohammedans, they were to increase their establishments of pundits and moollahs, and force the Christians to pay for them? Or if the celebrated Bramin, Ram Mohun Roy, now in this country, were to set up a Pagan shrine, and levy contributions on the Christians of England for its support? *Yet this was exactly what the Bill would do towards the natives of India: and, therefore, upon the true Christian principle, of doing unto others what we would they should do unto us, he should feel it his duty to resist so great an injustice.*
>
> Some had thought, however, that as the orientals were much impressed by pomp and rank, there was something in the dignity of a Bishop which would have an imposing effect upon the natives of India, and win them over to Christianity. No mistake could be greater than this. *This conversion of the natives to Christianity could only be effected by that familiar inter-course*

with them to which Bishops would never be likely to condescend. If they travelled, it was in a luxurious palanquin, borne on the shoulders of men, with umbrellas on either side to shield them from the rays of the sun; and a long retinue of pomp and state, which rendered the approach of the humble native, except in some menial capacity, wholly impossible. If they remained at home, they resided in a palace, receiving as companions only Europeans of the highest rank. The true instruments of conversion were the humble but zealous Missionaries, who, animated by a fervent and inextinguishable zeal, would go into the villages, invite and draw near to the people—converse with them in their own tongue, and endure sufferings and privations, to which no Bishop, archdeacon, or other dignitary of the Church would ever submit: and indeed it was by the Missionaries at Serampore, and in other parts of India, that whatever good had been already done in the way of education, or moral and religious improvement, had been wholly effected. The course was a very plain one, if the Ministers would only have the courage to adopt it. It was this: that every religion should be supported by those who believed in it, and who, on that ground, would be willing to give it their aid. If the Members of the Church of England in India wished to have an increase of bishops, let them be sent out, and those who called for them might fairly be left to pay for their support. If the Presbyterians and the Catholics wished an increase to their teachers, let them do the same. It was in this manner that Christianity was supported by the voluntary aid of its believers in the Apostolic age: it was, in this manner, that Christianity among the Dissenters of England was supported now: and it was his conviction that the nearer we approached to the truly Evangelical Spirit of the New Testament, and made its practice, as well as its percepts, the model of our imitation, the nearer we should approach perfection, and the sooner we should accomplish the great end of spreading the truth over every region of the earth.

We should be careful, however, not to introduce even the germ of Hierarchy into India; for in that prolific soil, though its first particle should be as small as the mustard seed, it would spread into a tree, large enough to afford shelter by its branches to all the fowls of the air. As an illustration of the manner in which the spirit of a dominant Church had already evinced itself in India, he would mention this anecdote. About the period of his first arrival in that country, a Presbyterian chapel was just about to be built in Bombay, the service having been previously held in the Court House there; when, a question arising about crowning the edifice with a steeple, Bishop Middle-ton protested against this, on the ground that Dissenters had no right to steeples, which were the distinguished characteristics of the privileged or Established Church; and maintained an obstinate controversy on this point; and that, too, in a country where the Hindoos might build pagodas till they touched the moon, and the Mahommedans might elevate their minarets till they lost their summits among the stars, as far at least as any Christian Bishop concerned himself about the matter; and in a community where the greater portion of the British-born subjects were either Irish Roman Catholics, or Scotch Presbyterians, or English Dissenters, who collectively formed a much greater number than the Members of the Episcopalian or English Established Church.

He repeated then his assertion, that the religion of the New Testament was conceived ill a different spirit from this; *and that the nearer we approached to the purity, economy, meekness, and piety of the Apostolic age, the greater would be the probability of our enlightening, moralising, and christianising, the whole Eastern world.* The last defect of the Bill that he would notice was this; that notwithstanding that the two great evils under which India laboured, were—first, excessive taxation, which ground the natives down to the dust, and deprived them of all physical enjoyment, by making existence so miserable as to be a burthen in itself; and—secondly, excessive ignorance, which rendered them the prey of superstition and all its

264   INDIA THAT IS BHARAT

odious vices: yet the Bill was wholly silent on the two great remedies—of relief from fiscal oppression, and the spread of education—without both of which, no improvement could be hoped for in their unfortunate and miserable condition. *He was glad to hear the right Honourable President of the India Board say, that the subjects of infanticide, and other human sacrifices still prevalent in India, were under consideration, and he hoped that in this case the terra would not be found a mere official evasion, without a sincere intention of coming to any speedy conclusion, but that the consideration would be pursued closely, until all these murderous rites and revolting abominations should be altogether abolished.* [emphasis added]

It must be noted that even when equal protection of all 'religions' was discussed, the reference was to all the religious denominations of Christianity and not to heathen and infidel faiths. This is all the more evident from the submissions of Richard Lalor Sheil, an Irish politician and MP, and Charles Grant, extracts of which are given below:

Mr. Sheil—'rose to propose a clause for making due provision in India for the Roman Catholic and other Churches dissenting from the Protestant Establishment, regard being had to the population of the various districts. He was one of those who were of opinion, that the wisest course would have been, not to make provision for any Ecclesiastical Establishment in India whatever. The Company had objected to any extension of the hierarchy. *Those points, however, having been disposed of, it was for the House now to consider whether it would not be expedient to place all forms of worship equally under the protection of Government. By the existing Act on the subject, provision was made for a Church Establishment in India, without stating whether that Establishment should be of the English Church alone, or not.* The present Bill extended the hierarchy. An Honourable Member for Scotland then called on his Majesty's Government to introduce a statutory provision for the protection of the Scottish Church in India. The President of the Board of Trade gave that Honourable Gentleman an assurance that a statutory provision should be introduced into the Bill for that purpose; and accordingly he (Mr. Sheil) found, that a most important change had been made in the Bill, and that a provision had been introduced into it for the protection of the Scotch Church.

He would ask what reason there was, that the Church of Scotland was to be protected by statute, when the Roman Catholics, who constituted so large a majority of the Christian population of India, were not to be protected? The whole amount of the Christian population of India was 800,000, of whom not less than 600,000 were Roman Catholics, besides a large population of Syrian Christians, whose tenets differed from those of the Roman Catholics by a very slight and evanescent line of demarcation. Thus there clearly appeared to be an infinite majority of Roman Catholics in the Christian population of India. In such a vast body of the population, of whom a great number were Irish soldiers, surely, in justice and good policy, there ought to be the same protection as for other classes. At the present moment the whole of the eight Roman Catholic bishops in India were maintained by the Portuguese government, and, as had been most justly observed by a competent authority, it was the worst policy to allow this hierarchy to be supported by a foreign government. He (Mr. Sheil) would therefore impress upon the House the propriety of consulting their interest and character by not depriving the Roman Catholics of the same protection as the other religious classes. This would be the only way of preventing those future dissensions which would otherwise inevitably result. There were quite sufficient precedents to authorise the House in granting to the Roman Catholics the protection of a statute. The Roman Catholic Establishment in Ireland in general, the college of Maynooth, and similar institutions, were all under the protection of the law, and there was no possible reason why the Roman Catholics abroad should be left unprotected.'

Mr. Charles Grant—'objected to the Honourable Gentleman's clause. It was rather remarkable that, after the strong denunciations made by the Honourable and learned Gentleman against imposing any additional load upon the Indians for the support of any other religion, the Honourable and learned Gentleman, notwithstanding, now strongly urged the imposition of a still further amount of taxation for the support of the Roman Catholic Church. The alteration which he had suggested was not with a view to establish any Ecclesiastical domination in India, but with a much higher and general view. *Besides, the clause of the Honourable and learned Gentleman could hardly be admitted, as being too general and indefinite in its nature, for it proposed that "all forms of worship should be equally under the protection of Government, and that due provision should be made for the maintenance of Churches dissenting from the Protestant Episcopal Church." This would bring under the protection of Government, not merely Christian forms of worship, but every description of religion, even the idolatrous creed of the Heathen sects, many of which were such, as, so far from calling for the protection of Government, loudly called for the most strenuous efforts to suppress them, such as those where human victims were sacrificed. The Honourable and learned Gentleman, too, had rather exaggerated the extent of the Catholic population. It would be the pride of the Protestant religion to make converts by the superior tone of its morality, and by the example given by its profession. The country might rest assured, however, that it was the desire and intention of Government to afford protection to all classes; and to make this apparent, he would propose to add as a proviso, that nothing in the Bill should be held to prevent the Governor of India in Council from advancing a sum of money for providing instruction for Christians of all classes, or from withholding due protection to all classes'.* [emphasis added]

The contents of these debates prove that Bharat was treated as a fertile territory for soul-harvesting by various Christian denominations, all of which sought a level playing field to compete for the status of the true champions of the one true religion, the one true God and His gospel. Therefore, this much can be said without equivocation—one of the primary intents behind the provisions of the 1833 Charter Act, as evidenced by the debates, was to lay the foundation of Christianity in Bharat through State support for conversion of the native (through a long-term Europeanisation project), with equal opportunity for evangelical work being assured to all Christian denominations.

The position under the Charter Act of 1833 was taken forward in the East India Company Act of 1853 for the most part, except for the following important changes:

1. Under the previous Charter Acts, term of each Charter was 20 years. However, under the 1853 Act, Section 1 expressly stated until the British Parliament provided otherwise, British Indian territories would be held in trust by the Company for the British Crown;

2. The legislative and executive functions of the Governor-General's councils were separated and a 12-member legislative council was created; and

3. The creation of an Indian Civil Service was envisaged, which led to the formation of the Macaulay Committee on Indian Civil Service in 1854.

The creation of a framework which the Indian elite could aspire to be a part of was the most significant contribution of the 1853 Act and the colonial consciousness behind it was stated categorically in the parliamentary debates prior to the passing of the Act. Following were the observations of the Earl of Derby, Edward Stanley, also the then British prime minister, on 2 April 1852 in the House of Lords[40]:

The Earl of Derby—'*With regard to that which I must look upon as one of the most leading objects connected with the affairs of India, though it is an establishment which has to contend with many obstacles, and work its way gradually through a mass of ignorance and superstition, and of conflicting difficulties, which render its advance slow and almost imperceptible, it is satisfactory to know that, whereas through the whole of the vast territories of India there were only employed in the service of the Company 31 chaplains of the Church of England, in 1813, when the episcopal authority was first introduced, in 1832 there were a bishop and 75 clergymen. The Act of 1833 multiplied the number of bishops, assigning its bishop to each separate Presidency. There are now, instead of 31 chaplains, as in 1812, or 75, as in 1832, three bishops, and no less than 130 chaplains of the Church of England, independent of the ministers of the Scotch Church.* Of the great social improvements which have taken place, cautiously and gradually introduced, since 1834, I cannot but mention, in the first place, that which had been the object of the constant and earnest attention of this country, namely, the total and entire abolition of slavery throughout its dominions; and, although great difficulties have had to be encountered, yet, by the Act passed in 1843, in India, as in the rest of Her Majesty's dominions, slavery was at once and completely abolished. Another not less gratifying change has taken place with regard to the administration of justice in India. In 1833 it was contemplated to establish, and there was established, a Legal Commission for the purpose of examining into the whole system of jurisprudence in India; the whole system of the penal and civil law, and reporting generally their opinions with regard to the necessary alterations.... . *But, although the Commission sent out in 1833 sat for some time, and laboured very industriously, and produced a most elaborate penal code, which is at the present moment, I believe, under the consideration of the Government of India, that Commission, from various circumstances, did not enter upon the discussion of the whole of the extensive subject committed to it; ... am quite sure, that this is your bounden duty in the interests of humanity, of benevolence, and of morality and religion—that as far and as fast as you can do it safely, wisely, and prudently, the inhabitants of India should be gradually intrusted with more and more of the superintendence of their own internal affairs, under the control of British authority, and taught to respect that authority which is vested in the law, and which they see judiciously and firmly enforced, temperately enforced also, by the superior British authority, which they may by long habit and practice learn to imitate, and, I would hope, even to surpass. And, my Lords, even if this gradual admission of the Indian race to the benefits of self-government, slowly and cautiously, should have the effect, not of consolidating and extending the great fabric of British dominion which has been built up in that country, but of leading a people accustomed to self-government to desire something more of control over their political, as well as their judicial affairs—I say that, even if the gigantic power of Britain over India should in the course of years, but centuries must first elapse, fall to the ground by the operation of our own hands, it will have been an achievement worthy of a nation like this to have rescued the native population from the state of ignorance, superstition, and debasement in which we found a large portion of them sunk, and to have placed them, at the expiration of the period of our dominion, in the capacity of administering the affairs of their own country as an independent nation, but under the influence of those laws, those principles, and those sound maxims which they ought ever to entertain gratitude to this country for having with care and pains instilled into their hearts. My Lords, I say this is not a work of months, or of years, nor it may be of centuries; but, though we may not live to see it, that does not absolve us from the duty, while we carefully abstain from placing in the hands of an ignorant population power which they are incapable of yielding for their own benefit; it does not absolve us from the obligation of endeavouring to raise that population in the social scale, and of carefully intrusting them with such an amount of the administration of their own local affairs as, not to their detriment but to their benefit, they may safely be enabled to carry on under the superintendence of this country'.* [emphasis added]

On 19 April 1852, John Charles Herries, a member of the House of Commons, highlighted the concrete impact of the missionary clause of the 1833 Charter Act as follows[41]:

Mr. Herries—'There was another subject of great importance, which he could not omit to notice, even at the risk of tiring the patience of the House; and this was the state of education in India, and the means adopted to promote it under the existing form of government. But in order to arrive at what had been done, it was necessary to consider what was the original number of public educational establishments, and what was the number at the present moment. He found that in 1823, the only really native endowments or educational establishments founded by the British Government were the Mahometan College at Calcutta, and the Sanscrit College at Benares. In 1835, there were fourteen of these establishments already in existence; and in 1852 in Bengal, and the North West Provinces alone there are about forty. Here was an augmentation from two years ago, to forty in 1852. But that was not all. Greater food for congratulation might be found in the evidence they possessed of the effects of these educational establishments in instructing and expanding the minds of those who have had recourse to them. He must here observe that in 1835 a very important change was made in the mode of imparting information from the system which had been previously adopted; and the beneficial results of that change may be inferred from the report of Mr. Bethune, published in 1849. Mr. Bethune says:- "There is no institution in England where the answerers are subjected to a severer test than in these institutions. I have no hesitation in saying that every succeeding examination has increased my admiration of the people, and of their attainments, both literary and scientific." In the Elphinstone Institution in Bombay the course of education is equal to a course for a degree at an English university; so that I think I may fairly refer to all these institutions, their progress and results, as a proof of the desire of the Indian Government to forward the great cause of education among the natives.... *He could also refer with great satisfaction to what had been done of late years in respect to the ecclesiastical establishment in India. The House was acquainted generally with that subject; but when we looked at what was the state of ecclesiastical establishments in India no further back than the year 1812, and compared them with what they were at the present day, he could not help seeing a very broad difference, and admitting that a very considerable anxiety had been exhibited for the spiritual instruction of so vast a body of people. In the year 1812 there were only 14 chaplains at Bengal, 12 at Madras, and 5 at Bombay. In 1813 a Bishop of Calcutta and three archdeacons for the Presidency were appointed; in 1832 there were in Bengal 37 chaplains, in Madras 23, and in Bombay 15; under the Act of 818 1833 the archdeacons ceased, and two additional bishops were appointed, and now there were 3 bishops and 68 chaplains in Bengal, 34 in Madras, and 28 in Bombay—making 3 bishops and 130 chaplains altogether, in addition to 6 of the Scotch Church. It cannot be denied that the statistics speak favourably of the exertions that have been made for the spiritual instruction of the people of India'.* [emphasis added]

Henry Goulburn, a Conservative member of the British Parliament, spoke of the manner in which the missionary clause of the 1833 Act was but a continuum of the original clause in the 1698 Charter. According to him, the entire purpose of the colonial government was to raise the morality and character of the people, and that this goal could be achieved only through the spread of the Gospel. Following were his thoughts in this regard:

Mr. Goulburn—'One great branch of the inquiry he conceived ought to be, what had been the results of *that system of religious instruction which was introduced in 1833?*

He said introduced, because previously the means were scarcely
worthy of notice. One great object to ascertain was, how far the
means of religious instruction for the people of India had been
carried out under the Act of 1833—whether those means had led
to the favourable results which were anticipated—and, if not,
how those means could be made adequate to the extension of the
Christian religion throughout the whole of that large population?
The noble Lord had told them that they had conferred great
advantages upon the people of India, and he enumerated
the reform of their judicial administration, the education of
the people in political matters, and the extension of general
education; *but he conceived the noble Lord felt it necessary on the*
occasion to forbear alluding to that which ought constantly to be
placed before them, the mode in which they could confer upon the
population of India the advantage of a knowledge of a purer faith
than any yet made known to them. He knew that great alarm had
formerly been felt on the subject of the introduction of Christianity
into India. It was supposed that excitement and insurrection
would follow if Christianity were attempted to be introduced;
but circumstances had since come to light which had dispelled
that opinion. In one of the earliest charters of the Company, in
1698, it was a specific injunction on the Company to place in
every garrison and settlement a minister of religion approved by
the Archbishop of Canterbury, not merely for the instruction of the
civil servants of the Company, to whom the noble Lord seemed
to intimate that religious instruction ought to be confined, but
it was provided also that those ministers should learn the native
language so as to convert the Hindoos and introduce, among the
inhabitants of India a purer faith Subsequently, owing to events
at home, it was thought fit to omit all allusion in the charters of
the Company to the subject of Christian instruction; but latterly
we had felt the pressing importance of communicating the blessing
of Christianity to the people of India, and he thought, therefore,
it ought to be one of the leading objects of the inquiry before the
Committee how that could be best effected. It appeared to him

that if there existed any difficulty on the subject, inquiry would expel it. At no time could inquiry be more effectually conducted. There were men in England competent to give the Committee the best information, from their experience in India, how the religion of the Church of England had been extended, and might be still further extended there, and to satisfy them that those restrictions which at present prohibited allusion to the Christian religion might be safely dispensed with. On former occasions it was urged that the prejudices of the people were such that by attempting to disseminate the principles of Christianity among them, we should incite rebellion and insurrection, and that it was in vain to attempt to overcome those prejudices, or to moderate them. But since then, many of these inveterate prejudices had been overcome; and one meritorious officer, by his own exertions and prudent management alone, had induced the Rajpoots, who were most bigoted in the practice of suttee, to abandon that practice, so revolting to all our feelings.

He considered that the empire of India had been confided to us for great and important objects. He was sure it was not given for the gratification of our national vanity, as a field on which to exercise the valour of our troops, as a means of increasing our national wealth, nor even for the improving the judicial and political relations of the different States of which that empire was composed. It imposed on us the high moral duty of taking such measures as prudence, combined with zeal, would justify for the purpose of spreading over a heathen continent the knowledge of that truth which was essential to our own happiness, and which, extended abroad, he believed might be essential to the happiness of millions yet unborn.

Sir Thomas Munro had said - "There is one great question to which we should look in all our arrangements—namely, what is to be the final result of our government on the character of the people, and whether that character will be raised or lowered. Are we to be satisfied with merely securing our power and protecting the inhabitants, leaving them to sink gradually in character lower than at present; or are we to endeavour to raise their character? It ought undoubtedly to be our aim to raise the minds of the natives, and to take care that whenever our connexion with India shall cease, it shall not appear that the only fruit of our dominion had been to leave the people more abject than when we found them. It would certainly be more desirable that we should be expelled from the country altogether, than that our system of government should be such an abasement of a whole people." *He (Mr. Goulburn) asserted this country could not fulfil the wishes and objects of that great statesman otherwise than by disseminating the truth of religion; and he trusted the result of the labours of this Committee would he, as it must be if prosecuted, to incite us to future exertions in spreading the Gospel without the fear of exciting those discontents which were so dreaded, but which experience had shown so far to be altogether groundless'.* [emphasis added]

While Ross Donnelly Mangles, a member of Parliament, was opposed to State support for the Christian establishment in India, his dissent only proves that the British Indian government was indeed actively aiding missionary work in Bharat. Not just that, his position is at best that of Christian tolerance, which is premised on the belief that as long as the State merely guaranteed the freedom of preaching the Gospel without being required to support it any further, it would produce converts of the first order as opposed to raising up 'a great body of hypocrites, seeking to curry favour by the simulated adoption of Christianity'. Following is an excerpt illustrating his views:

Mr. Mangles—'*said, that he was sincerely anxious that the blessings of Christianity should be extended to the people of India*; but he did not think that the Government, as a Government, should take any active part in its promotion. By doing so he thought they would baffle the object which they had in view; and he considered that it was the duty of the Government to hold the scales even, and afford fair play to the dissemination of the truth. This had been done hitherto. *It was perfectly notorious that under the present charter no restraint had been imposed upon the efforts of the missionaries, and these efforts had been made, and were making, not merely by missionaries connected with the Church of England, but by the Church of Scotland, and many denominations of Dissenters. If the Government undertook to attempt the conversion of the people of India, the only effect would be to raise up a great body of hypocrites, seeking to curry favour by the simulated adoption of Christianity. He considered that the Government should confine itself to its proper sphere of duty—the protection of all its subjects, including, of course, the preachers of the Gospel. The free preaching of the Gospel was all that should be secured; and as regarded its effects, he knew himself that from the free preaching of the missionaries many persons had been converted, and were as sincere and earnest Christians as any Members of that House'.* [emphasis added]

It is evident from the material discussed thus far that the events surrounding the *Inter Caetera* in 1493 until the Protestant Reformation, had a clear bearing on the colonisation of Bharat by European nations, including that of the British, whose colonial consciousness and evangelical intent are expressly reflected in no uncertain terms in legal instruments as well as the cogitations surrounding them—starting from 1600 until 1853. Therefore, it can be concluded, without reservation, that this inextricable enmeshing of the Christian obligation to proselytise and the civilising attitude of the British coloniser is a matter of fact, not subjective opinion. This had a direct bearing on the coloniser's understanding of Indic faith systems, societal structures, and on his education and language policies, as shall be seen in the next chapter.

Christian Colonial Consciousness, the Hindu Religion, Caste, Tribe and Education

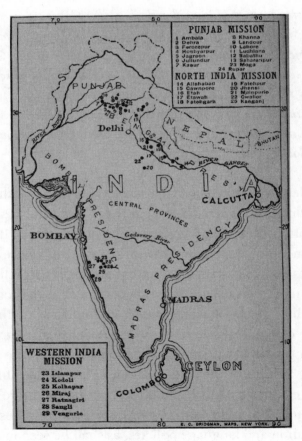

Missions in India

Source: *Reports of the Missionary and Benevolent Boards and Committees to the General Assembly of the Presbyterian Church in the United States of America* (1913).

G iven the inherently evangelical nature of Christian toleration practised by the European coloniser, what was the practical impact, if any, of such toleration on his understanding of Indic faith systems and its forms of social organisation? Did the Christian consciousness of the coloniser influence the shaping of his education and language policies in Bharat? To answer these questions, through the course of this chapter, I have relied on first-hand material, apart from the scholarly works of Dr. Jakob De Roover, Nicolas B. Dirks[1] and others who have expounded on these questions persuasively in great detail. At this juncture, I must clarify that my discussion on these aspects will be brief and limited to locating such literature in the broader context of coloniality.

In his must-read book *Europe, India, and the Limits of Secularism*[2], De Roover refers to a letter from the Collector and Magistrate of Karachi, Captain H.W. Preedy, to the Secretary to Government of Sindh, dated 28 November 1943, which according to me, pithily captures the essence of the British coloniser's policy of toleration. In the letter, Captain Preedy writes, 'We are bound to tolerate all religions, but not I conceive to support any but our own.' The letter is but an illustration of the clear distinction struck by the coloniser between toleration and support, wherein the former applied to the indigenous faith systems of the colonised society and the latter applied to his own religion, Christianity.[3]

Not only did this policy of Christian toleration translate to State support being provided to the spread of Christianity (as revealed by the legislative material discussed in the previous chapter), it also translated to the coloniser approaching Indic OET systems with the same anticlerical political theology that characterised the Protestant Reformation's approach to the Catholic Church and papal authority. As stated earlier, the consequence of this approach was that Brahmins, 'Brahminism' and 'Brahminical institutions' replaced the Pope and Catholic Church as the new objects of hatred and perpetual 'reform' at the hands of evangelical Christianity. Since temples were predominantly seen as 'Brahminical institutions', the narrative employed against pre-Christian pagan temples in Europe was pressed into service with respect to Hindu temples and their practices. For instance, the charge of 'sacred or cultic prostitution' that was employed by early Christians to malign and slander pagan temples in Europe was extended to the 'devadasi' practice in Bharat as well, which ultimately resulted in the legislative abolition of the practice. Despite its abolition, the narrative of temple prostitution continued to be advanced in order to strengthen the perception that the 'Hindoo religion' was so fundamentally debauched, corrupt and obsessed with sex that its places of worship were also sites of prostitution. This coupled with the caricature of the evil Brahmin, effectively painted a picture that women were being forced to become temple prostitutes to pander to the dictates of the 'Brahminical religion'.

No wonder the debates in the British Parliament pejoratively used 'priestcraft'[4] to refer to Brahmins and everything they subscribed to or were associated with, especially the Dharmashastras. This is corroborated by the view of Charles Grant, an evangelical-minded member of the British Parliament, on the Manusmriti[5], which is as follows:

> Nothing is more plain, than that this whole fabric is the work of a crafty and imperious priesthood, who feigned a divine revelation and appointment, to invest their own order, in perpetuity, with the most absolute empire over the civil state of the Hindoos, as well as over their minds.

De Roover argues that the Christian framework within which the British policy of toleration towards Indic faith systems and practices was adopted did not leave such systems untouched. On the contrary, indigenous/Indic OET was restructured to fit into the Christian idea of 'religion', which was embraced, unfortunately, by Hindu 'reform' movements as well. This translated to a doctrinal and scriptural approach to 'Hinduism', that is, only those practices which could be traced to the sacred texts of Hinduism would be tolerated by the colonial State, while the rest would be treated as superstitious and immoral, warranting State interference. To support this, the coloniser drew from the Protestant/Lockean position that struck a distinction between 'core' religious practices that did not warrant State interference, and 'false religion' and civil/secular aspects of religious practices that permitted State intervention. Here are a few educative excerpts on the said issue from De Roover's book:

> The framework underlying Locke's theory clarifies why it was so important to know whether the 'sacred laws of the Hindu religion' sanctioned sati and other practices. According to this Christian religious framework, all human souls have equal access to God and live to obey Him. Nevertheless, the devil and his priests corrupt this sense by imposing their fabrications as divinely revealed commandments upon innocent believers. In order to understand such people and go about with them, one should find out what they believe to be God's will for humanity. Which specific set of laws did the Hindus mistake for God's revelation? This was the obsession of early colonial scholars.[6]

> ....the toleration policy compelled colonial officials to determine which practices were truly religious and hence had to be tolerated. At this first level, Protestant notions of false religion operated implicitly. Even though the colonial government and its courts of law approached the Hindu traditions as religion tout court, without adding predicates of falsity, they nevertheless smuggled in the theological distinction between true religion as the revelation of God and false religion as human additions to religion. In fact, the Christian distinction between the religious, the secular, and the idolatrous was introduced as though it

concerned a distinction internal to Hindu religion. Some
practices were accepted as truly religious, while others
were rejected as illegitimate additions to religion.

The boundary was drawn along the lines of the Protestant
division between the essentials commanded by God in scripture
and indifferent things falsely superimposed as religion.... In
its secularized form, this division between pure religion and
human additions was viewed as a general characteristic of all
religions, including Hinduism. Since the task of locating this
boundary was displaced to the 'scriptures' and 'priests' of 'Hindu
religion', the colonial legal system effectively transplanted this
conceptual structure into the Hindu traditions.

Consequently, the normative framework behind the
colonial legal system compelled Hindu traditions to internalize
the Christian division between the religious, the secular and
the falsely religious.... All aspects of Indian traditions that
did not fit into the codified model of Hindu law were rejected
as illegitimate human additions to true 'Hindu religion' or
denounced as ceremonies and rites that had no role to play in
genuine 'Hindu law'. Thus, these aspects were relegated to a
hidden realm of false religion.[7]

Simply put, toleration meant that what constituted the 'Hindu
religion' was determined through the application of a manifestly
Christian framework. This blatantly Christian attempt to
understand the 'Hindu religion' also manifested itself in the
coloniser's understanding of the fundamental tenets or 'laws'
of Hinduism, leading to the quest for a Moses-like 'lawgiver'.
This quest yielded Manu, the author of the much-reviled
Manusmriti. Whether the Manusmriti, or for that matter the
Dharmashastras, constituted a religious commandment/law or
a descriptive recordal of customs and practices was never clearly
understood by the Christian coloniser since he was incapable
of viewing the indigenous society through an indigenous
perspective. Therefore, even conceptions of what constituted

'religious law' in the 'Hindu religion' were introduced through a Christian lens, which significantly affected both the coloniser's understanding of the native society as well as the colonialised natives' understanding of their own culture, since the Christian idea of seeking scriptural support for traditions was embraced by the latter. This led to attempts at converting the Hindu system of tradition to 'religion' in the Christian sense.

De Roover presents the 'Hindu reformer' Raja Rammohun Roy as one of the prime examples of those who actively applied the scriptural approach to Hinduism to rid it of its 'ills' in the interest of 'social reform'. Under this approach, Roy treated the Vedas as the Hindu 'Bible' and attempted to draw structural parallels between the 'Hindu religion' and Christianity. On a related note, in the ensuing discussion on the introduction of English education in Bharat, we shall see that Roy's views on indigenous education, its pedagogy and its worth were no less colonialised.[8]

In practical terms, the application of the Christian framework to understand what constituted the 'Hindoo religion' translated to its 'essentials' being distilled. This had the following two consequences that are of patent relevance to contemporary debates surrounding Hinduism, both in society as well as in judicial treatment:

1. The Essential Religious Practices (ERP) test, as applied by the Indian Supreme Court in matters involving protection of religious practices and institutions under Articles 25 and 26 of the Constitution may be traced to the Christian colonial distinction between essential tenets of a religion and its non-essential aspects; and
2. The application of the Christian concept of 'religion' to Indic OET gave rise to the debate as to whether Hinduism was a 'religion' or 'a way of life'.

I will now elaborate further upon each of these positions and demonstrate them through a few landmark judgments of the Supreme Court of India.

First, the application of the ERP test by the Supreme Court broadly translates to an exercise undertaken to identify whether a certain practice falls within the realm of religion or in the secular realm, in order to determine the extent of protection accorded to it from State interference under the Constitution. This test was laid down by the Supreme Court in the landmark judgment delivered by a seven-Judge Bench in 1954, in the case of *The Commissioner, Hindu Religious Endowments, Madras* v. *Sri Lakshmindra Tirtha Swamiar of Sri Shirur Mutt*, popularly known as the 'Shirur Math Judgment'.[9] This judgment was delivered in the context of a challenge to the constitutionality of the Madras Hindu Religious and Charitable Endowments Act of 1951. However, before I proceed to discuss the Shirur Math Judgment, a brief history of the Madras Hindu Religious and Charitable Endowments Act, 1951, itself is important to demonstrate the coloniality in the treatment of Indic religious institutions by the independent Indian State.

Owing to the significant resources attached to temples, the East India Company began interfering with the administrative structures of temples citing corruption in their administration as the primary pretext. After all, the colonial assumption was that since heathens were inherently corrupt, their institutions too must be dens of corruption and avarice. This led to the British policy of centralised collection as well as distribution of all temple revenues within the territories under its control. The policy also included audit of funds used by temple authorities and bureaucratic control over temple administrators. This policy resulted in undermining the autonomous, localised, community-driven and self-sufficient nature of temple administration by making it increasingly dependent on a centralised bureaucracy. By 1789, a Board of Revenue was established by the Company to take charge of temples in the Madras Presidency, which was then followed by the Madras Endowments and Escheats Regulation of 1817 whose preamble reads as follows:

> Considerable endowments have been granted in money, or by assignments of land or of the produce of the land by the former Governments of this country as well as by the British Government, and by individuals for the support of *mosques, Hindu temples,* colleges and choultries, and for other pious and beneficial purposes; and ... endowments [are] in many instances appropriated, contrary to the intentions of the donors, to the personal use of the individuals in immediate charge and possession of such endowments; and... it is the duty of the government to provide that such endowments be applied according to the real intent and will of the granter. [emphasis added]

Pertinently, this regulation applied to both Hindu and Muslim religious institutions. It was in force until 1839, when Christian missionaries back in England started protesting against administration of the religious institutions of 'heathens' by the Christian colonial government. In 1863, the Regulation of 1817 was replaced by the Religious Endowments Act, which applied to temples and mosques. The 1863 Act was then replaced by the Madras Hindu Religious Endowments Act of 1923, which was the first legislation to apply solely to Hindu religious institutions, in contrast to previous legislations. Perhaps, in the eyes of the coloniser, Muslims, being 'people of the book', were deemed less corrupt and immoral than idol-worshipping heathen, and hence were exempt from State interference. In 1927, the 1923 legislation was replaced by the Madras Hindu Religious Endowments Act of 1926 (the 1927 Act), which too applied solely to Hindu religious institutions. The 1927 Act was in force until 1951.

It was the 1927 Act whose constitutionality was originally challenged in writ petitions in 1951 by the Shirur Math from Udupi (in present-day Karnataka) and the Nataraja Temple in Chidambaram (in present-day Tamil Nadu) before the Madras High Court in what has come to be known as the Shirur Math case. The challenge to the 1927 Act was on the grounds that after the Constitution came into force on 26 January 1950, the framework of the 1927 Act had to be tested on the anvils of the Constitution. During the pendency of the writ petitions, the then Madras government repealed the 1927 Act and passed the Madras Hindu Religious and Charitable Endowments Act, 1951, which too, as the name reflects, applied exclusively to Hindu religious institutions. Accordingly, the writ petitions were amended to challenge the 1951 Act on the ground that it violated Articles 19(1)(f), 25, 26 and 27 of the Constitution. The central provisions of the Act were struck down by the Madras High Court in 1951 as being unconstitutional, and the judgment of the High Court was largely upheld by the Supreme Court in 1954 in its landmark Shirur Math Judgment.

Ironically, the very same provisions of the 1951 Madras HRCE Act, which were struck down by the Supreme Court as unconstitutional in 1954, were reintroduced in sum and substance in the Tamil Nadu Hindu Religious and Charitable Endowments Act, 1959, which is still in force to date. These reintroduced provisions, along with the corresponding provisions of the HRCE legislations of Andhra Pradesh and Puducherry, are currently under challenge before the Supreme Court in a Writ Petition filed in 2012 by the late Swami Dayananda Saraswathi, founder of Arsha Vidya Gurukulam. Clearly, the Indian State in general has no qualms or compunctions in circumventing or contravening the verdict of even the highest court of the land when it comes to Indic religious institutions.

This is but one of the examples of the manner in which concepts such as 'secularism' and 'equality' have played out in so-called independent, decolonised Bharat—to the extreme detriment of its indigenous consciousness. This is in stark contrast to the Christian secularism of Europe which protects Christian institutions from

State interference. In other words, the coloniality of the Indian State is evidenced by the fact that as opposed to preserving and respecting the space of Indic consciousness, which would have been consistent with the policy of Christian toleration and secularism of the coloniser that accorded primacy to Christianity, the Indian State acts as the successor of the coloniser in its stepmotherly treatment of native consciousness. Consequently, non-Indic institutions and practices enjoy better protection from State interference than their Indic counterparts. This is supported by the fact that the Indian State has enacted at least 15 Hindu-specific legislations that enable State control and facilitate State entrenchment in Hindu institutions. Clearly, this is attributable to the Indian State's embracing of the colonial assumption that the 'Hindoo' is corrupt, debauched and backward, especially if Brahmin, and therefore, such institutions must be under State control in order to 'reform' them.

Coming back to the Supreme Court's Shirur Math Judgment in the context of the ERP test, it continues to be the ruling precedent on the interpretation of religious versus secular under Article 25(2)(a) of the Constitution to date, which led to the formulation of the Test. At this juncture, it becomes important to broadly understand the intent and import of Article 25, which will help better comprehend the judgment. As we shall see, it could be argued based on the language of Article 25 that the distinction between 'religious' and 'secular' is directly embedded in it, which resonates with the Christian or Lockean position.

Article 25(1) of the Constitution guarantees to all persons the freedom of conscience and the right to freely profess, practise and propagate 'religion' subject to public order, morality, health and other provisions of that part of the Constitution. Article 25(2)(a) enables the State to make laws 'regulating or restricting any economic, financial, political or *other secular activity which may be associated with religious practice*'. Effectively, Article 25(2)(a) strikes the very same distinction between the religious and the secular that is inherent to the Christian framework. I would find it exceedingly difficult to dismiss this as mere coincidence. Whether the language of this provision is attributable to Christian colonial consciousness of the framers of the Constitution and whether they were aware of its Christian normative framework are aspects that will be explored in the sequel to this book.

What is, however, relevant for the current discussion is that it is this distinction between the religious and the secular that enables the Indian State to enact laws that regulate religious and charitable activities. While this power is available to the Indian State in relation to institutions of *all* faiths, thus far it has chosen to exercise this power primarily in relation to Hindu institutions. The claimed ideological proclivities of no dispensation has made a difference to this pattern, underscoring the presence of colonial consciousness across the political spectrum with the difference being in degree, at best.

Here is the relevant extract from the Shirur Math Judgment that captures the genesis of the ERP test based on the religious versus secular distinction reflected in the language of Article 25(2)(a):

The learned Attorney-General lays stress upon clause (2)(a) of the article and his contention is that *all secular activities, which may be associated with religion but do not really constitute an essential part of it, are amenable to State regulation.*

The contention formulated in such broad terms cannot, we think, be supported. *In the first place, what constitutes the essential part of a religion is primarily to be ascertained with reference to the doctrines of that religion itself. If the tenets of any religious sect of the Hindus prescribe that offerings of food should be given to the idol at particular hours of the day, that periodical ceremonies should be performed in a certain way at certain periods of the year or that there should be daily recital of sacred texts or ablations to the sacred fire, all these would be regarded as parts of religion and the mere fact that they involve expenditure of money or employment of priests and servants or the use of marketable commodities would not make them secular activities partaking of a commercial or economic character; all of them are religious practices and should be regarded as matters of religion within the meaning of article 26(b). What article 25(2)(a) contemplates is not regulation by the State of religious practices as such, the freedom of which is guaranteed by the Constitution except when they run counter to public order, health and morality, but regulation of activities which are economic, commercial or political in their character though they are associated with religious practices.* [emphasis added]

As is evident, the above test was originally formulated to distinguish between the religious and the secular in the context of determining the scope of State powers to regulate the secular aspects of a religious institution under Article 25(2)(a). However, it would ultimately morph in subsequent judgments of the Supreme Court into a test to determine the 'essential aspects' of a religion for the very purpose of the enjoyment of fundamental religious freedoms under Article 25(1). In other words, thenceforth, the State or more often than not, constitutional courts, would determine what constituted 'essential' aspects of a religion despite professing to be secular bodies with no institutionalised training in the OET of any faith. The irony is compounded by the fact that the religious versus secular divide was conceived of in the Christian faith to limit the scope of State interference in matters of religion, which, in Bharat, has yielded diametrically opposite results particularly with respect to Indic faith systems.

Even if the ERP test may validly be applied to other scripture-based faiths that are closer to the coloniser's faith, the application of such a test to Indic OETs, which are not fully bound by scripture, is to impose the Christian theological framework on indigenous faith systems. The fact that native faith systems are not fully bound by scripture and have evolved as much through custom, practice and context flummoxed the Christian European coloniser just as much as it seems to confound contemporary Indian institutions, including the judiciary. It bears noting that this colonialised understanding of Indic faith systems forms the bedrock of the eternal project of 'reform' of the 'Hindu religion' and society in 'independent' Bharat.

Coming to the second issue of whether Hinduism is a 'religion' or a way of life, the debate invariably ends up stoking emotions for several reasons. The adherents of Indic faith systems are concerned, and rightly so, that the treatment of Hinduism as 'a way of life' and not a 'religion' by the Indian State might deprive them of their fundamental religious freedoms under the Constitution that are guaranteed to the followers of other religions. At the same time, they do not want 'Sanatana Dharma' or 'Dharma' to be equated with the Christian or Islamic idea of 'religion', again rightly so, since their OETs are very different. Nor do they want to be told that the 'Hindu religion' is essentially a Christian colonial construct because they understand that by calling it a colonial construct, some call into question the very precolonial existence of Dharmic belief systems and the notion of Dharmic oneness underlying the various Hindu sampradayas. There is more than an element of truth in these strands, each of which warrants unpacking.

First, it is important to distinguish between (*a*) the need for legal/constitutional approximation of Indic faith systems as 'religion' to ensure the enjoyment of fundamental freedoms, and (*b*) OET-based differences between Indic faith systems and the coloniser's religion. Interestingly, this brings out the coloniality inherent in the mechanical application of the concept of 'religion' as well as the use of the word 'religion' in contemporary legal and constitutional framework, both domestic and international. Whether this indicates the acceptance of the colonial worldview by the framers of the Constitution, again, will be discussed in the sequel to this book; however, what is evident is the problem underlying the use of colonial linguistics and the connotations they carry when extended to Indic OET systems. Therefore, the existence of this problem must be acknowledged and a decolonial approach to it must be employed.

Second, in so far as OET is concerned, the adherents of Indic OET systems are justified in taking the position that their OETs are vastly different from that of Christianity, and therefore, except for the purposes of enjoyment of equal rights under the Constitution, the conceptual and theoretical frameworks of Indic OET and Christian OET are not and cannot be treated as the same. It is in this context that the assertion is typically made that 'Hinduism', given its approach to the concept of soul and consciousness, its relationship with nature, and its diverse and federal character reflected by the nature of the Indic civilisation, is vastly different from monochromatic, monotheistic and centrally organised religions, such as Islam and Christianity. It is this distinction that leads to the widely misunderstood summation that Hinduism is more a 'way of life' and therefore, comparisons with Christianity and Islam are misplaced.

This summation can be traced to the judgments of the Supreme Court of India in *Shastri Yagnapurushdasji and others* v. *Muldas Bhundardas vaishya and another*[10] and *Bramchari Sidheswar Bhai and others* v. *State of West Bengal*[11], wherein the Apex Court distinguished Hinduism from the Islamic and Christian understanding of 'religion'. A reading of the said judgments reveals that, surprisingly, the position of the Supreme Court is largely consistent with the decolonial position that Indic faith systems are distinct from both Abrahamic religions, and yet qualify for protection under the Constitution as 'the Hindu religion'. In other words, the Supreme Court, while recognising that Sanatana Dharma cannot be understood through the Abrahamic construct of 'religion', has not taken away the right of Dharmic OET systems to be treated as 'religion' for the purposes of enjoyment and exercise of constitutionally guaranteed fundamental freedoms.

Extracted below are a few relevant excerpts from *Shastri Yagnapurushdasji* judgment:

When we think of the Hindu religion, we find it difficult, if not impossible, to define Hindu religion or even adequately describe it. Unlike other religions in the world, the Hindu religion does not claim any one prophet; it does not worship any one God; it does not subscribe to any one dogma; it does not believe in any one philosophic concept; it does not follow any one set of religious rites or performances; in fact, it does not appear to satisfy the narrow traditional features of any religion or creed. It may broadly be described as a way of life and nothing more.

Whilst we are dealing with this broad and comprehensive, aspect of Hindu religion, it may be permissible to enquire what according to this religion, is the ultimate goal of humanity? It is the release and freedom from the unceasing cycle of births and rebirths; Moksha or Nirvana, which is the ultimate aim of Hindu religion and philosophy, represents the state of absolute absorption and assimilation of the individual soul with the infinite. What are the means to attain this end? On this vital issue, there is great divergence of views; some emphasise the importance of Gyan or knowledge, while others extol the virtues of Bhakti or devotion; and yet others insist upon the paramount importance of the performance of duties with a heart full of devotion and mind inspired by true knowledge. In this sphere again, there is diversity of opinion, though all are agreed about the ultimate goal. Therefore, it would be inappropriate to apply the traditional tests in determining the extent of the jurisdiction of Hindu religion. It can be safely described as a way of life based on certain basic concepts to which we have already referred. Tilak faced this complex and difficult problem of defining or at least describing adequately Hindu religion and he evolved a working formula which may be regarded as fairly adequate and satisfactory. Said Tilak: 'Acceptance of the Vedas with reverence; recognition of the fact that the means or ways to salvation are diverse and realisation of the truth that the number of gods to be worshipped is large, that indeed is the distinguishing feature of Hindu religion'(1). This definition brings out succinctly the broad distinctive features of Hindu religion. It is somewhat remarkable that this broad sweep of Hindu religion has been eloquently described by Toynbee. Says Toynbee: 'When we pass from the plane of social practice to the plane of intellectual outlook, Hinduism too comes out well by comparison with the religions and ideologies of the South-West Asian group. In contrast to these Hinduism has the same outlook as the pre-Christian and pre-Muslim religions and philosophies of the Western half of the old world. Like them, Hinduism takes it for granted that there is more than one valid approach to truth and to salvation and that these different approaches are not only compatible with each other, but are complementary.'

The Constitution-makers were fully conscious of this broad and comprehensive character of Hindu religion; and so, while guaranteeing the fundamental right to freedom of religion, Explanation II to Art. 25 has made it clear that in sub-clause (b) of clause (2), the reference to Hindus shall be construed as including a reference to persons professing the Sikh, Jaina or Buddhist religion, and the reference to Hindu religious institutions shall be construed accordingly. Consistently with this constitutional provision, the Hindu Marriage Act, 1955; the Hindu Succession Act, 1956; the Hindu Minority and Guardianship Act, 1956; and the Hindu Adoptions and Maintenance Act, 1956 have extended the application of these Acts to all persons who can be regarded as Hindus in this broad and comprehensive sense.

The above-mentioned judgment was delivered by the Supreme Court in the context of the Swaminarayan sect taking the position that its followers did not profess the Hindu religion, a contention which the Court rejected. When a similar position was sought to be taken by the Ramakrishna Mission in *Bramchari Sidheswar Bhai and others* v. *State of West Bengal*, the Supreme

Court reiterated the position set out in *Shastri Yagnapurushdasji*. Therefore, at least in two landmark judgments, the Supreme Court has recognised that Dharmic OET is different from the Christian and Islamic OETs, and that its approximation as 'religion' is only for the purposes of equal enjoyment of fundamental religious freedoms under the Constitution.

Moving to the next limb, that is, colonial reshaping of Indic faith systems, while it is true that the Christian coloniser did seek to reconstruct the Indic OET by applying the Christian standard of 'religion', it would be incorrect to state that Indic sects or sampradayas did not exist or lacked unity under the umbrella of Sanatana Dharma prior to colonisation. Simply stated, the coloniser's attempt to redefine the 'Hindu religion' cannot and does not render 'Dharma' or 'Dharmic unity' an artificial colonial construct. On this specific subject, Dr. S.N. Balagangadhara[12] is of the view that be it 'Hindu*ism*', 'Buddh*ism*' or 'Jain*ism*', each of these is a colonial construct in an empirical sense, but *not* in the epistemological sense. In other words, the existence of Dharmic OET systems or sampradayas obviously predates the Christian European coloniser, while only their reconstruction as 'religions' in the Christian sense is attributable to him. Critically, this must be understood in the context of the global application of the concept of 'religion' by Christian Europe or the West to approximate the nature of non-Christian or non-Abrahamic indigenous faith systems in order to make sense of them through a Christian theological framework. Therefore, the reconstruction of indigenous OET systems on the lines of 'religion' is a global consequence of European colonisation, not limited to Indic OET systems, and this does not take away from the precolonial antiquity of Sanatana Dharma.

On this aspect, the views of Dr. Balagandhara and Dr. Roover, and the views of decolonial scholars, such as Nelson Maldonado-Torres[13], echo one another. According to Maldonado-Torres, 'the concept of religion most used in the

West by scholars and laypeople alike is a specifically modern concept forged in the context of imperialism and colonial expansion'. He even goes a step further to criticise the postcolonial school for having reinforced this by according a special place to 'secular' authors from Europe and the Third World over the views of native practitioners of indigenous faith systems. Extracted below is an excerpt from his work on the subject[14]:

> Postcolonial theory has made some contributions to the understanding of the links between religion, modernity, and coloniality, but it has tended to side with modern secularism in its characterization of religion, and it has equally privileged conversations with European and, to some extent, Third World secular authors. That is, the views of religious thinkers themselves, and experiences grounded in religious practices, rituals, narratives, or forms of organization, tend to be less present than the perspectives of secular authors in the understanding of the meaning of religion, modernity, or coloniality. Another tendency in postcolonial theory, due in part to the collective impact of renowned theorists, such as Edward Said, Gayatri Spivak, and Homi Bhabha, has been to identify sources for postcolonial theorizing in the specific histories of eighteenth- and nineteenth-century English and French colonialism and in the regions of the Middle East and South Asia. Less attention has been paid to fifteenth- to seventeenth-century formations of coloniality, and to colonies in the West, where the Spanish, the Portuguese, the Dutch, and more recently the United States, among other imperial powers, have had enduring influences. One of the consequences of this is that religious studies scholars who are in conversation with post-colonial theory tend to be well versed in the postcolonial critique of Orientalism, but much less informed about the theorization of Occidentalism or Americanity.

This is yet another reason why the decolonial approach is better than the postcolonial in the critical realm of religion, since the latter privileges modern secularism without exploring or acknowledging its Christian OET foundations and applies the construct of 'religion' as well as 'secularism' to native OET systems. According to Balagangadhara, De Roover and Sarah Claerhout[15], the application of this framework can be traced to the Christian premise 'that religion would exist among all nations, because God had gifted religion to humanity at the time of creation'. In fact, these scholars take the considered position that the application of Christian theology led to misplaced deductions which pass off as historical facts, such as 'Brahmins are the priests of Hinduism' or 'Buddhism was a reform movement against Brahmanism and its caste hierarchy'. The following is a relevant excerpt from a paper by Dr. Roover and Claerhout[16], which captures the decolonial question in the realm of 'religion':

> One could simply accept that 'Hinduism' does not name a unitary phenomenon, but picks out a super set that includes many different sets of practices and beliefs.... One could even add that the claim that Hinduism cannot be one religion, because it is not a coherent unit, presupposes a Christian model of religion as a coherent doctrinal entity and then assesses Hinduism according to this model.
>
> Did Indians, with their own background framework and cultural experience, understand what the British meant when the latter said 'religion', 'law', 'scripture', 'priests' or 'caste'? Did the British and other Europeans, with their specific background framework and cultural experience, understand Indians when they spoke of 'dharma', 'shastra', 'puja', 'brahmanas' or 'jati'?
>
> Whenever Europeans invoked notions like 'religion', 'worship', 'gods' or 'priesthood' in order to describe India, their reasoning operated against a background

theology, which had determined the semantic content and systematic relations of these terms. Over many centuries, this background theology had shaped natural language use in European vernaculars. Naturally, Indians had their own cultural experiences, linguistic practices and semantic schemes. Trying to make sense of the queries of the coloniser, Indians learned to use English-language words ('religion', 'revelation', 'God', 'worship', 'priest', 'idolatry'), without having access to the background theology that related these terms to each other in a systematic way.

For instance, while puja rituals are not in any sense the equivalent of worship in Christianity, Europeans misunderstood these rituals as worship and mistranslated 'puja' as 'worship'. In the next step, Indians learned English and accepted that 'worship' meant 'puja', without understanding what worship is in Christianity and without having access to the linguistic practices and conceptual schemes, which related this notion of worship to other theological concepts like God, idolatry and religion. Given our current lack of insight into this process, we cannot grasp the distortions that occurred when the term 'worship' was mapped onto 'puja'.

A similar process occurred for all such appropriations of English-language terms and theological notions. As Indians took over these words, their original meanings were distorted, accordingly as European-language terms were mapped onto terms and semantic schemes from Indian languages (e.g., 'dharma', 'apaurusheya', 'deva', 'puja', 'purohit', 'murtipuja').

This extract succinctly highlights the problematic use of Christian colonial linguistics or semantics and the underlying Protestant experience to describe and understand Indic systems, institutions and practices, which results in the superimposition of the Christian framework on native consciousness. In this regard, once again the Shirur Math Judgment is useful to demonstrate the way Indian constitutional courts have applied Christian colonial linguistics to Indic institutions and practices.

In the Shirur Math Judgment, apart from setting out the ERP test based on the religious versus secular divide, the Supreme Court also laid down the criteria for what constitutes a 'religious denomination' under Article 26, which is the law on this issue to date. Here is the relevant excerpt from the judgment:

> *As regards article 26, the first question is, what is the precise meaning or connotation of the expression 'religious denomination' and whether a Math could come within this expression. The word 'denomination' has been defined in the Oxford Dictionary to mean 'a collection of individuals classed together under the same name: a religious sect or body having a common faith and Organisation and designated by a distinctive name'.* It is well known that the practice of setting up Maths as centres of the logical teaching was started by Shri Sankaracharya and was followed by various teachers since then. After Sankara, came a galaxy of religious teachers and philosophers who founded the different sects and sub-sects of the Hindu religion that we find in India at the present day. Each one of such sects or sub-sects can certainly be balled a religious denomination, as it is designated by a distinctive name—in many cases it is the name of the founder— and has a common faith and common spiritual organization. The followers of Ramanuja, who are known by the name of Shri Vaishnavas, undoubtedly constitute a religious denomination; and so do the followers of Madhwacharya and other religious teachers. It is a fact well established by tradition that the eight Udipi Maths were founded by Madhwacharya himself and the trustees and the beneficiaries of these Maths profess to be followers of that teacher. The High Court has found that the Math in question is in charge of the Sivalli Brahmins who constitute a section of the followers of Madhwacharya. As article 26 contemplates not merely a religious denomination

but also a section thereof, the Math or the spiritual fraternity represented by it can legitimately come within the purview of this article. [emphasis added]

There are multiple problems with this excerpt, the first of which is that, as opposed to using Indic commentaries to understand the contours of a 'sampradaya' from a Dharmic perspective in the context of a Dharmic institution, the Supreme Court chose to rely on the Oxford Dictionary. This is because the language in which the Constitution is understood and interpreted is the British coloniser's native tongue, English. Second, the Oxford Dictionary of the 1950s surely could not have been expected to reflect anything other than the Christian understanding of things, in particular, religious concepts. Therefore, while it could be argued that the Supreme Court was only operating within the rules of interpretation accepted in English law (which is its standard practice even today), the fact is that owing to the Christian backdrop of the coloniser's lexicon, the Court unconsciously applied a manifestly Christian concept and definition of religious denomination to a Dharmic institution. After all, as discussed in the first section of the book, the concept of a religious denomination is a direct consequence of the Protestant Reformation, which led to the recognition of Lutheranism and Calvinism as the other two permanent Christian religious denominations alongside Roman Catholicism.

This clearly brings out the problem with the application of Christian colonial linguistics, semantics and framework to Indic institutions, groups and practices since those sampradayas, which do not satisfy the test prescribed by the Supreme Court for a 'religious denomination' but can otherwise broadly be considered sects, stand to lose out on the fundamental rights guaranteed under Article 26 that envisages institutional religious autonomy of sects/groups. In this regard, as someone who has been a part of matters of civilisational importance before the Supreme Court, I have experienced, first-hand, the problem with such an application of a Christian framework to a Hindu religious institution, which resulted in the institution being denied the status of a denominational institution and, accordingly, the freedoms under Article 26.

Interestingly, on the issue of interpretation of a 'religious denomination', the following is the difference between the Madras High Court's position in the Shirur Math case in its judgment of 1951 and the Supreme Court's position in 1954 in the very same case. Extracted below is the definition of religious denomination from the Webster Dictionary used by the Madras High Court in 1951:

> of action of naming from or after something;
>> giving a name to, calling by a name;
>> a characteristic or qualifying name given to a thing or class
> of things;
>> that by which anything is called;
>> an appellation, designation or title;
>> a collection of individuals classed together under the same
> name; *now almost always specifically a religious sect or body having a common faith and organisation and designated by a distinctive name.* [emphasis added]

While the Madras High Court's verdict enumerated at least seven possible definitions of religious denomination from the Webster Dictionary, including the last two, namely 'a collection of individuals classed together under the same name' and '*now almost always specifically a religious sect or body having a common faith and organisation and designated by a distinctive name*', which were separated by a semicolon, the Supreme Court relied on the Oxford version which defined it as '*a collection of individuals classed together under the same name: a religious sect or body having a common faith and organisation and designated by a distinctive name*', which connected the two parts with a colon.[17] This difference in punctuation has made a world of difference, since the Supreme Court appears to have latched on to the narrower definition which, apart from being Christian-inspired, has effectively truncated the group rights of Dharmic sampradayas. It remains to be seen if such issues of colonial linguistics/semantics receive due attention from the Supreme Court in pending matters of civilisational/ Dharmic importance.

What emerges from a reading of the Shirur Math Judgment along with the judgments in *Shastri Yagnapurushdasji* and *Bramchari Sidheswar Bhai* is a curious mixture wherein the colonial framework enmeshes with a partly colonial and partly decolonial understanding of native/Indic OET systems. As stated earlier, whether or not this duality has its genesis in the Constitution and its making will be examined in the sequel to this book in greater detail.

The other colonial attitude that the Indian State appears to have embraced is the need to codify and systematise indigenous 'personal laws' in order to make them 'uniform' and 'consistent', in the process ossifying and centralising them. The 'Hindu Code' legislations passed between 1955 and 1956, which resulted in the Hindu Marriage Act, Hindu Succession Act, Hindu Minority and Guardianship Act, and Hindu Adoptions and Maintenance Act, are cases in point. In the process of this codification, the Indian State, which presides over a civilisational society that values context, subjectivity and custom, has stifled the evolution of custom at the altar of uniformity, homogeneity and codification.

This was highlighted and analysed powerfully by Dr. Madhu Kishwar in her article titled 'Codified Hindu Law: Myth and Reality'[18]. Dr. Kishwar captured brilliantly the colonial obsession with codification of 'Hindu law', which the first government of independent Bharat under Jawaharlal Nehru, ably aided by Dr. Ambedkar's earlier work on the subject, took forward with the zeal of a new convert. Here are a few instructive excerpts from her article that capture the Indian State's colonial consciousness as reflected in its bull-headed pursuit of codification and standardisation of Hindu 'personal laws' in the early years of its independence. Interestingly, although she does not use the terms coloniality or decoloniality, Dr. Kishwar clearly recognises its presence and influence in the Indian State's mental constitution:

> Why then the insistence on codifying and unifying Hindu law? There seems to be a fascination, among the social reformers in particular and the English educated elite in general, with uniformity as a vehicle of national unity. In the vein of British distaste for polytheism and glorification of monotheism as somehow intrinsically morally superior, the reformers express disgust with the diversity of Hindu law as practised in different regions and with its complexities. The reformers perceive themselves as modernising woodcutters wielding the axe against the mystifying jungle of Hindu law.... .
>
> Time and again, the reformers put forward the argument that uniformity is necessary, without explaining why, simply assuming that uniformity is an un-questioned good. One such typical statement by S C Shah: 'We have had Hindu law varying from place to place, province to province, having all kinds of local customs and family customs ... it is a very great thing that we will, for the first time, have a uniform code at least for the Hindu community.' All who questioned that uniformity was a great thing were labelled and dismissed by the 'progressives' led by Nehru as reactionaries.
>
> Some argued that diversity was not itself an evil, and, more important, that Hindu law had not been imposed by the state or other authority from above but had grown from popular consensus and that this character should be preserved.
>
> This perception of the state as an instrument of social reform to be imposed on people without creating a

social consensus derives essentially from the norms of functioning inherent in colonialist state machinery and ideology. The English educated elite among the Indians had faithfully imbibed the colonial state's ideology, projecting itself as the most progressive instrument of social reform, failing to realise that many of these enactments (such as, the Sharada Act) remained paper tigers of which people were not even aware. The contempt for Indian society, labelled backward, uncivilised and degenerate, was all pervasive. Notice the words used by Ambedkar: '....some communities like the Hindu community needed the reform so badly- it was a slum clearance'.

This discussion based on scholarly literature is sufficient for the purview of this book to demonstrate the manifest hand of Christian European coloniality, 'the hand of G_d', so to speak, in the reshaping of Indic consciousness. What is important to note is the critical similarity and equally critical difference between Middle Eastern coloniality and European coloniality. While both believe in the concept of 'false religion' in the context of native societies which do not share their faith, the former destroys 'false religions' root and branch through overt subjugation, while the latter attempts to convert, failing which, it subtly moulds and reconstructs other faith systems in its own image by applying its framework to bring them in line with Christian consciousness. The former's direct and visible aggression invited fierce resistance from Indic consciousness, while the latter's attempt to Christianise it through its policy of toleration and secularism resulted in the integration of the native Indic consciousness in a Eurocentric 'modern' global order. This has made it much more difficult for Indic consciousness and its way of life to be understood on its own terms without suffering labels, such as 'ancient', 'traditional', 'conservative' and the like. Critically, De Roover points out that this model of Christian reconstruction of indigenous faith systems and societies has been secularised, and goes by the name of 'secularism', wherein the colonial framework with its distinct religious/scriptural origin is projected as 'universal' for all societies and cultures.

I will elaborate on the British coloniser's movement from the policy of toleration to adoption of secularism in the next section where I address the period between 1858 and 1919, but first, the impact of the coloniser's Christian reconstructionism on native OET needs to be understood.

Every society's subjective experience leads to the formation of its own views on ontology, which ultimately forms the basis of its epistemology and theology, including its social organisation. In this regard, broadly speaking, the ontology of Indic consciousness rests, among other things, on the belief in the laws of 'karma' and rebirth which manifest in its knowledge production structures, its faith systems, its relationship with nature and its societal structures. The Christianisation of Indic consciousness through the use of a secularised Christian framework has impacted not just the external edifice of the Indic society but has also pushed to extinction specific groups, communities and ways of life, which have long preserved the indigenous ontology upon which the civilisation was built. Specifically, the application of the Protestant Reformation's hatred of clergy to Brahmins and 'Brahminism', who the Christian coloniser and accompanying missionary groups categorically reviled as impediments to the Christianisation of Bharat, has ensured that a significant cross-section of the native society today, regardless of stated political or ideological proclivities (Left, Right or Centre) now shares the coloniser's hatred of Brahmins and 'Brahminism'. This shared hatred of an Indic sub-identity based on colonial versions of Bharat's history and consciousness is proof of coloniality at work.

Further, in my opinion, it is also proof of the success of the European coloniser's approach, since he managed to achieve what the Middle Eastern coloniser could not. The European coloniser ensured that even the indigenous discourse on consciousness-related issues takes place *within* a secularised Christian framework, albeit unconsciously, since the natives treat the coloniser's version of their history as Bible speak, pun intended. When an internal conversation among natives happens within a framework rooted in foreign consciousness, which is accepted as being universally valid without its premise being examined or critiqued, it effectively proves the deep-seated entrenchment of colonial consciousness.

This observation may invite predictable ad hominem reactions and caste-based epithets, which would only prove my point of ingrained coloniality in the native discourse. It would demonstrate how the *varnashrama* system and Indic knowledge traditions have been successfully boxed in the colonial category of 'caste', which takes us to the next related sub-issues of caste and tribe.

The Colonial Categories of Caste and Tribe

That 'caste' is the product of the reconstructionist attitude of the Christian European coloniser in the realm of religion and social organisation is again evidenced by scholarly literature. The literature demonstrates that the coloniser's ethnocentric approach to social organisation was foisted on the Indic society as in other colonised indigenous societies, which gave birth to colonial identities, such as 'caste'[19] and 'tribe'[20], through conflation of Indic lexicon, such as varna and jati, with caste. On the subject of caste as a colonial construct, Nicholas B. Dirks' *Castes of Mind: Colonialism and the Making of Modern India*[21] charts the evolution of caste *as we know it today*, as a marker of identity, starting from the Portuguese, who introduced the term 'casta' to describe the Hindu social structure, which was institutionalised under the British through the creation of an ethnographic state in Bharat. While I do not fully agree with some of the views expressed by Dirk, given my position as a learner and not an expert on the subject, I will

limit my agreement to his central thesis which is captured in
the following excerpt from the book:

> This book will ask why it is that caste has become for so many
> the core symbol of community in India, whereas for others,
> even in serious critique, caste is still the defining feature of
> Indian social organization. As we shall see, views of caste differ
> markedly: from those who see it as a religious system to those
> who view it as merely social or economic; from those who view
> it as the Indian equivalent of community to those who see it as
> the primary impediment to community. But an extraordinary
> range of commentators, from James Mill to Herbert Risley,
> from Hegel to Weber, from G.S. Ghurye to M.N. Srinivas, from
> Louis Dumont to McKim Marriott, from E.V. Ramaswamy
> Naicker to B.R. Ambedkar, from Gandhi to Nehru, among
> many others who will populate the text that follows, accept that
> caste—specifically caste forms of hierarchy, whether valorized
> or despised—is somehow fundamental to Indian civilization,
> Indian culture, and Indian tradition.[22]
>
> *This book will address this question by suggesting that caste, as*
> *we know it today, is not in fact some unchanged survival of ancient*
> *India, not some single system that reflects a core civilizational*
> *value, not a basic expression of Indian tradition. Rather, I*
> *will argue that caste (again, as we know it today) is a modern*
> *phenomenon, that it is, specifically, the product of a historical*
> *encounter between India and Western colonial rule.* By this I do
> not mean to imply that it was simply invented by the too clever
> British, now credited with so many imperial patents that what
> began as colonial critique has turned into another form of
> imperial adulation. *But I am suggesting that it was under the*
> *British that 'caste' became a single term capable of expressing,*
> *organizing, and above all 'systematizing' India's diverse forms of*
> *social identity, community, and organization. This was achieved*
> *through an identifiable (if contested) ideological canon as the*
> *result of a concrete encounter with colonial modernity during two*

hundred years of British domination. In short, colonialism made caste what it is today. It produced the conditions that made possible the opening lines of this book, by making caste the central symbol of Indian society… [emphasis added]

While the book's focus on the colonial creation of 'caste' makes it a must-read, what is of relevance to the discussion at hand is Dirks' unequivocal and extensive identification of the role of Christian missionaries as the British coloniser's go-to ethnographers of Bharat and how they saw the 'caste system', in particular Brahmins, as the chief impediment to the Christianisation of Bharat. In this regard, he cites the influential work of French Catholic missionary Abbe Dubois, titled *Description of the Character, Manners, and Customs of the People of India, and of Their Institutions, Religious and Civil,* which was published in 1816. This book was treated as the most comprehensive authority on the caste system, so much so that the Madras government bought the copyright for the book from Dubois for a fortune, which provided him with a source of regular pension for years. In fact, William Bentinck, the then Governor of Madras, showered effusive praise on Dubois' work. Following are Dirks' views on the 'anthropological service' provided by Dubois to the British administration in Bharat and its use for the purpose of conversion[23]:

Dubois performed an anthropological service to the British rulers of India, doing so in part because as a French Jesuit missionary he was thought to be able to cross social worlds far more readily than the imperial British themselves. *But, as was true with all missionary perspectives, social worlds were crossed in order to convert souls, a social fact that led to very strong views on the subject of caste.*

… As we shall see, much early 'colonial' ethnography was in fact written by missionaries, who observed Indian society more closely than did British officials, but experienced it in relation to their primary concern with Christian conversion. Dubois was one of the first such missionary ethnographers and, as Bentick duly noted, a great authority at a time when the colonial administration knew so little. [emphasis added]

Dirks elucidates in great detail how the missionary role in ethnography resulted in the creation of 'criminal castes', 'martial castes'[24], 'martial races' and 'tribes', all with a view to harvest more souls for Christ and also to identify groups whose loyalty to the British coloniser could be trusted. The use of 'Aryan races' in George MacMunn's *The Martial Races of India*, published in 1933[25], too is underscored for its ethnocentrism based on missionary ethnography and White supremacism based on Christian OET. This is evident from MacMunn's belief that the martial races were 'largely the product of the original white (Aryan) races' and that 'the white invaders in the days of their early supremacy started the caste system, as a protection, it is believed, against the devastating effect on moral and ethics of miscegenation with Dravidian and aboriginal peoples'. Dirks also highlights the pivotal role played by missionaries, such as Robert Caldwell, in fanning 'virulent anti-Brahmanism' owing to which 'he became an extraordinary figure in the history of the Dravidian movement' in southern Bharat. Given the connections drawn by Dirks whose relevance to raging contemporary debates are self-evident, I would urge readers to read his work before forming their views on the subject of 'caste' and to recognise the deep-seated coloniality in contemporary perceptions of caste.

Similarly, on the creation of the 'tribal' identity, the works of S.K. Chaube and Susana B.C. Devalle, which shed light on the creation of this colonial categorisation, are a must-read. While Chaube's work *Hill Politics in Northeast India* is of immense value in understanding the nexus between the creation of the tribal identity with specific reference to the Northeast and the facilitation of conversion of 'tribes' to Christianity, Devalle's work on the invention of the tribal construct as a colonial category provides broader perspective on the same lines as Dirks' work on caste. Sample this introduction from Devalle's work[26]:

> Tribe has been the most salient category used in the study of Indian indigenous ethnic formations: the adivasi societies. It is my contention that the tribal construct in India is a colonial category and that it formed part of the colonial legitimizing ideology. As such this category operated as a device to catalogue conquered populations, to reformulate control policies and to facilitate the incorporation of these populations into the colonial system. The ideology of tribe did not disintegrate in India with the end of colonialism. It has been reformulated in the context of the Hindu model of caste-ideology, a context observable in the conceptualization of adivasi 'backwardness' and in the alternatives espoused for social mobility
>
> ... In sum, I will argue that there were no 'tribes' in Jharkhand until the European perception of Indian reality constructed them and colonial authorities gave them their administrative sanction. In fact, the tribal paradigm is ill-suited to categorize both past and present adivasi societies. In Jharkhand, these societies arc now basically peasant societies inserted in a class society, possessing at the same time specific ethno-cultural styles....

Commenting brilliantly on how 'tribe' became one of the lenses for the European coloniser to understand Bharat, the following is what Devalle has to say, using the Jharkhand experience to make her case:

> Under colonialism, communities that evaded the other dominant cataloguing device -caste- were defined according to the tribal paradigm. It was then that 'the tribes' made their appearance in the Indian scenario. *A creation of European origin, tribe was one of the elements through which Europe constructed part of the Indian reality.*

A final factor must be considered for nineteenth century colonial Chotanagpur: the arrival of German Evangelican Lutheran, Anglican and Roman Catholic missions. In this way, the pillars that have classically sustained colonial penetration and ensured colonial hegemony: the military, a legal and administrative system, a capitalist economy, and the Church with its 'civilizing'/ educational mission were all present in Jharkhand.

The core of the Munda area was contained in the Quadrilateral, flanked by the Catholic churches at Bandgaon, Sarwada, Dolda and Buruduth. Although the Roman Catholic mission was the last to enter the area, it attained the fastest rate of conversions (15,000 converts in 1887; 71,270 by 1900). The German Evangelican Lutheran mission was the first to settle in Chotanagpur when it established stations in Munda territory in 1845. It had 40,000 converts by 1895... . Santals and Hos rarely converted; the bulk of adivasi Christians were Mundas and Oraons.

Education given by the different missions, based on European values, contributed to the adivasis' deculturation, and its effects are clearly observable today.

... Jharkhand's socioeconomic evolution in the course of history, summarily described above, gives evidence that supports my contention that it is erroneous to place Jharkhand's adivasi societies within the artificially created framework of tribe.

... In sum, given the qualitative aspects of the social and economic organization of the adivasi precapitalist societies of Jharkhand in pre-colonial India as well as after their subsumption under colonial capitalism, their categorization as 'tribal' is at best, out of place and, at worst, ahistorical and sociologically groundless. There were in fact no tribes in Jharkhand. In essence they were a parthenogenetic creation of British colonial administration. Only by a curious trick of historical reversion could there be tribes nowadays. Adivasis live in a class society, and exist in an economic formation where the capitalist mode

is dominant. What does exist, however, is the ideology of tribe which, in Wolpe's words, 'sustains and reproduces capitalist relations of production' (1972: 454). [emphasis added]

It is evident from the above excerpts that both Dirks and Devalle end up showcasing the undeniable hand of coloniality in the creation of 'caste' and 'tribe' *as we know and understand it today*. This qualification 'as we know and understand it today' is of vital importance because it underscores the impact of coloniality on aspects of indigenous society, which popular discourse treats as being representative of its unchanging character and nature. I must clarify that it is not my case that the precolonial past was perfect or that there were no instances of discrimination; instead, I am merely making the point, citing credible literature, that our understanding of the past is thoroughly colonialised, and only when the colonial strings are removed from the discourse, can we truly begin to understand *varna* and *jati* from the standpoint of their history as well as examining them for contemporary relevance, if any.

The unchanging character imputed to institutions, such as caste as well as to the stakeholders, is largely a product of Christian colonial reconstruction. Until a decolonial approach is employed by experts and 'intellectuals', we will continue to see the entrenchment of colonialised identities and fissures, which began with an anti-Brahmin slant but whose rapid movement towards an anti-Dharmic/anti-Hindu position is less veiled with each passing day—thereby revealing the end goal of European coloniality. Pertinently, Middle Eastern coloniality too now rides on the coat-tails of European coloniality in this regard, since the latter's secularised Christian framework provides it with optically sanitised means to gradually marginalise and eliminate Indic consciousness, which it failed to do despite the employment of savagery for centuries.

It is also evident from the literature discussed here that even education was used as a means to further the Christian civilising and reformist intent, since the nexus between education, language and religious conversion was thoroughly understood by the Christian establishment right from the inclusion of the first Missionary Clause in the Charter of 1698. Consequently, it is important to briefly examine the education and language policies of the British coloniser which also support the position that education was the secularised means to an unsecular evangelical end or the Christian colonial end.

Colonial Education for 'Moral and Religious Improvement' a.k.a. Proselytisation

Between 1715 and 1787, English-medium charity schools were set up in Madras, Bombay and Calcutta with the assistance of the Company largely for the purposes of educating European and Anglo-Indian children. In so far as the education of the natives was concerned, the Company started taking an interest from 1765 onwards, that is, after the Battle of Buxar, when its rise as a political power had become clear to the British government as well as to Indian rulers. As a measure of rapprochement with the Indian population, the Company adopted a conscious policy of taking forward the legacy of Hindu and Muslim rulers which led to the following measures, according to scholars J.P. Naik and Syed Nurullah[27]:

1. Establishment of madrassahs and *pathashalas*;
2. Giving marks of honour or pecuniary grants to learned Pandits and Moulvis; and
3. Endowing educational institutions for higher religious studies.

In addition to these, in order to co-opt the Indian upper classes into the British administration, the Company established the Banaras Sanskrit College and Calcutta Madrassah. The intent behind the establishment of such institutions and the role that was envisaged for their products was captured in a letter dated 1 January 1792 from Jonathan Duncan, the British Resident in Benares, to the Earl of Cornwallis, K.G., Governor-General in Council.[28]

> The 2nd principal advantage that may be derived from this Institution will be felt in its effects more immediately by the natives, though not without being participated in by the British subjects, who are to rule over them, by pre-serving and disseminating a knowledge of the Hindoo Law and proving a nursery of future doctors and expounders thereof, to assist the European judges in the due, regular, and uniform administration of its genuine letter and spirit to the body of the people.

At the other end of the spectrum were those, such as Charles Grant, who were obsessed with the idea of using colonial education to cure the 'Hindoos' of the error of their ways and the darkness which was attributed to the 'Hindoo religion', of course.[29] Here are a few portions of Grant's views from his 'Observations' dated 16 August 1797, which laid the foundations for the strengthening of the Church establishment in Bharat through the 1813 Charter Act[30]:

> We now proceed to the main object of this work, for the sake of which all the preceding topics and discussions have been brought forward—*an enquiry into the means of remedying disorders, which have become thus inveterate in the state of society among our Asiatic subjects, which destroy their happiness, and obstruct every species of improvement among them.*
> *The true cure of darkness, is the introduction of light. The Hindoos err, because they are ignorant; and their errors have never fairly been laid before them. The communication of our light and knowledge to them, would prove the best remedy*

*for their disorders; and this remedy is proposed, from a full
conviction that if judiciously and patiently applied, it would
have great and happy effects upon them, effects honourable and
advantageous for us.*

... There are two ways of making this communication: the
one is, by the medium of the languages of those countries;
the other is by the medium of our own. In general, when
foreign teachers have proposed to instruct the inhabitants
of any country, they have used the vernacular tongue of
that people, for a natural and necessary reason, that they
could not hope to make any other mean of communication
intelligible to them. This is not our case in respect of our
eastern dependencies. They are our own, we have possessed
them long, many Englishmen reside among the natives, our
language is not unknown there, and it is practicable to diffuse
it more widely. The choice therefore of either mode, lies open
to us; and we are at liberty to consider which is entitled to a
preference. Upon this subject, it is not intended to pass an
exclusive decision here; the points absolutely to be contended
for are, that we ought to impart our superior lights, and that
this is practicable; that it is practicable by two ways, can never
be an argument why neither should be attempted. Indeed no
great reason appears why either should be systematically
interdicted, since particular cases may recommend even that
which is generally least eligible.

... *We proceed then to observe, that it is perfectly in the power
of this country, by degrees, to impart to the Hindoos our language;
afterwards through that medium, to make them acquainted with
our easy literary compositions, upon variety of subjects ; and,
let not the idea hastily excite derision, progressively with the
simple elements of our arts, our philosophy and religion. These
acquisitions would silently undermine, and at length subvert, the
fabric of error; and all the objections that may be apprehended
against Such a change, are, it is confidently believed, capable of
a solid answer.*

The first communication, and the instrument of introducing the rest, must be the English language; this is a key which will open to them a world of new ideas, and policy alone might have impelled us, long since, to put it into their hands. It would be extremely easy for Government to establish, at a moderate expense, in various parts of the provinces, places of gratuitous instruction in reading and writing English: multitudes, especially of the young, would flock to them; and the easy books used in teaching, might at the same time convey obvious truths on different subjects. The teachers should be persons of knowledge, morals and discretion; and men of this character could impart to their pupils much useful information in discourse: and to facilitate the attainment of that object, they might at first make use of the Bengalese tongue. The Hindoos would, in time, become teachers of English themselves; and the employment of our language in public business, for which every political reason remains in full force, would, in the course of another generation, make it very general throughout the country. There is nothing wanting to the success of this plan, but the hearty patronage of Government. If they wish it to succeed, it can and must succeed. *The introduction of English in the administration of the revenue, in judicial proceedings, and in other business of Government, wherein Persian is now used, and the establishment of free-schools for instruction in this language, would insure its diffusion over the country, for the reason already suggested, that the interest of the natives would induce them to acquire it.*

With our language, much of our useful literature might, and would, in time be communicated. The art of Printing, would enable us to disseminate our writings in a way the Persians never could have done, though their compositions had been as numerous as ours. *Hence the Hindus would see the great use we make of reason on all subjects, and in all affairs; they also would learn to reason, they would become acquainted with the history of their own species, the past and present state of the world; their affections would gradually become interested by various engaging works, composed to recommend virtue, and to deter from vice; the general mass of their opinions would be rectified; and above all, they would see a better system of principles and morals. New views of duty as rational creatures would open upon them; and that mental bondage in which they have long been holden would gradually dissolve.*

To this change the true knowledge of nature would contribute; and some of our easy explanations of natural philosophy might, undoubtedly, by proper means, be made intelligible to them. *Except a few Brahmins, who consider the concealment of their learning as part of their religion, *the people are totally misled as to the system and phenomena of nature; and their errors in this branch of science, upon which divers important conclusions rest, may be more easily demonstrated to them, than the absurdity and falsehood of their mythological legends. From the demonstration of the true cause of eclipses, the story of Ragoo and Ketoo, the dragons, who when the sun and moon are obscured are supposed to be assaulting them, a story which has hitherto been an article of religious faith, productive of religious services among the Hindoos, would fall to the ground; the removal of one pillar would weaken the fabric of falsehood; the discovery of one palpable error, would open the mind to farther conviction; and the progressive discovery of truths, hitherto unknown, would dissipate as many superstitious chimeras, the parents of false fears, and false hopes. Every branch of natural philosophy might in time be introduced and diffused among the Hindoos. Their understandings would then be strengthened, as well as their minds informed, and error be dispelled in proportion.* [emphasis added]

On the introduction of Christianity, Grant had the following to say:

It is not asserted, that such effects would be immediate or universal; but admitting them to be progressive, and partial only, yet how great would the change be, and how happy at length for the outward prosperity, and internal peace of society among the Hindoos! Men would be restored to the use of their reason; all the advantages of happy soil, climate, and situation, would be observed and improved; the comforts and conveniences of life would be increased; the cultivation of the mind, and rational intercourse, valued; the people would rise in the scale of human beings; and as they found their character, their state, and their comforts, improved, they would prize more highly, the security and the happiness of a well-ordered society. Such a change would correct those sad disorders which have been described, and for which no other remedy has been proposed, nor is in the nature of things to be found.

Grant's views are the perfect response to those that contend that language is merely a medium of instruction or communication and that it must not be associated with any particular religion. Critically, between the Company's policy of setting up the Benares Sanskrit College and the Calcutta Madrassah, and the views of evangelical Christians like Charles Grant, one can see the tussle from the 1790s to the mid-1800s between two predominant schools of thought on what must be the Christian British coloniser's education-cum-language policy in Bharat.[31]

The first school, namely the Orientalist school, believed in amalgamating indigenous forms of knowledge production, content and pedagogy with the European system, which led to the establishment of the Benares Sanskrit College and the Calcutta Madrassah, so as to co-opt Indians into the British administrative structure. The second school, namely the Evangelical/Anglicist school, led by Charles Grant and other like-minded individuals, such as William Wilberforce, associated the English language with Christianity and Western civilisation. This school was acutely aware of the role language played as the carrier of a worldview and, therefore, pushed for the introduction of English education. It is important to underscore the fact that both schools subscribed to the notion of Christian

European superiority in all respects; the only difference was that
the former was more driven by certain pragmatic and mercantile
considerations and therefore, believed in employing subtler
means to Europeanise natives while being seen as supportive of
native institutions, whereas the latter school wore its Christian
colonial consciousness and evangelising nature on its sleeve.

Ultimately, in the tussle between the Company's Orientalism
and Grant's evangelism, the latter clearly dominated, since it was
responsible for the express and enhanced support of the British
government to the advancement of Christianity in Bharat under
the 1813 Charter Act, a position which was carried forward
and strengthened at least until 1853. While Grant's views were
proof of evangelical intent prior to and underlying the 1813 Act,
here is an extract from a Minute issued by Lord Moira, dated 2
October 1815[32]:

119. *In looking for a remedy to these evils, the moral and
intellectual improvement of the natives will necessarily form a
prominent feature of any plan which may arise from the above
suggestions, and I have therefore not failed to turn my most
solicitous attention to the important object of public education.*

121. As the public money would be ill-appropriated in
merely providing gratuitous access to that quantum of
education which is already attainable, any intervention
of government either by superintendence, or by contribution,
should be directed to the improvement of existing tuition,
and to the diffusion of it to places and persons now out of its
reach. Improvement and diffusion may go hand in hand; yet
the latter is to be considered matter of calculation, while the
former should be deemed positively incumbent. The general,
the sad defect of this education is, that the inculcation of
moral principle forms no part of it. This radical want is not
imputable to us. The necessities of self-defence (for all our
extensions of territory have been achieved in repelling efforts
made for the subversion of our power) and our occupation in

securing the new possessions, have allowed us till lately, but little leisure to examine deliberately the state of the population which we had been gradually bringing beneath our sway. It was already vitiated. The unceasing wars which had harassed all parts of India, left everywhere their invariable effects, a disorganization of that frame-work of habit and opinion, which enforces moral conduct, and an emancipation of all those irregular impulses which revolt at its restraint. *The village school-masters could not teach that in which they had themselves never been instructed;* and universal debasement of mind, the constant concomitant of subjugation to despotic rule, left no chance that an innate sense of equity should in those confined circles suggest the recommendation of principles not thought worthy of cultivation by the government. *The remedy for this is to furnish the village school-masters with little manuals of religious sentiments and ethic maxims, conveyed in such a shape as may be attractive to the scholars; taking care that while awe and adoration of the Supreme Being are earnestly instilled no jealousy be excited by pointing out any particular Creed. The absence of such an objection, and small pecuniary rewards for zeal occasionally administered by the magistrates, would induce the school-masters to use those compilations readily.*

122. *To those who are anxious to propagate among the vast population of this empire the inestimable lights of true religion, it may be confidently maintained that there is no hope of success but by rendering the people capable of understanding that which is proposed to them; open the minds of the rising generation by due instruction; give them a habit of reverencing the principles which the Christian doctrine enjoins without stimulating the parents into opposition by teaching on point adverse to their superstitions; and their inevitable rejection of beliefs irreconcilable to the reason which you will have enabled them to exercise, and repugnant to the probity which you will have taught them to admire, must render certain their transition to the path you wish. As it is, their ignorance insures their tenaciousness of their earlier impressions,*

*and pledges their implicit submission to the dictates with which
the Brahmins would counteract the object were they alarmed into
contest. The progress to be effectual, must be patient and silent;
like every other beneficial change, it must rise out of the general
sense of society, not be imposed upon it; and to produce that sense,
I know no mode but education.*

123. The next gradation in public tuition is the higher
class of teachers to be found in the principal towns, and the
only question in regard to them appears to be the expediency
of furnishing them with the means of inculcating more
accurate ideas of general science and sounder principles of
morality.

135. The lapse of half a century and the operation of that
principle have produced a new state of society, which calls for
a more enlarged and liberal policy. The moral duties require
encouragement and experiment. The arts which *Minute
by Lord* adorn and embellish life, will follow in ordinary
course. It is for the credit of the British name, that this
beneficial revolution should arise under British sway. To be
the source of blessings to the immense population of India is
an ambition worthy of our country. In proportion as we have
found intellect neglected and sterile here, the obligation is the
stronger on us to cultivate it. The field is noble: may we till it
worthily! [emphasis added]

Paragraph 122 of this Minute could not have been clearer in the
intent behind the introduction of Christian education in Bharat.
The hope was that 'reason', that is, 'Christian reason' would
slowly and silently but surely bring to the native population
'the inestimable lights of true religion' by counteracting the
'dictates of Brahmins'. Would it not be fair to say that the stated
object behind introduction of Christian education in Bharat
appears to have been achieved to a significant extent? Again, I
leave it to the reader to draw their own conclusions while I place
first-hand material before them.

By July 1823, the Governor-General in Council had passed a resolution for the creation of a Committee for Public Instruction 'with a view to the better instruction of the people, to the introduction among them of useful knowledge and to the improvement of their moral character'.[33] In that very same month, Holt Mackenzie, a British colonial administrator, wrote a note on the government's scheme to pursue public education, wherein he stressed the need for a Christian scheme of education for the native elites in order to influence the 'lower orders', evidenced by the following extract[34]:

The education indeed of the great body of the people can never, I think, be expected to extend beyond what is necessary for the business of life; and it is only therefore through religious exercises, which form a great part of the business of life, that the labourer will turn his thoughts on things above the common drudgery, by which he earns his subsistence. *Hence it is under the Christian scheme alone, that I should expect to find the labouring classes really educated: and their station in the scale of instructed and humanized beings will, I imagine, be pretty closely proportioned to their piety. We have no such instrument, with which to work beneficially on the lower orders here. Further the natural course of things in all countries seems to be that knowledge introduced from abroad should descend from the higher or educated classes and gradually spread through their example. We surely cannot here, at least expect the servant to prize a learning, which his master despises or hates. The influence of Europeans, if they use not the influential classes of the native community, must necessarily be very confined. What is taught in our schools will only be thought of there.* Our scholars, if of the common people when they enter the world, will find no sympathy among their fellows, and until the lessons of the master, or professor become the subject of habitual thought and conversation, they cannot touch the heart, they will little affect the understanding. The acquirement will be an act

320 INDIA THAT IS BHARAT

of memory, with little more of feeling or reflection than if nonsense verses were the theme. [emphasis added]

Interestingly, the indigenous pedagogy and curriculum are discussed in great detail in a letter dated 17 August 1823 from A.D. Campbell, Collector of Bellary, to the President and Members of the Board of Revenue, Fort St. George.[35] Here are a few extracts which are telling in their demonstration of how far the contemporary Indian education system has travelled from its civilisational character, which existed even as recently as 1823, that is, less than two centuries ago:

2. The population of this district is specified in the enclosed statement at 927,857, or little less than a million of souls. The number of schools is only 533, containing no more than 6,641 scholars, or about 12 to each school, and not seven individuals in a thousand of the entire population.

3. The Hindoo scholars are in number 6,398, the Mussulman scholars only 213, and the whole of these are males, with the exception of only 60 girls, who are all Hindoos exclusively.

4. The English language is taught in one school only; the Tamil in four; the Persian in 21; the Mahratta in 23; the Teloogoo in 226, and the Carnataca in 235. Besides these there are 23 places of instruction attended by Brahmins exclusively, in which some of the Hindoo sciences, such as theology, astronomy, logic and law, are still imperfectly taught in the Sanscrit language.

5. In these places of Sanscrit instruction in the Hindoo sciences, attended by youths, and often by persons far advanced in life, education is conducted on a plan entirely different from that pursued in the schools, in which children are taught reading, writing and arithmetic only, in the several vernacular dialects of the country. I shall endeavour to give a brief outline of the latter, as to them the general population of the country is confined; and as that population consists chiefly

of Hindoos I shall not dwell upon the few Mussulman schools in which Persian is taught.

6. The education of the Hindoo youths generally commences when they are five years old; on reaching this age, the master and scholars of the school to which the boy is to be sent, are invited to the house of his parents; the whole are seated in a circle round an image of Gunasee and the child to be initiated is placed exactly opposite to it. The schoolmaster sitting by his side, after having burnt incense and presented offerings, causes the child to repeat a prayer to Gunasee, entreating wisdom. He then guides the child to write with its finger in rice the mystic names of the deity, and is dismissed with a present from the parents according to their ability. The child next morning commences the great work of his education.

12. The three books which are most common in all the schools, and which are used indiscriminately by the several castes, are the Ramayannm, Maha Bharata and Bhagavata; but the children of manufacturing class of people have, in addition to the above, books peculiar to their own religious tenets, such as the Nagalingayna, Kutha Vishvakurma, Poorana, Kamalesherra Ralikamahata; and those who wear the lingum, such as the Buwapoorana Raghavan-kimkanya, Keeruja Gullana, Unabhavamoorta, Chenna Busavaswara Poorana, Jurilagooloo, etc., which are all considered sacred, and are studied with a view of subserving their several religious creeds.

13. The lighter kind of stories, which are read for amusement, are generally the Punchatantra Bhatalapunchavunsatee, Punklee-soopooktahuller, Mahantarungenee. The books on the principles of the vernacular languages themselves, are the several dictionaries and grammars, such as the Nighantoo, Umara, Suddamumburee, Shuddeemanee, Durpana, Vyacurna, Andradeepeca, Andranamasangraha, etc., etc., but these last and similar books which are most

essential, and without which no accurate or extensive
knowledge of the vernacular languages can be attained, are,
from the high price of manuscripts and the general poverty
of the masters, of all the books the most uncommon in the
native schools, and such of them as are found there, are, in
consequence of the ignorance, carelessness and indolence
of copyists in general, full of blunders, and in every way
most incorrect and imperfect.

One of the reasons that this letter is educative is that it informs
us that at least until 1823, indigenous consciousness and
epistemology had survived twelve centuries of genocidal
campaigns by Middle Eastern coloniality. In stark contrast, in
less than two centuries, European coloniality has made deep
inroads which Middle Eastern coloniality could not. The extent
of entrenchment of European coloniality can perhaps be gauged
from a letter dated 11 December 1823 written by Raja Rammohun
Roy to the then Governor-General of India, William Pitt.[36] Raja
Rammohun Roy was known as a 'Hindoo social reformer' and
as one of the founders of the Brahmo Sabha. The following is
a reproduction of Roy's letter to Pitt, which reflected his views
on indigenous education and his fervent appeal for European
education:

> Sir,
> I beg leave to send you the accompanying address and shall
> feel obliged if you will have the goodness to lay it before the
> Right Hon'ble the Governor-General in Council.
> I have, etc.,
> RAMMOHUN ROY.
> Calcutta;
> The 11th December 1823.
>
> To
>   His Excellency the Right Hon'ble William Pitt, Lord Amherst.

My Lord,

Humbly reluctant as the natives of India are to obtrude upon the notice of Government the sentiments they entertain on any public measure, there are circumstances when silence would be carrying this respectful feeling to culpable excess.

The present Rulers of India, coming from a distance of many thousand miles to govern a people whose language, literature, manners, customs, and ideas are almost entirely new and strange to them, cannot easily become so intimately acquainted with their real circumstances, as the natives of the country are themselves. We should therefore be guilty of a gross dereliction of duty to ourselves, and afford our Rulers just ground of complaint at our apathy, did we omit on occasions of importance like the present to supply them with such accurate information as might enable them to devise and adopt measures calculated to be beneficial to the country, and thus second by our local knowledge and experience their declared benevolent intentions for its improvement.

The establishment of a new Sangscrit School in Calcutta evinces the laudable desire of Government to improve the Natives of India by Education—a blessing for which they must ever be grateful; and every well wisher of the human race must be desirous that the efforts made to promote it should be guided by the most enlightened principles, so that the stream of intelligence may flow into the most useful channels.

When this Seminary of learning was proposed, we understood that the Government in England had ordered a considerable sum of money to be annually devoted to the instruction of its Indian Subjects. *We were filled with sanguine hopes that this sum would be laid out in employing European Gentlemen of talents and education to instruct the natives of India in Mathematics, Natural Philosophy, Chemistry, Anatomy and other useful Sciences, which the Nations of Europe have carried to a degree of perfection that has raised them above the inhabitants of other parts of the world.*

While we looked forward with pleasing hope to the dawn of knowledge thus promised to the rising generation, our hearts were filled with mingled feelings of delight and gratitude; we already offered up thanks to Providence for inspiring the most generous and enlightened of the Nations of the West with the glorious ambitions of planting in Asia the Arts and Sciences of modern Europe.

We now find that the Government are establishing a Sangscrit school under Hindoo Pundits to impart such knowledge as is already current in India. *This Seminary (similar in character to those which existed in Europe before the time of Lord Bacon) can only be expected to load the minds of youth with grammatical niceties and metaphysical distinctions of little or no practicable use to the possessors or to society. The pupils will there acquire what was known two thousand years ago, with the addition of vain and empty Subtilties since produced by speculative men, such as is already commonly taught in all parts of India.*

The Sangscrit language, so difficult that almost a life time is necessary for its perfect acquisition, is well known to have been for ages a lamentable check on the diffusion of knowledge; and the learning concealed under this almost, impervious veil is far from sufficient to reward the labour of acquiring it. But if it were thought necessary to perpetuate this language for the sake of the portion of the valuable information it contains, this might be much more easily accomplished by other means than the establishment of a new Sangscrit College; for there have been always and are now numerous professors of Sangscrit in the different parts of the country, engaged in teaching this language as well as the other branches of literature which are to be the object of the new Seminary. Therefore their more diligent cultivation, if desirable, would be effectually promoted by holding out premiums and granting certain allowances to those most eminent Professors, who have already undertaken on their own account to teach them, and would by such rewards be stimulated to still greater exertions.

From these considerations, as the sum set apart for the instruction of the Natives of India was intended by the Government in England, for the improvement of its Indian subjects, I beg leave to state, with due deference to your Lordship's exalted situation, that if the plan now adopted be followed, it will completely defeat the object proposed; *since no improvement can be expected from inducing young men to consume a dozen of years of the most valuable period of their lives in acquiring the niceties of the Byakurun or Sangscrit Grammar. For instance, in learning to discuss such points as the following: Khad signifying to eat, khaduti, he or she or it eats. Query, whether does the word khaduti, taken as a whole, convey [sic] the meaning he, she, or it eats, or are separate parts of this meaning conveyed by distinct portions of the word? As if in the English language it were asked, how much meaning is there in the eat, how much in the s? and is the whole meaning of the word conveyed by those two portions of it distinctly, or by them taken jointly?*

Neither can much improvement arise from such speculations as the following, which are the themes Suggested by the Vedant:- In what manner is the soul absorbed into the deity? What relation does it bear to the divine essence? Nor will youths be fitted to be better members of Society by the Vedantic doctrines, which teach them to believe that all visible things have no real existence; that as father, brother, etc., have no actual entirety, they consequently deserve no real affection, and therefore the sooner we escape from them and leave the world the better.

Again, no essential benefit can be derived by the student of the Meemangsa from knowing what it is that makes the killer of a goat sinless on pronouncing certain passages of the Veds, and what is the real nature and operative influence of passages of the Ved, etc.

Again the student of the Nyaya Shastra cannot be said to have improved his mind after he has learned from it into how many ideal classes the objects in the Universe are divided, and what speculative relation the Soul bears to the body, the body to the Soul, the eye to the ear, etc.

In order to enable your Lordship to appreciate the utility of encouraging such imaginary learning as above characterised, I beg your Lordship will be pleased to compare the state of science and literature in Europe before the time of Lord Bacon, with the progress of knowledge made since he wrote.

If it had been intended to keep the British nation in ignorance of real knowledge the Baconian philosophy would not have been allowed to displace the system of the schoolmen, which was the beat calculated to perpetuate ignorance. In the same manner the Sangscrit system of education would be the best calculated to keep this country in darkness, if such had been the policy of the British Legislature.

But as the improvement of the native population is the object of the Government, it will consequently promote a more liberal and enlightened system of instruction, embracing mathematics, natural philosophy, chemistry and anatomy, with other useful sciences which may be accomplished with the sum proposed by employing a few gentlemen of talents and learning educated in Europe, and providing a college furnished with the necessary books, instruments and other apparatus.

In representing this subject to your Lordship I conceive myself discharging a solemn duty which I owe to my countrymen and also to that enlightened Sovereign and Legislature which have extended their benevolent cares to this distant land actuated by a desire to improve its inhabitants and I therefore humbly trust you will excuse the liberty I have taken in thus expressing my sentiments to your Lordship.

I have, etc.,

RAMMOHUN ROY.

Calcutta;

The 11th December 1823. [emphasis added]

This letter tells us quite a few things about Raja Rammohun Roy as well as about the two-way nature of coloniality as observed by Dr. Balagangadhara. First, there is a clear consistency of coloniality between Roy's Christianised views of the 'Hindu religion', reflected in the principles and beliefs of the Brahmo Movement, and his views on what constituted 'useful' knowledge on the other. Second, as Dr. Balagangadhara observed on the role of the coloniser and the colonised in creating and perpetuating coloniality, it could be said that Roy's letter is a textbook example of the role of the colonised. Therefore, in adopting a decolonial approach, as much as it is important to identify the role of the coloniser in altering the state of affairs as it existed prior to his arrival, it is equally important to acknowledge the role of the colonised in aiding the spread and entrenchment of the coloniser's colonial consciousness, especially after having achieved decolonisation or 'independence'.

One of the reasons that this must be underscored is that in popular discourse in contemporary India, Macaulay's infamous speech on the intention behind the introduction of colonial education is often cited (which I will discuss shortly), but the role played by 'Hindoo social reformers' of the colonial era is rarely known, let alone acknowledged or examined. This is not to pin the blame on the past, which has become a fad today, but to draw attention to existence and impact of colonial consciousness on the attitudes of the colonised natives, even those who sought the upliftment of the natives. The irony is that such 'Hindoo social reformers' were perhaps much closer to the Evangelical school in their positions on the 'Hindu religion' and its 'ills'.

The period until March 1835 witnessed frequent exchanges between members of the Orientalist and Evangelical schools, which are illustratively captured in the Minutes of H.T. Prinsep, a member of the Indian Civil Service, on the one hand, and T.B. Macaulay on the other, which included the latter's infamous Minute of 1835 on the need for Christian English-medium education in Bharat. This exchange culminated in the adoption of a resolution in March 1835 by William Bentinck, which was skewed in favour of Macaulay's position. Extracted below are the relevant excerpts from the Minutes of Prinsep, Macaulay and the Resolution of Bentinck.

Extract from the Minute of H.T. Prinsep, dated 9 July 1834:

I now first learn that on the 26th April 1834 at a meeting of the sub-committee at which only Messrs. Shakespear and Colvin were present the following resolution was passed:

'The Committee being of opinion that the time has arrived for encouraging more openly and decidedly the study of English in the Madrissa resolved that from the present date no student be elected to a scholarship) unless on the express condition of studying English as well as Arabic.'

This Resolution if allowed to stand, will have the effect of converting an institution established and endowed specifically for the revival and encouragement of Arabic literature for the education of Kazees and Moulvies into a mere seminary for the teaching of English. I protest against this measure as hasty and indiscreet, as preventing the funds of an endowment from the purposes to which they were specifically assigned and as involving nothing less than a breach of trust. If the teaching of English be attempted to be put on any other footing than a course of study thrown open to the students of the Madrissa to be undertaken or not at their perfect option; if a preference of any be given to it in the distribution of jageers, we shall be making a change in the character of the Institution such as nothing but an order of the Government which made the endowment could justify.

But the resolution goes further than this. *It not only gives preference to those who study English but gives to them a monopoly of the jageers, that is, it makes English the sine qua non of Study at a College of Moulvies. The next step will be to transfer the Professors' allowances to teachers of English and then will follow in due course the voting of Arabic and Persian to be dead and damned. I protest against this course of proceeding at the first step and feel so strongly on the subject that unless this resolution be rescinded I cannot retain my seat in this Subcommittee.* [emphasis added]

Extracts from the Minute of T.B. Macaulay, dated 2 February 1835[37]:

[1] As it seems to be the opinion of some of the gentlemen who compose the Committee of Public Instruction that the course which they have hitherto pursued was strictly prescribed by the British Parliament in 1813 and as, if that opinion be correct, a legislative act will be necessary to warrant a change, I have thought it right to refrain from taking any part in the preparation of the adverse statements which are now before us, and to reserve what I had to say on the subject till it should come before me as a Member of the Council of India.

[2] It does not appear to me that the Act of Parliament can by any art of contraction be made to bear the meaning which has been assigned to it. It contains nothing about the particular languages or sciences which are to be studied. A sum is set apart 'for the revival and promotion of literature, and the encouragement of the learned natives of India, and for the introduction and promotion of a knowledge of the sciences among the inhabitants of the British territories.' It is argued, or rather taken for granted, that by literature the Parliament can have meant only Arabic and Sanscrit literature; that they never would have given the honourable appellation of 'a learned native' to a native who was familiar with the poetry of Milton, the metaphysics of Locke, and the physics of Newton; but that they meant to designate by that name only such persons as might have studied in the sacred books of the Hindoos all the uses of cusa-grass, and all the mysteries of absorption into the Deity. This does not appear to be a very satisfactory interpretation. To take a parallel case: Suppose that the Pacha of Egypt, a country once superior in knowledge to the nations of Europe, but now sunk far below

them, were to appropriate a sum for the purpose 'of reviving and promoting literature, and encouraging learned natives of Egypt,' would anybody infer that he meant the youth of his Pachalik to give years to the study of hieroglyphics, to search into all the doctrines disguised under the fable of Osiris, and to ascertain with all possible accuracy the ritual with which cats and onions were anciently adored? Would he be justly charged with inconsistency if, instead of employing his young subjects in deciphering obelisks, he were to order them to be instructed in the English and French languages, and in all the sciences to which those languages are the chief keys?

[3] The words on which the supporters of the old system rely do not bear them out, and other words follow which seem be quite decisive on the other side. This lakh of rupees is set apart not only for 'reviving literature in India,' the phrase on which their whole interpretation is founded, but also 'for the introduction and promotion of a knowledge of the sciences among the inhabitants of the British territories'—words which are alone sufficient to authorize all the changes for which I contend.

[4] If the Council agree in my construction no legislative act will be necessary. If they differ from me, I will propose a short act rescinding that I clause of the Charter of 1813 from which the difficulty arises.

[5] The argument which I have been considering affects only the form of proceeding. But the admirers of the oriental system of education have used another argument, which, if we admit it to be valid, is decisive against all change. They conceive that the public faith is pledged to the present system, and that to alter the appropriation of any of the funds which have hitherto been spent in encouraging the study of Arabic and Sanscrit would be downright spoliation. It is not easy to understand by what process of reasoning they can have arrived at this conclusion. The grants which are made from the public

purse for the encouragement of literature differ in no respect from the grants which are made from the same purse for other objects of real or supposed utility. We found a sanitarium on a spot which we suppose to be healthy. Do we thereby pledge ourselves to keep a sanitarium there if the result should not answer our expectations? We commence the erection of a pier. Is it a violation of the public faith to stop the works, if we afterwards see reason to believe that the building will be useless? The rights of property are undoubtedly sacred. But nothing endangers those rights so much as the practice, now unhappily too common, of attributing them to things to which they do not belong. Those who would impart to abuses the sanctity of property are in truth imparting to the institution of property the unpopularity and the fragility of abuses. If the Government has given to any person a formal assurance—nay, if the Government has excited in any person's mind a reasonable expectation— that he shall receive a certain income as a teacher or a learner of Sanscrit or Arabic, I would respect that person's pecuniary interests. I would rather err on the side of liberality to individuals than suffer the public faith to be called in question. But to talk of a Government pledging itself to teach certain languages and certain sciences, though those languages may become useless, though those sciences may be exploded, seems to me quite unmeaning. There is not a single word in any public instrument from which it can be inferred that the Indian Government ever intended to give any pledge on this subject, or ever considered the destination of these funds as unalterably fixed. But, had it been otherwise, I should have denied the competence of our predecessors to bind us by any pledge on such a subject. Suppose that a Government had in the last century enacted in the most solemn manner that all its subjects should, to the end of time, be inoculated for the small-pox, would that Government be bound to persist in the practice after

Jenner's discovery? These promises of which nobody claims the performance, and from which nobody can grant a release, these vested rights which vest in nobody, this property without proprietors, this robbery which makes nobody poorer, may be comprehended by persons of higher faculties than mine. I consider this plea merely as a set form of words, regularly used both in England and in India, in defence of every abuse for which no other plea can be set up.

[7] We now come to the gist of the matter. We have a fund to be employed as Government shall direct for the intellectual improvement of the people of this country. The simple question is, what is the most useful way of employing it?

[8] All parties seem to be agreed on one point, that the dialects commonly spoken among the natives of this part of India contain neither literary nor scientific information, and are moreover so poor and rude that, until they are enriched from some other quarter, it will not be easy to translate any valuable work into them. It seems to be admitted on all sides, that the intellectual improvement of those classes of the people who have the means of pursuing higher studies can at present be affected only by means of some language not vernacular amongst them.

[9] What then shall that language be? One-half of the committee maintain that it should be the English. The other half strongly recommend the Arabic and Sanscrit. The whole question seems to me to be-- which language is the best worth knowing?

[10] I have no knowledge of either Sanscrit or Arabic. But I have done what I could to form a correct estimate of their value. I have read translations of the most celebrated Arabic and Sanscrit works. I have conversed, both here and at home, with men distinguished by their proficiency in the Eastern tongues. I am quite ready to take the oriental learning at the valuation of the orientalists themselves. I have never found one among them who could deny that a single shelf of a good European library was worth the whole native literature of India and Arabia. The intrinsic superiority of the Western literature is indeed fully

admitted by those members of the committee who support the oriental plan of education.

[11] It will hardly be disputed, I suppose, that the department of literature in which the Eastern writers stand highest is poetry. And I certainly never met with any orientalist who ventured to maintain that the Arabic and Sanscrit poetry could be compared to that of the great European nations. But when we pass from works of imagination to works in which facts are recorded and general principles investigated, the superiority of the Europeans becomes absolutely immeasurable. It is, I believe, no exaggeration to say that all the historical information which has been collected from all the books written in the Sanscrit language is less valuable than what may be found in the most paltry abridgments used at preparatory schools in England. In every branch of physical or moral philosophy, the relative position of the two nations is nearly the same.

[12] How then stands the case? We have to educate a people who cannot at present be educated by means of their mother-tongue. We must teach them some foreign language. The claims of our own language it is hardly necessary to recapitulate. It stands preeminent even among the languages of the West. It abounds with works of imagination not inferior to the noblest which Greece has bequeathed to us—with models of every species of eloquence—with historical composition, which, considered merely as narratives, have seldom been surpassed, and which, considered as vehicles of ethical and political instruction, have never been equaled—with just and lively representations of human life and human nature—with the most profound speculations on metaphysics, morals, government, jurisprudence, trade—with full and correct information respecting every experimental science which tends to preserve the health, to increase the comfort, or to expand the intellect of man. Whoever knows that language has ready access to all the vast intellectual wealth which all the wisest nations of the earth have created and hoarded in the course of ninety generations. It may safely be said that the literature now extant in that language is of greater

value than all the literature which three hundred years ago was extant in all the languages of the world together. Nor is this all. In India, English is the language spoken by the ruling class. It is spoken by the higher class of natives at the seats of Government. It is likely to become the language of commerce throughout the seas of the East. It is the language of two great European communities which are rising, the one in the south of Africa, the other in Australia—communities which are every year becoming more important and more closely connected with our Indian empire. Whether we look at the intrinsic value of our literature, or at the particular situation of this country, we shall see the strongest reason to think that, of all foreign tongues, the English tongue is that which would be the most useful to our native subjects.

[13] The question now before us is simply whether, when it is in our power to teach this language, we shall teach languages in which, by universal confession, there are no books on any subject which deserve to be compared to our own, whether, when we can teach European science, we shall teach systems which, by universal confession, wherever they differ from those of Europe differ for the worse, and whether, when we can patronize sound philosophy and true history, we shall countenance, at the public expense, medical doctrines which would disgrace an English farrier, astronomy which would move laughter in girls at an English boarding school, history abounding with kings thirty feet high and reigns thirty thousand years long, and geography made of seas of treacle and seas of butter.

[14] We are not without experience to guide us. History furnishes several analogous cases, and they all teach the same lesson. There are, in modern times, to go no further, two memorable instances of a great impulse given to the mind of a whole society, of prejudices overthrown, of knowledge diffused, of taste purified, of arts and sciences planted in countries which had recently been ignorant and barbarous.

[15] The first instance to which I refer is the great revival of letters among the Western nations at the close of the fifteenth and the beginning of the sixteenth century. At that time almost everything that was worth reading was contained in the writings of the ancient Greeks and Romans. Had our ancestors acted as the Committee of Public Instruction has hitherto noted, had they neglected the language of Thucydides and Plato, and the language of Cicero and Tacitus, had they confined their attention to the old dialects of our own island, had they printed nothing and taught nothing at the universities but chronicles in Anglo-Saxon and romances in Norman French—would England ever have been what she now is? What the Greek and Latin were to the contemporaries of More and Ascham, our tongue is to the people of India. The literature of England is now more valuable than that of classical antiquity. *I doubt whether the Sanscrit literature be as valuable as that of our Saxon and Norman progenitors. In some departments— in history for example—I am certain that it is much less so.*

[17] And what are the arguments against that course which seems to be alike recommended by theory and by experience? It is said that we ought to secure the cooperation of the native public, and that we can do this only by teaching Sanscrit and Arabic.

[18] I can by no means admit that, when a nation of high intellectual attainments undertakes to superintend the education of a nation comparatively ignorant, the learners are absolutely to prescribe the course which is to be taken by the teachers. It is not necessary however to say anything on this subject. For it is proved by unanswerable evidence, that we are not at present securing the co-operation of the natives. It would be bad enough to consult their intellectual taste at the expense of their intellectual health. But we are consulting neither. We are withholding from them the learning which is palatable to them. We are forcing on them the mock learning which they nauseate.

[21] I have been told that it is merely from want of local experience that I am surprised at these phenomena, and that it is not the fashion for students in India to study at their own charges. This only confirms me in my opinions. Nothing is more certain than that it never can in any part of the world be necessary to pay men for doing what they think pleasant or profitable. India is no exception to this rule. The people of India do not require to be paid for eating rice when they are hungry, or for wearing woollen cloth in the cold season. To come nearer to the case before us: --The children who learn their letters and a little elementary arithmetic from the village schoolmaster are not paid by him. He is paid for teaching them. *Why then is it necessary to pay people to learn Sanscrit and Arabic? Evidently because it is universally felt that the Sanscrit and Arabic are languages the knowledge of which does not compensate for the trouble of acquiring them. On all such subjects the state of the market is the detective test.*

[22] Other evidence is not wanting, if other evidence were required. A petition was presented last year to the committee by several ex-students of the Sanscrit College. The petitioners stated that they had studied in the college ten or twelve years, that they had made themselves acquainted with Hindoo literature and science, that they had received certificates of proficiency. And what is the fruit of all this? *'Notwithstanding such testimonials,'* they say, *'we have but little prospect of bettering our condition without the kind assistance of your honourable committee, the indifference with which we are generally looked upon by our countrymen leaving no hope of encouragement and assistance from them.'* They therefore beg that they may be *recommended to the Governor-General for places under the Government—not places of high dignity or emolument, but such as may just enable them to exist. 'We want means,'* they say, *'for a decent living, and for our progressive improvement,*

which, however, we cannot obtain without the assistance of Government, by whom we have been educated and maintained from childhood.' They conclude by representing very pathetically that they are sure that it was never the intention of Government, after behaving so liberally to them during their education, to abandon them to destitution and neglect.

[23] I have been used to see petitions to Government for compensation. All those petitions, even the most unreasonable of them, proceeded on the supposition that some loss had been sustained, that some wrong had been inflicted. These are surely the first petitioners who ever demanded compensation for having been educated gratis, for having been supported by the public during twelve years, and then sent forth into the world well furnished with literature and science. They represent their education as an injury which gives them a claim on the Government for redress, as an injury for which the stipends paid to them during the infliction were a very inadequate compensation. And I doubt not that they are in the right. They have wasted the best years of life in learning what procures for them neither bread nor respect. Surely we might with advantage have saved the cost of making these persons useless and miserable. Surely, men may be brought up to be burdens to the public and objects of contempt to their neighbours at a somewhat smaller charge to the State. But such is our policy. We do not even stand neuter in the contest between truth and falsehood. We are not content to leave the natives to the influence of their own hereditary prejudices. To the natural difficulties which obstruct the progress of sound science in the East, we add great difficulties of our own making. *Bounties and premiums, such as ought not to be given even for the propagation of truth, we lavish on false texts and false philosophy.*

[31] But there is yet another argument which seems even more untenable. It is said that the Sanscrit and the Arabic are the languages in which the sacred books of a hundred millions of people are written, and that they are on that account entitled

to peculiar encouragement. Assuredly it is the duty of the British Government in India to be not only tolerant but neutral on all religious questions. *But to encourage the study of a literature, admitted to be of small intrinsic value, only because that literature inculcated the most serious errors on the most important subjects, is a course hardly reconcilable with reason, with morality, or even with that very neutrality which ought, as we all agree, to be sacredly preserved. It is confined that a language is barren of useful knowledge. We are to teach it because it is fruitful of monstrous superstitions. We are to teach false history, false astronomy, false medicine, because we find them in company with a false religion. We abstain, and I trust shall always abstain, from giving any public encouragement to those who are engaged in the work of converting the natives to Christianity. And while we act thus, can we reasonably or decently bribe men, out of the revenues of the State, to waste their youth in learning how they are to purify themselves after touching an ass or what texts of the Vedas they are to repeat to expiate the crime of killing a goat?*

[34] In one point I fully agree with the gentlemen to whose general views I am opposed. I feel with them that it is impossible for us, with our limited means, to attempt to educate the body of the people. We must at present do our best to form a class who may be interpreters between us and the millions whom we govern,—a class of persons Indian in blood and colour, but English in tastes, in opinions, in morals and in intellect. To that class we may leave it to refine the vernacular dialects of the country, to enrich those dialects with terms of science borrowed from the Western nomenclature, and to render them by degrees fit vehicles for conveying knowledge to the great mass of the population.

[36] If the decision of His Lordship in Council should be such as I anticipate, I shall enter on the performance of my duties with the greatest zeal and alacrity. *If, on the other hand, it be the opinion of the Government that the present system ought to remain unchanged, I beg that I may be permitted to retire from the chair of the Committee. I feel that I could not be of the smallest*

use there. I feel also that I should be lending my countenance to what I firmly believe to be a mere delusion. I believe that the present system tends not to accelerate the progress of truth but to delay the natural death of expiring errors. I conceive that we have at present no right to the respectable name of a Board of Public Instruction. We are a Board for wasting the public money, for printing books which are of less value than the paper on which they are printed was while it was blank—for giving artificial encouragement to absurd history, absurd metaphysics, absurd physics, absurd theology—for raising up a breed of scholars who find their scholarship an incumbrance and blemish, who live on the public while they are receiving their education, and whose education is so utterly useless to them that, when they have received it, they must either starve or live on the public all the rest of their lives. Entertaining these opinions, I am naturally desirous to decline all share in the responsibility of a body which, unless it alters its whole mode of proceedings, I must consider, not merely as useless, but as positively noxious.

T.B. Macaulay
2nd February 1835. [emphasis added]

While I could have simply referred to and summarised the preceding exchange, I chose to extract the relevant portions of the same so as to pre-empt the argument that I was reading more into the primary source than warranted. As we can see, the material speaks for itself, displaying the utter contempt of the British coloniser for the Indic OET. The hypocrisy of the coloniser is writ large in the fact that Indic scriptures were being judged on the anvils of European philosophy and science instead of applying the very same standards of science and reason to the European coloniser's religion and its scripture. After all, if Indic OET is the subject of examination and criticism, it must be compared with Christian OET and the latter's claims of being the exclusive repository of reason and rationality. Also, when questioning the practical value of native learning and using the market as a test of its utility, the Christian coloniser turned a blind eye to the fact that knowledge of native OET was rendered unmarketable as a consequence of the alteration in the native worldview and way of life caused by the very factum of colonisation. Instead, he conveniently concludes that such learning had always been futile since it lacked intrinsic value. In any case, the Christian coloniser never deemed it fit to ask as to what was the market utility of being trained in Christian scripture. On the contrary, the British establishment was happy to financially support the Christian establishment in Bharat, which included pensionary benefits, using revenues earned from Bharat.

Between the Orientalist and Evangelical positions, William Bentinck threw his unreserved weight behind the latter, which is evidenced as follows:

give my entire concurrence to the sentiments expressed in this Minute.

W.C. BENTINCK

This reference is to Macaulay's Minute. Bentinck's concurrence was further reflected in the Resolution dated 7 March 1835, which is reproduced below[38]:

On the 7th of March 1835 the following Resolution was issued:—

'The Governor-General of India in Council has attentively considered the two letters from the Secretary to the Committee of Public Instruction, dated the 21st and 22nd January last, and the papers referred to in them.

First—His Lordship in Council is of opinion that the great object of the British Government ought to be the promotion of European literature and science among the natives of India; and that all the funds appropriated for the purpose of education would be best employed on English education alone.

Second—But it is not the intention of His Lordship in Council to abolish any College or School of native learning, while the native population shall appear to be inclined to avail themselves of the advantages which it affords, and His Lordship in Council directs that all the existing professors and students at all the institutions under the superintendence of the Committee shall continue to receive their stipends.

But his Lordship in Council decidedly objects to the practice which has hitherto prevailed of supporting the students during the period of their education. He conceives that the only effect of such a system can be to give artificial encouragement to branches of learning which, in the natural course of things, would be superseded by more useful studies; and he directs that no stipend shall be given to any student that may hereafter enter at any of these institutions; and that when any professor of Oriental learning shall vacate his situation, the Committee shall report to the Government the number and state Resolution, of the class in order that the Government may be able to decide upon the expediency of appointing a successor.

Third—It has come to the knowledge of the Governor-General in Council that a large sum has been expended by the Committee on the printing of Oriental works; his Lordship in Council directs that no portion of the funds shall hereafter be so employed.

Fourth—His Lordship in Council directs that all the funds which these reforms will leave at the disposal of the Committee be henceforth employed in imparting to the native population a knowledge of English literature and science through the medium of the English language; and His Lordship in Council requests the Committee to submit to Government, with all expedition, a plan for the accomplishment of this purpose.

Between this resolution passed in 1835 and the year 1839, the churn between the Orientalist and Evangelical schools continued, resulting in a compromise captured in the minute of Lord Auckland, dated 24 November 1839.[39] Among the measures proposed to address the grievances of both parties, additional funds were allocated to both, apart from directing that 'the first duty of the Oriental Colleges was to impart instruction in Oriental learning and that they may conduct English classes, if necessary, after that duty had been properly discharged'. However, as the Minute reflects and as confirmed by Naik and Nurullah in their seminal work on Indian education, the following positions of the Evangelical school were accepted:

1. Only partial and imperfect results could be expected from the attempts to teach European science through the medium of Sanskrit or Arabic;

2. The principal aim of educational policy should be to communicate, through the English language, a complete education in European literature, philosophy and science to the greatest number of students who may be found ready to accept it; and

3. Attempts of the government should be restricted to the extension of higher education to the upper classes of society who have leisure for study and whose culture would filter down to the masses.

Clearly, while increasing the allocation of funds to the Orientalist cause, the emphasis still remained on advancing the cause of English education and the spread of English ideas, apart from adopting a conscious policy of co-opting the Indian upper classes into higher education in the hope that the rest of the Indian society would aspire to follow their lead. This, according to scholars, such as Naik and Nurullah, was the Downward Filtration Theory in official action, which would characterise British education policy in Bharat at least until 1870.

The long and short of the preceding discussion on religion, caste, tribe and education, based on primary sources as well as scholarly literature, is that at least until 1853, the intention of the Christian European coloniser was to establish a politico-legal and social infrastructure which aided the spread of Christian colonial consciousness in every aspect of the native society. Therefore, in contemporary conversations and debates which touch upon religion, caste/tribe, education or any other aspect for that matter, the first step should be to check for the influence of colonial assumptions and colonial consciousness before proceeding to pass judgments on the past or evaluating contemporary practices and structures for relevance. Until and unless this exercise is undertaken, it must be presumed that our conversations happen within the Christian colonial framework *and* based on Christian colonialised versions of native OET.

Also, sometimes members of the indigenous society take pride and comfort in the fact that despite the best efforts of the Christian European coloniser, Bharat has remained un-proselytised for the most part. While I understand where this sense of optimism comes from, given that unlike Bharat, vast swathes of the 'New World' have turned Christian post the advent of the European coloniser, to err on the side of caution I would adopt a policy of civilisational vigilance for two reasons:

1. Given that the Indian State as well as the colonialised indigenous native are only too happy to wear the secularised Christian framework as a badge of honour, even if Bharat does not convert to Christianity, it would be equally bad or perhaps worse if Indic OET systems are completely Christianised; and

2. Conventional proselytisation has effectively alienated large parts of Bharat from the Indic consciousness and has, in fact, turned a significant cross-section of Bharat against it.

Therefore, I would not draw too much comfort from a mere paper identity when the native Indic consciousness is buried under layers of colonial consciousness without even realising it. As stated earlier, the decolonial 'option' is not just an option but an existential imperative for Indic civilisational consciousness; and since the Constitution is being pushed as a 'secular' document without examining it for colonial consciousness, a decolonial evaluation of the document and its antecedents is an exercise that must be undertaken without any further protraction. After all, the Constitution is capable of creating a multiplier effect either in favour of Indic consciousness or to its detriment.

Accordingly, in the next and final section of this book, I will examine the period between 1858 and 1919 to understand the influence of the colonial infrastructure in Bharat as well as that of international developments on Bharat's gradual movement towards a constitutional framework. One of the reasons for choosing the time frame from 1858 is because it is typically assumed that the so-called policy of Christian toleration morphed into a policy of irreligious secularism, thanks to the landmark events of 1857. Among other things, this assumption too will be put to test in the next section.

Section III

CONSTITUTION

Coloniality, Civilisation and Constitution

Blowing Mutinous Sepoys from the Guns, 8 September 1857

This is a hand-coloured steel engraving, detailing one of the activities post the suppression of the Uprising of 1857 (courtesy of London Printing and Publishing Company, 1858).

The discussions undertaken hitherto in the previous two sections on coloniality and civilisation are meant to serve as twin lenses to understand the influence of European coloniality/colonial consciousness on Bharat's journey as an indigenous civilisation towards constitutionalism. This section is, in fact, the intended culmination of the previous sections and the specific object of my examination. One of the reasons for using coloniality as the broader canvas within which this journey is sought to be placed is to drive home the point that to limit the study of the history of Bharat's Constitution to the Constituent Assembly and its cogitations would be a truncated analysis. This is because it is important to examine the OET-framework within which the Assembly operated, consciously or unconsciously. Accordingly, while the previous section covered the period until 1853 in order to underscore the distinctly Christian character of the politico-legal and social infrastructure established by the Christian European coloniser in Bharat, the current section will examine the period between 1858 and 1919–1920.

The importance of this time period is that 1858 marks the assumption of complete control of British India by the British Crown through the Government of India Act of 1858 and the Company's complete metamorphosis into an extension of the British State. That is, in case even a smidgen of autonomy remained after the 1853 Act, it was eclipsed by the Act of 1858. As for the outer limit of 1919–1920, not only does it mark the founding of the League of Nations, it is also the period of enactment of the Government of India Act of 1919—the first British-made Constitution for India—whose tacit nexus with international developments, including the founding of the League, is rarely discussed and warrants close study.

Between 1853 and 1858, the Government of India Act of 1854 too was passed but it need not be discussed in detail because for all practical purposes, the Act was an extension of the 1853 Act as evidenced by Section 8 of the 1854 Act, which reads as follows:[1]

This Act shall be read and construed as part of the Government of India Act, 1853.

Clearly, the 1854 Act took forward the intent of the 1853 Act by vesting in the Governor-General of India in Council the power to assume control of any province that was in the possession of the Company, which included the power to define and redraw the boundaries of those provinces. Therefore, the 1854 Act in itself contained nothing much further apart from expanding the scope of the Governor-General's territorial and administrative powers already granted under the 1853 Act.

Coming to the Government of India Act of 1858[2], the watershed event which led to it was, of course, the Indian Rebellion of 1857. The Rebellion itself was the making of several political and religious factors, with the episode involving the greased cartridges providing the necessary flammable material. The role played by increased Christian missionary activity under State patronage at least from 1813, which fuelled apprehensions of forced conversions of Indians by the British, must not be underestimated in triggering the Rebellion. What is worse is that the conduct of the British in putting down the Rebellion had religious bigotry written all over it. While the Muslims among the rebels were sewed in pigskins smeared with pork fat before execution, after which their bodies were burnt, the Hindus were forced to defile themselves by consuming beef. As for the civilian population, the conduct of English troops should have denuded the British of the authority to hold forth on 'civilisation' for eternity. Thousands of civilians were massacred and villages that were suspected of helping the Indian rebels were destroyed with the men being slaughtered and the women being subjected to all forms of sexual violence. Clearly, the unprovoked massacre at Jallianwala Bagh was not an aberration and not without precedent. The role played by the European coloniser's utter contempt for the natives, their religion and race must not be ruled out as a contributing factor to the barbarity and savagery meted out to the rebels and the civilian population.

While the origin of the Rebellion is usually traced to Meerut in May 1857, according to some scholars it began on 23 January 1857 at Dumdum near Calcutta, which spread to Barrackpore in March, Ambala in April, and Meerut, Lucknow and Delhi

in May. 'Peace' was restored in November 1858; however, the
Company was blamed for the Rebellion and the manner of
its handling. By December 1857, Henry John Temple (Lord
Palmerston), the then British prime minister, informed the
Company that a Bill would soon be introduced in the British
Parliament to abolish the Company and transfer all territories of
British India and the Government of India itself to the Crown.
Naturally, the Company begged and pleaded and even pitched its
case through the philosopher and politician John Stuart Mill, but
to no avail. On 12 February 1858, Lord Palmerston introduced
the Bill in the British Parliament to end the dual government of the
Company and the Crown. He lamented that 'the management of
such extensive territories, such vast interests, and such numerous
populations' had been 'deliberately consigned to the care of a small
body of commercial men'. Excoriating the Company, he said[3]:

> The principle of our political system is that all
> administrative functions should be accompanied by
> ministerial responsibility—responsibility to Parliament,
> responsibility to public opinion, responsibility to the Crown;
> but in this case the chief functions in the government of India
> are committed to a body not responsible to Parliament, not
> appointed by the Crown, but elected by persons who have
> no more connection with India than consists in the simple
> possession of so much stock.

He felt that the dual form of government, namely the Company
and the Crown, was among the biggest stumbling blocks for
'unity of purpose' and expeditious decision-making. There was
a significant cross-section of the British Parliament that shared
the views of Palmerston; however, he was out of office within
a week of the Bill's introduction in the Parliament and was
succeeded by Edward Smith-Stanley, the Earl of Derby. The
Bill was ultimately passed in August 1858 and the Act came into
force on 2 August 1858.[4]

Before we discuss the salient provisions of the 1858 Act, I will place before the reader extracts from the debates preceding the Act to demonstrate continuity in coloniality. In fact, the debates establish beyond an iota of doubt that the so-called policy of religious neutrality that was adopted by the British after the events of 1857 was, in fact, a restatement of the policy of 'toleration', which was discussed in the previous chapters. That this policy translated to grudging and pragmatic toleration of the false religion of the heathen and a tacit support of the true religion of the coloniser was said in as many words during the debates by several members of the British Parliament, in particular by the Archbishop of Canterbury and the bishops of London and Oxford, who clearly spelt out the nature of their 'neutrality', that is, Christian neutrality.

At the third reading of the Bill on 8 July 1858, Samuel Gregson, a member of the House of Commons, observed as under[5]:

It was a source of satisfaction to him that it had fallen to the lot of the noble Lord (Lord Stanley) to legislate for India, for he had visited India, and knew something about the population over which he was called to rule. *The three great points to which the attention of the Indian Government should be directed, as the seeds of the future prosperity of that empire, were commerce, civilization, and Christianity. He believed the first two would lead to the third, without any extraordinary pressure or exertion.* He had lived amongst the people of India for many years, and believed them to be intelligent, docile, and honest. For many years he had been surrounded by Native servants, and had never lost even so much as a pocket handkerchief. [emphasis added]

On the same day, Sir Erskine Perry pointed out,

... There was only one other point to which he wished to refer. It was singular that *the Bill did not contain a single allusion to the native interests of India, which he thought was an omission greatly to be deplored, as in every previous Act the people of India had been assured that their religion and customs would not be disturbed.* [emphasis added]

Similarly, at the second reading of the Bill in the House of Lords on 15 July 1858, the Earl of Ellenborough said[6]:

... My Lords, I have never looked forward to the future of India with more anxiety than I do at the present moment. I feel perfectly satisfied that it is absolutely necessary to send out for operations at the commencement of the cold season a very much larger force than it is possible, with due consideration to other equally vital interests, to detach front this country, without a material change in all our military establishments. But, however valuable it may be to send out a strong reinforcement of troops, I do not believe that that reinforcement will enable us to maintain our position in that country unless we send out also a policy intelligible and acceptable to the Natives. *The first act of the Government—when Her Majesty assumes in her own person the direction of affairs in India—ought to be to issue in the most solemn manner—and the Queen's word must be sacred—a proclamation with respect to the religion and the rights of the Natives.* That proclamation must not be written to please the House of Commons, nor to please people on the hustings, still less people on a platform; it must be addressed to the people and the armies of India. We have to govern India for India, not to please a party here, and we must make a declaration of the principles on which we intend to govern it, such as will be thoroughly acceptable and intelligible to the people. But, whatever policy you may declare, however great your additions to the army of India may be, neither one nor the other will effect your object unless you have in India at the head of the Government a man who has the confidence of the Natives and of the Europeans, who is capable of directing military operations, and who, by his personal authority, which in India is everything, can compel all his subordinate officials to co-operate in his policy and in carrying out the wishes of Her Majesty's Government. [emphasis added]

In fact, a Proclamation dated 1 November 1858 was indeed issued by Queen Victoria, which is often cited as the proof of British neutrality in matters of religion. The relevant portion of the Proclamation which contains cues on the nature of this toleration and neutrality[7] is as follows:

> *Firmly relying ourselves on the truth of Christianity,* and acknowledging with gratitude the solace of religion, we disclaim alike the right and desire to impose our convictions on any of our subjects. We declare it to be our royal will and pleasure that none be in anywise favoured, none molested or disquieted, by reason of their religious faith or observances, but that all alike shall enjoy the equal and impartial protection of the law; and we do strictly charge and enjoin all those who may be in authority under us that they abstain from all interference with the religious belief or worship of any of our subjects on pain of our highest displeasure. [emphasis added]

The language of the Proclamation itself is proof of the fact that the freedom of religion promised therein was rooted in the political theology of Christian freedom, as De Roover puts it. This is also evidenced by the language of the debates preceding the 1858 Act, as shall be seen in the ensuing portions. On 16 July 1858[8], the Bishop of Oxford proposed

> an addition to the clause vesting the right of nominating to chaplaincies in India in future alternately in the Crown and in the Bishop of the diocese in which the chaplaincies were situated. He hoped he should have

the concurrence of Her Majesty's Government on the subject. *From the commencement of legislation in connection with the East India Company they were bound to maintain and provide certain chaplains and ministers for their principal factories. Hitherto these appointments had been made by the Board of Directors at home, but under this clause they would transfer the appointment of all these chaplains to the Secretary of India. He, however, would propose that this should be done alternately by the Secretary of State and by the Bishop of the diocese. This would assimilate the ecclesiastical system in India to that of the system at home; and there was precedent for it in an Act passed by the late Sir R. Peel. It was desirable the resident Bishop should exercise this power, seeing that there were many missionaries whose fitness and whose merits could not come duly under the cognizance of the Secretary of State; and by the method he proposed one-half the patronage would be in the hands of the Government and the other half in the Bishop.* [emphasis added]

This was opposed by the Earl of Ellenborough on the grounds that *'it would be a most injudicious act at the present moment to permit the bishops in India to take gentlemen from the missionary body and connect them by chaplaincies with the Government'* [emphasis added]. Obviously, he was concerned about the sentiments of the natives in light of the 1857 Rebellion. However, the Bishop of London supported the Bishop of Oxford:

The Bishop of London—*supported the Amendment. It had been said that it was in the power of the bishops already to distribute patronage; but the only patronage he knew of was that of the Bishop of Calcutta to nominate his own archdeacon. He was far from wishing to import into this discussion the tone of the platform, but the feelings of the religious community ought not to be ignored, and it was generally thought that we ought to show a more manly and straightforward policy in regard to the Christian religion.*

The Earl of Derby—thought it would be exceedingly disadvantageous to have chaplains situated at such a distance dependent, not on the Government, but on their bishops, thus giving rise to a conflict of authorities. The chaplains were stipendiaries of the Government, and it was of great importance that the present relations between them should be maintained.

The Bishop of Oxford—said, the noble Earl had not met his arguments in any way. The question did not relate to the dependence of the chaplains either on the bishops or the Government. His proposal simply was, that the bishops should have an alternate share with the Secretary of state in the appointment of the chaplains. [emphasis added]

Of course, it could be argued that this discussion was in the context of the appointment of chaplains; however, it goes on to show that the Christian religion and its continued relationship with the State mattered enough to the lawmakers of Britain for it to figure extensively in their parliamentary debates. What is more interesting and relevant is their so-called policy of neutrality in relation to freedom of religion in Bharat, which is a restatement of 'secularism' as we shall see in the following pages. At the third reading of the Bill in the House of Lords on 23 July 1858, the following were the candid views of the Archbishop of Canterbury[9]:

The Archbishop of Canterbury—*My Lords, before this Bill leaves I wish to address a few words to your Lordships on a subject which, though not making any part of the Bill, is closely connected with the government of our Indian empire; but to which, nevertheless, very little allusion has been made in the course of the discussion—I mean the subject of religion, and the singular and responsible position which England holds as a Christian nation ruling over a nation of heathens. My Lords, I make no complaint that the Bill is silent on this important subject. It could not be otherwise.* The purpose of the Bill is to frame a government, not to declare how that government is to be administered—to create a machinery which is to be worked elsewhere. I also agree in the principle that has been so often laid down, that India must be governed in India, and not from England. *Still, my Lords, the subject to which I allude is one on which strong and conscientious convictions are entertained by a very large portion of the community, who deeply feel the anomalous and responsible position in which we are placed as a Christian nation ruling over a vast population of idolaters. My Lords, we are as far as possible from desiring any open attempt on the part of Government either to overthrow the false religion with which, unhappily, we have to deal, or to establish that which we know to be true. So far are we from desiring any such interference that we should think nothing gained by the conversion of the whole peninsula, supposing that it could possibly be effected through bribery or compulsion. But, while we grant to the religion of the Natives complete toleration, it is not necessary to conceal or compromise our own, or to let it appear to be a matter of indifference to us whether the Natives become converts to truth or not. And undoubtedly there is in this country a strong opinion prevailing that the course which has hitherto been pursued may wisely and safely be modified. My Lords I venture to specify a few points which I trust will be hereafter observed in the administration of affairs in India. First, that no distinction of caste be any longer recognized. Secondly, that in all schools to which aid is given by the Government the Bible shall be read—not commented upon for its doctrines, but read for its facts. Thirdly, that all connection on the part of the Government with the rites and customs of an idolatrous religion be entirely abolished, even if the object of such connection be simply the preservation of order; that those lands which have hitherto been employed for idolatrous purposes, and of which I believe the Company have become trustees, should be made over entirely to the Natives themselves, so that this nation may be altogether released from any participation in things which are*

detestable in themselves, and scandalous to the reputation of a
Christian country. Fourthly, that Native converts to Christianity
should be admitted to all employments the duties of which they
can adequately fulfil. In measures like these there is nothing that
ought to excite the suspicion of the Natives, nothing contrary to
the most perfect toleration, nothing savouring of proselytism—it
is merely an acknowledgment of the religion we ourselves profess.
And surely, my Lords, we ought to look forward to the time when,
under the providence of God, India shall form no exception to
the multitude of countries in which truth has prevailed against
falsehood, and the Gospel has triumphed over idolatry and
superstition, so that in the end it may appear why a remote country
like England should have been allowed to have dominion over the
vast territory of India. [emphasis added]

The Archbishop of Canterbury has saved me the trouble of
having to explain the fundamental Christian premise behind the
policy of 'toleration'. The Earl of Derby, the then British prime
minister Edward Smith-Stanley, who was in favour of protection
of all religions in Bharat, too was of the view that missionary
efforts in Bharat to Christianise the native population should not
be discouraged. The gulf between the two points of view was
merely a difference between the overt and the covert, the express
and the tacit. Following were the views of the then British prime
minister:

The Earl of Derby—*My Lords, after what has fallen from the*
most rev. Prelate, I may be permitted to observe, that while I think
that due protection ought to be given to the professors of all religions
in India, and nothing should be done to discourage the efforts of
Christian missionaries in that country; on the other hand, I am quite
certain that it is essential to the interests, the peace, and the well-
being of India, if not also to the very existence of our empire in
India, that the Government should carefully abstain from doing
anything except to give indiscriminate and impartial protection to

all sects and all creeds; and that nothing could be more inconvenient or more dangerous on the part of the State than any open and active assistance to any, or any attempt to convert the Native population from their own religions, however false and superstitious. My Lords, I hope I misunderstood the most rev. Prelate when he said that he should recommend the Government not in the slightest degree to recognize the distinction of caste. On that subject I will say, as far as the interest of the public service is concerned, it is not desirable that the same indulgence and punctilious deference for the caste of the Natives entering that service as was previously observed should be continued for the future; but to say that you will not recognize caste at all in India is to say that you will not recognize that which is intimately interwoven with all the cherished feelings, habits, associations, and most vital principles of the people. Therefore, my Lords, while in the public service I certainly would not allow prejudices of caste to interfere with the discharge of the duties which any person may voluntarily take upon himself, I say it is the bounden duty of the Government to pay that attention to caste which even in this country we pay, though not in the same degree, to the different ranks of society, and which any Government must, more or less, respect, if it would not be brought into constant collision with all classes of its subjects. *There was one topic touched upon by the most rev. Prelate in his observations with which I entirely concur. Wherever property in land or in any other form has been assigned to religious purposes, however repugnant to our feelings, provided they do not violate every principle of morality and decency, I think that that property ought to continue to be scrupulously applied to the ends to which it was dedicated. But I agree with the most rev. Prelate that it is most desirable that the Government and its officials should, as far as possible, separate themselves from any active interference in the detailed management of the property devoted to the support of idolatrous ceremonies in India. When I had the honour to hold the seals of the Colonial Department I introduced this principle into Ceylon, and required the arrangements under which the Government officials in that island had previously acted in regard to the Native rites and ceremonies to be modified, while the management of the funds applicable to such purposes was handed over to those with whose opinions they better accorded. I think the Government did its duty with credit then, as it will do its duty with credit now, by withdrawing as much as possible from any active participation in the detailed management of property of this description, while it at the same time strictly maintains the existing application of the endowments.* [emphasis added]

To this, the Archbishop of Canterbury responded as follows:

The Archbishop of Canterbury—I wish, my Lords, to explain that in speaking of caste I entirely referred to the public services.

The Archbishop of Canterbury was committed to the abolition of caste distinctions in the context of public services, which on the face of it, is not objectionable. However, the true objective behind the proposal was that no native public employee would be allowed to observe the rules of his caste during the course of public employment, which was contrary to the policy prior to the 1857 Rebellion that was caused by, among other things, the fear of caste rules being violated by the use of greased cartridges.

Coming back to the debates, the Earl of Shaftesbury was clear in his position that the British government should not shy away from calling itself a Christian government and proclaiming the superiority of the Christian religion as well as it being the basis for the 'best civilisation'. He also elaborated on the meaning of 'neutrality' as follows:

The Earl of Shaftesbury—My Lords, I think it due to the feelings of the country, which though recently silent, has by no means been asleep on this subject, that some expression of opinion should be given by your Lordships before the Bill to regulate the future government of India leaves this House. To nothing which has just fallen from the noble Earl can any exception be reasonably taken. I am exceedingly gratified, and I believe the public will also be gratified, with the sentiments which he has enunciated. *Those sentiments are very much in accordance with the petition which I had the honour to present to your Lordships signed by the representatives of all the bodies in this country engaged in the diffusion of Christian knowledge and in the encouragement of missionary operations. In that petition there is nothing violent, nothing fanatical. The demand of the petitioners is confined to what is strictly moderate and reasonable. What they require is the assertion of the most unbounded religious liberty in India; that the professors of all religions without distinction, should be put upon a footing of perfect equality. They say that in that country in the eye of the law the professors of all religions must be placed on a footing of equality; and they maintain that in the selection of candidates for the public service, there must be no rule but that of fitness for the public service. No man must be chosen or rejected simply because he is a Hindoo, a Parsee, a Mahommedan, or a Christian: all must have an equal claim to serve the State. I believe it would be prejudicial rather than otherwise if the Government were to come forward and give any direct assistance to the propagation of Christianity. What the petitioners ask is that the Government should neither promote that faith by active measures, nor in any way retard it—that it should neither be a favourer nor an opponent of Christianity. They expect that reasonable protection shall be given to all sects who conduct themselves with propriety. They hope the Government will not be ashamed to avow by its acts and in its official documents that it is a Christian Government; that it looks upon Christianity as the best form of religion and the best basis of all civilization; but that, neither directly nor indirectly—by force, bribery, or any other such inducement, great or small—will it endeavour to turn any Native from the religion to which he belongs. And this was the concluding prayer of the petitioners:— 'That all existing lets and hindrances being removed, and no new ones being opposed, free scope and action be given to the diffusion of Christianity through Her Majesty's territories in the East Indies.'... My Lords, I believe that the Asiatics will submit to much—to rapine, violence, spoliation, and oppression—but submit to insult they will not; and I know of no one single tiling that is more likely to retard the civilization of that country and endanger the peace and security of our empire than the continuance of such a state of things. A great many preach the Gospel with their mouths and others preach it by their lives. I am glad to see the Gospel advanced by both these means; but I am quite sure that no one single thing will more tend to advance civilization, even more than the exertions of the missionaries themselves, than that the language and conduct of all persons should be in harmony with the Gospel. The noble Earl will excuse me for having brought forward this subject, but I felt that a continuance of the present state of things would produce such serious results that I could not help expressing a hope that he will direct his attention to the subject.* [emphasis added]

The following were the words of caution from the Earl of Ellenborough:

The Earl of Ellenborough—... With regard to a most important matter—that of the future policy of the Government with respect to religion in India—I ask your Lordships to permit me to read a few sentences from the last authoritative exposition of their policy, dated only on the 13th of April last, in a letter from the Court of Directors to the Governor General, published for the information of your Lordships. In that letter are these words:— 'The Government will adhere with good faith to its ancient policy of perfect neutrality in matters affecting the religion of the people of India; and we most earnestly caution all those in authority under it not to afford by their conduct the least colour to the suspicion that that policy has undergone or will undergo any change. It is perilous for men in authority to do as individuals that which they officially condemn. The real intention of the

Government will be inferred from their acts, and they may unwittingly expose it to the greatest of all dangers, that of being regarded with general distrust by the people. We rely upon the honourable feelings which have ever distinguished our service for the furtherance of the views which we express. When the Government of India makes a promise to the people there must not be afforded to them grounds for a doubt as to its fidelity to its word.'

The Bishop of London voiced his objections to the management of Hindu temples by British officials, which was the predecessor to the Hindu Religious and Charitable Endowment legislations that are in force even today in contemporary Bharat, as discussed in the previous chapter. It is interesting how the Bishop balanced his views on the so-called commitment to impartiality in matters of religion and the superseding commitment to Christian truth, Christian justice and Christian civilisation. That truth and justice have a religious character, as opposed to the religious neutrality that is imputed to them, is underscored categorically by the words of the Bishop, which were as follows:

The Bishop of London—Before your Lordships pass this Bill I hope I may be permitted to make one or two remarks. *I understand that the point to which my most rev. Brother alluded was the practice that has existed for some years, of the Government taking into its own hands the management of the lands by which the heathen temples are supported. That practice has not as yet altogether ceased, and the result is, that these lands are kept in a far better state, and the heathen temples are, therefore, much better maintained than if the lands were under the control of those who would squander the proceeds and use them to their own advantage. The Government ought no longer to be responsible for the maintenance of that religion in any way. This is a matter of some importance, and we know that, notwithstanding what we have often heard, some change in this respect is desirable. The ancient traditional policy and management in India, as to religion, is not, indeed, likely to be altered; but there is a deep feeling in the hearts of religious people in this country that in that policy for many years back there has been some mistake.* I do not mean to say that exaggerated statements were not from time to time made upon this subject during the pressure of the calamities of last year. But I think that when all allowance is made for exaggeration it will still be found that there is a deep-seated feeling in the hearts of Englishmen that we do require some change in some of these matters, and I think the speech of the noble Earl at the head of the Government shows that we really are disposed to look this matter fairly in the face. It would not, I think, satisfy the feeling of the English nation if this year were to pass over without our future administration of India bearing upon it the shadow of that great event which has so deeply afflicted the nation, and which we cannot but regard as being in some degree a visitation from God. *No doubt, my Lords, we ought to exercise the utmost impartiality towards our heathen fellow-subjects. No doubt we ought to show the greatest forbearance to them. No doubt the Church of England and the Christian religion itself can never be advanced by a policy of mere force and power on the part of the Government. But we ought to show to the people of India that we wish to give them, not only Christian justice and Christian civilization, but, above all, ultimately the inheritance of Christian truth.* [emphasis added]

Building on the views of the Bishop of London, the Bishop of Oxford expounded on the difference between 'Christian truth' and 'wicked neutrality', obviously imputing the former meaning to the official policy of toleration and neutrality.

The Bishop of Oxford—*I think, my Lords, that we can have very little doubt what the conduct of a Christian Government ought to be; but I confess that I heard with some misgivings the extract which was read by the noble Earl below me (the Earl of*

Shaftesbury), especially when accompanied with the emphasis which the noble Earl threw upon certain expressions which are well capable of being understood in two different ways. If by the 'neutrality' which was referred to nothing more was meant than that there should be no attempt on the part of the Government as a Government, directly or indirectly to interfere with the religious belief of its heathen subjects, I for one cannot object to that word being taken in its fullest sense. But if by 'neutrality' is secretly meant that there shall be stamped on the English Government and their representatives in India an aspect of entire indifference as to whether this religion or that is to prosper and abide—if by 'neutrality' is meant that their characters are to exhibit that happy indifference as to Christianity which shall impress on the heathen mind the conviction that they care not whether they are Christians or heathens, then I believe that such neutrality would be fatal and false to the religion we profess, and that ultimately it would destroy the empire that has been entrusted to us. It seems to me that the distinction is plain and intelligible between making the Indian people feel that we do not by force and fraud, by policy or by violence, interfere with their religious belief, because our own religion teaches us that such interference would be wrong, and impressing them with the conviction that we withhold our interference because we have ourselves no distinct preference for our own faith. One seems to me to be the line of Christian truth, and the other to be the line of a wicked neutrality; and I am only most anxious that nothing should go forth to mar the impression that we do not mean the English Government in India to be ashamed of its Christianity; but that we wish it to make due provision for the supply of the Christian necessities of its own troops and civil servants, because it believes Christianity to be true, and is not afraid in the face of its heathen subjects to show that it believes it to be true, and that it builds its own expectations of its continued prosperity upon the blessing of that God whom it professes to serve. I trust that that is the only sense in which neutrality as to the Christian religion is to be admitted into the future Government of India; and I think it the more important to declare this, because I cannot but feel that there have been in times past many instances in which neutrality was understood to mean carelessness about the truth of Christianity and a fear to avow in the face of heathendom that we were ourselves firm believers in the Christian revelation. [emphasis added]

That the policy of neutrality advocated by the then prime minister was conducive to the gradual spread of Christianity is corroborated by the views of Earl Granville, who said it in as many words as follows:

Earl Granville—*I think that the meaning of the words quoted by the noble Earl is very obvious—that the Government is not to interfere in any manner with the religion of its subjects in India; that it is not in its official capacity to use either force or corruption for the purposes of proselytism. I may say that it gave me great pleasure to hear the declaration which was made by the noble Earl at the head of the Government. I think that it was most useful and important—most useful with regard to the influence which it will produce upon the opinions of people in this country, and most important not only with respect to the temporal interests of the government in India, but as indicating the most advantageous system for the gradual spread of Christianity in that large kingdom.* With regard to the policy of mercy which has been advocated this evening, I feel no distrust of Her Majesty's Government in that respect, and I am quite sure that there need be no fear of Lord Canning. It gives me great satisfaction to find the general concurrence which is now expressed by all in regard to that discrimination of punishment and to those principles of mercy for which the noble Lord made himself so very conspicuous last autumn, and then subjected himself to so much rebuke. [emphasis added]

It is evident from this that the Christian hope that Christian freedom/toleration and Christian neutrality would gradually bring the idolatrous heathen from the darkness of his/her false religion into the light of the one true religion is a constant undercurrent that runs through each of the views. In light of all of this irrefutable material, it is my considered position that there is no reason to read and understand the Queen's Proclamation of 1 November 1858 as being any different in its intent and import from the views of the members of the British Parliament, including the then prime minister. It is in this context that the passing of the 1858 Act must be understood, instead of making the erroneous assumption that the administrative structure laid down by the Act was intended to address only issues of 'secular' governance. If anything, the word 'secular' must always be understood as 'Christian secular', since the Christian worldview was inherent to the colonial infrastructure. Therefore, the transfer of territories and Government of British India to the Crown under the Act marked the beginning of a direct Christian 'civilising' phase for Bharat, which was partially held back until then due to the mercantile pragmatism of the Company. After all, the missionary clauses in the Charter Acts of 1813 and 1833 were not included at the behest of the Company, but were included at the behest of the British Parliament, which would thenceforth directly govern Bharat by virtue of the 1858 Act. In any case, perhaps, what most people do not pay attention to is the Preamble of these Acts, which inevitably contained the following portion:

> And whereas it is expedient that the said Territories should be governed by and in the Name of Her Majesty: *Be it therefore enacted by the Queen's most Excellent Majesty, by and with the Advice and Consent of the Lords Spiritual and Temporal, and Commons in this present Parliament assembled,* and by the Authority of the same, as follows; that is to say, Transfer of the Government of India to Her Majesty. [emphasis added]

The reference to 'Lords Spiritual' precedes Temporal and Commons; the Lords Spiritual, of course, being the bishops of

the Church of England, numbering 26 since the early nineteenth
century, with the Archbishops of Canterbury and York holding
a higher rank than the other bishops. Critically, the Christian
divide between the spiritual and temporal or secular, which I have
discussed extensively in the earlier chapters, is expressly captured
in the very language of the Charter Act and the Government
of India Acts. There was certainly no attempt on the part of the
British government to conceal or skirt around its Christian identity
and the foundations of its infrastructure in Christian political
theology. Surely it cannot be contended that a Parliament which
legally provided (*and still does*) for the presence of 26 bishops
representing Christianity was a secular Parliament. Why, then, do
we attempt to hyper-secularise what was essentially a Christian
establishment when statutory facts, not merely opinion, coming
straight from the horse's mouth, speak for themselves? Is this not
coloniality or colonial consciousness at work?

Coming to the 1858 Act, in over 40 provisions, the Act
stripped the Company of all and any powers of consequence over
Bharat and transferred it to the Crown of the Christian British
Empire. While the issue of granting representation to Indians
arose during the debates in the British Parliament relating to the
1858 Act, the Parliament decided against it on the grounds that
a significant cross-section of natives were still up in arms against
the British on account of the latter's barbarity in quelling the
1857 Rebellion. Following are some of the salient provisions of
the 1858 Act:

Section 01: Territories under the Government of the East
India Company to Be Vested in Her Majesty and Powers to
Be Exercised in Her Name
The Government of the Territories now in the Possession
or under the Government of the East India Company, and
all Powers in relation to Government vested in or exercised
by the said Company in trust for Her Majesty, shall cease
to be vested in or exercised by the said Company; and all

territories in the possession or under the government of the said Company, and all rights vested in or which if this Act had not been passed might have been exercised by the said Company in relation to any territories, shall become vested in Her Majesty, and be exercised in her name; and for the purposes of this Act India shall mean the territories vested in Her Majesty as aforesaid, and all Territories which may become vested in Her Majesty by virtue of any such Rights as aforesaid.

Section 02: India to Be Governed By and in the Name of Her Majesty

India shall be governed by and in the Name of Her Majesty, and all rights in relation to any territories which might have been exercised by the said Company if this Act had not been passed shall and may be exercised by and in the name of Her Majesty as rights incidental to the government of India; and all the territorial and other revenues of or arising in India, and all tributes and other payments in respect of any territories which would have been receivable by or in the name of the said Company if this Act had not been passed, shall be received for and in the name of Her Majesty, and shall be applied and disposed of for the purposes of the government of India alone, subject to the provisions of this Act.

Section 03: Secretary of State to Exercise Powers Now Exercised by the Company, Etc

Save as herein otherwise provided, one of Her Majesty's Principal Secretaries of State shall have and perform all such or the like powers and duties in anywise relating to the government or revenues of India, and all such or the like powers over all officers appointed or continued under this Act, as might or should have been exercised or performed by the East India Company, or by the Court of Directors or Court of Proprietors of the said Company, either alone or by the direction or with the sanction or Approbation of the Commissioners for the Affairs of India in relation to such government or revenues, and the officers and servants of the said Company respectively, and also all such powers as might have been exercised by the said Commissioners alone: Countersigning of warrants—and any warrant or writing under Her Majesty's Royal Sign Manual, which by the Government of India Act, 1854, or otherwise is required to be countersigned by the President of the Commissioners for the Affairs of India, shall in lieu of being so countersigned be countersigned by one of Her Majesty's Principal Secretaries of State.

Section 29: Appointments to Be Made by or with the Approbation of Her Majesty

The Appointments of Governor-General of India, Fourth Ordinary Member of the Council of the Governor-General of India, and Governors of Presidencies in India, now made by the Court of Directors with the Approbation of Her Majesty, and the Appointments of Advocate-General for the several Presidencies now made with the Approbation of the Commissioners for the affairs of India, shall be made by Her Majesty by Warrant under Her Royal Sign Manual; the Appointments of the Ordinary Members of the Council of the Governor-General of India, except the Fourth Ordinary Member and the Appointments of the Members of the Council of the several Presidencies, shall be made by the Secretary of State in Council; the Appointments of the Lieutenant Governors of Provinces or Territories shall be made by the Governor-General of India, subject to the Approbation of Her Majesty; and all such Appointments shall be subject to the Qualifications now by Law affecting such Offices respectively.

Section 32: Secretary of State in Council to Make Regulations for the Admission of Candidates to the Civil Service of India

With all convenient Speed after the passing of this Act, Regulations shall be made by the Secretary of State in Council, with the Advice and Assistance of the Commissioners for the Time being acting in execution of Her Majesty's Order in Council of Twenty-first May One thousand eight hundred and fifty-five, 'for regulating the Admission of Persons to the Civil Service of the Crown', for admitting all Persons being natural-born Subjects of Her Majesty (and of such Age and Qualifications as may be prescribed in this Behalf) who may be desirous of becoming Candidates for Appointment to the Civil Service of India to be examined as Candidates accordingly, and for prescribing the Branches of Knowledge in which such Candidates shall be examined, and generally for regulating and conducting such Examinations under the Superintendence of the said last-mentioned Commissioners, or of the Persons for the Time being entrusted with the carrying out of such Regulations as may be from Time to Time established by her Majesty for Examination, Certificate, or other Test of Fitness in relation to Appointments to Junior Situations in the Civil Service of the Crown; and the Candidates who may be certified by the said Commissioners or other Persons as aforesaid to be entitled under such Regulations shall be recommended for Appointment according to the Order of their Proficiency as shown by such Examinations, and such Persons only as shall have been so certified as aforesaid shall be appointed or admitted to the Civil Service of India by the Secretary of State in Council: Provided always, that all Regulations to be made by the said Secretary of State in Council under this Act shall be laid before Parliament within Fourteen Days after the making thereof, if Parliament be sitting, and, if Parliament be not sitting, then. within Fourteen Days after the next Meeting thereof.

Between 1858 and 1919–1920, a few more Government of India Acts were passed, which built on the basic template of the 1858 Act, apart from representative legislative councils which were constituted under the Indian Councils Acts of 1861, 1874, 1892 and 1909 (also known as Minto–Morley

Reforms) and the Government of India Act of 1915.[10] This period also saw the Home Rule Scheme of 1889, which was the first attempt towards securing the right of franchise to Indians and Indian representation in the legislative councils, and the preparation of the Constitution of India Bill, 1895 (also known as the Home Rule Bill), most probably drafted under the stewardship of Lokamanya Balgangadhar Tilak.[11]

However, given the specific focus of the discussion at hand, namely the examination of Bharat's constitutional journey for the influence of coloniality, I will discuss only those developments, which prove that over the years, there was no change in the colonial consciousness of the coloniser notwithstanding the setting up of representative legislative bodies. This is because these bodies operated within the political theology of Christianity, as we shall see from the literature, and Indians participated in these institutions, perhaps without paying attention to the unsecular nature of the underlying theology that informed such institutions. In a nutshell, my intention is to demonstrate that the 1858 Proclamation of religious neutrality by Queen Victoria provided an optically convenient veneer to the evangelical and civilising tendencies of the colonial administration, evident from their conduct as well as their own discussions in both international fora and in the British Parliament.

For instance, this petition moved by the Bishop of Oxford on behalf of the residents of Ham in the House of Lords on 6 July 1860 demonstrates the clear intentions to fully Christianise education in India by introducing the study of the Bible in government schools across the country[12]:

The Bishop of Oxford *presented a Petition from Inhabitants of Ham, praying that the Holy Scriptures may not be excluded by Authority from the Government Schools in India.* He said he did not intend to enter at length upon the great question to which the petition referred. Their Lordships had recently had an opportunity of hearing all that could be said upon the subject stated ably, completely, and temperately by the noble Duke on

the cross-benches (the Duke of Marlborough), and he felt it
would be improper for him to attempt to repeat the arguments
and statements which had been already submitted to the House.
He was, however, anxious, in the first place, to do away with an
impression which might probably prevail in the public mind
from the mode in which the discussion on a previous evening
had terminated. It might appear to the country that the noble
Duke (the Duke of Marlborough) stood alone in that House
in the opinions which he had expressed. Now, that was very
far from being the case. He (the Bishop of Oxford) had been
ready and desirous of stating how entirely he concurred in the
sentiments expressed by the noble Duke, but the mode in which
the discussion terminated prevented his doing so. He was also
anxious to suggest two grave considerations to the Government
in connection with the subject. *He had laid upon the table fifty
petitions from various parts of the country with the same prayer as
that of the petition he now held in his hand, that the Bible might
be introduced into the schools in India; but he was fully persuaded
they were not a tithe of the petitions which would pour in upon both
Houses of Parliament upon this grave subject, and he would venture
to predict that in a matter like this, upon which the religious mind of
the people of this country was to a remarkable degree unanimous—
when those who differed upon many points of Church government
were united in opinion that the Bible ought not to be excluded from
the Government schools in India, but that it should be accessible in
school hours to all those who desired to study it—that at no distant
day that question would be brought to a practical and a successful
issue. If there was any danger at all to be apprehended, it would
arise from a belief being raised in India that the Government
resisted the demand that was made because they thought it would
be an infraction of the fair dealing which had been guaranteed to
those who differed from us in religion, and that if the demand were
carried it would be carried by the religious mind of this country in
spite of the wishes of the Government. Such a belief would lead to
an impression, untrue, indeed, that the admission of the Bible into*

schools was something at which they had ground to be alarmed, and which constituted a violation of religious liberty. For his own part he believed that sooner or later the Bible would have to be introduced into these schools, and he was of opinion that it would be much safer to introduce it now, than to postpone it to a later period. It would be a danger in its worst form if the question was left as a subject for agitation in this country. He thought, also, that the introduction of the Bible taking place after an interval would be an evil, because the Native mind would form an opinion that we feared to do so as long as the recollection of the late mutiny remained in our minds, but that only when the memory of that event had passed away did we venture to take the step. There was another consideration he would urge upon the Government. He did not undervalue the dangers of our Indian Empire, but he was convinced that those dangers did not rest upon our simply giving fair play to Christianity, while we cautiously abstained from attempting to inflict Christianity by force, and from entrapping the Natives into Christianity by fraud. Our security would he greater if the Native mind could be taught that we abstained from those courses, not from fear, but because our consciences forbade them. The great danger was that in turning our attention to a false danger, we might overlook the real source of danger. The mode in which the question of Native adoption had been treated was, he believed, full of danger, as also was the annexation policy, and he believed also the proposed change in our army system in India. He was therefore most anxious, without reopening this great subject, to urge as earnestly as he could upon the Government a reconsideration of the position they had taken upon this grave question. [emphasis added]

The Earl of Galloway enthusiastically endorsed this proposal thus:

The Earl of Galloway

sincerely hoped the Government would give their earnest attention to the appeal of the right rev. Prelate. It was highly

inconsistent with our promise to elevate and improve the condition
of the Natives of India if we excluded from our schools in that
country the Bible, which was the only standard of right and wrong.
It was said that the fear of exciting distrust among the Natives and
of weakening our hold upon. India was a necessity for excluding the
Bible; but that would imply that we valued the material welfare of
England more than we cared for the moral condition of India. In a
speech lately delivered by Sir Herbert Edwardes on the propagation
of Christianity among the Natives that distinguished officer had
expressed opinions which he commended to the consideration of the
Government, and which he earnestly hoped would have their due
influence. [emphasis added]

It bears noting from the extracted portions here that this
discussion took place in 1860, that is, barely under two years of
the end of the 1857 Rebellion and the Proclamation of November
1858. If the Proclamation was truly intended to prevent and deter
further missionary work in Bharat, the proposal of the Bishop of
Oxford proves otherwise. In fact, it demonstrates the artificial
separation that the British Christian mind had created for itself.
It distinguished between interference with the religion of the
natives and the proselytising work carried out by missionaries in
Bharat. The latter was not seen as an infraction of the former.
This convenient distinction allowed the British coloniser to
continue with the façade of neutrality and was further proof
of the actual meaning of Christian toleration. It effectively
meant, 'Sure, practice your heathen faith but I will continue to
denigrate and undermine it through my missionary work until
you yield and have a change of heart and conscience.' That they
were utterly convinced of the inextricability of conversion to
Christianity and moral improvement of the natives, underscores
the Christianisation of morality and secularisation of Christianity
at the same time.

In any case, did the British government stop its expenditure
from revenues earned in Bharat on the Church establishment in

Bharat after the Proclamation of 1858 to prove its secular and neutral credentials? No. This is demonstrated by the question raised in the House of Commons on 28 September 1915 in relation to the Ecclesiastical establishment in India, which is extracted below[13]:

> Mr. Dundas White
>
> asked the Secretary of State for India whether, in view of the financial provisions as to the *ecclesiastical establishment which are now consolidated in Part X. of the Government of India Act, 1915, he will give a detailed statement showing what were the payments out of the revenues of India during the last financial year* for which figures are available in respect of the salary and allowances to each bishop and archdeacon mentioned in Section 118 (1); of the expenses of episcopal visitations in Section 118 (3); of payments of representatives of bishops in Section 119; of the pensions to bishops in Section 120; of the salaries to chaplains of the Church of Scotland in Section 122; and of the Grants to any other sect, persuasion, or community of Christians, under Section 123; and if he will state the aggregate for that year of these ecclesiastical endowments out of the revenues of India? [emphasis added]

To this, the then Secretary of State for India, Joseph Austen Chamberlain, gave a detailed break-up for the financial year in question which is as follows:

> Towards stipends of bishops of Calcutta, Madras and Bombay and the allowances of Archdeacons of the said Presidencies— Rupees 1,05,543
>
> The allowances of the Archdeacons were in addition to their salaries as Senior Chaplains on the Ecclesiastical Establishments.
>
> > Towards expenses of episcopal visitations—Rupees 15,611
> > Towards payments of pensions to bishops—£1,800

Towards salaries of Chaplains of Church of Scotland (exclusive of payments to Presbyterian Chaplains attached to regiments which are treated as Army expenditure)—Rupees 94,404

Grants to religious bodies other than Church of England and Church of Scotland—Allowances to bishops and Priests of Church of Rome and for upkeep of churches (exclusive of payments to Priests attached to regiments which are treated as Army expenditure)—Rupees 20,122

This cumulatively amounted to £17,512 in 1914–1915. Clearly, a portion of the revenues earned from Bharat, no matter how miniscule the quantum may seem, was being diverted towards maintenance of the Christian establishment in Bharat, a full 57 years after the Queen's Proclamation of 1858. Either there was a slip between the cup and the lip, or it was an intended slip. In short, it can be stated objectively that a government with an avowedly Christian character was and remains fundamentally incapable of being neutral and impartial in matters of religion, much less in relation to the 'false religion' of the 'heathen native'.

As we shall see in the next chapter, this fact is clearly demonstrated yet again in the convergence of international events leading to the founding of the League of Nations, such as the Paris Peace Conference of 1919, and the debates in the British Parliament surrounding the passing of the Government of India Act of 1919. The ensuing material will show that international law was used as a springboard and a force multiplier to give effect to universalisation of the Christian political theology which forms the basis of the European/Western civilisation. To assume that Bharat was an outlier to this global development would be ahistorical in light of the cogitations held in the British Parliament prior to and in relation to the Government of India Act of 1919.

The Standard of Civilisation, the League of Nations and the Government of India Act, 1919

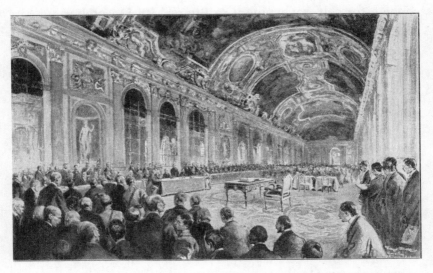

The Peace Congress at the Hall of Mirrors, Versailles, 29 June 1919

(Drawing by George Scott from L'Illustration)

'Nationalist' attempts to secure 'Home Rule' for Indians were active at least since 1889; however, the movement towards greater democratic participation of Indians in the business of law-making and administration of Bharat, albeit as part of the British Empire, picked up steam upon the outbreak of the First World War in 1914. Indian nationalists sensed an opportunity to present to the British a scheme for post-war reforms in response to growing political discontent in Bharat. Gopal Krishna Gokhale's 'Political Testament of 1914' stands out in this regard since it addressed the issue of 'provincial autonomy' with a certain degree of specificity. Subsequently, in October 1916, a Memorandum of post-war reforms was presented to the then Viceroy of India, Lord Chelmsford, by 19 non-elected members of the Imperial Legislative Council, which included Mahamana Madan Mohan Malaviya and Mohammed Ali Jinnah. The Memorandum outlined a 13-point scheme for self-government in Bharat. By December 1916, a scheme for self-government devised and formally approved by members of both the Indian National Congress and the Muslim League, known as the Congress–League Scheme, was passed at their respective annual sessions.[1]

The consequence of the growing chorus for self-government and the recognition of Bharat's contribution to the British war effort, both in terms of human resources and capital, was a declaration on 20 August 1917[2] in the House of Commons by the then Secretary of State for India Edwin Samuel Montagu, which read as follows:

The policy of His Majesty's Government, which the government of India are in complete accord is that of increasing association of Indians in every branch of administration, and the Gradual development of self-governing Institutions with a view to the progressive realization of *responsible governments in India as an Integral part of the British Empire.* They have decided that substantial steps in this direction should be taken as soon as possible.

I would add that progress in this policy can only be achieved by successive stages. The British Government and the

Government of India, on whom the responsibility lies for the welfare and advancement of the Indian peoples, must be the judges of the time and measure of each advance. [emphasis added]

Indian nationalists saw this Declaration as an attempt by the British to defer 'self-government' by replacing it with 'responsible government', which was obviously not acceptable. Therefore, when Montagu arrived in India in November 1917 to ostensibly hold parleys with various groups, the Congress–League Scheme on self-government was pitched to him by various organisations. These and other efforts by a variety of stakeholders, primarily the Congress and the Muslim League, ultimately culminated in the preparation of the Report on Indian Constitutional Reforms by Montagu along with the Viceroy Lord Chelmsford, which was completed in Simla on 22 April 1918 and published on 8 July 1918.[3] The importance of these Reforms, which were popularly known as the Montagu–Chelmsford Reforms, or the Montford Reforms for short, in Bharat's constitutional journey is evident from the fact that they formed the direct basis of the Government of India Act of 1919.[4]

For all practical purposes, it could be said that the Government of India Act of 1919 was the first British-made Constitution for India, which provided the foundation for the Government of India Act of 1935. The 1935 Act, in turn, provided the broader framework for the Constitution of independent India, as admitted by the Chairman of the Drafting Committee of the Constitution, Dr. Ambedkar, in the Constituent Assembly Debates.[5] Since the foundational document is the Montford Report, those who wish to understand the origins of independent Bharat's constitutional framework must read the 256-page Report which, among other things, is a one-stop shop of sorts to understand the evolution of the British politico-legal and administrative infrastructure in Bharat. The Report consists of 11 chapters and a conclusion, but I will discuss only those portions that are relevant to the theme of the discussion at hand, namely colonial consciousness and its influence on contemporary constitutionalism.

In Chapter VII of Part I of the Report, the authors rejected the Congress–League Scheme for self-government citing its 'unworkability in practice' and its 'negation of responsible government'. In short, according to Montagu and Chelmsford, Bharat was not ready for self-government even within the British Empire. In Part II of the Report, the proposals of the authors are set out along with the reasons in Paragraphs 178–199. These portions of the Report, according to me, are mandatory reading to understand the continuing colonial consciousness and civilising tendencies of the Christian coloniser. Here are a few extracts which speak for themselves, lest it is assumed that I am reading the document with a confirmation bias:

Reasons for a new policy
178. ... It is evident that the present machinery of government no longer meets the needs of the time; it works slowly, and it produces irritation; there is a widespread demand on the part of educated Indian opinion for its alteration; and the need for advance is recognized by official opinion also. One hundred and twenty years ago Sir Thomas Munro wrote:-
'What is to be the final result of our arrangements on the character of the people? Is it to be raised, or is it to be lowered? Are we to be satisfied with merely securing our power and protecting the inhabitants, *or are we to endeavour*

to raise their character, to render them worthy of filling higher stations in the management of their country, and devising plans for its improvement? .... We should look on India not as a temporary possession, but as one which is to be maintained permanently, until the natives shall in some future age have abandoned most of their superstitions and prejudices, and become sufficiently enlightened to frame a regular government for themselves, and to conduct and preserve it.'

The logical outcome of the past

179. Thus the vision of a persistent endeavour to train the people of India for the task of governing themselves was present to the minds of some advanced Englishmen four generations ago; and we since have pursued it more constantly than our critics always admit, more constantly perhaps than we have always perceived ourselves. The inevitable result of education in the history and thought of Europe is the desire for self-determination; and the demand that now meets us from the educated classes of India is no more than the right and natural outcome of the work of a hundred years. There can be no question of going back, or of withholding the education and enlightenment in which we ourselves believe; and yet, the more we pursue our present course without at the same time providing the opportunities for the satisfaction of the desires which it creates, the more unpopular and difficult must our present government become and the worse must be the effect upon the mind of India. On the other hand, if we make it plain that, when we start on the new lines, education, capacity, and good-will will have their reward in power, then we shall set the seal upon the work of past years. Unless we are right, in going forward now the whole of our past policy in India has been a mistake. *We believe, however, that no other policy was either right or possible, and therefore we must now face its logical consequences. Indians must be enabled, in so far as they attain responsibility, to determine*

for themselves what they want done. The process will begin in
local affairs which we have long since intended and promised
to make over to them; the time has come for advance also
in some subjects of provincial concern; and it will proceed
to the complete control of provincial matters and thence,
in the course of time, and subject to the proper discharge
of Imperial responsibilities, to the control of matters
concerning all India.. *We make it plain that such limitations
on powers as we are now proposing are due only to the obvious
fact that time is necessary in order to train both ·representatives
and electorates for the work which we desire them to undertake;
and that we offer Indians opportunities at short intervals to prove
the progress they are making and to make good their claim not
by the method of agitation, but by positive demonstration, to the
further stages in self-government which we have just indicated.*

*180. Further, we have every reason to hope that as the result of
this process, India's connexion with the Empire will be confirmed
by the wishes of her people. The experience of a century of
experiments within the Empire goes all in one direction. As power
is given to the people of a province or of a dominion to manage
their own local affairs, their attachment becomes the stronger to
the Empire which comprehends them all in a common bond of
union. The existence of national feeling, or the love of, and pride
in, a national culture need not conflict with, and may indeed
strengthen, the sense of membership in a wider commonwealth.
The obstacles to a growth in India of this sense of partnership in the
Empire are obvious enough.* Differences of race, religion, past
history, and civilization have to be overcome. But the Empire,
which includes the French of Canada and the Dutch of South
Africa—to go no further—cannot in any case be based on
ties of race alone. *It must depend on a common realization of the
ends for which the Empire exists, the maintenance of peace and
order over wide spaces of territory, the maintenance of freedom,
and the development of the culture of each national unity of*

which the Empire is composed. These are aims which appeal to the imagination of India and, in proportion as self-government develops patriotism in India, we may hope to see the growth of a conscious feeling of organic unity with the Empire as a whole. [emphasis added]

From this quote, it is clear that one of the primary goals behind the proposal of constitutional reforms, which finally found their way into the Government of India Act of 1919, was to rid the natives of their 'superstitions and prejudices' and strengthen their bonds with the British Empire. It was a project of eternal 'reform' through the means of a constitution whose ultimate goal was the colonialisation of the natives, which was inbuilt in the Montford scheme. The authors of the Report were also aware that the education system introduced in Bharat by the British had unexpectedly backfired since it had only served to strengthen existing ideas of freedom. Therefore, to offset the effect of the English education system without altering it altogether, 'responsible government' as opposed to 'self-government' *within the British Empire* was being proposed, to gradually 'educate' and 'prepare' natives for self-governance without losing any of their love for the British imperial commonwealth. It goes without saying that the authors of the Report clearly understood the causal relationship between the education system and ideas that drive a society's polity.

Of course, the Montford Report must also be read for its impact on the structure of Bharat's Constitution, such as the introduction of Central and Provincial Legislatures, the creation of Central and Provincial Lists (that is, lists of subjects they could legislate on), streamlining of the Indian Civil Service and so on and so forth. But its underlying objective, which was to strengthen the bonds between the natives and the British commonwealth, must not be lost sight of. The purpose of the proposed politico-legal framework was to co-opt the native into

the coloniser's worldview. This is evident from the Conclusion
of the Report in Paragraph 349, which is as follows:

CONCLUSION
Conception of India's future
349. We may conveniently now gather up our proposals, so as
to, present a general picture of the progress which we intend
and of the nature and order of the steps to be taken on the road.
Our conception of the eventual future of India is a sisterhood of
States, self-governing in all matters of purely local or provincial
interest, in some cases corresponding to existing provinces,
in others perhaps modified in area according to the character
and economic interests of their people. Over this congeries
of States would preside a central Government, increasingly
representative of and responsible to the people of all of them;
dealing with matters, both internal and external, of common
interest to the whole of India; acting as arbiter in inter-state
relations; and representing the interests of all India *on equal
terms with the self-governing units of the British Empire*. In this
picture there is a place also for the Native States (Princely
States). It is possible that they too will wish to be associated
for certain purposes with the organization of British India in
such a way as to dedicate their peculiar qualities to the common
service without loss of individuality. [emphasis added]

The sanctimony of the British coloniser, his concern for the
'European community' and his expectation of gratitude from
Indians for 'India's material prosperity', which is *owed* to
Europeans, is captured brilliantly in Paragraph 344 of the
Report, extracted as follows:

(iv) THE NON-OFFICIAL COMMUNITY.
The European commercial community
344. We cannot conclude without taking into due account
the presence of a considerable community of non-official

Europeans in India. In the main, they are engaged in commercial enterprises; but besides these are *the missions, European and American, which in furthering education, building up character and inculcating healthier domestic habits have done work for which India should be grateful.* There are also an appreciable number of retired Officials and others whose working life has been given to India, settled in the cooler parts of the country. *When complaints are rife that European commercial interests are selfish and drain the country of wealth which it ought to retain, it is well to remind ourselves how much of, India's material prosperity is due to European commerce.* It is true that those engaged in commerce mix less than officials with educated Indians, and that may be a reason why the latter do not always recognize their claim on India's consideration. Like commercial people all the world over Englishmen in business in India are frankly uninterested in politics; many of them would readily admit that they have taken insufficient part both in municipal business and the business of government. Our concern, however, is not so much with the past as with the future. From discussions with them we know that many of them accept the trend of events, and are fully prepared to see Indian political development proceed. *India has benefited enormously by her commercial development in European hands: nor is the benefit less because it was incidental and not the purpose of the undertaking.* What then are the obligations of the various parties? Clearly it is the duty of British commerce in India to identify itself with the interests of India, which are higher than the interests of any community; to take part in political life; to use its considerable wealth and opportunities to commend itself to India; and having demonstrated both its value and its good intentions, to be content to rest like other industries on the new foundation of government in the wishes of the people. *No less is it the duty of Indian politicians to respect the expectations which have been implicitly held out; to remember how India has profited by commercial development which only*

British capital and enterprise achieved; to bethink themselves
that though the capital invested in private enterprises was
not borrowed under any assurance that the existing form
of government would endure. Yet the favourable terms on
which money was obtained for India's development were
undoubtedly affected by the fact of British rule; *and to abstain
from advocating preferential treatment aimed not so much at
promoting Indian as at injuring British commerce. Finally it is
our duty to reserve to the Government the power to protect any
industry from prejudiced attack or privileged competition. This
obligation is imposed upon it, if not by history, at least by the
duty of protecting capital, credit and indeed property without
discrimination.* [emphasis added]

Was there anything in the Report on Christian missionary
activity in Bharat? Of course there was. Here is Paragraph 345,
which captures in a nutshell the British policy of 'toleration' and
'neutrality':

Mission Work

345. To the missions we would apply the same principle.
*It is difficult to overestimate the devoted and creative work
which missionary money and enterprise are doing in the fields
of education, morals and sanitation. Here also we reserve to the
Government a power of judgment and of effective intervention. If
missionary efforts were to assume a form that aroused widespread
alarm in Indian minds, or if orthodox Hindu or Muslim zeal sought
to impose disabilities which would lead to India's necessities losing
the material and moral benefits which missions afford, we should
hold it to be the duty ·or the Government which is responsible to
Parliament to step in and apply the remedy.* [emphasis added]

The support to Christian missionary work, the veiled threat
of government intervention in the event of disruption and the
expectation of gratitude from the natives for missionary work

could not have been more express, even after 60 years of the Queen's Proclamation of 1858, which ostensibly guaranteed protection to the native's faith. Since it is undisputed that the Montford Reforms directly influenced the framework and provisions of the 1919 Act, it must be presumed that the Christian 'civilising' intent of the Reforms were meant to and did indeed inform the 1919 Act. Some may contend that such a conclusion is tenuous because there was nothing in the 1919 Act to suggest this intent. To foreclose such an argument, here's Section 25(3)(v) of the Act which speaks for itself:

(3) The proposals of the Governor-General in Council for the appropriation of revenue or moneys relating to the following heads of expenditure shall not be submitted to the vote of the legislative assembly, nor shall they be open to discussion by either chamber at the time when the annual statement is under consideration, unless the Governor-General otherwise directs—

(v) expenditure classified by the order of the Governor-General in Council as—

(a) ecclesiastical [emphasis added]

This provision clearly exempts the decision of the Governor-General in Council in relation to ecclesiastical expenditure from any scrutiny except at the discretion of the Governor-General. This alone is sufficient to underscore the Christian character of the Government of India Act of 1919.

From the debates held in the British Parliament during the passing of the Act, what is relevant is the reference to Bharat's founding membership of the League of Nations, which was brought up by Montagu on 5 June 1919 in the House of Commons during the second reading of the Government of India Bill of 1919[6]:

I come now to the Bill itself. What I would like to do, if I may, is to start afresh and try to take the House with me, if I can and if it is not too ambitious a project, in realising that if you start from the place where the authors of this Bill started, the form of the Bill and the recommendations of the Bill are inevitable. Where did we start? We started with the pronouncement of the 20th August, 1917. I propose to ask: Is there anybody who questions to-day the policy of that pronouncement? It is no use accepting it unless you mean it; it is no use meaning it unless you act upon it; and it is no use acting upon it unless your actions are in conformity with it. Therefore, I take it that Parliament, or at any rate this House, will agree that the policy of the pronouncement of the 20th August must be the basis of our discussion—the progressive realisation of responsible government, progressive realisation, realisation by degrees, by stages, by steps—and those steps must at the outset be substantial. That pronouncement was made in order to achieve what I believe is the only logical, the only possible, the only acceptable meaning of Empire and Democracy, namely, an opportunity to all nations flying the Imperial flag to control their own destinies. [An Honourable Member: 'Nations!'] I will come to nations in a moment. I will beg no question. The Honourable Member raises the question of nations. *Whether it be a nation or not, we have promised to India the progressive realisation of responsible government. We have promised to India and given to India a representation like that of the Dominions on our Imperial Conference. India is to be an original member of the League of Nations. Therefore I say, whatever difficulties there may be in your path, your Imperial task is to overcome those difficulties and to help India on the path of nationality, however much you may recognise—and I propose to ask the House to consider them—the difficulties which lie in the path.*

... Perorations on Indian affairs have a tendency to great similarity; at least the perorations of my speeches on Indian affairs always seem so. I cannot, however—and I say it once again—believe that Parliament is going to afford any obstacle to the partnership of India in the British Empire.

We have recently been so sympathetic to the national aspirations of Arabs, of Czecho-Slovaks, of Serbs, of Croats, and of Slovenes. *Here is a country desirous of achieving nationality once again, I repeat, an original member of the League of Nations, developed under our protecting care, imbued to a greater and greater degree with our political thought. Let us pass this Bill and start it, under the ages of the British flag, on the road which we ourselves have travelled, despite all the acknowledged difficulties of area, of caste, of religion, of race and of education. If you do that, if you pass this Bill and modify it until it becomes a great Statute, I can say—we can say—as I should like to say with the authority of the House to the peoples of India, 'The future and the date upon which you realise the future goal of self-government are with you. You are being given great responsibility to-day, and opportunities of consultation and influence on other matters in which for the present we keep responsibility. You will find in Parliament every desire to help and to complete the task which this Bill attempts, if you devote yourselves to use with wisdom, with self-restraint, with respect for minorities, the great opportunities with which Parliament is entrusting you.' That is the message which it seems to me—I say with all deference—this House should send to the Indian peoples to-day, when you are starting to fulfil the pronouncement of the 20th of August.* That message cannot be sent unless the House is determined to pass without delay, and with every desire that it should be improved before it is passed, a Statute which means the beginning of self-government, responsible government, in the Indian Empire. [emphasis added]

Why does Montagu refer to the League of Nations in the context of the Government of India Act of 1919? What was the reason for making Bharat a founding member of the League? This takes us to the Paris Peace Conference of 1919–1920, which led to the founding of the League of Nations and requires us to understand terms, such as Standard of Civilisation, 'civilised nations', 'self-determination' and 'nation-state'. Readers may recollect that earlier, in Chapter 4, I had discussed the role of the Standard of Civilisation as a legal standard for the entry of only civilised nations into the international society that laid down international law. In this chapter, I will build on that discussion and demonstrate how that standard was specifically applied in the League of Nations in order to globally advance the Christian colonial consciousness of the West, especially in colonised countries including Bharat, through the medium of national constitutions.

Importantly, the timeline shows a significant overlap between (*a*) the Paris Peace Conference proceedings and the debates relating to that in the British Parliament, and (*b*) the preparation of the Montford Report for a constitutional scheme for Bharat, and the passing of Government of India Act of 1919. Therefore, the preparation of a constitutional framework for Bharat in 1918–1919 must be viewed in the larger context of framing and enforcing national constitutions to universalise European coloniality and Christian universalisms.

The Paris Peace Conference, Nation-States and Civilised Nations

Much before Samuel Huntington spoke of the 'Clash of Civilisations' in the 1990s,[7] it had already taken place when European colonisers sought to impose their Standard of Civilisation on colonised societies, which defined the in-group, namely civilised nations, and the out-group, namely the 'uncivilised' or 'not-civilised nations'. As discussed in Chapter 4, the Standard of Civilisation has its roots in Westphalian thought and became the basis for international relations since it stood for a certain degree of commonality between 'nations', such as their 'common interests and values, commonly binding rules and common institutions'. While between two European nations, it was easier to apply the standard given a shared

Christian civilisational mooring, between European nations and non-European societies, the application of the standard was a function of the power imbalance, which enabled the European to impose the Christian Standard of Civilisation as a pre-requisite for the establishment of bilateral relations. Whether motivated by the transactional need for reciprocity or driven by coloniality, the standard came to signify the civilising attitudes of European nations. Implicit in this position is the requirement of a 'nation-state', that is, only a group that was a 'nation' could aspire to become a 'nation-state', which, as explained in the first section of this book, was a direct consequence of the Westphalian model as well.

Therefore, calling a nation 'civilised' is a secularised way of labelling it a 'Christian nation' or a Europeanised nation that has organised itself on the lines of a nation-state. The literature shows that for non-Christian non-European countries, the path to being treated as a 'civilised nation' was obviously more arduous, and therefore they had to effect a fundamental change in their systems to be accepted into this elite European/Western club of nations. The following are a few relevant excerpts from a seminal work on the topic, 'The Standard of "Civilisation" in International Society' by scholar Gerrit Gong[8], which supports the position enumerated above:

Paralleling the expansion of the European international system, the international society of European states—those countries which had European civilization in common—also began to extend its boundaries. Interaction with non-Christian and non-European countries underscored the international society's need for a universally acceptable identity. Thus, in extending its domain, the international society which had earlier identified itself with Christendom and then with Europe came gradually to characterize itself as 'civilized'.

According to the logic of a standard of 'civilization', the nineteenth-century international lawyers (then referred to as publicists) divided the countries of the world into 'civilized', barbarous, and savage spheres ....

... Indeed, some non-European countries had to learn the hard way. Until they fulfilled the standard's requirements, these non-European countries remained outside the law's pale and protection.[9]

It is true that every nation or culture had its own definitions of who was civilised and who was the savage; the difference, however, was that Europe sought to universalise its definitions whereas others used it primarily to provide or restrict access to their societies and territories. That the distinction struck by the Christian White European was based on his obsession with race and ethnicity, especially his superiority thereof—which he believed as an anthropological fact—is evident from the historical treatment of 'inferior' races. The view is summed up by James Lorimer, a Scottish advocate, professor of public law and an authority on international law in the nineteenth century[10]:'No modern contribution to science seems destined to influence international politics and jurisprudence to so great an extent as that which is known as ethnology, or the science of races.'

It is no wonder that, as Gong points out, Lorimer divided humanity into three zones or spheres—civilised humanity, barbarous humanity and savage humanity. In the same vein are the following views of the Chief of the colonial division of the American delegation to the Paris Peace negotiations, G.L. Beer[11]:

The negro race has hitherto shown no capacity for progressive development except when under the tutelage of other peoples. The 'new science' seemed to substantiate his position. According to many scientists, it is an established physiological fact that the cranial structures of the negro close at an early age, which condition, it has been contended, prevents organic intellectual progress thereafter. Hence, many have denied the capacity of the negro to advance far on the path of civilization.

These views were not exceptions, but were the norm. With time, Europe's ideas of Christian civilisation were secularised as 'universal' ideas of civilisation which were sought to be shared with all, keeping with the Christian injunction to spread the gospel. Here are a few extracts from Gong's work which support this observation and are consistent with the discussion undertaken in the first section of this book:

Another nineteenth-century trend which focused attention on 'civilization' was the general secularization of European society. Owen Chadwick defines secularization in the following terms[12]: 'the relation (whatever that is, which can only be shown by historical inquiry) in which modem European civilization and society stands to the Christian elements of its past and the continuing Christian elements of its present'. ...

... One element of the Christian tradition which the trend toward secularization not only maintained but intensified was the universality manifest in the biblical injunction to take the good news to every nation. Christianity's universalist aspirations were easily transformed into notions of a universal civilization which could progress by adhering to scientific principles.

... Because Europe thought itself the epitome both of scientific law and of Christian principle, its standards were self-consciously declared to represent universal values. Barbarians might therefore acquire 'civilization'. Combined with the eighteenth-century belief that human misery was to some degree preventable, the idea that progress could be shared by all contributed to the notion of the 'civilizing' mission where secular reformers, even enlightened believers, could share the missionary zeal and rally around the standard of 'civilization' to carry the light of 'civilization' to dark places.[13]

These extracts from Gong's work capture the sum and substance of Christian European coloniality. Gong even cites the life and views of Cecil Rhodes, the British diamond magnate from South Africa who instituted the Rhodes Scholarship, as an illustration of the movement from Christian civilisation to secularised Christian civilisation. This is corroborated by other scholars as well.[14]

Those in Bharat who aspire to the Rhodes Scholarship or are beneficiaries of it and hold forth on 'constitutional morality' and 'transformative constitutionalism' should consider reading more of Rhodes' views and those of other like-minded individuals who saw national constitutions as conduits to advance the cause of secularised Christian civilisational values. That would be a good decolonial beginning since it is well-known that scholarships, such as Rhodes, were typically employed by the Christian European coloniser to groom and co-opt natives into his worldview and values. The objective was that such Westernised natives would return to their countries of origin to 'reform' their fellow natives by instilling respect for 'constitutional morality' and 'civilisation'.

Coming back to the standard of civilisation, as Europe reached the heights of its colonisation, an 'international society' began to take shape. The system bestowed certain benefits upon its Christian and European members, and colonised societies too sought to reorient themselves in order to be accepted as 'civilised' members of the international society and enjoy the benefits of a Eurocentric global order. Following were the broad legal requirements of the Standard of Civilisation, as enumerated by Gong:

1. A 'civilised' State guarantees basic rights, that is, life, dignity and property; freedom of travel, commerce and religion, especially that of foreign nationals;

2. A 'civilised' State exists as an organised political bureaucracy with some efficiency in running the state machinery, and with some capacity to organise for self-defence;

3. A 'civilised' State adheres to generally accepted international law, including the laws of war; it also maintains a domestic system of courts, codes and published laws, which guarantee legal justice for all within its jurisdiction, foreigners and native citizens alike;

4. A 'civilised' State fulfils the obligations of the international system by maintaining adequate and permanent avenues for diplomatic interchange and communication; and

5. A 'civilised' State, by and large, conforms to the accepted norms and practices of the 'civilised' international society; for example, *suttee (Sati)*, polygamy and slavery were considered 'uncivilised', and therefore unacceptable.

The reference to 'suttee/Sati' in the proscriptions under the standard of civilisation is proof of the success of the Christian missionaries in Bharat in having internationalised their stereotypes of Bharat. The fact that the above-mentioned requirements were rooted in Christendom is widely accepted by scholars of international law. It is also evident from these requirements that they necessitated a fundamental change in the political, legal, social and economic infrastructure of non-European nations in order for them to be accepted as civilised nations in the global order.

One of these changes was to have a constitution to prove a nation's civilised credentials as a nation of laws. For instance, Gong points out that Japan adopted a constitutional form of government with representative institutions to impress the West and to convince it of its eligibility for membership in the international order. In fact, the Standard of Civilisation extended not just to the broad institutional framework but also to specific legal principles to be followed by national courts. This was evident from the fact that principles of 'natural justice', 'good conscience and morality', while appearing to be capable of accommodating the subjective values of each society, in reality translated to the application of European values and ethics or at the very least, treating them as benchmarks to be measured against. This practice continues to date in Bharat as Indian courts continue to refer to and rely on English common law to distil principles of natural justice, which are widely applied to a range of legal issues.

This was a consequence of, among other things, using international law as a means to treat the Standard of Civilisation as a juridical/legal prerequisite for membership in the international society. I have already demonstrated this in Chapter 4 citing the use of 'civilisation' in Articles 9 and 38 of the Statute of the International Court of Justice[15], which was established under the Charter of United Nations. The presence of the Standard of Civilisation, at least until the founding of the United Nations in 1945, lends credence to the position that it was equally prevalent at the time of the Paris Peace Conference of 1919–1920, which led to the founding of the League of Nations in 1920. The application of the standard to the League of Nations is evident from Article 22 of the League's Covenant, which reads as follows[16]:

ARTICLE 22.

To those colonies and territories which as a consequence of the late war have ceased to be under the sovereignty of the States which formerly governed them and *which are inhabited by peoples not yet able to stand by themselves under the strenuous conditions of the modern world,* there should be applied the principle that the well-being and development of such peoples form a *sacred trust of civilisation* and that securities for the performance of this trust should be embodied in this Covenant.

The best method of giving practical effect to this principle is that the tutelage of such peoples should be entrusted to advanced nations who by reason of their resources, their experience or their geographical position can best undertake this responsibility, and who are willing to accept it, and that this tutelage should be exercised by them as Mandatories on behalf of the League.

The character of the mandate must differ according to the stage of the development of the people, the geographical situation of the territory, its economic conditions and other similar circumstances.

Certain communities formerly belonging to the Turkish Empire have reached a stage of development where their existence as independent nations can be provisionally recognized subject to the rendering of administrative advice and assistance by a Mandatory until such time as they are able to stand alone. The wishes of these communities must be a principal consideration in the selection of the Mandatory.

Other peoples, especially those of Central Africa, are at such a stage that the Mandatory must be responsible for the administration of the territory under conditions which will guarantee freedom of conscience and religion, subject only to the maintenance of public order and morals, the prohibition of abuses, such as the slave trade, the arms traffic and the liquor traffic, and the prevention of the establishment of fortifications or military and naval bases and of military training of the natives for other than police purposes and the defence of territory, and will also secure equal opportunities for the trade and commerce of other Members of the League.

There are territories, such as South-West Africa and certain of the South Pacific Islands, which, owing to the sparseness of their population, or their small size, or their remoteness from the centres of civilisation, or their geographical contiguity to the territory of the Mandatory, and other circumstances, can be best administered under the laws of the Mandatory as integral portions of its territory, subject to the safeguards above mentioned in the interests of the indigenous population.

In every case of mandate, the Mandatory shall render to the Council an annual report in reference to the territory committed to its charge.

The degree of authority, control, or administration to be exercised by the Mandatory shall, if not previously agreed

upon by the Members of the League, be explicitly defined in
each case by the Council.

A permanent Commission shall be constituted to receive
and examine the annual reports of the Mandatories and to
advise the Council on all matters relating to the observance
of the mandates. [emphasis added]

That the 'sacred trust of civilisation' required 'advanced nations'
to hand-hold and tutor former colonies (which were referred to
as 'backward' instead of 'uncivilised') so that they could deal
with 'modernity', a condition distinctly created by the Christian
European coloniser, represents coloniality at its peak.

I will now place before the reader extracts from material
leading to the Paris Peace Conference of 1919 to show that the
reference to civilisation in Article 22 of the League's Covenant
was not without significance or context. For starters, although
the United States of America chose not to become a formal
member of the League, here is an extract from the Bible-inspired
speech delivered by the 27th President of the United States
(1909–1913), Howard William Taft, on 4 March 1919, on the
need for the League[17]:

*We are here tonight in sight of a League of Peace, of what
I have ever regarded as the 'Promised Land.' Such a war as
the last is a hideous blot on our Christian civilization. The
inconsistency is as foul as was slavery under the Declaration
of Independence. If Christian nations cannot now be brought
into a united effort to suppress a recurrence it will be a shame
to modern society.*

This covenant of Paris bears on its face the evidences that
it is the result of compromise; that it has been produced by
an earnest effort of the President and other representatives
of the nations who have won this war and thereby have made
themselves responsible for future peace to adopt machinery
through which the peace now to be formulated may be

THE STANDARD OF CIVILISATION

maintained and the united force of the nations making the treaty can be directed to discouraging war.

.... Unless there be some means for authoritatively interpreting the treaty and applying it, and unless the power of the League be behind it to give effect to such interpretation and application, the treaty instead of producing peace will produce a state of continued war.

More than this, in the dark background is the threatened spectre of Bolshevism, hard, cruel, murderous, uncompromising and destructive of Christian civilization, militant in pressing its hideous doctrines upon other peoples and insidious in its propaganda among the lowest element in every country. Against the war, the chaos and the explosive dangers of Bolshevism, throughout all the countries of Europe, a League of Nations must be established to settle controversies peaceably, and when settled to enforce the settlement. It must stand as the living evidence of the united power of Christian civilization to make this treaty a real treaty of peace. [emphasis added]

Perhaps it could be argued that Taft was not the US President during the Paris Peace Conference and, therefore, his views did not reflect the official position. To meet such an argument, here is an extract from 'The Triumph of Ideals' speech given by Woodrow Wilson, the then President of the United States, on 7 May 1919, which indicates that he saw the League as an opportunity to showcase the 'civilised' world as well as its Christian unity before 'heathen countries' so that they look up to the Christian civilisation[18]:

... The arrangements of the present peace cannot stand a generation unless they are guaranteed by the united forces of the civilized world. And if we do not guarantee them cannot you see the picture? Your hearts have instructed you where the burden of this war fell. It did not fall upon the national treasuries, it did not fall upon the instruments of administration, it did not

fall upon the resources of the nation. It fell upon the victims' homes everywhere, where women were toiling in hope that their men would come back.

I do not know when I have been more impressed than by the conferences of the commission set up by the conference of peace to draw up a covenant for the League of Nations. *The representatives of fourteen nations sat around that board—not new men, not men inexperienced in the affairs of their own countries, not men inexperienced in the politics of the world—and the inspiring influence of every meeting was the concurrence of purpose on the part of all those men to come to an agreement, and an effective working agreement, with regard to this league of the civilized world.*

…. I remember not long ago attending a very interesting meeting which was held in the interest of combining Christian missionary effort throughout the world. I mean eliminating the rivalry between churches and agreeing that Christian missionaries should not represent this, that, or the other church, but represent the general Christian impulse and principle of the world. I said I was thoroughly in sympathy with the principle, but that I hoped, if it was adopted, the inhabitants of the heathen countries would not come to look at us, because we were not ourselves united, but divided; that while we were asking them to unite, we ourselves did not set the example. My moral from that recollection is this: We, among other friends of liberty, are asking the world to unite in the interest of brotherhood and mutual service and the genuine advancement of individual and corporate liberty throughout the world; therefore we must set the example.

…. These men did not come across the sea merely to defeat Germany and her associated powers in the war. They came to defeat forever the things for which the Central Powers stood, the sort of power they meant to assert in the world, the arrogant, selfish domination which they meant to establish; and they came, moreover, to see to it that there should never be a war like this again. *It is for us, particularly for us who are civilized, to use our proper weapons of counsel and agreement, to see to it that there never is such a war again.* The nation that should now fling out of this common concord of counsel would betray the human race.

.... The nation that wishes to use the League of Nations for its convenience, and not for the service of the rest of the world, deliberately chooses to turn back to those bad days of selfish contest when every nation thought first and always of itself, and not of its neighbors; thought of its rights and forgot its duties; thought of its power and overlooked its responsibility.

Those bad days, I hope, are gone, and the great moral power, backed, if need be, by the great physical power of the civilized nations of the world, will now stand firm for the maintenance of the fine partnership which we have thus inaugurated. [emphasis added]

It is evident that the Standard of Civilisation was a concept that was very much alive and kicking between 1917 and 1920, when it was expressly used by the League as a criterion for membership to avail the right to self-determination as a 'nation-state'. In other words, only a group that qualified as a 'nation' could exercise its right to self-determination and become a nation-state, provided it met the standard of civilisation and was eligible for treatment as a 'civilised nation'. Those groups which were not 'civilised' would be either protectorates or mandates. Therefore, the Christian Western powers of the world arrogated to themselves the power to determine who could aspire for statehood and who could not, depending on the Standard of Civilisation laid down by them. The Chinese Empire, the Siamese Kingdom and the Japanese Empire, all had to transition to being 'nation-states' in order for them to be accepted by the international society. Clearly, this transition was largely global owing to the universalisation of the European politico-theological thought and institutions through the medium of international law.

Naturally, Bharat was no exception to this rule. Pertinently for Bharat, the build-up to the Paris Peace Conference and the founding of the League not merely coincided but overlapped with the preparation of the Montford Report on Constitutional Reforms for Bharat in 1917–1918 and the passing of the Government of India Act of 1919. The Government of India Bill of 1919 was introduced in the British House of Commons on 29 May 1919[19] and received Royal Assent on 28 December 1919[20], while the Paris Peace Conference, the Treaty of Versailles and the League of Nations were being discussed in the British Parliament at least between March 1918 and June 1920 as an international platform to give effect to the civilising project and to usher in Christian Peace.

It is precisely for this reason that the multiple references to Bharat's membership of the League of Nations in Montagu's submissions in the British Parliament during the passing of the Government of India Act of 1919 are particularly significant. The debates in the British Parliament demonstrate that the Act, the first British-made Constitution for Bharat, was imbued with the Standard of Civilisation that was the not-so-unwritten civilising code amongst Christian European colonising nations for non-Christian non-European societies.

Here are a few excerpts from the debates that took place in the British Parliament between March 1918 and June 1920 which reflect the Christian character of the League and its use as a springboard for universalising the Christian standard of civilisation. On 19 March 1918, the motion approving the principle of the League of Nations was moved in the British House of Lords by Lord Parmoor as follows[21]:

That this House approves the principle of a League of Nations and the constitution of a Tribunal, whose orders shall be enforceable by an adequate sanction.

Introducing the motion, Lord Parmoor said the following while liberally quoting Kant, who, as we saw earlier, was a Christian White supremacist, to put it in contemporary terms:

> As far as I can gauge opinion, it comes to this—that we have suffered and are suffering from what I may call international anarchy, and that the time has come when we should put a more settled order in place of the existing international anarchy, founded on the restraint which comes from the recognition of mutual obligation as between one country and another. The principle, as I should put it, is that ordinary restraint means freedom as between nations when properly adjusted, as it is recognised to be the only basis of true freedom as between individuals in any particular country....
>
> .... It was rejected in the time of Grotius, who was at once the earliest and the greatest of our international lawyers, and who insisted—and that is part of the form of my Resolution today—that no League of Nations could be effective unless it were enforceable by an adequate sanction. *But I will give one quotation from a later thinker of great eminence, Kant. I give it, again, in order to avoid any necessity for repetition. Speaking of States in their relations to one another, Kant said— 'There can be, according to reason, no other way of advancing from the lawless conditions which war implies than by States yielding up their savage lawless freedom, just as individuals have done, and yielding to the coercion of a public law.' There is no reason why that principle should not be made effective.... Kant goes on to say that he 'regarded the want of a common public law amongst nations as barbarism, the negation of civilisation, and the brutal degradation of humanity.' I do not think that those words are too strong; and if they were not too strong in the time of Kant, certainly the conditions of the present warfare have emphasised every particular to which Kant called attention....*
>
> .... Now the difficulty which stands in the way of accepting the principle which I ask your Lordships to affirm must be

fairly stated. I am not now dealing with difficulties of detail, because that is no part of my Resolution at the present time, but there is a difficulty in principle which I think ought to be met and which I desire to anticipate in case it should be raised as against the principle of my Resolution. It is this. That you cannot have any League of Nations without some interference with the sovereign rights of individual parties. *Unless a League of Nations did, in some respects at any rate, restrain the rights of individual sovereignty it would be ineffective, and I do not deny that there is a strong school of thought which would object, and strongly object, to any interference with the rights of individual sovereignty which particular nations enjoy. That doctrine has been carried further in Germany than in any other country. In fact, it has been carried to the extent of a State worship. It has been carried to the extent of saying that as regards international relationship no morality, and no Christian morality, ought to prevail at all, and that the reign of force should be supreme. The result of a principle of that kind is to justify any brutality which you may desire, provided only it is to the advantage of the particular State.* ... If you assume for a moment, as I am willing to assume, that nations approach one another on the basis that they ought not to be influenced in international relationship by moral conditions of any kind, but only by conditions of force, it appears to me you make in the strongest way a case for some restraint and coercion to which they shall be bound to submit in the cause of order and humanity.

I may say one word further whilst I am referring to the United States of America. They and we form the two great Anglo-Saxon communities of the world. *They and we have carried the principle of the rule of law and the supremacy of law further than any other country. They and we have put our legal systems substantially on the same basis—the old common law principles which prevail in England—and what I hope is this, particularly having regard to the work which is going on at this time both in this country and in the United States, that it may be to the glory of those two countries that by joint effort they may bring to fruition a League of nations on the best principle and on the soundest foundation....* [emphasis added]

On 26 June 1918, in the House of Lords, the Bishop of Oxford advocated for 'profound conversion of nations' using the pacifying nature of democracy to do so[22]:

My Lords, I hope that as a clergyman, and as one quite unversed in International Law, it will not be thought inopportune if I intrude for a few minutes in your Lordships discussion, because no one at all acquainted with the principles of the Christian religion can doubt the extraordinary affinity between those principles as originally expressed and the aspirations and intentions which under-lie the present scheme for a League of Nations. It is from this point of view that I have taken a great interest—indeed, what thinking man could fail to take a great interest?—in these various proposals, and have given them as much detailed study as I have been able to give to the subject.

.... I hope that the concentration and efforts of all branches of the Christian Church may cooperate towards this end. Christianity embarked on the most momentous scheme of being supernational and proclaiming the idea of supernationalism. In the strength of St. Paul's argument, and the enthusiasm he put into the proclamation of this idea, you see the force of the opposition with which he was encountered. The whole of the history of the Church has been a struggle against the narrowness of a false nationalism. It is a great mistake to suppose that the division and heresies of the early years of the Christian Church were merely about theological doctrines. They had behind them national movements. In the same way, when the East and the West separated, it was not nearly so much on a matter of doctrine, or on an ecclesiastical question, as it was a division between the political tendencies of the East and the political tendencies of the West. Though the Reformation

was at the beginning a great religious protest against scandals and abuses, yet the developed nationalities, which had grown up and strengthened themselves, seized hold of it, and the idea of the Catholic Church was imperiled, overwhelmed, and lost. So it has been ever since that time in England. We have been content with the idea of a national religion. But Christianity itself claims to constitute a tie between nations which shall be closer than the ties of blood and race. I believe there is an immense call for the Christian Church, and to the divided parts of the Christian Church, to realise what Christianity means, and to bring to bear a united pressure upon all Christian peoples that they should rise again to the height of the great idea. In this matter, it seems to me, we can ignore our divisions and act as one body, and I desire nothing more than that the whole divided forces of the Christian Church should be brought together, so that they may speak with a united voice and the nations might feel what the Christian religion really meant. [emphasis added]

One must be grateful to the Bishop of Oxford for putting in plain Christian terms what the leaders of the 'civilised world' went at lengths to put in the 'secular' language of the standard of civilisation. Endorsing the motion for a League of Nations and concurring with the views of the bishops in the House, following were the views of Earl Russell, wherein he expressed that he saw the League of Nations as an instrumentality of ushering in that elusive creature called 'Christian Peace' (Pax Christiana) in the world:

I am inclined to think that the feelings of patriotism, the feelings of nationality, and the feelings of independence of the various nations are hardly likely to reach such a complete internationalisation of their relations under at least a generation or two. I can hardly look forward to that as a thing likely to happen tomorrow, but I think we should all keep before us that real international view, in which the nations of the world, keeping their independence in all their domestic affairs, should be prepared to sacrifice a portion of that independence for the sake of the general world's peace. That, I think, is the ideal to which a League of Nations must ultimately tend, and I think that in constructing an imperfect approximation to that ideal, either now or hereafter, we should not do anything to make the ultimate realisation of that ideal impossible. I hope the House will not consider that in saying this I am adumbrating that which we cannot look for. *I do not drink we can look for it soon, but if that education to which the noble Earl referred is conducted and continued for a considerable time, that must be what we should look for as the ultimate device which alone can make for permanent peace and would unite the world in that Christian peace to which the right rev. Prelate alluded, but which unfortunately has never yet succeeded in uniting it. I wish to say nothing more beyond expressing the pleasure which the acceptance of the Motion, as amended, gives me.* [emphasis added]

Similarly, on 3 July 1919, when the Treaty of Versailles[23] (which was signed on 28 June 1919 between the Allied and Associated Powers and Germany) was taken up for discussion in the House of Lords, following were the views of the Archbishop of Canterbury, who saw the League of Nations as rooted in Christian principle[24]:

The work of Lord Robert Cecil, as we have constantly been told, has been of an invaluable kind, and those who look in detail into all that has been said with regard to the League of Nations will be able to say what leadership they have found in what he has taught us on that subject. *The framers of that scheme have resolved to put into the forefront of the new world plan what is already not only a sanguine political plan for the future but what has been from the first a well assured Christian principle. It is for that reason that I believe we have a right to expect a better result from the effort which is now being made than any result that could have been rightly expected from far-reaching and ambitious treaties of another kind in the days gone by.* The danger lies, I suppose, in the possibility that the provisions of the Treaty might here and there be so worked as to endanger the very principle which underlies the League of Nations. Against that peril we as a people, and not our statesmen only, have all to be watchful. The responsibility is shared by us all, for the peoples are now enlisted. In the stimulating and robust words which were written a few days ago by General Smuts—'The League is yet only a form. It still requires the quickening life which can only come from the active interest and vitalising contact of the peoples themselves.' *That is the primary fact upon which all this discussion rests, and, standing here in the position I occupy, I should be false indeed to every principle I have ever held, or to the faith for which I stand, if I doubted that that principle, put in the very forefront of a Treaty like this, will and must stand the strain. It lies at the root and basis of the creed of every Christian man. It is that which differentiates this effort, this pact of the peoples, from any that has ever gone before, and it is that which, above all, justifies us, as we peer forward into the future, in making it a part not only of our hopes but, I do not scruple to say here, of our prayers as well as of our thanksgivings, offered in confident expectation of the fruit that is to come. The origin of this is not human but divine. It stands in fundamental truth. Magna est veritas et proevalebit.* [emphasis added]

On 21 July 1919, when the Treaty of Peace Bill was taken up by the House of Commons for a second reading, Viscount Bryce was sanguine about the application of Christian principles to international relations through the League of Nations in order to replace enmity with friendship[25]:

> The League of Nations if it has any truth, or reality, or force, rests on the belief that the community of the world requires that a new spirit should prevail in international relations—a spirit which seeks to substitute friendship for enmity. Each of the European countries, our own included, emerged from the sanguinary welter of the Middle Ages by realising in its own domestic affairs that order and peace and respect by each individual for the rights and feelings of every other individual were better for all than ferocious strife. *All the nations now have to do the same thing; they have to try to apply, far as is possible, Christian principles to international relations—to work for reconciliation, and to make even the peoples that have been alienated feel that they are members of one great community in peace and good will. That will do more for the happiness of each and of all than strife has given or ever will give to even the strongest.* [emphasis added]

On 17 June 1920, the League's functions and purpose were discussed in the House of Lords. On the said date, Sir Henry Craik drew attention to the obligation of the 'higher races' and drew Biblical support for it, effectively restating the duty of the White man to carry the burden of the rest in the following words[26]:

> Sir H. Craik—'I yield to nobody in my enthusiasm as to what the League might possibly accomplish. Meanwhile we must be patient. I believe that the real value of the League—and here some Honourable Members may think that I am retrograde or reactionary—lies, not in all its stipulations, its recommendations, its machinery, and its councils, but lies in the hope that the Great Powers will in their strength, and bearing a responsibility corresponding to that greatness of strength, will rise to the occasion and make themselves the

real leaders of right all the world over. *I do believe that we in England, the great Anglo-Saxon race, have an ideal, which we have made real and practical, of un-selfishness in politics, and that we should bear that flag high, but we can only bear it high by virtue of our exercising our strength and our power. I believe that if the great Anglo-Saxon races of Britain and America, with our friends and Allies France, will rise to the height of their responsibility and hold up to the world a higher ideal of unselfish politics they will do more than all your schemes and all your stipulations by the respect they would gain from smaller nations. I would ask Honourable Members to remember that great message from the Lord to Joshua: 'Only be strong and very courageous; be strong and of good heart.' I believe it is that strength that will give us what Tennyson saw with the poet's eye: 'When the war drum throbs no longer, and the battle flag is furled' 'In the Parliament of man, the Federation of the world,' 'When the common sense of most shall keep a fretful realm in awe,' 'And the kindly earth shall slumber lapped in universal law.' Yes, the kindly earth may slumber, but it will be no slumbrous time for the Great Powers for the two Anglo-Saxon races, combined with our friends in France, if they are to ensure that peace and that tranquillity which we all desire, and which we hope this League of Nations will establish.*
[emphasis added]

Despite these categorical professions of the League standing for Christian peace and Christian unity based on Christian principles, some may point out that the Vatican was kept out of the League of Nations despite the papacy wanting to be a member of the League. Therefore, they could argue that the League was secular in character, but this would be historically incorrect for multiple reasons.

First, the Vatican was kept out of the League primarily because Italy resisted its entry fearing that the Vatican would seek return of the territories lost to Italy in the Italian wars of unification. Second, Pope Benedict XV's attempts at floating the

Vatican's own peace platform after the war, although successful to a significant extent through its 'Concordat diplomacy', put him in direct competition with the US President Woodrow Wilson's attempts to lead the peace efforts. As revealed by a letter from Eugenio Pacelli (future Pope Pius XII), a prominent Vatican jurist of the time, to the Secretary of State to Pope Benedict XV, Pietro Gasparri, it was feared that Wilson's 'fourteen points' peace programme was the brainchild of the Freemasons who opposed Catholicism and 'supplied the United States with one of the cornerstones of its government, namely the democratic spirit'.[27] In fact, it was feared that Allied victory would 'Americanise the whole world, making it Freemason so as to liberate it from its servitude to the kaiser, the pope, and the priesthood'. The Vatican's opposition to the US programme ensured that the UK and France too allied with the US. The third reason for the Vatican's exclusion from the League is that some of the obligations cast on the members of the League were forbidden by Vatican's religious beliefs.

Therefore, the absence of the Vatican in the League of Nations is not proof of the latter's secular credentials. If anything, it only reinforced Protestant Christian political theology, evident from the all-round affirmation of the Christian nature of the League by world leaders of the time, such as Woodrow Wilson, a devout Christian, and by members of the British Parliament. Again, the fact that the US ultimately opted to stay out of the League does not in any way take away from the Christian character of the League and its standard of civilisation since the US's decision was the consequence of isolationists in the US Congress who wanted the US to stay out of European affairs. From this, it is clear that the League was not 'secular', it was 'Christian secular'.

Circling back to Bharat, it is in this well-documented historical backdrop that the reference to Bharat's membership to the League by Montagu in his submissions in the British Parliament during the debates on the Government of India Bill 1919 must be understood, since it highlights the Christian underpinnings of the Government of India Act, 1919. But then, how did the 'nationalists' in Bharat respond to the application of the standard of civilisation to secure self-governing status? Did they oppose it for being unsecular and racist in its outlook? Did they challenge the imposition of Christian political theology and Christian values on Bharat? Did they accept the definition of 'nation' in its entirety to Bharat? Lala Lajpat Rai, who then headed the Indian Home Rule Movement in America, published a pamphlet titled 'Self-Determination for India'[28] in 1919 wherein he made out a case for Bharat as a 'nation'. To his credit, he distinguished it from the European definition. Here are some relevant extracts from his educative pamphlet:

> We believe the principle of Self-Determination alone can solve the great problem of peace, and we can claim the application of this principle to the case of India, which has contributed so much in men, money and materials to the triumph of the Allied Arms. *We do not advocate dismemberment or severance. We desire partnership on the footing of equality with the Overseas Dominions. Under the British aegis, we demand an absolutely unmolested opportunity of autonomous development for India similar to that accorded to various nationalities within the Austro-Hungarian and Ottoman Empires under President Wilson's 'fourteen points' assented to by the British Government with the approval of the people. Our claim is founded upon the ideals and rights of Self-Determination, Nationalism, Freedom of Nations, National dignity and self-respect. These immortal principles have infused a new life into India during the war, and the supreme object of this war, the peace of the world, cannot be achieved unless full scope be given to the principles of Self-Determination for gratifying the internal aspirations of India, and ending the external ambitions of foreign nations in relation to India. Without it the world can never be made safe for Democracy.*

THE STANDARD OF CIVILISATION

.... Her [India's] former fame as the mart and mint of the world allured invaders by land from the days of Alexander the Great. But the land invasion ended with the Mohammedan Occupation. The capture of Constantinople by the Ottomans in blockading the land way of Europe to India stimulated the mariners of Spain and Portugal to find a waterway. In the process Columbus discovered America and Vasco De Gama went to India. Then America and India both became battlefields of European nations ... England, no doubt drove the Dutch and the French from India and consolidated her power. But Russia and Germany in turn planned the conquest of India.

Few will have the temerity to deny that the present war [WWI] was partly caused by German designs on her. According to The Times of January 23, 1918, the ex-Kaiser is reported to have said: 'We shall not merely occupy India, but shall conquer it; and the vast revenues that the British allow to be taken by the Indian Princes, will, after our conquest, flow in a golden stream into the Fatherland.' The loyalty of India, and particularly of the intelligentsia of India, frustrated the German attempts to foment conspiracies. But clearly these external ambitions and internal aspirations render it absolutely imperative to settle Indian problems by enunciating a 'Monroe Doctrine' for Asia and Africa, and emancipating India from pupilage and democratizing the Government of India so as to remove rivalries and assure the world that India is governed by the sons of India, for the benefit of India and for the common welfare of all mankind. [emphasis added]

After this, Shri Lajpat Rai quoted the Montagu Declaration of 20 August 1917, which he saw as a denial of Bharat's right to self-determination as a dominion within the British Empire. Shri Rai pointed out that after the founding of the League, which treated the said right as one of its cornerstones, the Montagu

Declaration and its assumptions could no longer hold water since Bharat too was entitled to exercise its right to self-determination as a 'nation'. Saying so, he went on to make a case for Bharat as a 'nation', which read as follows:

India, a Nation
It is argued that India is not a nation, but congeries of nations, not a country but a continent. These epigrams obscure the truth and delude the ignorant.

What do we mean by a nation? Do the English, the French, the Poles severally constitute a nation? Then the Bengalis, the Punjabis, the Rajputs and the Mahrattas do also form a nation. The Bengalis inhabit the same region with a distinct name. Ethnologically they are descended from the same race. They have the same blood, the same language, the same civilization, literature, customs and traditions. These are the essential elements that constitute nationality in the popular sense. Castes do not divide a nation any more than classes do in England. Creeds do not rend a nation in two. If they did religious toleration would be impossible. There is less antagonism between the creeds of India than there is between the various sects of Christianity in England. There are hundreds of such sects in England, but there are five religions in the whole of India. Two of these cover 95 per cent of the population. The statement about Bengali group is equally true of all the other groups in India. there are about 12 such groups. Historically up to the advent of British rule each of them formed a distinct State, more or less exclusively governed by themselves. These distinct States were in some measure disturbed by the artificial arrangements of the Provinces by the British Government. Nevertheless the spirit of nationalism pervades every one of them, and manifests itself when violently attacked or assailed, as it did when Lord Curzon partitioned Bengal. Historically, each of these groups form a nation in the same sense as the English, the French, the Belgians and the Poles do. They are therefore entitled to

Self-Determination, and upon that principle also to federate to form the United States of India.

We have so far confined ourselves to the definition of nation in the popular sense of the word in dealing with the aforesaid groups. But as a matter of fact, in the broad sense of the word, the whole of India is one nation. India is said to be the epitome of the world; but there is unity in diversity. 'India encircled by seas and mountains, is indisputably a geographical unit' (V.A. Smith, Early History of India*). 'There is no part of the world better marked out by nature as a region by itself than India exclusive of Burmah' (Chisholm:* Geography*).*

Ethnologically they belong to the same Aryan race, except in some parts of India, but even there they have been assimilated. The whole of India was Hinduized long before Alexander invaded India in 315 B.C. The Hindu religion absorbed into its fold all the non-Aryan races, with the result that Hindu culture became the predominant culture of India. this culture was based upon the ancient traditions, impulses and sentiments preserved and sung in the great Epic of India, the Mahabharata, which is translated in most of the modern vernaculars.

Sanskrit was once the lingua franca of India. It was language of the learned, as Latin was in Europe in the Middle Ages. 'India, though it has more than 500 dialects, has only one sacred language, only one sacred literature, accepted and revered by all adherents of Hinduism alike, however diverse in race, dialect, rank and creed. That language and literature is Sanskrit, the most ancient language in the world' (Monier Williams). Three-fourths of the population speak dialects derived from Sanskrit, as French, Spanish and Portuguese are derived from Latin. Though there are many dialects, there are only about twelve which cover the whole of India.

Politically, the whole of India is now practically united, and had been so also in the past, notably in the days of Asoka. But the ancient Emperors of India, more liberal than the modern Tzars or Kaisers, never used force to standardize language, culture, creed or caste, but left each group to self-development suitable to its environments.

India, therefore, possesses all the elements of nationality— viz., same blood, same culture, same traditions and same faith.

This Hindu nationality was to a certain extent disturbed by the Mohammedan invasion and Moghul rule, but the overwhelming majority of Moslems are the descendants of Hindus who embraced Mohammedanism, and as such they have retained the language and customs of their respective regions, and are still influenced by the immemorial Hindu culture except in religious matters. 'Century after century our departed ancestors have fashioned our ideas and sentiments' (Le Bon). The change of faith cannot obliterate the work of centuries. 'Beneath the manifold diversities of physical and social type, language, and customs and religion, which strike the observer in India, there can still be discerned a certain underlying uniformity of life from the Himalayas to Cape Comorin' (Sir Herbert Risley).

The civilization of India 'has many features which differentiate from that of all other regions of the world, while they are common to the whole country in a degree sufficient to justify its treatment as a unit in the history of human social and intellectual development' (V.A. Smith, Early History of India*). So intense is the feeling of unity throughout India that any attempt to divide the country into independent States would provoke indignant remonstrances. In fact, so deep is this feeling that even a proposal to create racial Provinces is regarded by some Indians as a malicious manoeuvre at disruption.*

The allegation that India is not a nation is therefore untenable and unjustifiable. In political science, 'A nation is no longer what it had been in the ancient world, a progeny of common ancestors, or the aboriginal product of the a particular religion, a result of merely physical and material causes, but a moral and political being; not the creation of geographical or physiological unity, but developed in the course of history by the action of the State. It is derived from the State and not supreme over it. A State may, in the course of time, produce a nationality, but that a nationality should constitute a State is contrary to the nature of modern civilization' (Lord Acton). Such a nationality is constituted when the people are animated by sympathies which make them co-operate with one another more willingly than with other people and desire to be under the same Government. Such a desire for co-operation exists throughout India and has been accelerated and accentuated by British domination. Indeed, according to Sir Henry Maine, 'the idea of Nationality was first derived from India, and it travelled westwards'. It is this feeling that makes federal union feasible. In this respect the Bengalis, the Mahrattas the Madrasees, the Sikhs and other groups in India are more anxious to federate than the nations under the Dual Monarchy, or the defunct Russian Empire, or even the Irish and the English, or any other European nations. The Concordat between the Hindus and Mohammedans at Lucknow in 1916 illustrates the facility with which the Indians left to themselves settle differences.

But to require races of India to coalesce into a nation with one religion and one tongue, is midsummer madness. It would revive the medieval idea of one Empire, one people and one church, which engendered the despotisms of the blackest dye. The world is now happily rid of such tyranny. America has presented to the world the principle of federalism, the last of the political principles, but the richest in promise of peace and freedom. According to Lord Acton, it renders possible and practicable 'the highest degree of organisation, which Government is capable of receiving, with the fullest security for the preservation of local customs and ancient rights, where liberty would achieve its most glorious results, while centralization and absolutism would be destruction.' *There is no (foundation) whatever for the assumption that India is not capable of such organization. On the contrary, the conditions and capacity, postulated by Lord Acton, exist in a remarkable degree in India. if such federal organization has not hitherto been evolved in India it must be attributed to the neglect and the freezing and sterilizing influences of the Indian Bureaucracy with its excessive centralization, resulting from its rigid methods and notions of trusteeship.*

.... It is manifest that England cannot be a fit trustee for India, for a trustee, unlike an executor, enforces his own will as to what is good for the ward. The result is deplorable. India lags far behind Germany or Japan. In 150 years of British rule the progress in India is less than the progress in Germany or Japan in 50 years. Indians have as much intelligence and capacity as the Germans or the Japanese. The rapid strides of Germany in commerce and industry have made her one of the greatest workshops in the world. India, with her unrivalled resources is still in industrial swaddling clothes.

A century ago the percentage of literates in India was about the same as in England. Today 95 per cent can read and write in England, while in India scarcely 6 per cent can do so. It is unnecessary for us to specify other grave defects. .... India is not an infant nation, not a primitive people, but the eldest brother in the family of man, noted for her philosophy and for being the home of religions that console half of mankind.

This is no place to discuss the details, but we resent the implied slur on the patriotism, intelligence and capacity of the people of India. The people of India are admittedly as shrewd, law-abiding and intelligent as the people of Europe. The venerable civilisation of India has moulded their character and made them fit for citizenship in any civilised State. The only argument against their capacity is that a large majority of them cannot read and write. But this is no fault of theirs. It is a grievance against the Bureaucracy. It was their duty to teach them to read and write during the past 150 years of their rule....

.... We are told that the British took six hundred years to reach the present form of government. But the Athens did it in generation and France in six months. ... *Left to themselves there can be no doubt that Indians are capable of solving their Domestic Problems on democratic principles within a short time. It must not be easily assumed that Orientals are wedded to autocracy. The truth is that democracy is older than autocracy in India. Our ancestors were fully accustomed to democratic institutions. The great Epic of India not only mentions, but describes Indian democracies, and the Buddhist literature fully testifies to their existence in those early days. The Greeks found village republics in full force. For over 2,000 years, five hundred thousand (500,000) village republics, composed of all castes in the village, flourished in India from Megasthenes to Munro, till exterminated by Anglo-Indian centralisation. The vigorous Caste Panchayat of today contains the germs of republicanism. No people in the world have had a wider or longer experience in working popular institutions. It is therefore absurd to presume that Indians are incapable of working democratic institutions.*

Absolute freedom for autonomous development would enable India to advance as Japan did, by leaps and bounds, thereby becoming a source of strength to Great Britain and a valued contributor to the civilization of mankind. India is anxious to restore her pristine glory. Of this there is no doubt. Liberty will infuse a new soul into her. It is therefore hoped that the high-minded statesmanship of England will rise to the occasion and support this demand of India at the Congress of Peace and give her the longed-for opportunity of working, on her own lines, democratic institutions, and thereby becoming a source of strength to the British Commonwealth....

.... Upon the principles we have discussed we claim that the British Parliament should enact a complete Constitution for India conceding autonomy within the British Commonwealth, with transitory provisions for bringing the whole constitution into full operation within the time specified by the Congress and the Moslem League.

The autonomy we advocate may be briefly sketched as follows: The Peninsula of India should be divided into a number of provinces on the principle of nationality. The Province should administer the internal affairs of the Province and be entrusted with all powers requisite for the administration. The form of government should be democratic. These Provinces should be federated to form the United States of India, with democratic Central Executive and Legislative bodies having powers to deal with the internal affairs of the whole of India. The United States of India should form a unit of the British Commonwealth with equal status with any other constituent thereof.... [emphasis added]

The purpose of placing Rai's pamphlet before the readers in the context of the discussion at hand was to show that in 1919, that is, after close to 84 years of introduction of Macaulay's education policy, the awareness of Bharat's civilisational character and history was still alive, which brings Rai's position closer to that of historians of his time, such as Radha Kumud Mookerji, and others. Importantly, Rai drew attention to the existence of democratic and republican institutions in Bharat much before the arrival of both the Middle Eastern and European colonisers. As one of the leading lights of the Home Rule Movement, Rai's distinction between Bharat as a civilisation and Europe's construct of a nation indicates that at least until 1919, those who fought for this country's decolonisation, even if gradual, were aware of its roots and had not been fully colonialised. While this may point to the inherent strength of the Indic civilisation, colonial education and its version of Bharat's history had started showing results, evident from the references to the 'Aryan race' and 'caste' in Rai's pamphlet. Therefore, a certain degree of duality had begun to surface in Bharat's indigenous consciousness, at least by 1919.

In any case, despite such representations for self-government, albeit within the British Empire, the Government of India Act of 1919 was enacted, which was based on the idea of 'responsible government', evident from its Preamble that read as follows:

> Whereas it is the declared policy of Parliament to provide for the increasing, association of Indians in every branch of Indian administration, and for the gradual development of self-governing institutions, with a view to the progressive realization of responsible government in British India as an integral part of the empire:
>
> And whereas progress in giving effect to this policy can only be achieved by successive stages, and it is expedient that substantial steps in this direction should now be taken:
>
> And whereas the time and manner of each advance can be determined only by Parliament, upon whom responsibility lies for the welfare and advancement of the Indian peoples:
>
> And whereas the action of Parliament in such matters must be guided by the co-operation received from those on whom new opportunities of service will be conferred, and by the extent to which it is found that confidence can be reposed in their sense of responsibility:
>
> And whereas concurrently with the gradual development of self-governing institutions in the Provinces of India it is expedient to give to those Provinces in provincial matters the largest measure of independence of the Government of India which is compatible with the due discharge by the latter of its own responsibilities:
>
> Be it therefore enacted by the King's most Excellent Majesty, by and with the advice and consent of the Lords Spiritual and Temporal, and Commons, in this present Parliament assembled, and by the authority of the same, as follows....

Going by the material discussed in the previous as well as in the current section, this much is clear—the Christian secular character of the British colonial infrastructure in Bharat remained consistently evangelical in its outlook both before and *after* the Queen's Proclamation of 1858. None of the events between 1857 and 1919 had an impact on the British policy of 'Christian toleration', which was simply a euphemism for silent and gradual proselytisation without the overt use of force by the State, but with its tacit support. Effectively, their position remained the same from the insertion of the Missionary Clauses in the 1813 Charter Act, to the Montford Reforms, which led to the 1919 Government of India Act. The literature also demonstrates that the Government of India Act of 1919 was not merely the product of a clamour for self-government within Bharat in lieu of its services in the First World War; it was equally a product of the internationalisation of standard of civilisation and hence Christian colonial consciousness, through the League of Nations. It is clear that at least until 1919, the standard of civilisation, which emanates from Christian European coloniality, was in vogue and directly impacted Bharat's organisation as a political entity.

Conclusion

This concludes the scope of discussion outlined for this book. The direct causal nexus, *nay* umbilical cord, between the global history of European coloniality and Bharat's tryst with it, in particular in the realm of the Constitution until 1919–1920, has been reasonably fleshed out in order for the readers to use this book as a starting point for their individual enquiries into Bharat's indigenous Indic consciousness and its contemporary dual nature. The fervent hope is that readers would, at the very least, become aware of their own preconceived notions about Bharat brought about by unconscious and conscious coloniality before holding forth on the need for 'reform' or the virtues of 'secularism', and instead revisit their biases with respect to terms, such as 'traditional'. 'Reform' in the context of Bharat must be decolonial reform as opposed to a colonialising one.

It is also hoped that Bharat's institutions, whether executive, legislative or judicial, too would wear decolonial hats each time they preside over Indic traditions, faith systems and institutions so that they are not tempted to push Bharat further into the arms of coloniality in the name of constitutional morality and transformative constitutionalism. Hopefully, some day transformative constitutionalism will acquire a decolonial hue in Bharat, thereby strengthening indigeneity instead of shaming and silencing it through the unending and secularised Protestant project of 'reform'.

In the next book of this trilogy, I will take this decolonial discussion forward and cover Bharat's constitutional journey in the crucial period between 1920 and 1951. As part of this analysis, I will also examine the new avatars of the standard of civilisation, namely the standards of modernity and human rights and their impact on Indic consciousness. The end goal, of course, is to understand the degrees of separation, if any, between the Constitution as it stood on 26 January 1950 and the Indic civilisational worldview, and to examine whether the duality in Bharat's native consciousness, which already existed in 1919, was reinforced or minimised, if not fully eliminated.

ॐ असतो मा सद्गमय ।
तमसो मा ज्योतिर्गमय ।
मृत्योर्मा अमृतं गमय ।
ॐ शान्तिः शान्तिः शान्तिः ॥
Pavamana Mantra;
Brihadaranyaka Upanishad (1.3.28)

Om, lead us from the unreal to the real;
Lead us from darkness to light;
Lead us from death to immortality;
Om Peace, Peace, Peace.

NOTES

INTRODUCTION

1   Arun Shourie, *The World of Fatwas or the Shariah in Action*, New Delhi: ASA Publications, 1995; Arun Shourie, *Missionaries in India: Continuities, Changes, Dilemmas*, New Delhi: Harper Collins Publishers, 1998.

2   As a law student, my first blog on the popular IP blog, *SpicyIP*, had been cited and extensively relied upon by a Division Bench of the Madras High Court to vacate an interim injunction granted in a hotly contested patent dispute. See https://www.livemint.com/Industry/YfBnnhqMJOQiR5zfBGc7IJ/Indian-court-uses-blog-reference-to-solve-TVSBajaj-patent-i.html

3   *Tata Sons Limited* v. *Greenpeace International & Anr* (2011) 178 DLT 705.

4   *Shreya Singhal* v. *Union of India* AIR 2015 SC 1523.

5   See https://globalfreedomofexpression.columbia.edu/cases/shreya-singhal-v-union-of-india/

6   Shri C.S. Vaidyanathan subsequently represented the Deity Shri Ram Lalla in the Shri Ram Janmabhoomi title dispute before the Supreme Court.

7   *Shri Dayananda Saraswati Swamiji and others* v. *The State of Tamil Nadu and others*, W.P. (C). No. 476/2012, which is currently pending before the Hon'ble Supreme Court. In December 2019, another writ petition, W.P. (C). No. 1432/2019, was preferred on behalf of the guardians of the Sri Subramanya Swami Temple in Tamil Nadu and the Indic Collective Trust, challenging more provisions of the TNHRCE Act 1959 and the rules thereunder. The said petition was tagged with Swami Dayananda Saraswati ji's petition on 18 December 2019.

8   The founder of Arsha Vidya Gurukulam.

9   *Indian Young Lawyers Association and others* v. *State of Kerala and others*, W.P. (C). No. 373 of 2006.

10 The Reference proceedings in the Sabarimala Temple case commenced in February 2020, but had to be put on hold due to the COVID-19-induced lockdown on 24 March 2020 during which period one member of the nine-Judge Bench retired. As on date, the Reference Bench is yet to be re-constituted. I represent People for Dharma and two other parties in the Reference proceedings.

11 Sri Marthanda Varma (D) *Th. Lr.* v. *State Of Kerala* 2020 SCC Online SC 569.

12 J. Sai Deepak, 'Constitution is meant to preserve integrity of nation and institutions; romanticising it is like confusing medium for message', 2019. See https://www.firstpost.com/politics/constitution-is-meant-to-preserve-integrity-of-nation-and-institutions-romanticising-it-is-like-confusing-medium-for-message-6708421.html

13 J. Sai Deepak, 'The Sovereign State Versus the Globalized Citizenship Model', 2019. See https://openthemagazine.com/essays/sovereign-state-versus-globalized-citizenship-model/

CHAPTER 1 COLONISATION, COLONIALISM, COLONIALITY AND DECOLONIALITY: LANGUAGE MATTERS

1 Shishir Tripathi, 'A lawyer for Lord Ayyappa: Advocate Sai Deepak turns heads in SC arguing for Sabarimala deity's right to celibacy', 2018. See https://www.firstpost.com/india/a-lawyer-for-lord-ayyappa-advocate-sai-deepak-turns-heads-in-supreme-court-arguing-for-sabarimala-deitys-right-to-celibacy-4859291.html; 'SC praises lawyer for spirited defence in Sabarimala case', *Business Standard*, 26 July 2018. See https://www.business-standard.com/article/pti-stories/sc-praises-lawyer-for-spirited-defence-in-sabarimala-case-118072601333_1.html; 'SC praises lawyer for spirited defence in Sabarimala case', *India Today*, 26 July 2018. See https://www.indiatoday.in/pti-feed/story/sc-praises-lawyer-for-spirited-defence-in-sabarimala-case-1297435-2018-07-26

2 Belonging to a 'sampradaya', which means either a tradition or a school of philosophy or a religious denomination or a sect.

3 *M. Siddiq (D) through LRS* v. *Mahant Suresh Das and others,* (2019) 19 SCC 440.

4 Sowmya Sivakumar, 'Sabarimala: "Deity's Will" Cannot Trump the Constitution on Right to Equality', 2018. See https://thewire.in/law/sabarimala-is-temple-entry-a-destination

5 Chennai International Centre, 10 September 2018, '"A Tug of War between Constitution and Faith" : 7th Sept, 2018' [Video]. See https://www.youtube.com/watch?v=ozxQu_sQbO8&t=2347s

6   Aníbal Quijano, 'Coloniality of Power, Eurocentrism and Latin America', *Nepantla: Views from South*, 1:3 (2000), pp. 533–580.

7   Aníbal Quijano, 'Coloniality and Modernity/Rationality', *Cultural Studies*, 21:2 (2007), pp. 168–178.

8   Walter D. Mignolo and Catherine E. Walsh, *On Decoloniality: Concepts, Analytics, Praxis*, London: Duke University Press, 2018.

9   W. Mignolo, *The Idea of Latin America*, Oxford: Blackwell Publishers, 2005.

10 Anibal Quijano, 'Coloniality and Modernity/Rationality', *Cultural Studies*.

11 Walter D. Mignolo and Catherine E. Walsh, *On Decoloniality: Concepts, Analytics, Praxis*, London: Duke University Press, 2018.

12 Sylvia Wynter, '1492: A New World View', in *Race, Discourse, and the Origin of the Americas: A New World View*, edited by Vera L. Hyatt and Rex Nettleford, Washington, D.C.: Smithsonian Institution Press, 1995.

13 Jeffrey Hart, 'Feting the Lindbergh of the 15th Century', *San Francisco Examiner*, 1991.

14 Linda Hutcheon, 'Circling the Downspout of Empire', in *The Post-Colonial Studies Reader*, edited by Bill Ashcroft, Gareth Griffiths and Helen Tiffin, London: Routledge, 2003, pp. 130–135.

15 Madina Tlostanova, 'The Postcolonial Condition, the Decolonial Option and the Post-Socialist Intervention', in *Postcolonialism Cross-Examined: Multidirectional Perspectives on Imperial and Colonial Pasts and the Newcolonial Present*, edited by M. Albrecht, London: Routledge, 2019, pp. 165–178.

16 Nelson Maldonado-Torres, 'Race, Religion, and Ethics in the Modern/Colonial World', *The Journal of Religious Ethics*, 42:4 (December 2014), pp. 691–711.

CHAPTER 2   THE DISCOVERY OF COLONIALITY AND THE BIRTH OF DECOLONIALITY

1   Walter Mignolo, 'Coloniality Is Far from Over, and So Must Be Decoloniality', *Afterall: A Journal of Art Context and Enquiry*, 43 (2017), pp. 38–45.

2   Michael Baker, 'Modernity/Coloniality and Eurocentric Education: Towards a Post-Occidental Self-Understanding of the Present', *Policy Futures in Education*, 10:1 (2012).

3   Walter Mignolo, 'On Pluriversality and Multipolar World Order: Decoloniality after Decolonization; Dewesternisation after the Cold War', in *Constructing the Pluriverse*, edited by Bernd Reiter, London: Duke University Press, 2018.

4   Walter Mignolo, *The Darker Side of Western Modernity: Global Futures, Decolonial Options*, London: Duke University Press, 2011.

5   Aníbal Quijano, 'Coloniality of Power, Eurocentrism and Latin America', *Nepantla: Views from South*, 1:3 (2000), pp. 533–580.

6   Walter D. Mignolo and Catherine E. Walsh, *On Decoloniality: Concepts, Analytics, Praxis*, London: Duke University Press, 2018.

7   Aníbal Quijano, 'Coloniality and Modernity/Rationality', *Cultural Studies*, 21:2 (2007), pp. 168–178.

8   Enrique Dussel, Javier Krauel and Virginia Tuma, 'Europe, Modernity and Eurocentrism', *Nepantla: Views from South*, 1 (2000), pp. 465–478.

9   Ramón Grosfoguel, 'Colonial Difference, Geopolitics of Knowledge, and Global Coloniality in the Modern/Colonial Capitalist World-System', Review (Fernand Braudel Center), *Utopian Thinking*, New York: Research Foundation of State University, 25:3 (2002), pp. 203–224.

10 Walter Mignolo, 'The Geopolitics of Knowledge and the Colonial Difference', *The South Atlantic Quarterly*, London: Duke University Press, 101:1 (Winter 2002), pp. 57–96.

11 Patricia Seed, 'Early Modernity: The History of a Word', *CR: The New Centennial Review*, Michigan State University Press, 2:1 (Spring 2002).

12 E. Dussel, 'Eurocentrism and Modernity (Introduction to the Frankfurt Lectures)', in *The Postmodernism Debate in Latin America* by John Beverley-José Oviedo, London: Duke University Press, 20:3 (1993), pp. 65–76; 2a (1995), pp. 65–76.

13 An Yountae, 'A Decolonial Theory of Religion: Race, Coloniality, and Secularity in the Americas', *Journal of the American Academy of Religion*, 88: 4 (December 2020), pp. 947–980.

14 Sylvia Wynter, '1492: A New World View', in *Race, Discourse, and the Origin of the Americas: A New World View*, edited by Vera L. Hyatt and Rex Nettleford, Washington, D.C.: Smithsonian Institution Press, 1995.

15 *Inter Caetera*—Division of the undiscovered world between Spain and Portugal, Pope Alexander VI, 1493; See https://www.papalencyclicals.net/alex06/alex06inter.htm

16 Sylvia Wynter, 'Unsettling the Coloniality of Being/Power/Truth/Freedom: Towards the Human, After Man, Its Overrepresentation—An Argument', *CR: The New Centennial Review*, Michigan State University Press, 3:3 (Fall 2003), pp. 257–337.

17 Walter Mignolo, 'Racism as We Sense It Today', *PMLA*, 123:5, Special Topic: Comparative Racialization (October 2008), pp. 1737–1742.

18 Nelson Maldonado-Torres, 'Race, Religion, and Ethics in the Modern/Colonial World', *The Journal of Religious Ethics*, 42:4 (December 2014), pp. 691–711.

19 J.W. Martin, *The Land Looks After Us: A History of Native American Religion*, New York: Oxford University Press, 2001.

20 Nassima Dalal, 'The Impact of Colonial Contact on the Cultural Heritage of Native American Indian People', *Diffusion: The UCLan Journal of Undergraduate Research*, 4:2 (December 2011).

21 D.M. Grandbois and G.F. Sanders, 'The Resilience of Native American Elders', *Issues in Mental Health Nursing*, 30 (2009), pp. 569–580.

22 C. Palmiste, 'Forcible Removals: The Case of Australian Aboriginal and Native American Children', *Alternative*, 4 (2008), pp. 76–88.

23 D. Hightower-Langston, *The Native American World*, New Jersey: John Wiley, 2003.

24 C.F. Taylor and W.C. Sturtevant, *The Native Americans: The Indigenous Peoples of North America*, London: Salamander Books, 1996.

25 L. Spence, *North American Indians Myths & Legends*, London: Senate, 1994.

CHAPTER 3 COLONIALITY, INDIGENOUS FAITHS, NATURE AND KNOWLEDGE

1   Aníbal Quijano, 'Coloniality and Modernity/Rationality', *Cultural Studies*, 21:2 (2007), pp. 168–178.

2   Aníbal Quijano, 'Coloniality of Power and Eurocentrism in Latin America', *International Sociology*, 15:2 (2000), pp. 215–232.

3   R. Erdoes and A. Ortiz, *American Myths and Legends*, New York: Pantheon, 1984.

4   Clayton T. Russell, 'Use of Native American Oral Tradition in Environmental Education', *Graduate Student Theses, Dissertations, & Professional Papers*, 7905, 1988.

5   Joseph Epes Brown, *The Spiritual Legacy of the American Indian*, New York: Crossroad, 1982.

6   Ibid.

7   N. Scott Momaday, 'Native American Attitudes to the Environment', in *Seeing with the Native Eye: Essays on Native American Religion*, edited by Walter H. Capps, New York: Harper and Row, 1976.

8   Richard K. Nelson, *Make Prayers to the Raven*, Chicago: University of Chicago Press, 1983.

9   A. Versluis, *Native American Traditions*, Dorset: Element Books, 1995.

10 B.B. Mukumuri, 'Local Environmental Conservation Strategies: Karanga Religion, Politics and Environmental Control', *Environment and History*, 1 (1995), pp. 297–311.

11 Joseph Epes Brown, ed., *The Sacred Pipe: Black Elk's Account of the Seven Rites of the Oglala Sioux*, Norman: University of Oklahoma Press, 1953, p. 15.

12 Lina Álvarez and Brendan Coolsaet, 'Decolonizing Environmental Justice Studies: A Latin American Perspective', *Capitalism Nature Socialism*, 31:2 (2018), pp. 50–69.

13 William Adams, 'Nature and the Colonial Mind', in *Decolonizing Nature: Strategies for Conservation in a Post-Colonial Era*, edited by William M. Adams and Martin Mulligan, Earthscan Publications Ltd, 2003.

14 Val Plumwood, 'Decolonizing Relationships with Nature', in *Decolonizing Nature: Strategies for Conservation in a Post-Colonial Era*, edited by William M. Adams and Martin Mulligan, Earthscan Publications Ltd, 2003.

15 R. Drayton, *Nature's Government: Science, Imperial Britain and the 'Improvement' of the World*, New Haven: Yale University Press, 2000.

16 William M. Adams and Martin Mulligan, *Decolonizing Nature: Strategies for Conservation in a Post-Colonial Era*, edited by William M. Adams and Martin Mulligan, Earthscan Publications Ltd, 2003.

17 R. Murphy, *Rationality and Nature: A Sociological Inquiry into a Changing Relationship*, Colorado: Westview Press, 1994.

18 Ibid.

19 L.J. Zimmerman, *American Indians: The First Nations; Native North American Life, Myth and Art*, London: Duncan Baird, 2003.

20 C. Palmiste, 'Forcible Removals: The Case of Australian Aboriginal and Native American Children', *Alternative*, 4 (2008), pp. 76–88.

21 W.T. Hagan, *American Indians*, 3rd edition, Chicago: University of Chicago Press, 1993.

22 E.G. Anderson, 'The Presence of Early Native Studies: A Response to Stephanie Fitzgerald and Hilary E. Wyss', *Early American Literature*, 45 (2010), pp. 250–260.

23 J.W. Martin, *The Land Looks After Us: A History of Native American Religion*, New York: Oxford University Press, 2001.

24 Mark Malisa and Thelma Quardey Missedja, 'Schooled for Servitude: The Education of African Children in British Colonies, 1910–1990', *Genealogy*, 3:40 (2019). See https://doi.org/10.3390/genealogy3030040

25 Ibid.

26 Walton Johnson, 'Education: Keystone of Apartheid', *Anthropology & Education Quarterly*, 13 (1982), pp. 214–237.

27 Abraham Leslie Behr and R.G. Macmillan, *Education in South Africa*, Pretoria: J.L. van Schaik Ltd, 1966.

28 Ayi Kwei Armah, *Why Are We So Blest?*, London: Heinemann, 1972.

29 Pam Christie, *The Right to Learn: The Struggle for Education in South Africa*, Cape Town: Ravan Press, 1990.

30 James Collins, 'Social Reproduction in Classrooms and Schools', *Annual Review of Anthropology*, 38 (2009), pp. 33–48.

31 Pam Christie and C. Collins, 'Bantu Education: Apartheid Ideology of Labour Reproduction?', *Comparative Education*, 18 (1982), pp. 59–75.

32 Cynthia Kros, 'W.W.M. Eiselen: Architect of Apartheid Education', in *The History of Education under Apartheid 1948–94: The Doors of Learning and Culture Shall Be Opened*, edited by Peter Kallaway, Cape Town: Pearson, 2002.

33 A. Roberts, *South African Native Affairs Commission*, 2, Cape Town: Cape Times.

34 Chana Teeger, 'Ruptures in the Rainbow Nation: How Desegregated South African Schools Deal with Interpersonal and Structural Racism', *Sociology of Education*, 88 (2015), pp. 226–243.

35 Michael Omolewa, 'Educating the "Native": A Study of the Education Adaptation Strategy in British Colonial Africa, 1910–36', *The Journal of African American History*, 91 (2006), pp. 267–287.

36 Nelson Mandela, *Long Walk to Freedom: The Autobiography of Nelson Mandela*, Boston: Back Bay, 1994.

37 Richard Corby, 'Educating Africans for Inferiority under British Rule: Bo School in Sierra Leone', *Comparative Education Review*, 34 (1990), pp. 314–349.

38 Shoko Yamada, 'Educational Borrowing as Negotiation: Re-examining the Influence of the American Black Industrial Education Model on British Colonial Education in Africa', *Comparative Education*, 44 (2008), pp. 21–37.

39 D.M. Grandbois and G.F. Sanders, 'The Resilience of Native American Elders', *Issues in Mental Health Nursing*, 30 (2009), pp. 569–580.

40 Ayi Kwei Armah, *Osiris Rising*, Popenguine: Per Ankh, 2008.

41 L.A. French, 'Psychoactive Agents and Native American Spirituality: Past and Present', *Contemporary Justice Review*, 11 (2008), pp. 155–163.

42 C. Rybak and A. Decker-Fitts, 'Theory and Practice: Understanding Native American Healing Practices', *Counselling Psychology Quarterly*, 22 (2009), pp. 333–342.

43 D.M. Grandbois and G.F. Sanders, 'The Resilience of Native American Elders', *Issues in Mental Health Nursing*, 30 (2009), p. 570.

CHAPTER 4 ENTRENCHMENT OF COLONIALITY THROUGH EUROPEAN POLITICAL STRUCTURES

1 Patrick Ziltener, 'Impacts of Colonialism—A Research Survey', *Journal of World-Systems Research*, 19:2 (2013), pp. 290–311.

2   Robin M. Grier, 'Colonial Legacies and Economic Growth', *Public Choice*, 98 (1999), pp. 317–335.

3   Crawford Young, *The African Colonial State in Comparative Perspective*, New Haven: Yale University Press, 1994.

4   Valerie Phillips, 'Indigenous Peoples and the Role of the Nation-State', *Proceedings of the Annual Meeting (American Society of International Law)*, 101 (28–31 March 2007), pp. 319–323.

5   Jakob De Roover, *Europe, India, and the Limits of Secularism*, India: Oxford University Press, 2015.

6   Derek Croxton, 'The Peace of Westphalia of 1648 and the Origins of Sovereignty', *The International History Review*, 21:3 (September 1999), pp. 569–591.

7   Gerhart B. Ladner, *The Idea of Reform: Its Impact on Christian Thought and Action in the Age of the Fathers*, New York: Harper & Row, 1967.

8   Karl F. Morrison, *Understanding Conversion*, Charlottesville: University of Virginia Press, 1992.

9   Martin Luther, *Martin Luther's Basic Theological Writings*, Minneapolis: Fortress Press, 1989.

10   Hugh of Saint-Victor and R. Berndt, *De Sacramentis Christinae Fidei*, Germany: Monasterii Westfalorum, 2008.

11   Steven D. Smith, *Foreordained Failure: The Quest for a Constitutional Principle of Religious Freedom*, New York: Oxford University Press, 1995; Nomi Maya Stolzenberg, 'The Profanity of Law', in *Law and the Sacred*, edited by Austin Sarat, Lawrence Douglas and Martha Merrill Umphrey, Stanford University Press, 2007, p. 29; Nomi Maya Stolzenberg, 'Theses on Secularism', *San Diego Law Review*, 1041 (2010).

12   Jakob De Roover, *Europe, India, and the Limits of Secularism*, India: Oxford University Press, 2015, p. 94.

13   Nomi Maya Stolzenberg, 'Political Theology with a Difference', U.C. *Irvine Law Review*, 407 (2014).

14   James M. Estes, ed., *Whether Secular Government Has the Right to Wield the Sword in Matters of Faith: A Controversy in Nürnberg in 1530 over Freedom of Worship and the Authority of Secular Government in Spiritual Matters*, Toronto: Centre for Reformation and Renaissance Studies, 1994.

15   Lewis W. Spitz, 'Particularism and Peace Augsburg: 1555', *Church History*, 25:2 (1956), pp. 110–126.

16   Leo Gross, 'The Peace of Westphalia, 1648–1948', *American Journal of International Law*, 42:1 (January 1948).

17   Daniel Philpott, 'Religious Freedom and the Undoing of the Westphalian State', *Michigan Journal of International Law*, 25:4 (2004), pp. 981–998.

18 Montevideo Convention on the Rights and Duties of States, 26 December 1923. See https://www.jus.uio.no/english/services/library/treaties/01/1-02/rights-duties-states.xml

19 Ove Bring, 'The Westphalian Peace Tradition in International Law: From Jus ad Bellum to Jus contra Bellum', *International Law Studies*, 75 (2000).

20 Jason Farr, 'Point: The Westphalia Legacy and the Modern Nation-State', *International Social Science Review*, 80:3/4 (2005), pp. 156–159.

21 Statute of the International Court of Justice, articles 9 and 38(1), 26 June 1945. See https://www.icj-cij.org/en/statute

22 David P. Fidler, 'The Return of the Standard of Civilization', *Chicago Journal of International Law*, 2:1 (2001), pp. 137–157.

23 Georg Schwarzenberger, 'The Standard of Civilisation in International Law', *Current Legal Problems*, 8:1 (1955), pp. 212–234.

24 G.W. Gong, *The Standard of Civilization in International Society*, Oxford: Clarendon Press, 1984.

25 Daniel Philpot, 'The Religious Roots of Modern International Relations', *World Politics*, 52:2 (January 2000), p. 213.

26 G.J.S. Dei and J. Anamuah-Mensah, 'The Coloniality of Development', in *Indigenist African Development and Related Issues: Anti-colonial Educational Perspectives for Transformative Change*, edited by A. Asabere-Ameyaw, J. Anamuah-Mensah, G.J.S. Dei and K. Raheem, Rotterdam: Sense Publishers, 2014. See https://doi.org/10.1007/978-94-6209-659-2_3

27 Jakob De Roover and S.N. Balagangadhara, 'John Locke, Christian Liberty, and the Predicament of Liberal Toleration', *Political Theory*, 36:4 (2008), pp. 523–549.

28 Jeremy Waldron, *God, Locke, and Equality: Christian Foundations of John Locke's Political Thought*, Cambridge: Cambridge University Press, 2002.

29 Ibid., pp. 242–243.

30 Carl L. Becker, *The Heavenly City of the Eighteenth-Century Philosophers*, 2nd edition, New Haven: Yale University Press, 2003.

31 S.J. Barnett, *The Enlightenment and Religion: The Myths of Modernity*, Manchester: Manchester University Press, 2004.

32 Elizabeth S. Hurd, 'The Political Authority of Secularism in International Relations', *European Journal of International Relations*, 10:2 (2004), pp. 235–262.

33 Pauline Kleingeld, 'Kant's Second Thoughts on Race', *Philosophical Quarterly*, 229 (2007), pp. 573–592.

34 P. Frierson and P. Guyer, *Observations on the Feeling of the Beautiful and Sublime and Other Writings*, Cambridge: Cambridge University Press, 2011.

35 Pauline Kleingeld, 'Kant's Second Thoughts on Colonialism', in *Kant and Colonialism: Historical and Critical Perspectives*, edited by Katrin Flikschuh and Lea Ypi, Oxford: Oxford University Press, 2014, pp. 43–67.

36 Ramón Grosfoguel, 'Developmentalism, Modernity, and Dependency Theory in Latin America', *Nepantla: Views from South*, 1:2 (2000), pp. 347–374.

37 Britta Saal, 'How to Leave Modernity Behind: The Relationship between Colonialism and Enlightenment, and the Possibility of Altermodern Decoloniality', *Budhi: A Journal of Ideas and Culture*, 17 (2013), DOI: 10.13185/BU2013.17103.

38 Walter D. Mignolo, 'Delinking', *Cultural Studies*, 21:2–3 (2007), pp. 449–514.

39 Christine Schwöbel-Patel, '(Global) Constitutionalism and the Geopolitics of Knowledge', in *The Global South and Comparative Constitutional Law*, edited by Philipp Dann, Michael Riegner and Maxim Bönnemann, Oxford: Oxford University Press, 2020.

40 Pieter Heydenrych, 'Constitutionalism and Coloniality: A Case of Colonialism Continued or the Best of Both Worlds?', *New Contree*, 75 (2016), pp. 116–134.

41 D. Hightower-Langston, *The Native American World*, New Jersey: John Wiley, 2003.

CHAPTER 5 DECOLONIALITY, INDIGENEITY, SUBJECTIVITY AND RELATIONALITY

1 Gayatri Chakravorty Spivak, 'Can the Subaltern Speak?', in *Marxism and the Interpretation of Culture*, edited by Cary Nelson and Lawrence Grossberg, Chicago: University of Illinois Press, 1988; W.D. Mignolo, 'Coloniality of Power and Subalternity', in *The Latin American Subaltern Studies Reader*, edited by I. Rodríguez, London: Duke University Press, 2001; Ramón Grosfoguel, 'The Epistemic Decolonial Turn', *Cultural Studies*, 21:2–3 (2007), pp. 211–223.

2 Walter D. Mignolo, 'Delinking: The Rhetoric of Modernity, the Logic of Coloniality and the Grammar of De-coloniality', *Cultural Studies*, 21:2 (2007), pp. 449–514, 469.

3 Ramón Grosfoguel, 'Decolonising Post-Colonial Studies and Paradigms of Political-Economy: Transmodernity, Decolonial Thinking, and Global Coloniality', *Transmodernity: Journal of Peripheral Cultural Production of the Luso-Hispanic World*, 1:1 (2011).

4 José Domingues, 'Global Modernisation, "Coloniality" and a Critical Sociology for Contemporary Latin America', *Theory Culture & Society*, 26 (2009), pp. 112–133.

5   W.D. Mignolo and M. Tlostanova, 'The Logic of Coloniality and the Limits of Postcoloniality', in *The Postcolonial and the Global*, edited by R. Krishnaswamy and Hawley, pp. 109–123, Minneapolis: University of Minnesota Press, 2008.

6   M. Tlostanova, 'The Postcolonial Condition, the Decolonial Option and the Postsocialist Intervention', in *Postcolonialism Cross-Examined: Multidirectional Perspectives on Imperial and Colonial Pasts and the Neocolonial Present*, edited by M. Albrecht, pp. 165–178, London: Routledge, 2019.

7   G. McLennan, 'Sociology, Eurocentrism and Postcolonial Theory', *European Journal of Social Theory*, 6:1 (2003), pp. 69–86.

8   Gayatri Spivak, *In Other Worlds: Essays in Cultural Politics*, New York: Routledge, 1988; Homi K. Bhabha, *The Location of Culture*, London: Routledge, 1994.

9   Gurminder K. Bhambra, 'Postcolonial and Decolonial Dialogues', *Postcolonial Studies*, 17:2 (2014), pp. 115–121; Edward Said, *Orientalism*, New York: Vintage Books, 1979.

10 Walter Mignolo, 'Delinking, Decoloniality and Dewesternisation: Interview with Walter Mignolo', in *Critical Legal Thinking*, 2 May 2012. See http://criticallegalthinking.com/2012/05/02/delinking-decoloniality-dewesternisationinterview-with-walter-mignolo-part-ii/

11 Aníbal Quijano, 'Coloniality of Power, Ethnocentrism, and Latin America', *Nepantla*, 1:3 (2000), pp. 533–580.

12 Aníbal Quijano, 'Coloniality and Modernity/Rationality', *Cultural Studies*, 21:2 (2007), pp. 168–178.

13 Walter D. Mignolo, *Local Histories/Global Designs: Essays on the Coloniality of Power, Subaltern Knowledges and Border Thinking*, Princeton: Princeton University Press, 2000.

14 Walter D. Mignolo, 'Introduction: Coloniality of Power and Decolonial Thinking', *Cultural Studies*, 21:2–3 (2007), pp. 155–167.

15 Ramón Grosfoguel, 'Colonial Difference, Geopolitics of Knowledge and Global Coloniality in the Modern/Colonial Capitalist World-System', *Review*, 25:3 (2002), pp. 203–224; Walter D. Mignolo, 'Spirit Out of Bounds Returns to the East: The Closing of the Social Sciences and the Opening of Independent Thoughts', *Current Sociology*, 62 (2014), pp. 584–602.

16 Walter D. Mignolo and Catherine E. Walsh, *On Decoloniality: Concepts, Analytics, Praxis*, London: Duke University Press, 2018.

17 Ramón Grosfoguel, 'Transmodernity, Border Thinking, and Global Coloniality: Decolonising Political Economy and Postcolonial Studies', 4 July 2008. See https://www.eurozine.com/transmodernity-border-thinking-and-global-coloniality/

18 Ramón Grosfoguel, 'The Structure of Knowledge in Westernised Universities: Epistemic Racism/Sexism and the Four Genocides/Epistemicides of the Long 16th Century', *Human Architecture: Journal of the Sociology of Self-Knowledge*, 11:1, Article 8 (2013).

19 Ramón Grosfoguel, 'From Postcolonial Studies to Decolonial Studies: Decolonising Postcolonial Studies: A Preface', *Review*, 29 (2006).

20 Ronald Niezen, *The Origins of Indigenism, Human Rights and the Politics of Identity*, Berkeley: University of California Press, 2003.

21 Patrick Wolfe, *Settler Colonialism and the Transformation of Anthropology: The Politics and Poetics of an Ethnographic Event*, London: Cassell, 1999.

22 James S. Anaya, *Indigenous Peoples in International Law*, Oxford: Oxford University Press, 1996.

23 C107—Indigenous and Tribal Populations Convention, 1957 (No. 107). International Labour Organization. See https://www.ilo.org/dyn/normlex/en/f?p=NORMLEXPUB:12100:0::NO::P12100_ILO_CODE:C107

24 C169—Indigenous and Tribal Peoples Convention, 1989 (No. 169), International Labour Organization. See https://www.ilo.org/dyn/normlex/en/f?p=NORMLEXPUB:12100:0::NO::P12100_ILO_CODE:C169

25 Jodi A. Byrd and Michael Rothberg, 'Between Subalternity and Indigeneity', *Interventions*, 13:1 (2011), pp. 1–12.

26 Jose R. Martinez Cobo (Special Rapporteur of the Sub-Commission on Prevention of Discrimination and Protection of Minorities), 'Study on the Problem of Discrimination against Indigenous Populations', 1987. See https://digitallibrary.un.org/record/133666?ln=en and https://cendoc.docip.org/collect/cendocdo/index/assoc/HASH01a2/55590d02.dir/Martinez-Cobo-a-1.pdf

27 United Nations Declaration of the Rights of Indigenous Peoples (UNDRIP). See https://www.un.org/development/desa/indigenouspeoples/wp-content/uploads/sites/19/2019/01/UNDRIP_E_web.pdf

28 State of the World's Indigenous Peoples, ST/ESA/328, Department of Economic and Social Affairs (DESA), Secretariat of the Permanent Forum on Indigenous Issues, United Nations, 2009.

29 Walter Rodney, *How Europe Underdeveloped Africa*, Washington, D.C.: Howard University, 1972.

30 A. Escobar, *Encountering Development: The Making and Unmaking of the Third World*, Princeton: Princeton University Press, 1995.

31 A. Escobar, 'Imagining a Post-Development Era? Critical Thought, Development and Social Movements', *Social Text*, 31/32 (1992),

pp. 20–56; Frantz Fanon, *The Wretched of the Earth*, translated by Constance Farrington, New York: Grove, 1968, p. 169.

32 Mario Blaser, Glenn McRae and Harvey A. Feit, *In the Way of Development: Indigenous Peoples, Life Projects and Globalisation*, IDRC, 2004.

33 Mathias Guenther, Justin Kenrick, Adam Kuper, Evie Plaice, Trond Thuen, Patrick Wolfe, Werner Zips and Alan Barnard, 'The Concept of Indigeneity', *Social Anthropology*, 14 (2006).

34 Walter D. Mignolo, 'Coloniality Is Far from Over, and So Must Be Decoloniality', *Afterall*, 43 (2017), pp. 38–45.

35 Paul Berne Burow, Samara Brock and Michael R. Dove, 'Unsettling the Land: Indigeneity, Ontology, and Hybridity in Settler Colonialism', *Environment and Society*, 9 (2018), pp. 57–74.

36 Sarah Radcliffe, 'Geography and Indigeneity I: Indigeneity, Coloniality and Knowledge', *Progress in Human Geography*, 2015.

37 Adam Barker and Jenny Pickerill, 'Doings with the Land and Sea: Decolonising Geographies, Indigeneity, and Enacting Place-Agency', *Progress in Human Geography*, 44 (2019).

CHAPTER 6 BHARAT, COLONIALITY AND COLONIAL CONSCIOUSNESS

1 B. Rao, E. Bloch and J. De Roover, 'Rethinking Colonialism and Colonial Consciousness: The Case of Modern India', in *Forms of Knowledge in India: Critical Revaluations*, edited by S. Raval, G. Mehta and S. Yashaschandra, pp. 179–212, New Delhi: Pencraft International, 2008.

2 B. Rao and J. De Roover, 'The Secular State and Religious Conflict: Liberal Neutrality and the Indian Case of Pluralism', *Journal of Political Philosophy*, 15:1 (2007), pp. 67–92.

3 Sitaram Goel, *The Story of Islamic Imperialism in India*, New Delhi: Voice of India, 1982.

4 R.K. Ohri, *Long March of Islam: The Future Imperfect*, New Delhi: Manas Publications, 2004.

5 Koenraad Elst, *Negationism in India: Concealing the Record of Islam*, New Delhi: Voice of India, 1992.

6 Sitaram Goel, *Hindu Temples: What Happened to Them*, volumes 1 and 2, New Delhi: Voice of India, 1982.

7 Ram Swarup, *Understanding Islam through Hadis—Religious Faith or Fanaticism?*, New Delhi: Voice of India, 1982.

8 M.A. Khan, *Islamic Jihad: A Legacy of Forced Conversion, Imperialism, and Slavery*, New York: iUniverse, 2009.

9 Sitaram Goel, *Muslim Separatism: Causes and Consequences*, New Delhi: Voice of India, 1983.

10 Kolja Lindner, 'Marx's Eurocentrism: Postcolonial Studies and Marx Scholarship', *Radical Philosophy*, 161 (2010), pp. 27-41; P. Jani, 'Karl Marx, Eurocentrism, and the 1857 Revolt in British India', in *Marxism, Modernity and Postcolonial Studies*, edited by C. Bartolovich and N. Lazarus, Cambridge: Cambridge University Press, 2002, pp. 81–98.

11 J. Li, 'The Asiatic Mode of Production and the Marxist Theory of History', in *Chinese Civilization in the Making, 1766–221 BC*, London: Palgrave Macmillan, 1996.

12 T. Byres, 'Eurocentric Marxism and the Third World: View from the Academy in the Anglophone Metropolis', *Economic and Political Weekly*, 19:30 (1984), pp. 1199–1204.

13 K. Mathew Kurian, 'Marxism and Christianity', *Social Scientist*, 2:8 (1974), pp. 3–21; H.F. Ward, 'Christian Marxism', in *Trends in Protestant Social Idealism*, edited by J. Neal Hughley, New York: Columbia University Press, 1948.

14 Manfred Sing, 'The Tempestuous Affair between Marxism and Islam: Attraction, Hostility, and Accommodation since 1917', in *Muslims and Capitalism: An Uneasy Relationship?*, edited by Béatrice Hendrich, Baden-Baden: Ergon Verlag, 2018.

15 B. Rao, *Reconceptualizing India Studies*, India: Oxford University Press, 2012.

16 Koenraad Elst, *Decolonizing the Hindu Mind: Ideological Development of Hindu Revivalism*, India: Rupa & Co., 2001.

17 B.R. Ambedkar, *Pakistan or the Partition of India*, India: Thacker and Co., 1946.

18 Ibid.

19 Venkat Dhulipala, *Creating a New Medina: State Power, Islam, and the Quest for Pakistan in Late Colonial North India*, Cambridge: Cambridge University Press, 2015.

20 Christine C. Fair, *Fighting to the End: The Pakistan Army's Way of War*, Oxford: Oxford University Press, 2014.

21 Sandeep Balakrishna, *Invaders and Infidels: From Sindh to Delhi, The 500-Year Journey of Islamic Invasions*, India: Bloomsbury India, 2020.

CHAPTER 7 BHARAT AS A CIVILISATION

1 Martin Jacques, *When China Rules the World: The End of the Western World and the Birth of a New Global Order*, UK: Penguin, 2009.

2 Martin Jacques, 'Civilization State versus Nation-State', 2011. See http://www.martinjacques.com/articles/civilization-state-versus-nation-state-2/

3   Zhang Weiwei, *The China Wave: Rise of a Civilizational State*, World
    Scientific Publishing Company, 2012.

4   Koenraad Elst, 'India as a Civilization-State', 2014. See http://
    koenraadelst.blogspot.com/2014/07/india-as-civilization-state.html

5   'India Is a Civilisational State, Not Based on Religion or Language:
    NSA Doval', *DNA*, 2020. See https://www.dnaindia.com/india/
    report-india-is-a-civilisational-state-not-based-on-religion-or-
    language-nsa-doval-2852191

6   Har Bilas Sarda, *Hindu Superiority: An Attempt to Determine the Position
    of the Hindu Race in the Scale of Nations*, Rajputana Printing Works,
    1906.

7   Radha Kumud Mookerji, *Hindu Civilization: From the Earliest Times
    up to the Establishment of the Maurya Empire*, London and New York:
    Longmans, Green and Co., 1936; Radha Kumud Mookerji, *Hindu
    Civilization: From the Earliest Times up to the Establishment of the
    Maurya Empire*, Bombay: Bharatiya Vidya Bhavan, 1950.

8   Radha Kumud Mookerji, *A New Approach to the Communal Problem*,
    Bombay: Padma Publications, 1943.

9   Radha Kumud Mookerji, *Akhand Bharat*, Bombay: Hind Kitabs, 1945.

10 Radha Kumud Mookerji, *The Fundamental Unity of India (from Hindu
    Sources)*, London and New York: Longmans, Green and Co., 1914.

11 Strachey, quoted in Radha Kumud Mookerji, *The Fundamental Unity of
    India (from Hindu Sources)*, London and New York: Longmans, Green
    and Co., 1914, p. 5.

12 Radha Kumud Mookerji, *The Fundamental Unity of India (from Hindu
    Sources)*, London and New York: Longmans, Green and Co., 1914, p. 6.

13 Vincent Arthur Smith, quoted in Radha Kumud Mookerji, *The
    Fundamental Unity of India (from Hindu Sources)*, London and New
    York: Longmans, Green and Co., 1914, p. 14.

14 Radha Kumud Mookerji, *The Fundamental Unity of India (from Hindu
    Sources)*, London and New York: Longmans, Green and Co., 1914, p. 19.

15 Ibid., p. 37.

16 Radha Kumud Mookerji, *Nationalism in Hindu Culture*, London:
    Theosophical Publishing House, 1921.

17 Ibid., p. 57.

18 Objectives Resolution adopted by the Constituent Assembly on
    22 January 1947. See http://loksabhaph.nic.in/writereaddata/
    cadebatefiles/C22011947.pdf

19 The Draft Constitution prepared by the Drafting Committee under
    the Chairmanship of Dr. B.R. Ambedkar was based on the draft
    Constitution prepared by the Constitutional Advisor to the Constituent
    Assembly, Sir Benegal Narsing Rau.

20 Constituent Assembly of India Debates, 15 November 1948. See http://164.100.47.194/loksabha/writereaddata/cadebatefiles/C15111948.html

21 Constituent Assembly of India Debates, 17 November 1948. See http://164.100.47.194/loksabha/writereaddata/cadebatefiles/C17111948.html

22 Constituent Assembly of India Debates, 17 September 1949. See http://loksabhaph.nic.in/writereaddata/cadebatefiles/C17091949.html

23 Constituent Assembly of India Debates, 18 September 1949. See http://loksabhaph.nic.in/writereaddata/cadebatefiles/C18091949.html

24 Catherine Clémentin-Ojha, '"India, That Is Bharat....": One Country, Two Names', *South Asia Multidisciplinary Academic Journal,* 2014. See https://doi.org/10.4000/samaj.3717

25 Jadunath Sarkar, *India Through the Ages,* India: M.C. Sarkar & Sons, 1928.

26 R.C. Majumdar, Kalikinkar Datta and Hem Chandra Raychaudhuri, *An Advanced History of India*, India: Macmillan Publishers, 1946.

27 R.C. Majumdar, *Ancient India*, Banaras: Motilal Banarsidass, 1952.

28 Bruce T. McCully, 'The Origins of Indian Nationalism According to Native Writers', *The Journal of Modern History,* 7 (1935), pp. 295–314.

29 Nilakanta K.A. Sastri and G. Srinivasachari, *Advanced History of India*, Bombay: Allied Publishers, 1971.

30 S.K. Aiyangar, *Ancient India and South Indian History and Culture Papers on Indian History and Culture*, Poona: Oriental Book Agency, 1941; R.C. Dutt, *A History of Civilisation in Ancient India (Based on Sanscrit Literature)*, London: Kegan Paul, Trench, Trubner, & Co. Ltd, 1893.

31 Govind Chandra Pande, *Foundations of Indian Culture*, India: Motilal Banarsidass, 1990; K.P. Jayaswal and V.R. Sankrityayana, *An Imperial History of India in a Sanskrit Text [c. 700 B.C.–C. 770 A.D.] with a Special Commentary on Later Gupta Period*, Lahore: Motilal Banarsidass, 1934.

32 Diana L. Eck, *India: A Sacred Geography*, New York: Harmony, Random House, 2012.

CHAPTER 8 EUROPEAN COLONIALITY AND THE INDIC CIVILISATION

1 N.K. Sinha and A.C. Banerjee, *History of India*, Calcutta: A. Mukherjee & Co. Private Ltd, 1947.

2 A.B. Keith, *A Constitutional History of India, 1600–1935* (1st edition.), London: Routledge, 1937.

3 Gurumukh Nihal Singh, *Landmarks in Indian Constitutional and National Development, (1600–1919)*, Benares: Indian Book Shop, 1933.

4   Narendra Nath Law, *Promotion of Learning in India by Early European Settlers (up to about 1800 A.D.)*, London: Longmans, Green and Co., 1915.

5   Syed Nurullah and J.P. Naik, *A Students' History of Education in India (1800–1973)*, Delhi: S.G. Wasani for Macmillan Company of India, 1974.

6   M.B. Hooker, 'The East India Company and the Crown 1773–1858', *Malaya Law Review*, 11:1 (July 1969), pp. 1–37.

7   East India Company, *The Law Relating to India, and The East-India Company*, London: W.H. Allen & Co., 1841.

8   *East India Company* v. *Sandys* (1683) 90 ER 62.

9   Richard Tuck, 'Alliances with Infidels in the European Imperial Expansion,' in *Empire and Modern Political Thought*, edited by Sankar Muthu, Cambridge: Cambridge University Press, 2012, pp. 61–83.

10 James Muldoon, *Popes, Lawyers, and Infidels: The Church and the Non-Christian World, 1250–1550*, Pennsylvania: University of Pennsylvania Press, 1979.

11 Edward Cavanagh, 'Infidels in English Legal Thought: Conquest, Commerce and Slavery in the Common Law from Coke to Mansfield, 1603–1793', *Modern Intellectual History*, 16 (2017), pp. 1–35.

12 Letter Patents granted to the Governor and the Company of Merchants of London, trading into the East-Indies, 5 September 1698, IOR/A/1/56–57. Printed in Charters Granted to the East India Company from 1601, London, 1773.

13 S.C. Ilbert, *The Government of India: A Brief Historical Survey of parliamentary Legislations Relating to India*, India: Oxford University Press, 1922.

14 *A Collection of Statutes Relating to India in Two Volumes*, Calcutta: Office of the Superintendent of Government Printing, 1899.

15 *The Journals of the House of Commons* (from 26 November 1772 to 15 September 1774), 34 (1804). See https://babel.hathitrust.org/cgi/pt?id=chi.78147261&view=1up&seq=1

16 Jakob De Roover and S.N. Balagangadhara, 'Liberty, Tyranny and the Will of God: The Principle of Toleration in Early Modern Europe and Colonial India', *History of Political Thought*, 30:1 (Spring 2009), pp. 111–139.

17 John Shore (Baron Teignmouth), *Considerations on the Practicability, Policy, and Obligation of Communicating to the Natives of India the Knowledge of Christianity*, London, 1808.

18 Joshua Marshman, *Advantages of Christianity in Promoting the Establishment and Prosperity of the British Government in India*, London, 1813; Andrew Fuller, *An Apology for the Late Christian Missions to India*, London: J.W. Morris, 1808; John William Cunningham, *Christianity in*

India: An Essay on the Duty, Means and Consequences of Introducing the
Christian Religion among the Native Inhabitants of the British Dominions
of the East, London: J. Hatchard, 1808.

19   Roger H. Martin, 'Anglicans and Baptists in Conflict: The Bible Society,
     Bengal and the Baptizo Controversy', *The Journal of Ecclesiastical*
     History, 49 (1998), pp. 293–316.

20   William Carey, *An Enquiry into the Obligations of Christians to*
     Use Means for the Conversion of the Heathens, Ireland, 1792; Mary
     Drewery, *William Carey: A Biography*, Grand Rapids: Zondervan
     Publishing House, Michigan, 1979.

21   E. Daniel Potts, *British Baptist Missionaries in India, 1793–1837*,
     Cambridge: Cambridge University Press, 1967, p. 54.

22   William Wilberforce, *A Practical View of the Prevailing Religious System*
     of Professed Christians, in the Higher and Middle Classes, Contrasted with
     Real Christianity, New York: American Tract Society, 1830, 1839 [1797].

23   House of Commons (26 June 1811), 'Missionaries to the East', H.C.
     Deb, vol. 20, cc. 758–759. See https://api.parliament.uk/historic-
     hansard/commons/1811/jun/26/missionaries-to-the-east

24   Karen Chancey, 'The Star in the East: The Controversy over Christian
     Missions to India, 1805–1813', *The Historian*, 60:3 (Spring 1998),
     pp. 507–522.

25   L. Mani, *Contentious Traditions: The Debate on Sati in Colonial India*,
     Berkeley and Los Angeles, 1998.

26   Bennie R. Crockett and Myron C. Noonkester, 'The Chaplains'
     Plot: Charter Renewal in 1813 and the Reformation of British India',
     paper delivered at Southern Conference on British Studies, Memphis,
     Tennessee, November 2004. See https://www.wmcarey.edu/carey/
     lectures/chaplains-plot.pdf

27   House of Commons (22 February 1813), 'Petition of the East India
     Company for the Renewal of their Charter', H.C. Deb, vol. 24,
     cc. 659–676. See https://api.parliament.uk/historic-hansard/commons/
     1813/feb/22/petition-of-the-east-india-company-for

28   Claudius Buchanan, *'The Star in the East': A Sermon Preached in the*
     Parish Church of St. James, Bristol, England, Sunday, February 26, 1809,
     New York: Williams & Whiting, 1809, p. 29; Claudius Buchanan,
     Memoir of the Expediency of an Ecclesiastical Establishment for British
     India; both as a Means of Perpetuating the Christian Religion among our
     own Countrymen; and as a Foundation for the Ultimate Civilisation of the
     Natives, 2nd Edition, Cambridge: Hilliard and Metcalf, 1811, pp. 44–
     48; Claudius Buchanan, *Christian Researches in Asia*, New York, 1812;
     Claudius Buchanan, *An Apology for Promoting Christianity in India*,
     Boston: Nathaniel Willis, 1814.

29 Robert Hall, *Considerations on a Most Important Subject Connected with the Question of the Renewal of the Charter of the East India Company*, Glasgow: W. Turnbull and M. Ogle, 1813.

30 House of Commons (19 February 1813), 'Petition Respecting the East India Company, from the Society in Scotland for Propagating Christian Knowledge', H.C. Deb, vol. 24, cc. 654–655. See https://api.parliament.uk/historic-hansard/commons/1813/feb/19/petition-respecting-the-east-india

31 Andrea Major, *Pious Flames: European Encounters with Sati 1500–1830*, India: Oxford University Press, 2006.

32 Meenakshi Jain, *Sati: Evangelicals, Baptist Missionaries, and the Changing Colonial Discourse*, New Delhi: Aryan Books International, 2016.

33 One of the leading families of Bengal which led the Bengali Renaissance. Shri Rabindranath Tagore hailed from this family.

34 Further Papers respecting East India Company's Charter, 1833, General Court for the Information of the Proprietors, London.

35 House of Commons (13 June 1833), 'East India Company's Charter', H.C. Deb, vol 18, cc. 698–785. See https://api.parliament.uk/historic-hansard/commons/1833/jun/13/east-india-companys-charter

36 House of Lords (17 June 1833), 'East India Charter', H.L. Deb, vol. 18, cc. 851–852. See https://api.parliament.uk/historic-hansard/lords/1833/jun/17/east-india-charter

37 House of Commons (10 July 1833), 'East India Company's Charter', H.C. Deb, vol. 19, cc. 479–550. See https://api.parliament.uk/historic-hansard/commons/1833/jul/10/east-india-companys-charter

38 House of Commons (19 July 1833), 'East India Company's Charter', H.C. Deb, vol. 19, cc. 1031–1037. See https://api.parliament.uk/historic-hansard/commons/1833/jul/19/east-india-companys-charter-1

39 House of Commons (26 July 1833), 'East India Company's Charter', H.C. Deb, vol. 20, cc. 14–50. See https://api.parliament.uk/historic-hansard/commons/1833/jul/26/east-india-companys-charter

40 House of Commons (2 April 1852), 'The East India Company's Charter', H.L. Deb, vol. 120, cc. 546–580. See https://api.parliament.uk/historic-hansard/lords/1852/apr/02/the-east-india-companys-charter

41 House of Lords (19 April 1852), 'East India Company's Charter', H.C. Deb, vol. 120, cc. 806–868. See https://api.parliament.uk/historic-hansard/commons/1852/apr/19/east-india-companys-charter

CHAPTER 9 CHRISTIAN COLONIAL CONSCIOUSNESS, THE HINDU RELIGION, CASTE, TRIBE AND EDUCATION

1 Nicholas B. Dirks, *Colonialism and Culture*, Michigan: University of Michigan Press, 1992; Nicholas B. Dirks, 'The Original Caste:

Power, History and Hierarchy in South Asia', *Contributions to Indian Sociology*, 23:1(1989), pp. 59–77; Nicholas B. Dirks, 'The Invention of Caste: Civil Society in Colonial India', *Social Analysis: The International Journal of Social and Cultural Practice*, 25 (1989), pp. 42–52; Nicholas B. Dirks, 'The Policing of Tradition: Colonialism and Anthropology in Southern India', *Comparative Studies in Society and History*, 39:1 (1997), pp. 182–212; Nicholas B. Dirks, 'The Conversion of Caste: Location, Translation, and Appropriation', in *Conversion to Modernities,* edited by P. van der Veer, New York: Routledge, 1996, pp. 115–137.

2   Jakob De Roover, *Europe, India, and the Limits of Secularism*, India: Oxford University Press, 2015.

3   Peter van der Veer, *Conversion to Modernities: The Globalization of Christianity* [Conference on Conversion, Held at the Research Centre of Religion and Society of the University of Amsterdam, June 1994], New York: Routledge, 1996.

4   J. De Roover, 'A Nation of Tribes and Priests: The Jews and the Immorality of the Caste System', in *Western Foundations of the Caste System,* edited by M. Fárek, D. Jalki, S. Pathan and P. Shah, Palgrave Macmillan, 2017.

5   Jakob De Roover and S.N. Balagangadhara, 'Liberty, Tyranny and the Will of God: The Principle of Toleration in Early Modern Europe and Colonial India', *History of Political Thought*, 30:1 (March 2009), pp. 111–139.

6   Jakob De Roover, *Europe, India, and the Limits of Secularism*, India: Oxford University Press, 2015

7   Ibid., p. 187.

8   S.N. Balagangadhara and Jakob De Roover, 'The Dark Hour of Secularism, Hindu Fundamentalism and Colonial Liberalism in India', in *Making Sense of the Secular: Critical Perspectives from Europe to Asia,* edited by Ranjan Ghosh, New York: Routledge, 2012.

9   *The Commissioner, Hindu Religious Endowments, Madras* v. *Sri Lakshmindra Tirtha Swamiar of Sri Shirur Mutt*, AIR 1954 SC 282.

10 *Shastri Yagnapurushdasji and others* v. *Muldas Bhundardas vaishya and another*, AIR 1966 SC 1119.

11 *Bramchari Sidheswar Bhai and others* v. *State of West Bengal*, 1995 SCC (4) 646.

12 S.N. Balagangadhara and Jakob De Roover, 'John Locke, Christian Liberty and the Predicament of Liberal Toleration', *Political Theory*, 36:4 (August 2008), pp. 523–549.

13 Nelson Maldonado-Torres, 'Religion, Modernity, and Coloniality', in *Religion, Theory, Critique,* edited by Richard King, New York: Columbia University Press, 2017, pp. 547–554.

14 Nelson Maldonado-Torres, 'On the Coloniality of Being', *Cultural Studies,* 21:2–3 (2007), pp 240–270.

15 Sarah Claerhout and Jakob De Roover, 'Conversion of the World: Proselytization in India and the Universalization of Christianity', in *Rights Talk, Free Markets and Culture,* edited by Rosalind I.J. Hackett, London: Equinox, 2008.

16 Jakob De Roover and Sarah Claerhout, 'The Colonial Construction of What?', in *Rethinking Religion in India: The Colonial Construction of Hinduism,* edited by Esther Bloch, Marianne Keppens and Rajaram Hegde, London: Routledge, 2010, pp. 164–183.

17 The credit for bringing out this nuance goes to Shri T.R. Ramesh, a highly erudite champion of freedom of Hindu religious institutions from State control.

18 Madhu Kishwar, 'Codified Hindu Law: Myth and Reality', *Economic and Political Weekly,* 29 (1994), pp. 2145–2161.

19 Gloria Goodwin Raheja, 'Caste, Colonialism, and the Speech of the Colonized: Entextualization and Disciplinary Control in India', *American Ethnologist,* 23:3 (1996), pp. 494–513.

20 F.G. Bailey, '"Tribe" and "Caste" in India', *Contributions to Indian Sociology,* 5 (1961), pp. 7–19.

21 Nicholas B. Dirks, *Castes of Mind: Colonialism and the Making of Modern India,* Princeton: Princeton University Press, 2002.

22 Herbert H. Risley, *Manual of Ethnography for India: General Instructions, Definitions, and Ethnographic Questions,* Calcutta: Bengal Secretariat Press, 1907.

23 Nicholas B. Dirks, *Castes of Mind: Colonialism and the Making of Modern India,* Princeton: Princeton University Press, 2002, pp. 22, 24.

24 A.H. Bingley, *Caste Handbooks for the Indian Army: Rajputs,* Calcutta: Superintendent of Government Printing, 1918; A.H. Bingley and A. Nicholls, *Caste Handbooks for the Indian Army: Brahmans,* Calcutta: Superintendent of Government Printing, 1918.

25 George MacMunn, 'The Romance of the Martial Races of India', *Journal of the Royal Society of Arts,* 80:4128 (1932), pp. 171–193.

26 Susana B.C. Devalle, 'Tribe in India: The Fallacy of a Colonial Category', in *Studies on Asia and Africa from Latin America,* edited by David N. Lorenzen, 1st edition, México: El Colegio De Mexico, 1990.

27 Syed Nurullah and J.P. Naik, *A Students' History of Education in India (1800–1973),* Delhi: S.G. Wasani for Macmillan Company of India, 1974.

28 Printed in *Bengal: Past and Present*, VIII, 1914, pp. 130–133; and in
    G. Nicholls, *Sketch of the Rise and Progress of the Benares Patshalla or
    Sanskrit College*, Allahabad, 1907, p. 1; K. Raj, 'Colonial Encounters
    and the Forging of New Knowledge and National Identities: Great
    Britain and India, 1760–1850', Osiris, 15 (2000), pp. 119–134.
29 'Bureau of Education, Government of India', in *Selections from
    Educational Records, Part I: 1781–1839*, edited by W.H. Sharp,
    Superintendent Government Printing India, 1920.
30 In 1813, Grant's 'Observations, etc.' was laid before the House of
    Commons, by whose orders it was printed. It was regarded as the ablest
    answer to the arguments of the anti-missionary party headed by Major
    Scott Waring and Sydney Smith (Diet. Nat. Biog. VIII, 379). It appears in
    the Report from the Select Committee of the House of Commons on the
    affairs of the East India Company, 16 August 1832, Appendix I, pp. 82–87.
31 Lynn Zastoupil and Martin Moir, 'Introduction', in *The Great Indian
    Education Debate: Documents Relating to the Orientalist-Anglicist
    Controversy, 1781–1843*, Richmond: Curzon Press, 1999, pp. 1–72.
32 Extract from a Minute by Lord Moira, on the judicial administration of
    the Presidency of Fort William, 2 October 1815.
33 Printed in *Bengal: Past and Present*, VIII, 1914, p. 93; and in part in
    Howell, *Education in India, prior to 1854, etc.*, Calcutta: Office of the
    Superintendent of Government Printing, 1872, pp. 13–14.
34 Note dated 17 July 1823 by Mr Holt Mackenzie, Territorial Department,
    Revenue Consultations repetition.
35 Extract from a letter, dated 17 August 1823, from A.D. Campbell,
    Esq., Collector of Bellary, to the President and Members of the Board
    of Revenue, Fort St. George. Printed in Evidence of 1832, App. I,
    No. 15 [351/501]; also in the Madras Selections, ii, 1856, p. xiii.
36 Address dated 11 December 1823, from Raja Rammohun Roy. Printed
    in G. Trevelyan, *On the Education of the People of India*, London:
    Longman, Orme, Brown, Green & Longmans, 1838, pp. 65–11;
    and C.H. Cameron, *An Address to Parliament on the Duties of Great Britain to
    India in Respect of the Education of the Natives and Their Official Employment*,
    London: Longman, Brown, Green and Longmans, 1853, pp. 83–87.
37 H. Woodrow, Macaulay's Minutes on Education of India (Collection);
    C.B. Lewis, at the Baptist Mission Press, Calcutta, 1862.
38 Lord Bentinck's Resolution of 7 March 1835. Printed in Cameron's
    Address to Parliament, pp. 81–82; and Madras Selections, II,
    1855, pp. lxxxiii–lxxxiv.
39 Minute by the Right Hon'ble Lord Auckland, the Governor-General,
    dated 24 November 1839. Printed in the Revd. Dr. Duff's letters addressed
    to Lord Auckland on the subject of Native Education, etc., 1841.

CHAPTER 10 COLONIALITY, CIVILISATION AND CONSTITUTION

1   Government of India Act, 1854, 17 & 18 Vict. c. 77. See http://www. indianlegislation.in/BA/BaActToc.aspx?actid=2213

2   Government of India Act, 1858, 16 & 17 Vict. c. 95. See http://www. indianlegislation.in/BA/BaActToc.aspx?actid=2222

3   Gurumukh Nihal Singh, *Landmarks in Indian Constitutional and National Development, (1600–1919)*, Benares: Indian Book Shop, 1933.

4   A.B. Keith, *A Constitutional History of India, 1600–1935*, 1st edition, London: Routledge, 1937.

5   House of Commons, 8 July 1858, 'Order for Third Reading (of the Bill to Act of 1858)', H.C. Deb, vol. 151, cc. 1086–1096. See http:// api.parliament.uk/historic-hansard/commons/1858/jul/08/third-reading

6   House of Lords, 15 July 1858, 'Order of the day for the Second Reading (of the Bill to Act of 1858)', HL, vol. 151, cc. 1447–1481. See http://api.parliament.uk/historic-hansard/lords/1858/jul/15/ second-reading

7   Proclamation by the Queen in Council to the Princes, Chiefs and people of India (published by the Governor-General at Allahabad, 1 November 1858). See https://www.bl.uk/collection-items/ proclamation-by-the-queen-in-council-to-the-princes-chiefs-and-people-of-india

8   House of Lords, 16 July 1858, 'Order of the day for the House to be put into Committee (to review the Bill to Act of 1858)', HL, vol. 151, cc. 1561–1590. See https://api.parliament.uk/historic-hansard/ lords/1858/jul/16/committee

9   House of Lords, 23 July 1858, 'Bill (To Government of India Act 1858) read with the Amendments', HL, vol. 151, cc. 2007–2020. See https://api.parliament.uk/historic-hansard/lords/1858/jul/23/ third-reading 1

10 Sir Courtenay Ilbert, *The Government of India (supplementary chapter)*, India: Oxford University Press, 1910.

11 The Project Committee in Chairmanship of B. Shiva Rao, *The Framing of India's Constitution: Select Documents*, Vol. II, New Delhi: The Indian Institute of Public Administration, 1967.

12 House of Lords, 6 July 1860, 'Education (India)—Petition', H.L. Deb, vol. 159, cc. 1513–1518. See https://api.parliament.uk/historic-hansard/lords/1860/jul/06/education-india-petition

13 House of Commons, 28 September 1915, 'Ecclesiastical Establishment (India)', H.C. Deb, vol. 74, cc. 753–754 See https://api.parliament. uk/historic-hansard/written-answers/1915/sep/28/ecclesiastical-establishment-india

CHAPTER 11 THE STANDARD OF CIVILISATION, THE LEAGUE OF NATIONS AND THE GOVERNMENT OF INDIA ACT, 1919

1 The Project Committee in Chairmanship of B. Shiva Rao, *The Framing of India's Constitution: Select Documents*, vol. I, New Delhi: The Indian Institute of Public Administration.

2 House of Commons, 20 August 1917, 'India (Government Policy)', H.C. Deb, vol. 97, cc. 1695–1697; R. Danzig, 'The Announcement of August 20th, 1917', *The Journal of Asian Studies*, 28, no. 1 (1968).

3 Report on Indian Constitutional Reforms, India: Superintendent Government Printing, 1918. See https://upload.wikimedia.org/ wikipedia/commons/8/84/Report_on_Indian_Constitutional_ Reforms_%28Montagu-Chelmsford_Report%29.pdf

4 Government of India Act, 1919, 9 and 8, Geo. 5, Ch. 101.

5 Constituent Assembly of India Debates, 4 November 1948. See http://164.100.47.194/Loksabha/Debates/cadebatefiles/C04 111948.html

6 House of Commons, 5 June 1919, 'Government of India Bill', H.C., vol. 116, cc. 2295–2411. See https://api.parliament.uk/historic-hansard/commons/1919/jun/05/government-of-india-bill

7 Samuel P. Huntington, 'The Clash of Civilizations?', *Foreign Affairs*, 72:3 (1993), pp. 22–49.

8 G.W. Gong, *The Standard of Civilization in International Society*, Oxford: Clarendon Press, 1984.

9 James Mayall, *International Society and International Theory: The Reason of States*, edited by Michael Donelan, London: George Allen and Unwin, 1978.

10 James Lorimer, *The Institutes of the Law of Nations: A Treatise of the Jural Relations of Separate Political Communities*, Edinburgh and London: W. Blackwood and Sons, 1883.

11 G.L. Beer and H.L. Gray, *African Questions at the Paris Peace Conference, with Papers on Egypt, Mesopotamia, and the Colonial Settlement*, New York: Macmillan, 1923.

12 Owen Chadwick, *The Secularization of European Society in the Nineteenth Century*, Cambridge: Cambridge University Press, 1975.

13 Philip P. Curtin, *The Image of Africa*, University of Wisconsin Press, 1964.

14 John Flint, *Cecil Rhodes*, London: Hutchinson, 1976; J.G. Lockhart and C.M. Woodhouse, *Cecil Rhodes*, London: Macmillan, 1963.

15 Statute of the International Court of Justice, San Francisco, 26 June 1945. See https://www.icj-cij.org/en/statute

16 League of Nations, Covenant of the League of Nations, 28 April 1919.
    See https://www.refworld.org/docid/3dd8b9854.html

17 Old Colony Trust Company, *The League of Nations*, Cambridge: The
    University Press, 1919.

18 Woodrow Wilson, *The Triumph of Ideals*, New York and London:
    Harper & Brothers Publishers, 1919.

19 House of Commons, 29 May 1919, 'Bill Presented', H.C., vol.116, c.1428.
    See https://api.parliament.uk/historic-hansard/commons/1919/
    may/29/bill-presented

20 House of Commons, 28 December 1919, 'Royal Assent', H.C., vol.
    123, cc. 1300–1302. See https://api.parliament.uk/historic-hansard/
    commons/1919/dec/28/royal-assent

21 House of Lords, 19 March 1918, 'A League of Nations', H.L., vol. 29, cc.
    476–510. See https://api.parliament.uk/historic-hansard/lords/
    1918/mar/19/a-league-of-nations

22 House of Lords, 26 June 1918, 'League of Nations', H.L., vol. 30, cc.
    383–429. See https://api.parliament.uk/historic-hansard/lords/
    1918/jun/26/league-of-nations

23 Treaty of Peace with Germany (Treaty of Versailles), Paris, 28 June
    1919. See https://www.loc.gov/law/help/us-treaties/bevans/m-
    ust000002-0043.pdf

24 House of Lords, 3 July 1919, 'The Treaty of Peace', H.L., vol.
    35, cc. 155–188. See https://api.parliament.uk/historic-hansard/
    lords/1919/jul/03/the-treaty-of-peace

25 House of Commons, 21 July 1919, 'Treaty of Peace Bill', H.C., vol.
    118, cc. 951–1077. See https://api.parliament.uk/historic-hansard/
    commons/1919/jul/21/treaty-of-peace-bill

26 House of Commons, 17 June 1920, 'Statement by Mr. Balfour', H.C., vol
    130, cc. 1491–1602. See https://api.parliament.uk/historic-hansard/
    commons/1920/jun/17/statement-by-mr-balfour

27 G. Chamedes, 'The Vatican and the Reshaping of the European
    International Order after the First World War', *The Historical Journal*,
    56:4 (2013), pp. 955–976; P. Steinbicker, 'The Papacy and the League
    of Nations', *The Irish Monthly*, 64:756, pp. 369–375.

28 Lala Lajpat Rai, *Self-Determination for India*, New York: India Home
    Rule League of America. See https://www.saada.org/item/20130123-
    1240

INDEX

Westphalian nation-state system, 81,
    95
Westphalian Peace, 95
Westphalian principles, 99
Westphalian system, 100
White European Christian, 180
White European Christian coloniser,
    179
William, Fort, 234
Word of God, 115

Wynter, Sylvia, 39

X
Xenophobia, 119

Z
Zel Domus, 93
Ziltener, Patrick, 76

ABOUT THE AUTHOR

 J. Sai Deepak is an engineer-turned-lawyer with a bachelor's degree in mechanical engineering from Anna University (2002–2006) and a bachelor's degree in law from IIT Kharagpur (2006–2009). From July 2009 to June 2016, Sai practised as a litigator primarily before the High Court of Delhi and the Supreme Court of India as part of a leading National Capital Region-based law firm, reaching the position of an associate partner in 2015. In June 2016, he founded Law Chambers of J. Sai Deepak and set up an independent practice as an arguing counsel. Ever since, Sai has been engaged by law firms and solicitors to appear and argue on behalf of their clients before the Delhi High Court, the Supreme Court, the Madras High Court, the Competition Commission of India, NCLAT, the NCLTs and arbitral tribunals. In 12 years of practice, Sai has carved a niche for himself as a litigator in matters relating to civil commercial laws, intellectual property laws, constitutional law and competition law. Over the years, he has been a part of several landmark cases, such as the Sabarimala Ayyappa Temple and Sree Padmanabhaswamy Temple matters, and the dispute over Basmati Geographical Indication.